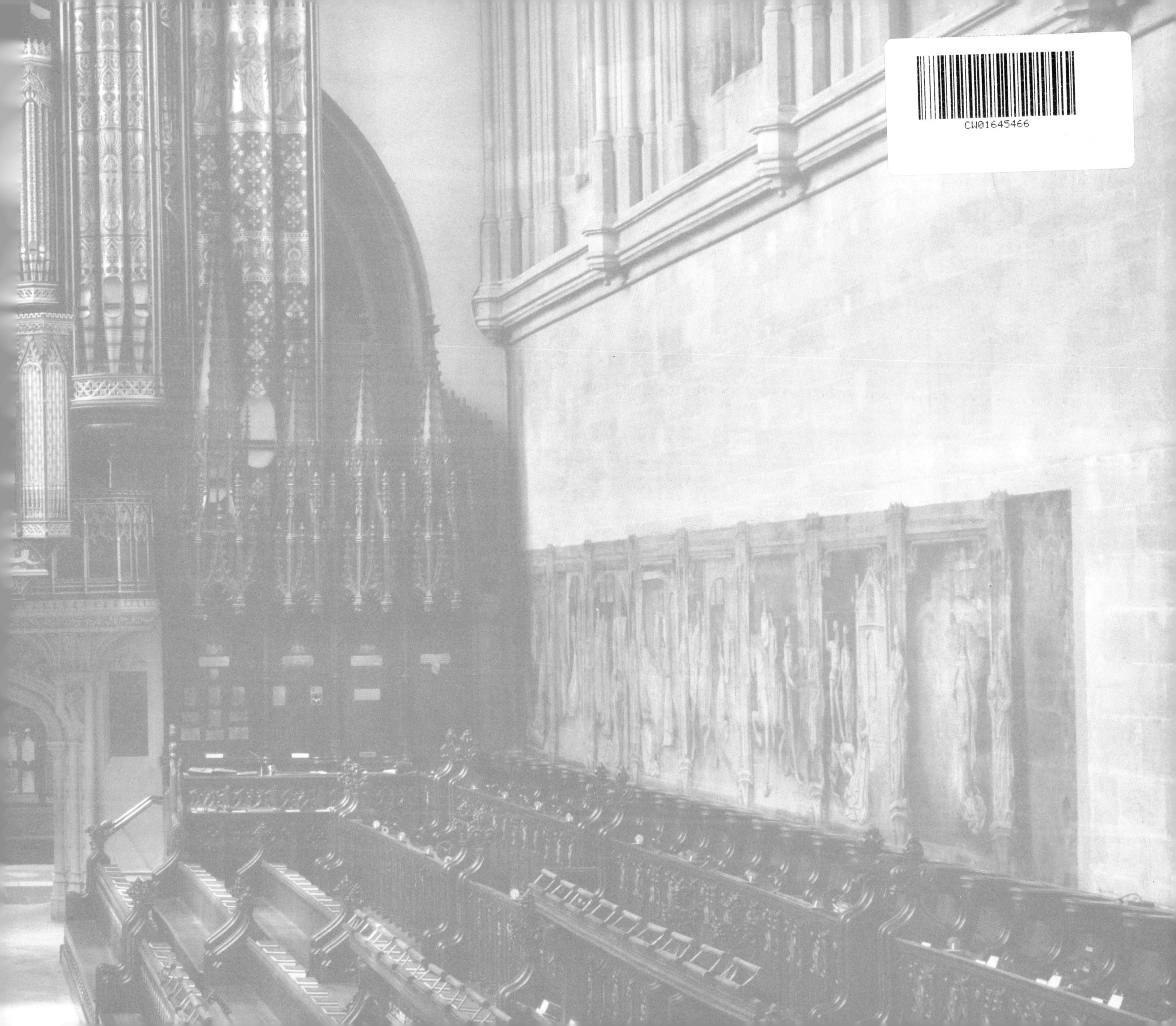

Wall Paintings of Eton

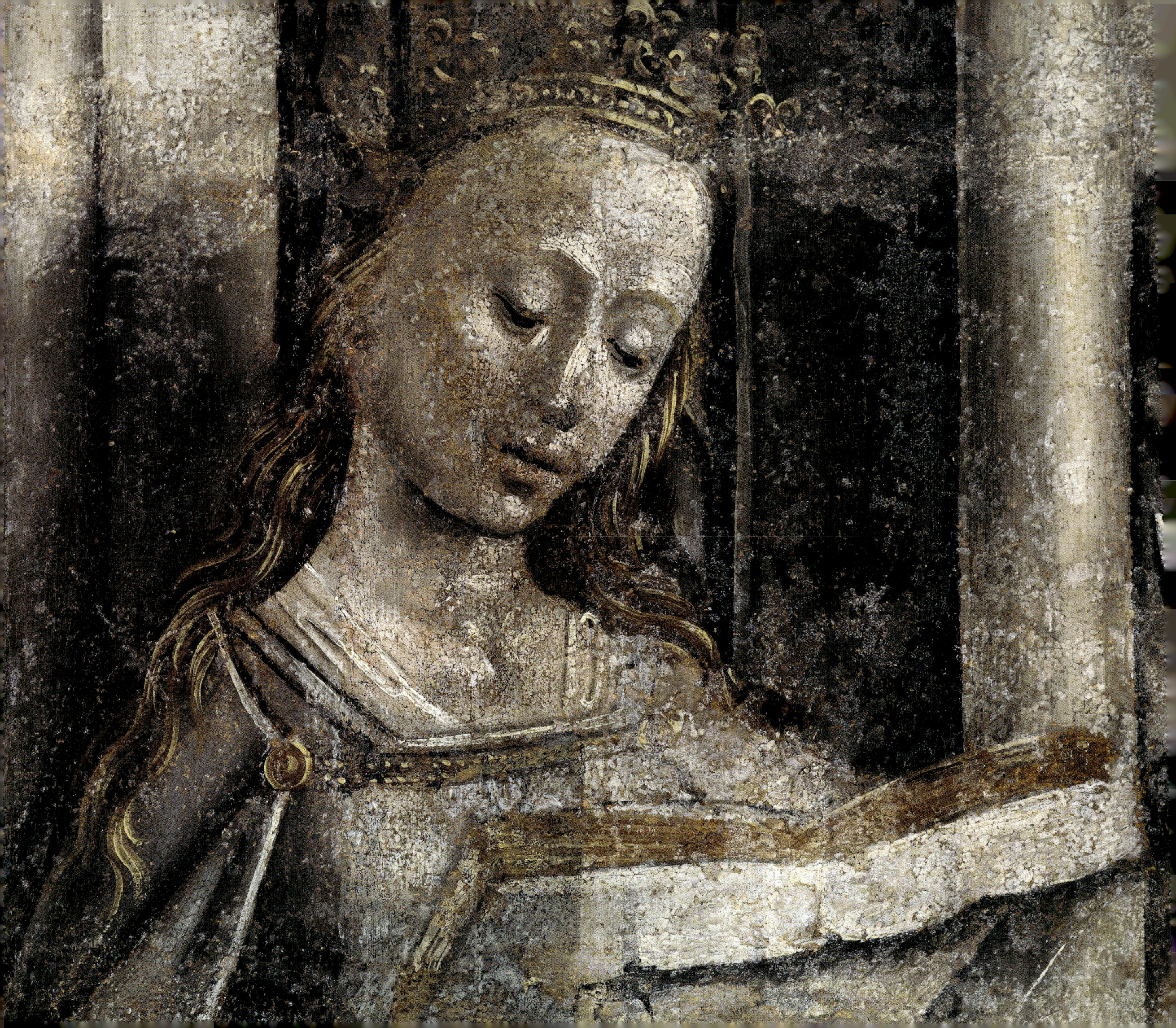

Wall Paintings of Eton

Emily Howe
Henrietta McBurney
David Park
Stephen Rickerby
Lisa Shekede

Preface by Lord Waldegrave of North Hill

SCALA

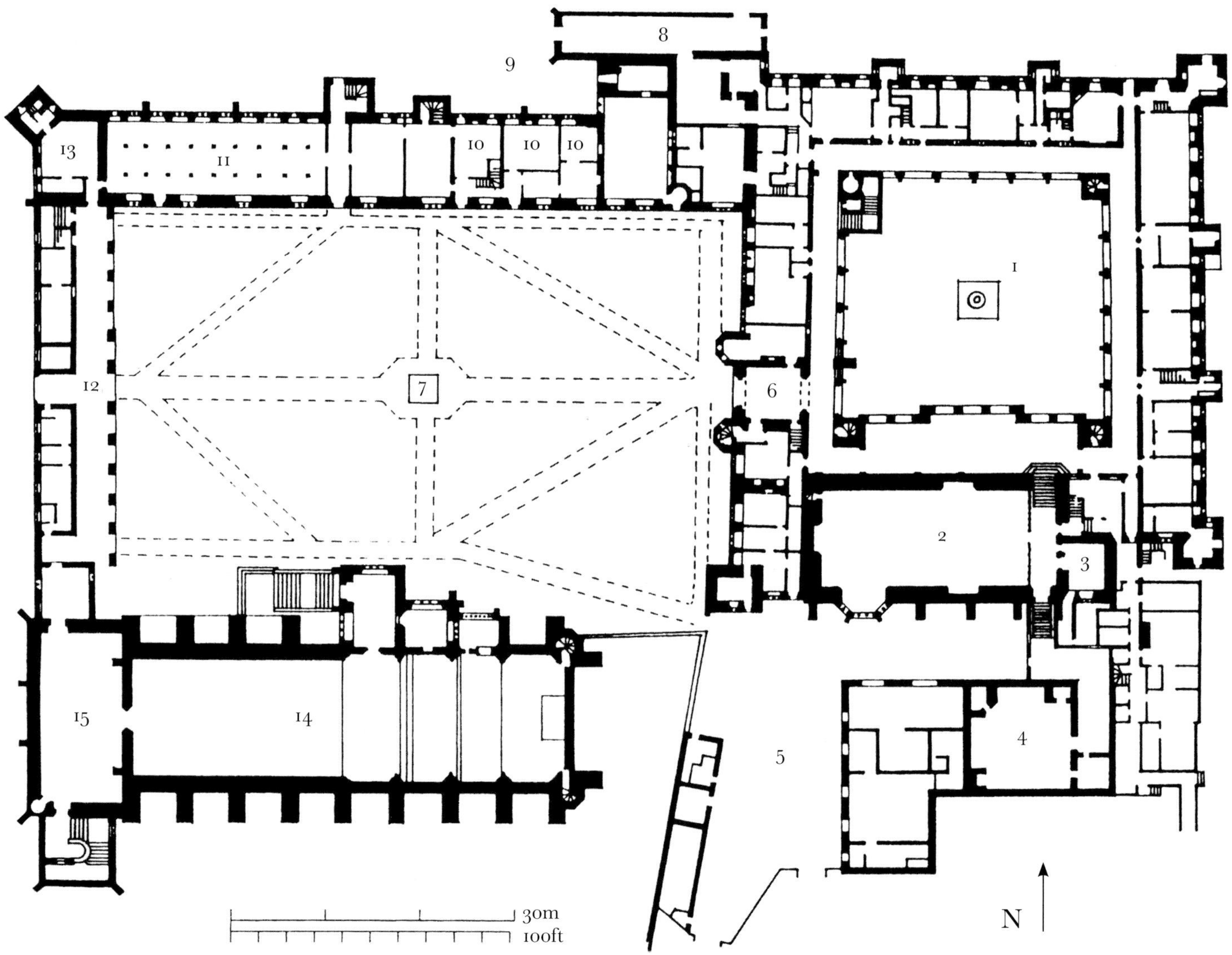

Ground plan of Eton College today.

1 Cloister Court
2 College Hall
3 Buttery
4 Kitchen
5 Brewhouse Yard
6 Lupton's Range
7 School Yard
8 Provost's Lodge entrance
9 Weston's Yard
10 Master in College
11 Lower School
12 Upper School (over)
13 Head Master's Chambers
14 Chapel
15 Ante-chapel

Contents

Preface

Many of the buildings which have the strongest power to move us are, paradoxically, utterly different now compared to what their builders intended. What would we think of the Parthenon if its original vermilions and blues still disguised the serene Pentelic marble we see today? How would we react to those austere, calm English country churches if we saw, through a haze of incense and beeswax-candle smoke, their brightly coloured plasterwork and the richly draped and painted devotional statues which the vicar of Morebath, Christopher Trychay, describes so vividly in his remote Devon parish in the 1520s?

Eton, uniquely, offers an immensely evocative partial glimpse of what a pre-Reformation church would have been like before Christianity's equivalent of Taliban iconoclasm smashed and whitewashed away the traditions of a thousand years. There is nothing, as Emily Howe writes, like our College chapel wall paintings anywhere north of the Alps. There is almost nothing like our Choirbook, which gives us the music which would have filled the richly decorated, incense-filled space to which the wall paintings provided the backdrop.

My predecessors, whose narrower Protestantism saw nothing but mumbo-jumbo and superstitious darkness in the old world, were wrong. The fifteenth and early sixteenth century was a time of intellectual and educational excitement. Henry VI would have been remembered in a peaceful time as a magnificent patron of educational expansion, rather than as a militarily disastrous leader. In his own foundations and in those of his circle, such as Archbishop Chichele's All Souls College in Oxford, the new learning spread by Gutenberg's great invention thrived. No better symbol of this could be imagined than the wall painting recently discovered in the Head Master's Chambers, and described by Henrietta McBurney and others in Part II of this book, showing Etonian pupils at work under the eye of their teacher, whose painted slogan comes not from scripture but from Quintilian and is one to which we are proud still to adhere: the task of the teacher is to bring out the talent of the child.

The hero of the story of the chapel paintings – sadly, he never knew of the Head Master's Chambers painting – is my great predecessor Montague Rhodes James, as Emily Howe makes clear. My wife Caroline is James's double great-niece and I first saw Richard Hamilton Essex's drawings of the paintings, and read James's commentary on them, when her father Richard Burrows gave me James's *Frescoes in the Chapel at Eton College* after we were married. Richard Burrows, a small boy in the school when James was Provost, heard him tell the famous ghost stories in our drawing room, where they are still told. It seemed to us therefore that it would be a fitting act of family piety that we should sponsor a new volume, to bring together an account of all that has been learned from modern scholarship about the chapel paintings since James wrote more than a century ago; to have it illustrated by modern photography; and to include an account of the newly found wall painting. The Courtauld Institute of Art, the Paul Mellon Centre and the College itself have generously helped us to bring our plan to fruition, and Henrietta McBurney has both co-authored a section and overseen the production of the book, for which we are very grateful.

We would like to dedicate the book to the memory of Montague Rhodes James, Provost 1918 to 1936.

William Waldegrave, Provost of Eton

Acknowledgements: Part I

This study draws upon the work of many distinguished scholars, not least those enumerated in the lengthy bibliography at the end of this book. Particular thanks, however, are due to Henrietta McBurney, Keeper of Fine and Decorative Art at Eton College, for her invaluable assistance and encouragement throughout this project. I am also greatly indebted to Professor David Park, Director of the Conservation of Wall Painting Department, Courtauld Institute of Art, for permitting me unfettered access to the National Survey of Medieval Wall Paintings and for so generously supporting my examination of the paintings through access to the Courtauld's analytical facilities. Both have been kind enough to read and comment upon my text, which is much improved by their suggestions. I am also grateful to Dr Christopher de Hamel, Gaylord Donnelley Fellow Librarian, Corpus Christi College, Cambridge, who valiantly undertook to re-examine what remains of the Latin inscriptions which form part of the chapel scheme, extensive passages of which have been recovered since the texts were last transcribed. Professor Jean Michel Massing of King's College, Cambridge, very kindly agreed to read my text at a late stage in its preparation and made most helpful comments. In my time on site at Eton, I have benefited tremendously from the practical support of Lynn Sanders, Reg Harberd, Tim Woods and Simon Shergold, and all those who work with Graham Buckland in the Porters' Lodge.

The staff at Deddington Library, the Courtauld Institute Library and the British Library have been consistently accommodating and considerate in fielding my many queries and requests. Dr Karin Kyburz at the Courtauld Institute and Charlotte Villiers at Eton assisted me greatly by sourcing many of the images featured in this book. Beautiful new photography of the wall paintings was undertaken by James Davies. Penny Hatfield, Archivist at Eton College, provided thoughtful clarification of several matters relating to the College accounts, and Penny Brading kindly checked the details of some of the historical sources upon which I have drawn. Jo Bartholomew, Curator and Librarian at Winchester Cathedral, was kind enough to afford me access to the paintings in the Lady Chapel and to material from the choir screen at very short notice. For their suggestions on matters technical, I am grateful to Sharon Cather, Tobit Curteis and Dr Helen Howard. I am especially obliged to Jo Kirby Atkinson and Dr David Peggie at the National Gallery, London, for so kindly undertaking to examine the organic colorants from the scheme, and to Jo for her invigorating discussion on many other aspects of the paintings' technique. For his assistance with SEM-EDX analysis, I am extremely grateful to Jim Davy at University College, London. Analysis of the paintings' binding media was undertaken with great efficiency by Dr Brian Singer at the University of Northumbria. My thanks are due, finally, to my family, without whose support and forbearance this project would never have reached fruition.

E.H.

Acknowledgements: Part II

Among colleagues at the Courtauld Institute of Art, we are particularly indebted to Sharon Cather of the Conservation of Wall Painting Department, whose expertise has been invaluable at all stages of the research. Karin Kyburz has been immensely helpful in procuring comparative illustrations, and we are also very grateful to the Institute's Director, Professor Deborah Swallow, for the interest she has shown throughout the project.

At Eton, Lynn Sanders has provided unfailing support throughout the writing of this section, and in particular with her invaluable help in assembling the illustrations. We also owe thanks to Rachel Bond, Lucy Gwynn, Reg Harberd, Penny Hatfield, Serena Hedley-Dent, Bob Hutton, Paul Maher, Andrew Maynard, Ian Mellor, Simon Shergold, Charlotte Villiers, Lord and Lady Waldegrave, Janet Walker, the Revd Canon Keith Wilkinson, Tim Woods and Sue Young. Peter Jones and Professor Jean Michel Massing of King's College, Cambridge, and Stephen Anderson, John Falconer and Suzanne Foster of Winchester College have all been most kind in giving us their time, suggestions and advice.

Among many other individuals who have kindly provided expertise are: David Alexander, Sir Eric and Lady Anderson, Jo Kirby Atkinson, David Broomfield, Sophie Connor, Dr Tim Connor, Dr Emily Dourish, Anna Eavis, Dr John Goodall, Professor Tim Gowers, Phillipa Grimstone, Dr Christopher de Hamel, Helen Hills, Emily Howe, Michael Hyland, Cristina Neagu, Susan North, Professor Christopher Norton, Ed Potten, the staff of the Rare Books Room at Cambridge University Library, Christopher Rowell, Dr Giovanni Verri, Dr Géraldine Victoir, Claire Welford, Anthony Wells-Cole, Dr Paul Williamson, and Professor Christopher Wilson.

James Davies was responsible for undertaking the excellent new photography of the wall painting in the Head Master's Chambers, while Dennis Wallis kindly provided some of the comparative illustrations. We are particularly grateful to Dr Annemarieke Willemsen, who has been most generous in providing one of her own comparative illustrations, as well as her enormous expertise. We are also very grateful to Stephen Conlin, for his reconstruction drawings of the wall painting and of one of the stained glass roundels in Election Hall. Finally the thanks of all the authors in this volume are due to Jessica Hodge for her enthusiasm and care in preparing the text of this book for publication.

H.McB., D.P., S.R. and L.S.

Introduction

The two wall painting schemes which form the focus of this book are each connected with one of the two major early phases of building works at Eton, as personified in two of the College's early Provosts, William Waynflete and Roger Lupton. The scheme illustrating the *Miracles of the Virgin*, created over a period of about 10 years between *c*.1477 and *c*.1487, marked the completion, under the patronage of Waynflete, of the choir of the chapel dedicated to Our Lady of Eton, begun but never completed by Henry VI. The second scheme, a single wall painting recently discovered in the Head Master's Chambers, depicts a school scene in about 1520. It coincides with the next major building phase under Provost Lupton, which was concerned with the improvement of the secular buildings: the schoolroom and the accommodation of pupils and schoolmaster; new accommodation for the Provost; and a new library for the Fellows. Separated in time from each other by about 30 years, the religious murals in the chapel represent a flowering of late medieval art in England, while the secular scene in the Head Master's Chambers, with its classical quotations and interest in characterisation, reflects the humanist ideals of the Tudor period. In terms of style and technique, the two mural schemes can be seen to demonstrate, on the one hand, a lavish, sophisticated commission designed for public consumption as part of an elaborate and ostentatious religious setting, and, on the other, a painting designed for a private audience but of similarly superb quality, as revealed by recent scientific examination.

While the two mural schemes are artistically speaking very different, Waynflete and Lupton, the figures connected with each building phase, are linked in an important respect. Each was deeply involved in the humanist encouragement of the teaching of grammar.[1] Waynflete was working in the early 1480s, just as a revolution in grammar teaching began in England, spread partly by means of the printing press and partly

1 Both founded schools; Waynflete's was Magdalen College School, Oxford, and Lupton's was Sedbergh Grammar School in the town of his birth in Yorkshire. For Waynflete's foundation see Davis 1993, 57-73, and for Lupton's see *ODNB*, 34, 784-5.

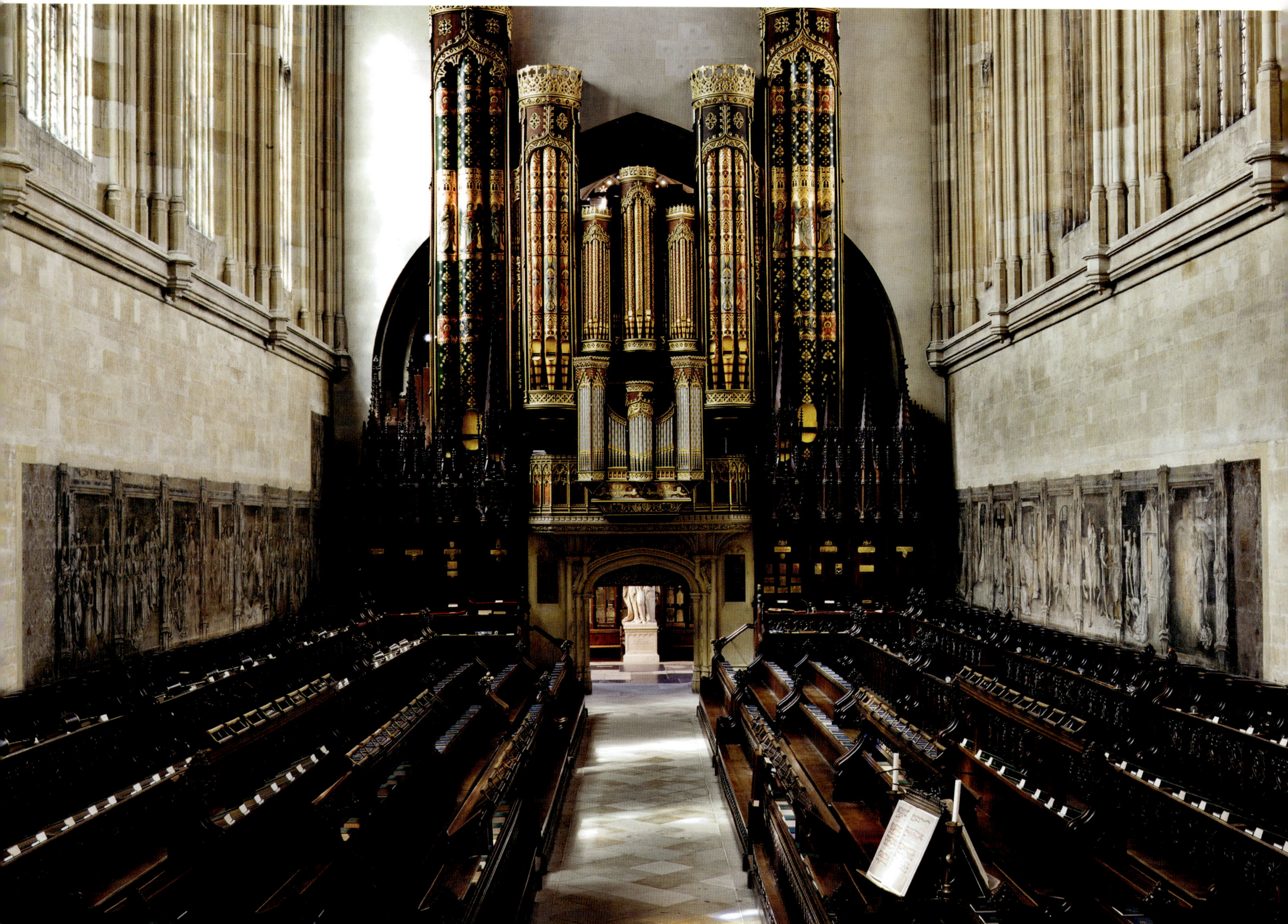

through the influence of contemporary Italian grammarians. Lupton was Provost of Eton during the influential period of the humanists John Colet, Thomas More and Erasmus, of whose circle Eton's schoolmaster Robert Aldrich, the likely patron of the school scene mural, was a member. While Waynflete's interest in education was a moving force behind his patronage of Henry VI's foundation, including the adornment of the chapel walls, Lupton's was concerned with the enhancement of the school buildings and the encouragement of humanist learning, as reflected in the classical inscriptions which form part of the wall painting in the Head Master's Chambers.

A more recent link between the two mural schemes is provided by Montague Rhodes James, scholar, author, and Provost of Eton from 1918 until his death in 1936. It was thanks to his enlightened intervention that the chapel wall paintings were exposed, published, and subsequently conserved. James never knew of the school scene mural in the Head Master's Chambers; had it been discovered during his lifetime, he would surely have been delighted, not least because of the painting's connections with the schoolmaster and grammarian William Horman, whose Latin phrase book, the *Vulgaria* of 1519, he edited for the Roxburghe Club in 1926. Had he known of the painting he would undoubtedly have written his own scholarly account of it.

Fig. 1. General view of the surviving wall paintings, looking west in the chapel.

James's interest in the College chapel murals, which form the subject of Part I of this book, began in 1881 when, as an 18-year-old scholar in the last year of his studies at Eton, he first caught a glimpse of two female saints painted on the chapel's north and south walls in the far western corner. The figures were depicted life-size, bare-headed and dressed in long white robes, standing on pedestals beneath ornate canopied niches. The masonry had been exposed only briefly from beneath the wooden stalls during the construction of a new organ screen at the junction of the choir with the ante-chapel.[2] James already knew, from an account in Maxwell Lyte's recently published *History of Eton College* (1875), that a far more extensive cycle of medieval wall paintings depicting the *Miracles of the Virgin* was preserved beneath the woodwork.[3] These were first chanced upon in 1847 during a previous refurbishment of the chapel, partially obliterated, and the remainder then hidden by new seating.[4] From the moment of this sighting, however, James was smitten with 'a great desire to see what was hidden behind the canopies' and, fuelled by this ambition, worked tirelessly throughout his career to bring the chapel paintings to the attention

2 See James & Tristram 1929, 10-11; also Maxwell Lyte 1911, 538.
3 See Maxwell Lyte 1911, 83-90.
4 On the discovery and destruction of the paintings in 1847, see chapter 5 below.

of a wider public.[5] In 1894, during his tenure as Director of the Fitzwilliam Museum in Cambridge, James presented a paper on the wall paintings to the Cambridge Antiquarian Society.[6] Some years later, in 1907, he published his first full description of *The Frescoes in the Chapel at Eton College*, accompanied by fine pencil drawings made by the artist Richard Hamilton Essex in 1847. It was not, however, until the summer of 1923, by which time James had returned to Eton to assume the position of Provost, that he was to see his ambition fulfilled and the paintings finally exposed.[7]

Obscured for the greater part of their lifetime, the wall paintings in the chapel at Eton College constitute arguably the most important surviving late medieval mural scheme in northern Europe.[8] Nowhere in England, certainly, does a scheme survive on this enormous scale and of such high quality (Figure 1). The vast body of literature which has grown up around the paintings since their discovery is surely testament to their enormous significance. It is just over a century since James published his monograph on the paintings, and almost 40 years since they underwent an extensive programme of conservation by Pauline Plummer,[9] and it seemed both desirable and timely that the wide range of scholarship relating to them should now be brought together in a single volume. As part of this project, and in order to advance further our appreciation and understanding of the wall paintings, the College took the initiative of commissioning the first comprehensive scientific examination of the murals' original painting materials and technique.[10]

The creation and patronage of the chapel wall paintings forms the focus of the opening chapter of Part I. Drawing upon Maxwell Lyte's celebrated history of Eton and Willis and Clark's architectural history of the College (published shortly afterwards in 1886), as well as recent biographical studies, it considers the motivation behind Henry VI's ambitious foundation and charts the completion of Eton's new church, following the king's death, under the patronage of William Waynflete, Bishop of Winchester.[11] Revisiting evidence in the College audit rolls, consideration is given to the question of the murals' date and to the evidence for the authorship of the programme and the identities of those who executed it. The iconography of the wall paintings, comprising two dozen Marian miracles and 36 intervening figures of saints, and the rationale behind these choices, is discussed in detail in chapter 2. A full catalogue of the painting programme, with specially commissioned photography of each of the scenes, is located at the end of this study and incorporates both extensive revisions to James's original identifications and up-to-

5 James & Tristram 1929, 10.
6 While his paper was reproduced in the *Proceedings of the Cambridge Antiquarian Society* in the following year (James 1895b), there appears to be some confusion over the event, as James himself recollects that he did not make this presentation until 1906 (James & Tristram 1929, 11).
7 The discovery was followed, a few years later, by a far more comprehensive paper on the paintings and a similar derivative scheme in the Lady Chapel of Winchester Cathedral; see James & Tristram 1929.
8 See Martindale 1995, 136.
9 The paintings were conserved between 1961 and 1975, see chapter 5 below; also Plummer 1986.
10 This technical study was undertaken by Emily Howe in November 2010 and generously supported by the Courtauld Institute of Art's Conservation of Wall Painting Department; see chapter 6 below.
11 See, in particular, Wolffe's biography of Henry VI, Wolffe 2001, and Davis's of William Waynflete, Davis 1993. A comprehensive treatment of Eton's foundation history and pioneering architectural style is also found in Goodall 2002.

date transcriptions of the scheme's Latin inscriptions.[12]

The devotional context of the wall paintings, both at Eton and more broadly in England at the close of the fifteenth century, forms the focus of chapter 3. Building on observations made by Andrew Martindale in his two seminal papers on the chapel,[13] consideration is given both to the paintings' audience and to the ways in which the murals functioned within their architectural setting. Magnus Williamson's illuminating account of the roughly contemporary Eton Choirbook has proved invaluable in reflecting upon the scheme's relationship with the liturgy performed in the church.[14] Viewed against the backdrop of Lollard insurgency which threatened the established church around this time, the wider theological significance of Eton's *Miracles* is re-evaluated through comparison with other expressions of contemporary Marian beliefs and devotional practices.[15]

In reassessing the range of influences which informed the murals' format, palette and style, chapter 4 reflects upon the 'Netherlandish' character of the paintings in the context of England's social, economic and artistic connections with the Low Countries. In exploring the scheme's affinity with contemporary English and northern European works of art – not only wall paintings, but also illuminated manuscripts and block books, sculpture and carving, stained glass and painted panels – this study draws on a wealth of recent scholarship.[16] The vicissitudes suffered by the paintings, including their whitewashing by the College barber in 1560, are recounted in chapter 5. The details of the scheme's treatment by the renowned wall painting expert Professor E.W. Tristram in the 1920s, and its conservation by Pauline Plummer in the 1960s and 1970s, are also reported.

Chapters 6 and 7 recount the findings of the recent technical examination of the paintings, and evaluate their significance in the context of painting techniques employed across a variety of media around this time. Consideration is given not only to the surprisingly varied range of pigments and binding media identified, but also to the sophisticated ways in which these have been employed. Particular attention is devoted to the issue of whether the stylistic differences between the north and south walls are corroborated by differences in painting technique. Comparison of the technique of the murals with recent analyses of other contemporary wall paintings, sculptural polychromy and painted panels,[17] together with evidence from recent studies of surviving documentary sources,[18] affords valuable new insights into the influence of northern European painting practices in England towards the close of the fifteenth century.

12 These revisions, which relate primarily to the identification of the saints between the Marian scenes, are based largely on recent research by Anderson 1989 and Gill 2003. The Latin inscriptions, so much more of which are now visible than they were to James in the 1920s, have been kindly re-transcribed by Dr Christopher de Hamel.

13 Martindale 1971 and 1995.

14 Williamson 2000.

15 Themes most recently explored by Gill 2003 and Glover 2007.

16 In particular, Martindale 1995, Gill 2003, Anderson 1989, Kidd 1987 and Noad 1997.

17 See, in particular, Howard's seminal publication on medieval wall painting pigments, Howard 2003, and the work of the National Gallery, London, on the materials and techniques of northern European panel paintings (see Billinge *et al.* 1997), including Kirby's groundbreaking analyses of red lake pigments (Kirby & White 1996, Kirby *et al.* 2005 and 2006); on painted sculpture, see especially Brodrick & Darrah 1986 and 1989 on the funerary effigies at Arundel and the Winchester screen.

18 See Kirby *et al.* 2010 (in particular articles by Childs, Nash and Kirby) for in-depth analysis of documentary sources pertaining to the trade and purchase of painting materials in England and on the Continent at this time.

Part II of the book concerns the remarkable mural of a school scene in the Head Master's Chambers, which was discovered by chance during building repairs in December 2005, and conserved by Stephen Rickerby and Lisa Shekede in 2006-7. The different elements of the painting are described, including its allusions to the historical association of Eton with Winchester. Chief among the classical inscriptions included in the scene is a quotation from William Horman's *Vulgaria* of 1519, itself quoting the well-known humanist text of Quintilian's *Istitutio oratoria*. The relationship between William Horman, Robert Aldrich and Roger Lupton is examined, their shared interests in scholarship and education is discussed, and Aldrich is proposed as the likely patron of the wall painting. The style of the mural, and its materials and technique, are discussed in the light of the scientific examination of the painting undertaken in 2006-7.

Although the scene provides a portrait of school life at Eton in around 1520, the painting's dependence on an earlier iconographical tradition is clear, and is discussed in the next section. Details of the scene reflecting the structure and character of school life at Eton in the early sixteenth century, including the curriculum and dress, are described in the light of surviving contemporary documents. Finally, a discussion of the mural in the context of other depictions of school scenes reveals its status as the only painting of its type to survive from the monumental art of Renaissance Europe.

This book has come about thanks to the initiative of the present Provost of Eton, William Waldegrave, who believed that the discovery of the mural in the Head Master's Chambers provided the ideal opportunity not only to publish that immensely important new find, but also to bring together the scholarship on the chapel wall paintings that had accumulated since the time of M.R. James, and to enhance this with a detailed scientific study of both painting schemes. Lord and Lady Waldegrave's personal financial support, together with that of the Provost and Fellows of Eton, the Courtauld Institute of Art and the Paul Mellon Centre, has been invaluable in bringing this project to fruition. That two mural schemes of such rarity and importance can be found adorning the walls of one institution is truly remarkable, and it is hoped that this volume will bring them to the wide audience they deserve.

Emily Howe and Henrietta McBurney, December 2011

Part I: The fifteenth-century Marian scheme in the College chapel

Emily Howe

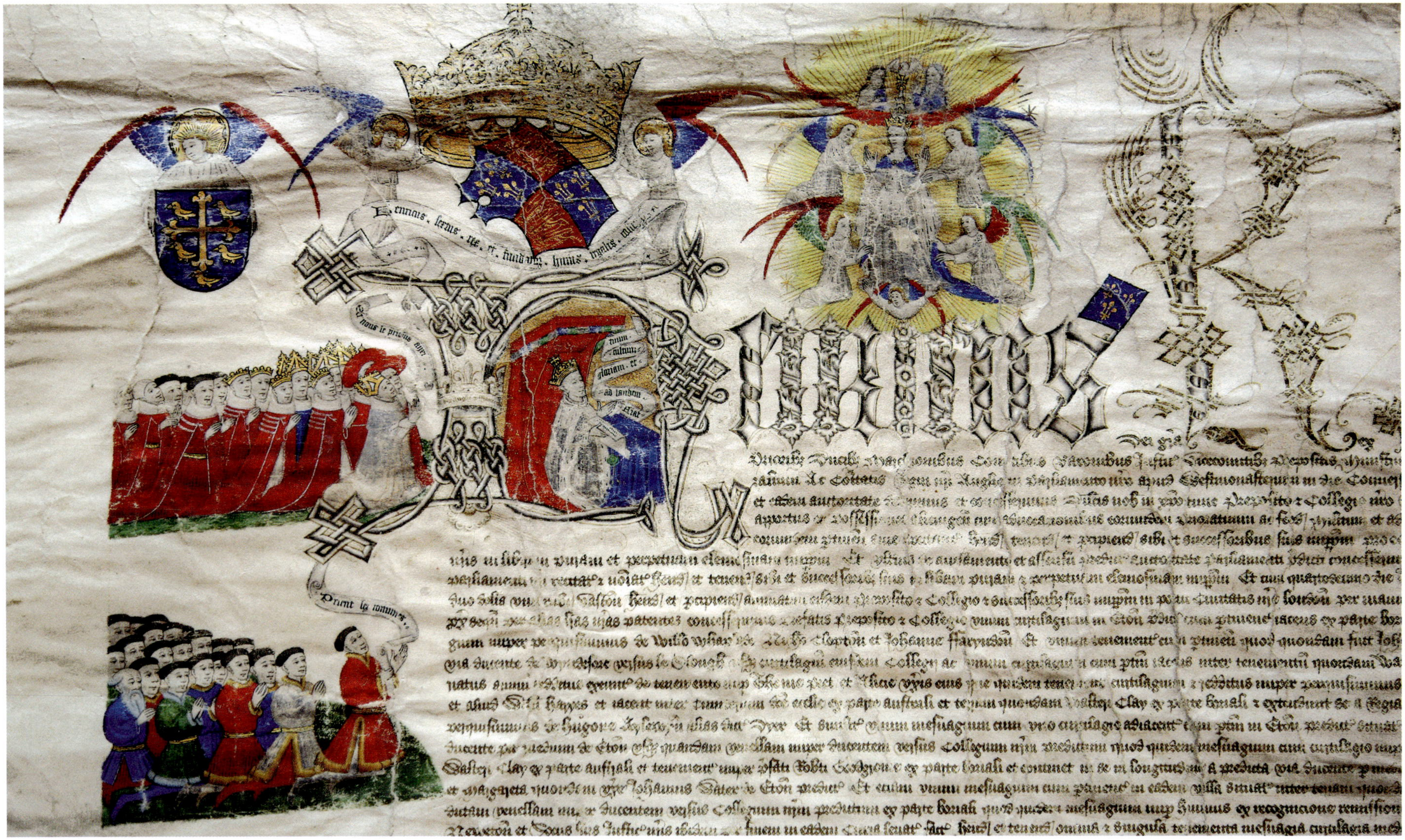

Fig. 2. Charter upon Act of Parliament for the foundation of Eton College, known as the 'Consolidation Charter', 5 March 1446 (ECR 39/57).

1. Patrons and painters

For Henry VI, who had only recently attained the full powers of his kingship, the foundation of Eton College was an act of ostentatious and self-affirming piety.[1] In his charter of foundation, dated 11 October 1440, the king declares that:

> ...Wherefore we also, who, by the disposition of the same King of kings (through whom all kings do reign), have now taken into our own hands the government of both our realms, have from the very beginning of our riper age carefully revolved in our mind how, or in what manner, or by what royal gift, according to the measure of our devotion and the example of our ancestors, we could do fitting honour to that our same Mistress and most Holy Mother, to the pleasure of that her great Spouse. And at length, while we were thinking over these things with the most profound attention, it hath become a fixed purpose in our heart to found a college, in honour and in support of that our Mother, who is so great and so holy, in the parochial church of Eton near Windsor, not far from our birthplace.[2]

A later, more lavishly illuminated document, which records the ratification of Henry's foundation by Act of Parliament, depicts the young king kneeling within the niche of his initial, as if in a small private chapel.[3] In his hands he holds the charter which he offers up towards the Virgin who, encircled by sun rays and supported by angels, ascends to heaven (Figure 2). It is an image perpetuated on Eton's first seal (Figures 3 and 4).[4] Clearly, Henry's aspirations for his new foundation were great. A drawing in a book belonging to the king's biographer and priest, John Blacman, captures the solemn moment when, kneeling with his queen at the altar of Eton's incomplete church, Henry bestowed upon the College a host of relics, among which were 'portions of the precious blood of our Lord, of His cross, of "the glorious Virgin Mary His mother, and of His most blessed Confessor Nicholas, and of Catherine the Virgin, and of other martyrs, confessors and virgins"'.[5] Against such a backdrop, it is easy to forget that Henry VI never envisaged the extraordinary scheme of paintings depicting the *Miracles of the Virgin* that was commissioned shortly after his death to adorn the walls of his extravagant new

1 For a critique of Henry VI's intentions at Eton, see Wolffe 2001, 135-45.

2 Cal. Pat. Rolls 1436-41, 455. The assignment of a site for the proposed College is announced in Royal Letters Patent, dated from Shene, 11 October (19 Henry VI., 1440), which were incorporated into a charter confirmed by the Parliament of the following year; see Willis & Clark 1886, 313-14.

3 This charter, which is known as the Consolidation Charter, dates from 5 March 1446 and is still held in the College archives (ECR 39/57); it is transcribed in Heywood & Wright 1850, 414-59. The illumination was undertaken by the London limner William Abel, for which he was paid 26*s.* 8*d.*; see Auerbach 1954, 20-1. A similar and contemporary charter, also thought to have been illuminated by Abel, is held by Eton's twin foundation, King's College, Cambridge; see Bovey in Marks & Williamson 2003, 162, cat. no.20; also Binski & Panayotova 2005, 379-81, cat. no.181.

4 Maxwell Lyte 1911, 15 and 70-2. The only impression of this seal to survive intact is attached to British Library Additional Charter 7210, a document issued by William Westbury on 5 July 1446; see Birch 1887-1900, cat. entry 4906.

5 Taken from Maxwell Lyte 1911, 28-9, who cites Bentley's *Excerpta historica*, 44-6; see also James 1920, 402, for the chapel inventories. The drawing, the date of which is uncertain, was inserted in Blacman's copy of the *Polychronicon*; see Wolffe 2001, fig.7(a).

church. While there is little doubt that Eton's founder would have approved of such a monumental display of his patron's intercessory powers,[6] records attest that his own intentions for these walls had been quite different.

By September 1440, the king had acquired the advowson of the parish church of Eton, and he resolved to make provision for a foundation comprising a provost, 10 priest-fellows, four clerks, six choristers, 25 poor scholars, a schoolmaster and 25 poor or 'enfeebled men' to pray for the souls of himself and his forebears.[7] Assiduous petitioning in Rome on behalf of the king over the ensuing years secured not only papal confirmation of his new foundation, but also the power to grant, unconditionally and in perpetuity, those pilgrims visiting Eton on the feast of the Assumption of the Virgin a plenary indulgence in remission of their sins.[8] Indeed, by 1447, Henry VI was able to boast that the papacy had granted to penitents visiting Eton indulgences more remarkable than any previously granted to any other ruler or kingdom.[9] Henry VI's ambitious aspirations for his foundation at Eton meant, however, that progress with building work was slow, the plans being subject to continual and increasingly extravagant revision.[10] While the precise date is elusive, it would seem likely that Henry laid the foundation stone of the new collegiate church at Eton before Easter 1441, with work on site commencing that summer.[11] By August 1443, a further 11 acres of land had been granted by the crown to the College and the population of its chapter had expanded to number some 70 scholars, with the addition of an usher to assist the schoolmaster, 10 extra priests (or fellows), six additional clerks and 10 more choristers. Most significantly for the character of the foundation, however, there had also been a substantial reduction, from 25 to 13, in the number of almsmen sustained by the college.[12]

Knowing, as we now do, that the College was soon to become part of a dual educational foundation with a new royal college founded by Henry VI at Cambridge, it is difficult to deduce the king's original intentions

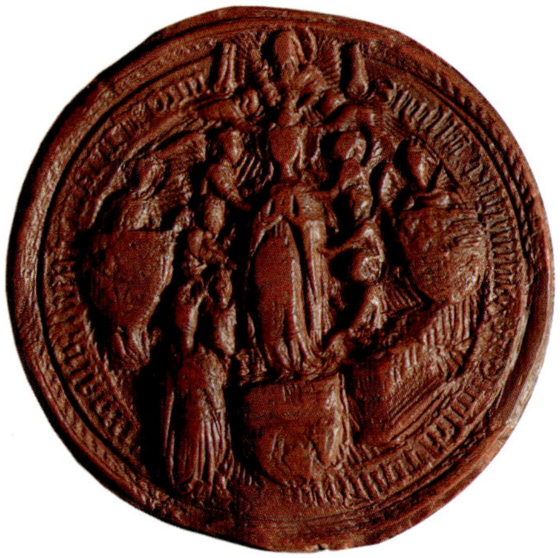

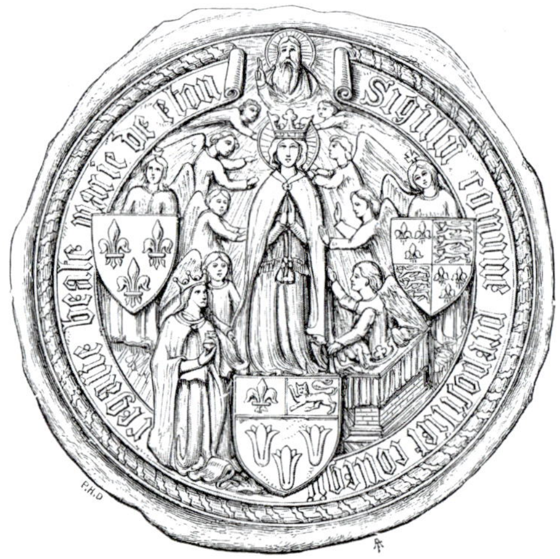

Left Fig. 3. An impression of the first seal of Eton College, attached to a document issued by the headmaster, William Westbury, 5 July 1446 (British Library, Additional Charter 7210).
Right Fig. 4. Drawing of the first seal of Eton College (reproduced from Maxwell Lyte 1911).

6 On Henry VI's devotion to the Virgin as a royal and dynastic patron, see Rubin 2009, 286-7.

7 See Willis & Clark 1886, 313-14, and Maxwell Lyte 1911, 3-4, who cite letters patent dated 3 September (19 Henry VI. 1440), and Henry's charter of foundation in Williams 1872, II, 279-85, respectively.

8 These exceptional privileges, for which Henry VI is reputed to have paid at least 1000 ducats, were granted in a papal bull dated 11 May 1444; Bekynton, I, lxxxi-lxxxviii, cited by Wolffe 2001, 137-8. See also Maxwell Lyte 1911, 6-10 and 23-4, on the papacy's ratification of the project.

9 Maxwell Lyte 1911, 24.

10 For the building history of Eton College, see Willis & Clark 1886, especially chapters I, IV, V and VI; also Colvin 1963, 279-92; and Goodall 2002.

11 Willis & Clark 1886, 380; also Maxwell Lyte 1911, 12. Wolffe 2001, 137 and n.11, cites two sources which state that when the king laid the foundation stone at King's College, Cambridge, on 2 April 1441, he had already done so at Eton. The clerk of the works' journal (or wage book), cited by Willis & Clark 1886, 383, indicates that work proper was not begun on site until July.

12 Wolffe 2001, 140. By 1447, the number of 'bedesmen' had been reduced to just six; see Davis 1993, 40.

for Eton. At the outset, at least, with an existing royal chapel school and Edward II's college of King's Hall at Cambridge providing for the educational needs of the crown, the emphasis seems to have been primarily on an ecclesiastical foundation, in pious imitation of those established by his ancestors.[13] It is not certain whether Henry, in the months before he founded Eton, had paid a visit to Wykeham's famous collegiate foundation at Winchester, and still less clear whether, at this early stage, the latter's affiliation with New College, Oxford, had influenced the king's model for his own foundation.[14] Within six months of founding Eton, however, Henry VI had proceeded to establish his new college at Cambridge, comprising a rector and 12 scholars,[15] and in the following August (1441) he visited Winchester and enlisted the headmaster, William Waynflete, to assume the same post at Eton, from which office he was almost immediately elevated to Provost.[16] A relationship of close trust developed between the two men and when the formal statutes of Eton College were drawn up in 1443, the character of Henry VI's foundation at Eton was, almost inevitably, modelled closely on that of Winchester.[17] The increasingly educational focus of the new college, a transformation undoubtedly presided over by Waynflete, was confirmed when, on 15 September 1443, a public contract of perpetual alliance was concluded between Henry's college at Eton and the newly founded royal college of St Mary and St Nicholas (later to become King's College) at Cambridge.[18]

Waynflete, having been taken into the king's closest confidence, assumed a pivotal role in overseeing the building work during his time at Eton. While none of the College's early accounts records contain a detailed plan for the new church, Henry VI's requirements for the structure – revised since the foundation of the College in favour of a far more grandiose edifice – are set out in painstaking detail in the king's 'Will and intent' dated 12 March 1448.[19] It was at this time that Waynflete, who had in the previous year been dramatically promoted to the see of Winchester, and William de la Pole, Marquess (and later Duke) of Suffolk, were formally entrusted with managing the project on behalf of the king, assisted by a succession of clerks and, later, masters of the works.[20] Progress with the project, despite their best efforts, was neither fast nor smooth. Within nine months of issuing this 'Will', Henry instructed that the choir and nave of the new minster were each to be extended by some 4.5m (15ft) and widened by 1m (3ft) and the aisles by an additional 30cm (1ft),[21] alterations that – quite astonishingly – required the destruction of the previous seven years' work, including the by now almost complete choir.[22] In January of the following year

13 This point is persuasively argued by Davis 1993, 35-56; also Wolffe 2001, 137. Goodall 2002, 247-8, observes that it had become common practice to establish religious foundations in association with important residences, and that it was not unusual for schools to be included within such secular colleges.

14 In the 3rd edition of his *History of Eton College*, Maxwell Lyte (citing Kirby's *Annals of Winchester*, 192) states that Henry VI paid a visit to Winchester College on 30 July 1440 and 'attended several services in the Chapel' (Maxwell Lyte 1899, 5). This reference was, however, conspicuously removed by the author from the 1911 edition of his book, although Griffiths 2004, 243, also refers to this visit. Wolffe 2001, 141, however, attests that the king did not make his first visit to Winchester College until 5-7 August 1441. On the influence of the Wykehamist model, see also Goodall 2002, 249.

15 Davis 1993, 36, citing *VCH Cambridgeshire*, iii, 376-7.

16 Davis 1993, 36-8; it is suggested that the king's secretary, Thomas Bekynton [sic], a former Wykehamist, had recommended Waynflete to Henry VI.

17 See Davis 1993, 38-9.

18 Davis 1993, 39, citing ECR 39/30, which states that the poor scholars of Eton, 'when sufficiently grounded in grammar, should be received for further education at the college of the Blessed Mary and St Nicholas and that no others should be admitted until these had first been admitted'. On the wider ranging *Amicabilis concordia* between Eton, King's, Winchester and New College, made in the following July (1444), see also Davis 1993, 45; Maxwell Lyte 1911, 20-1; and Wolffe 2001, 139.

19 Henry VI's 'Will' is reproduced in its entirety in Willis & Clark 1886, 350-7; see also Maxwell Lyte 1911, 38-9; also Colvin 1963, 284. Long mislaid, the building accounts of Eton College – which are unusually complete – were rediscovered in 1866 (see Willis & Clark 1886, 381 and ch.5 *passim* where the accounts are perused in great detail). While the accounts afford only glimpses of work undertaken on the new church prior to 1448, money seems to have been spent freely during this period in adapting the fabric of the existing parish church for use by the College; see Colvin 1963, 283, 285; also Willis & Clark 1886, 393-5.

20 See Maxwell Lyte 1911, 39; also Colvin 1963, 279-80.

21 Willis & Clark 1886, 364-5.

22 Willis & Clark 1886, 402, cite accounts which attest that this first choir was already being roofed and the choir stalls

(1449), Roger Keys (or Keyes), then clerk of works, was dispatched by the king with three servants to measure Winchester and Salisbury cathedrals, following which a third and final design was issued for Eton in which the dimensions of the choir were, incredibly, increased in length by a further 10m (32ft) and 1.6m (5ft) in width, and the nave by 15m (49ft) and 1.6m (5ft) respectively.[23] The proportions of the present-day chapel represent what would have constituted the choir of Henry VI's ultimate design for Eton, had his gargantuan project ever reached fruition (Figure 5).[24]

It is during this period, between 1448 and 1450, that the works accounts record the period of greatest activity on site.[25] Accounts from ensuing years, though fragmentary, attest that work tailed off dramatically from 1453, reflecting the decline of the king's own fortunes, and while the east end of the choir was apparently complete and the great window ready to receive its ironwork by 1459-60, the western end lay unfinished on Henry's deposition from power in 1461.[26] Indeed, the Lancastrian's project was nearly scuppered for good when, in 1463, Pius II issued a bull dissolving the college at Eton, and resources were subsumed into the building of a new chapel to St George at the palace in neighbouring Windsor.[27] Thanks in large part to the judicious leadership of Provost Westbury, who remained staunchly opposed to the proposed union with Edward IV's new foundation and undertook to petition those in the confidence of the new king, the fortunes of the beleaguered college eventually rallied.[28] In 1467 the crown restored to Eton some of its former landed possessions. Two years later building work resumed and, in 1470, the devastating papal decree was rescinded. Despite this, Eton found its revenues reduced to almost a quarter of its previous income and the choir's west end and roof were only completed,

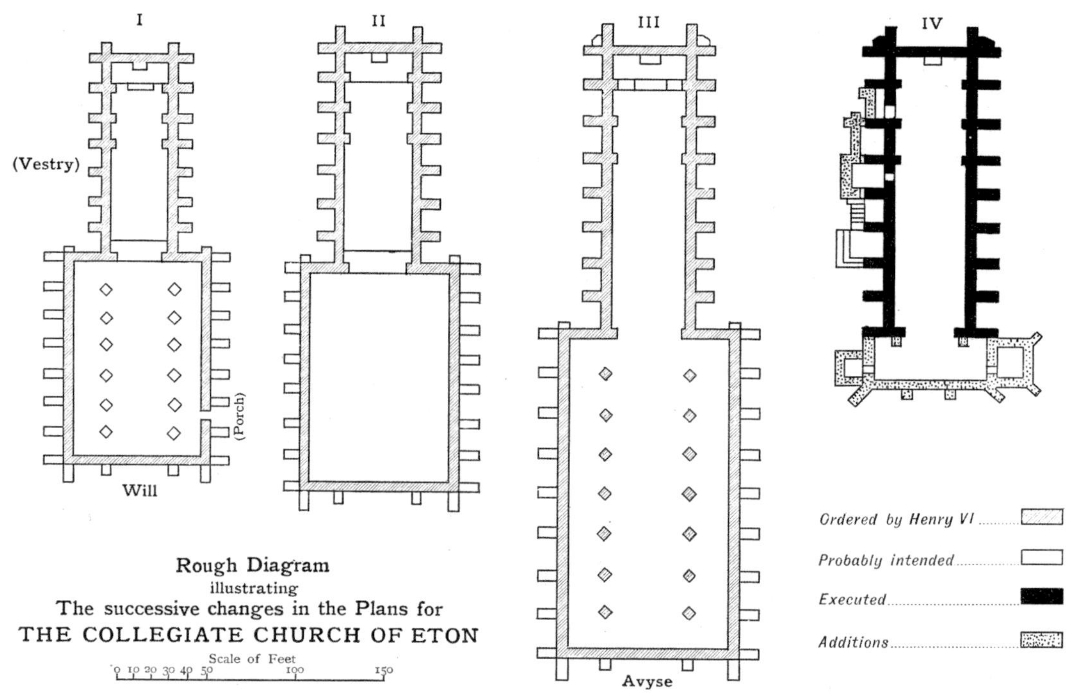

Fig. 5. Successive changes in the plans for Eton College chapel (reproduced from Maxwell Lyte 1911).

constructed; see also Wolffe 2001, 142-3. Colvin suggests that the foundations may have been undermined by water, causing the entire project to be revised (Colvin 1963, 288).

23 This document is commonly referred to as 'The King's Avyse'; see Willis & Clark 1886, 398 and 365-8; also Goodall 2002, 252-3.

24 The nave of the proposed structure, comprising eight bays and measuring some 51.2 x 12m (168 x 40ft), would have been one of the largest naves in England; see Martindale 1995, 134, and Willis & Clark 1886, 368.

25 See accounts in Willis & Clark 1886, 396 ff.

26 See Willis & Clark 1886, 404-5; also Wolffe 2001, 144, who cites Knoop & Jones 1933, 70-114; also Colvin 1963, 281. It seems that Waynflete's subvention of the building work similarly dwindled around this time, presumably as his resources were focused on his own new foundation of Magdalen College at Oxford; see Davis 1993, 46-51.

27 Martindale 1971, 179, and 1995, 134; also Davis 1993, 51-2.

28 Maxwell Lyte 1911, 62-4, 66.

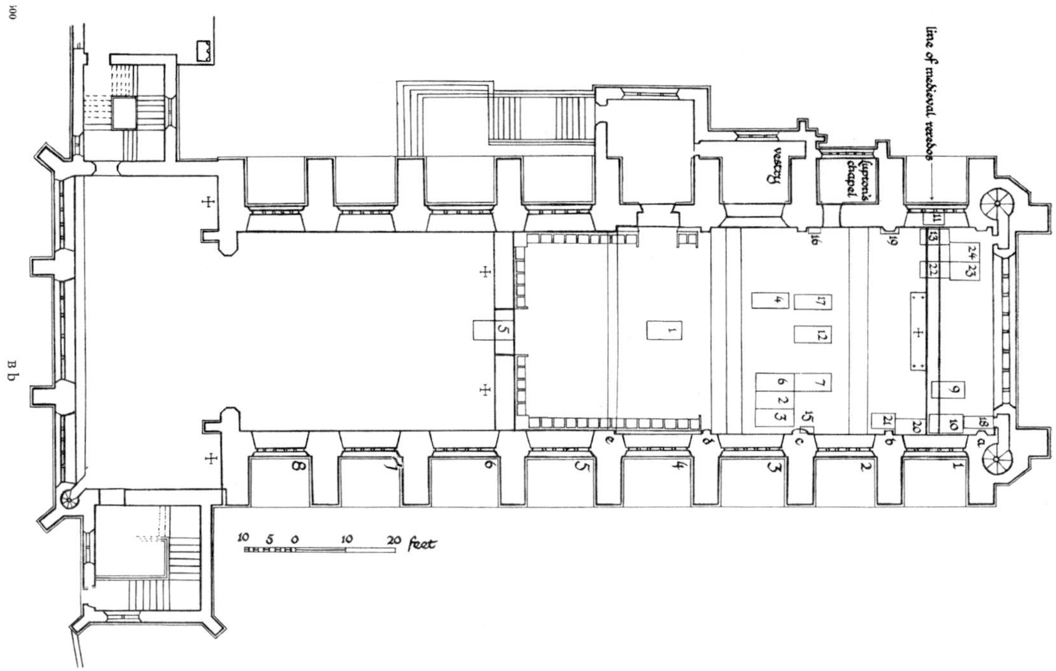

Fig. 6. Plan of Eton College chapel *c.*1500, showing the configuration of the nave (reproduced from Martindale 1971).

between 1469 and 1475, under the generous patronage of Bishop Waynflete.[29] The audit rolls from 1468 onwards record frequent journeys made by the Provost and other Fellows of the College to the Bishop of Winchester 'in order to begin the works on the church' (*pro operibus ecclesie inchoandi*) or 'to obtain money' for this work (*pro pecuniis adquirendi pro operibus ecclesie*).[30] Frustratingly, no mention is made of the sums of money acquired, nor of the ways in which they were spent.[31] Surviving documentation attests that the chapel rood screen and choir stalls were also commissioned by Waynflete in 1475, and that in the same year the bishop's glazier, Thomas, made no fewer than three visits 'to measure the windows of the new church'.[32] Constructed between 1479 and 1483, a relatively modest transverse ante-chapel was substituted for the cavernous nave intended by Henry VI, but with a congregation of about 200 parishioners, such a space proved inadequate.[33] As a result, the new rood screen was erected not at the west end of the choir where the current organ loft now stands, but three bays eastward, thereby creating a parochial nave (Figure 6).[34] The expanses of flat unornamented wall which formed the north and south elevations of this space, and which according to Henry VI's original plans ought to have been covered by the canopies of ornately carved choir stalls, now demanded urgent attention.

While it was customary for the care of the nave to fall to the parish, Waynflete doubtless considered the completion of the king's prestigious building project to be incumbent upon himself, not only as executor of the king's 'Will', but also as the benefactor of an institution that was in no small measure responsible for his personal advancement.[35] The walls beneath the great glass windows – measuring some 20m (65ft) wide and over 8m (26ft) high – were vast, and devoid of the

29 See Willis & Clark 1886, 406-11; also Davis 1993, 53-4; Colvin 1963, 291; also Martindale 1995, 134-5.
30 Willis & Clark 1886, 406-11; also Davis 1993, 53-4.
31 Davis 1993, 54, suggests that the frequency of the visits indicate that Waynflete paid out money in small amounts, thereby retaining considerable personal control over the works.
32 Willis & Clark 1886, 408-9 (the contract with the carpenter Walter Nicholl is reproduced in full in appendix I.C.); also Colvin 1963, 291.
33 The figure of 200 is proposed by Martindale 1971, 189, n.2, based on the tax records for Eton in 1523. The ante-chapel was of the kind appearing at some of the Oxford college chapels around this time, including those of New College, All Souls and Waynflete's own foundation, Magdalen College; see Martindale 1971, 189 and Martindale 1995, 135. On the ante-chapel see also Lindley 1988.
34 Martindale 1971, 182, 189, draws our attention to the high curving line on the eastern edge of the wall paintings, which marks the point where the rood screen was originally installed; see also Gill 2003, 176.
35 See Davis 1993, 55-6, who observes that Waynflete went so far as to adopt the lilies of Eton College in his episcopal arms as a means of conveying his enduring attachment to the foundation. The responsibility of parishioners for the nave of a church dates back to statutes promulgated in the thirteenth century; see Cragoe 2010.

ornate sculptural detail which articulates such areas in Henry VI's chapel at King's College. While an elaborate mural programme was, arguably, excessive in a nave to be used predominantly by parishioners, this was no ordinary parish church and the decoration of the nave needed to be sufficiently sumptuous to complement the level of ornament employed elsewhere in the building. By this late stage the options open to Waynflete were limited. Tapestries were exorbitantly expensive, and painted murals would certainly have presented the fastest and most affordable solution, given the large area that required decoration.[36]

No contract or other surviving document attests to the authorship of the iconographically complex programme which was ultimately devised to decorate the nave walls,[37] nor to the date at which painters were first engaged to undertake this project. The series of accounts relating to work undertaken at Eton over this period is exasperatingly fragmentary, permitting only occasional glimpses of those working in the church.[38] The first mention of painters engaged in the College appears in a quite recently discovered fragment of the account roll relating to 1477, though it is not clear in which area of the College these men were working.[39] A similarly vague reference is made in the roll for 1479-80, but again there is no specific mention of either the church or of wall paintings.[40] While the next two rolls are missing, reference is made in 1482-3 to a priest who is 'master of the painters' (*presbiter magister pictorum*),[41] the inference being that a group of painters were engaged in work on a scheme sufficiently complex to demand that a man of some learning should oversee its execution. An appealing though as yet unsubstantiated suggestion, first ventured by James, is that such a master may have been a member of Waynflete's own household.[42] More recent scholarship has proposed, however, that that this individual may in fact have been the Eton Fellow William Whyther, whom James considered synonymous with the 'magister operis sive fabrice ecclesie' mentioned in the roll for 1484-5.[43] Compelling evidence for this assertion is, however, lacking and Whyther's repeated trips to Winchester to collect funds would seem to fit better with the role of clerk of the works.[44] The absence from the accounts of any wages paid to the aforementioned painters, or of payments for materials used by them, suggests in any case that all such costs were defrayed by Waynflete. It seems certain that at least some of the wall paintings had been completed by 1482-3, as account is given in the rolls for this year of a payment to one 'Lodovico Palmer' for sponges with which to 'wash the paintings in the nave of the church in preparation for the feast of the Assumption'.[45] Willis

36 Gill 2002, 192-3, notes that while this configuration of wall paintings beneath windows was born of necessity in response to an architectural change of plan, the model was emulated in the Marian scheme of *c.*1500 in Winchester's Lady Chapel (see Figures 33 and 34) as well as in the nave of the Guild chapel at Stratford-upon-Avon (*c.*1496) where hagiographic scenes with textual commentaries were surmounted by windows interspersed by fictive statues painted beneath architectural canopies.

37 The iconography of the paintings is treated in some depth in chapter 2 of this study.

38 The accounts are treated in scrupulous detail by James; see James & Tristram 1929, 1-4.

39 The rolls for 1476-8 were believed missing until Martindale first brought this fragment to our attention; see Martindale 1995, 151, n.11. It would seem that the last two manuscripts of the lost audit roll for 1477 were re-used as the wrapper for an Elizabethan bursar's roll (ECR 61/BR/K/6); they were catalogued in 1982 by the then archivist, Patrick Strong. Under the heading 'Custus forinseci' the costs of board and lodging for one *dominus Ricardus Seywell* and four other painters are noted; this is quite possibly the same *Ricardus* who receives frequent mention in the household accounts of Provost Bost (COLL/HB1), apparently also dating from that year.

40 Roll 18 (ECR 61/AR/C/6) cited by James (James & Tristram 1929, 1-2), records, under the heading *Ecclesia*, '… iij s. vj d. pro iij duodenis et dimid. in candelis datis pictoribus isto anno operantibus infra collegium..'

41 Roll 19 (ECR 61/AR/D/1) also cited by James (James & Tristram 1929, 1-2).

42 James & Tristram 1929, 2; see also Davis 1993, 102; Marks 1979, 147.

43 Roll 20 (ECR 61/AR/D/2). See Anderson 1989, 14-15, who notes that Whyther was bursar in the years 1478-9, 1480-1 and 1482-3. In the nominal roll for 1485-6 (ECR 61/NR/2), Whyther is styled 'provisor operis' and receives payment 'pro supervisione operas hoc anno'.

44 See James & Tristram 1929, 3; also Willis & Clark 1886, 411.

45 Roll 19 (ECR 61/AR/D/1) cited by James (James & Tristram 1929, 2): 'Lodovico Palmer… pro spongiis emptis pro picturis mundandis erga festum assumpcionis beate Marie et pro labore eiusdem Palmer et unius secum laborantis ad pisas pictures in naue ecclesie mundandas xxij[d]'.

and Clark identify Palmer as the sacristan,[46] but it is perhaps not beyond the realms of possibility that the Italian-sounding 'Lodovico' was, in fact, a foreign painter.[47] Indeed Tristram asserts that, rather than washing the paintings to clean them (which could hardly have been necessary given how recently they had been executed), Palmer was probably pursuing the customary workshop practice of washing down paintings executed in oil to harden the surface of the paint.[48]

In the years following this, evidence of painting activity in the church is scant. The roll for 1483-4 is missing, and by 1484-5 there is no further reference to the aforementioned master of the painters. While an isolated entry in the rolls for this year alludes to the purchase of candles for an unspecified number of glaziers and painters at work in the chapel,[49] it is only on Waynflete's death in 1486 that we observe a significant increase in entries pertaining to painting in the church, the costs of which – along with all other building work at Eton – thereafter fall entirely to the College.[50] The account roll for 1486-7 is particularly illuminating in this respect, and is worth examining in detail, recounting as it does not only an extensive list of painting materials, but also the name of 'ipsius pictoris', one Willelmi Baker, and the wages paid to other unnamed men engaged in this work in the 'lower part' (we must presume the nave) of the church.[51] Beneath the heading 'Ecclesia', Lodovico Palmer is again remunerated for washing the wall paintings in the church.[52] Then, alongside the marginal inscription 'pictura ecclesie', we find the following account:

> Et pro expensis factis circa picturam ecclesie. In primis pro scansiliis factis et planacione tabularum in inferiori parte ecclesie xiij^{d}.
> Et pro viij lagenis Potell et Pynt olei pictorum precium lagene xvj^{d} summa xij^{s}.
> Et pro i li. vernacii viij^{d}.
> Et pro x li. plumbi albi et rubei empt. ad diuersa tempora ij^{s} iiij^{d}.
> Et pro xj li. de colore viridi anglice vertegrece x^{s} x^{d}.
> Et pro v li. de colore fuluo scilicet oker xij^{d} ob.
> Et pro v li. de colore blodio scil. anglice blew orch (erch?) et blew yende viij^{d}.
> Et pro ix li. de colore fuluo anglice generall iij^{s}.
> Et pro iij quart. li. de ly vermelon xij^{d}.
> Et pro iij quart. de auro puro iiij^{s} vj^{d}.
> Et pro expensis factis circa empcionem predictorum colorum et vecturam iij^{s} viij^{d} ob.
> Et pro laboribus diuersorum pictorum in opera predicto viij^{li}. vij^{s}. iiij^{d}.
> Et pro diuersis aliis coloribus ocupatis de coloribu propriis ipsius pictoris scilicet Willelmi Baker iij^{s}.

The materials cited include 8 gallons of painter's oil, 1lb of varnish, 10lb of red and white lead, 11lb of English verdigris, 5lb of 'tawny' ochre, 5lb of vivianite and indigo, 9lb of 'the tawny colour called generall', ¾lb of vermilion, and ¾lb of pure gold. Whether this inventory of materials relates specifically and exclusively to

46 See Willis & Clark 1886. In the college audit rolls for 1479-80 (ECR 61/AR/C/6) Palmer is, for example, mentioned in the context of repairing church vestments.

47 While Tudor-Craig 1973, 21, has postulated that Palmer may have been an anglicised version of '*da Palma*', David Park observes (pers. comm.), that Palmer was a relatively common surname in England at this time, derived from the term for pilgrims (who traditionally carried palm branches). Given that Eton was a centre for pilgrimage, it may be that 'Lodovico' originally came to Eton under this guise, only to take up more permanent duties. Regrettably, research yields no further leads in this matter.

48 James & Tristram 1929, 42. If this was indeed the case, it is not clear why the cost of these sponges and of Palmer's time were not met by Waynflete, along with all other expenses relating to the paintings.

49 ECR 61/AR/D/2, cited by James & Tristram 1929, 3 ('pro iiij duodenis candelarum paris. liberates pictoribus et vitratoribus laborantibus in ecclesia hoc anno iiij^{s}.')

50 See Davis 1993, 55.

51 Roll 22 (ECR 61/AR/F/2, m2), cited by James (James & Tristram 1929, 3-4).

52 Roll 22 (ECR 61/AR/F/2, m2), 'Lodowyco Palmer pro locione parietum depictarum in ecclesie ijs vid.'

the execution of the wall paintings in the nave is contested.[53] Recent scientific analysis of the paintings confirms that most of the materials employed in the scheme, with the conspicuous exceptions of red lake, lead-tin yellow, lime white and carbon black, are indeed itemised. It may well be, given the predominantly grisaille palette of the paintings and the quantities of brightly coloured pigments here specified, that the materials listed also include those required for painting being undertaken elsewhere in the church. This extensive entry seems, in any case, to have comprised something of a closing account for painting within the church, the main work of which was evidently complete by this time. The identity of William Baker remains both tantalising and elusive.[54] Though the manner in which he is singled out may reasonably suggest that he enjoyed prominent status among those working in the church at this time, it is conspicuous and puzzling that there is no itemised payment for Baker's work here. Martindale, who has analysed this passage in some detail, concludes that Baker receives mention in this entry only in as much as he was the supplier of pigments; he is 'ipse pictor' (the painter) not 'magister pictor' (the master painter).[55] It does not, however, seem unreasonable to suppose that an artist might charge for the use of painting materials already in his possession, and that Baker – as the principal painter – may have been remunerated for his labour from some other source, even by Waynflete, prior to his death.

Establishing a timeframe for the execution of Waynflete's mural programme at Eton is far from straightforward. The wall paintings must certainly post-date the insertion, in 1475, of the rood screen, the silhouette of which is preserved in a high curving line just visible on the upper eastern edges of the scheme.[56] The copious provision of furnishings and fittings in the College records for the year 1479-80 strongly suggests that it was around this time that the nave of the church began to be used for lay worship.[57] From the accounts evidence we may further deduce that paintings of some sort – almost certainly wall paintings – existed in the nave of the church by 1482, and that significant numbers of painters were again at work in the 'lower church' between 1486 and 1487. While James seems to have construed from this that painting continued in the nave steadily throughout this period (albeit largely undocumented at Eton owing to the fact that Waynflete was absorbing the main cost of the work), Martindale has since hypothesised that there were two distinct phases of painting, with the north wall being painted first, in about 1480, and the south in 1486, a pause which, though unexplained, may account for the discontinuity in style between the two walls.[58]

53 This point, which is made by Martindale 1995, 149-50, is given further consideration in chapter 6 below.

54 Though it may be no more than coincidence, it seems that the chief carver working at St George's Chapel at Windsor in the period 1479-83 was one William Berkeley – also sometimes referred to as William Baker; see Harvey 1984, 20-1.

55 Martindale 1995, 149-50. Gill 2003, 177, concurs that Baker may have been no more than a 'colour-man'. Recent work on the trade in painters' materials in sixteenth-century London suggests, however, that the appearance of specialist colour merchants occurred much later here than on the Continent, with most pigments being supplied through general grocers up until the late 1500s; see Kirby 2010.

56 Martindale 1971, 182, 189; see also Gill 2003, 176.

57 Willis & Clark 1886, 411; also Gill 2003, 176; also Martindale 1971, 197-8, who cites the onset of offerings to altars and images by parishioners visiting the church, along with a dramatic increase in expenses for the daily provision of services.

58 See James & Tristram 1929, 1-4; also Martindale 1995, 149. This date for the south wall paintings would accord well with Tudor-Craig's hypothesis that the distinctive pendant worn by the Emperor's brother in scene s7, comprising a crescent suspended from a sunburst or *rose-en-soleil*, makes derogatory reference to the recently defeated Yorkist regime; see Tudor-Craig 1973, 21; also Martindale 1995, 148-9, and Anderson 1989, 28-9.

While the extent of Waynflete's personal involvement in designing the programme of the wall paintings at Eton is far from clear, his influence in the choice of subject matter, if not the detail, cannot be doubted. Although there is no evidence that Waynflete overtly sought to advertise his patronage in the paintings, some of the subjects depicted quite obviously reflect his own devotional preoccupations.[59] Indeed, Waynflete's particular allegiance to Mary Magdalene – an affinity rooted in the dedication of the Winchester hospital of which he long stood master, and confirmed in the dedication of his own collegiate foundation at Oxford – resonates at Eton, where the saint is depicted in a position of prominence at the far east end of the north wall.[60] As a patron at Eton and elsewhere, Waynflete reveals himself to have been at once conservative and progressive. While he was undoubtedly traditionalist in terms of his own faith and training, he also enjoyed a reputation for being an energetic advocate of learning, particularly in English humanist circles.[61] Even in old age, he seems to have remained open-minded towards new ideas, embracing technological developments such as the printing press. At Winchester, Oxford, Eton and the collegiate foundation of Tattershall in Lincolnshire (for which he became responsible on the death of Henry VI's treasurer, Ralph, Lord Cromwell), Waynflete proved himself an ambitious and actively involved patron of architecture.[62] In the church at Tattershall, in particular, he seems to have been personally involved in the composition of the complex programme of stained glass which, until the Reformation, adorned its great windows.[63] The iconography of this scheme, which dates from almost exactly the same period as the Eton wall paintings and has been shown to include elements of the life of Christ, as well as episodes from the Old Testament, the lives of the saints and the Catechism, is believed to have been closely derived from a Netherlandish block book, the *Biblia pauperum*. It is quite possible that this work, which had been published on the Continent only very recently, was in the bishop's possession.[64] It does not require a huge leap of the imagination to postulate that such a model may also have been made available by Waynflete when he commissioned the wall paintings in the new nave at Eton.[65]

59 See Gill 2003, 177.
60 Davis 1993, 13; also Maxwell Lyte 1911, 14.
61 See Davis 1993, 90-9.
62 On Tattershall, see Marks 1979. Waynflete showed himself to be particularly innovative in his deployment of brick in many of his buildings (see Davis 1993, 99-106; also Goodall 2002), and was actively involved in the selection of craftsmen working on his projects (see Marks 1979, 136-7). While the glass workers employed at Tattershall College have not been directly linked to Waynflete, we do know that Thomas, the bishop's own glazier, was deployed in the chapel at Eton; see Willis & Clark 1886, 408-9.
63 Davis 1993, 101; also Marks 1979, 145-8.
64 Marks 1979, 150-2.
65 This suggestion is made by Davis 1993, 101. On the Netherlandish style of the paintings, see chapter 4 below.

2. The wall painting programme

Nineteenth-century drawings of the wall paintings in Eton's chapel reveal that Waynflete's original scheme entirely covered the unpunctuated north and south walls of the new nave up to the height of the string course beneath its vast stained glass windows (Figures 7 and 8, see also Figure 1). Comprising 32 scenes ranged in two registers, the paintings set forth a sequence of miracles which according to legend were performed by the Virgin following her death. Each miraculous episode is depicted within a rectangular frame and bordered, on either side, by an elaborate hexagonal canopied niche in which stands one of 36 fictive statues of saints (Figure 9). While both the figurative elements of the scheme and the micro-architectural framework in which they are depicted are executed in a predominantly grisaille palette, in imitation of stonework, extensive touches of colour are employed to enliven such elements as the figures' hair, skin tone, costumes and identifying attributes. The two registers of the scheme are articulated by an intervening horizontal band of simulated stone, from which ornately carved foliate corbels project into the upper corners of each scene.[66] It has been suggested that the designer's intention was to evoke the sense of space that the aisles in

Fig. 7. The surviving lower register of painting on the chapel's north wall.

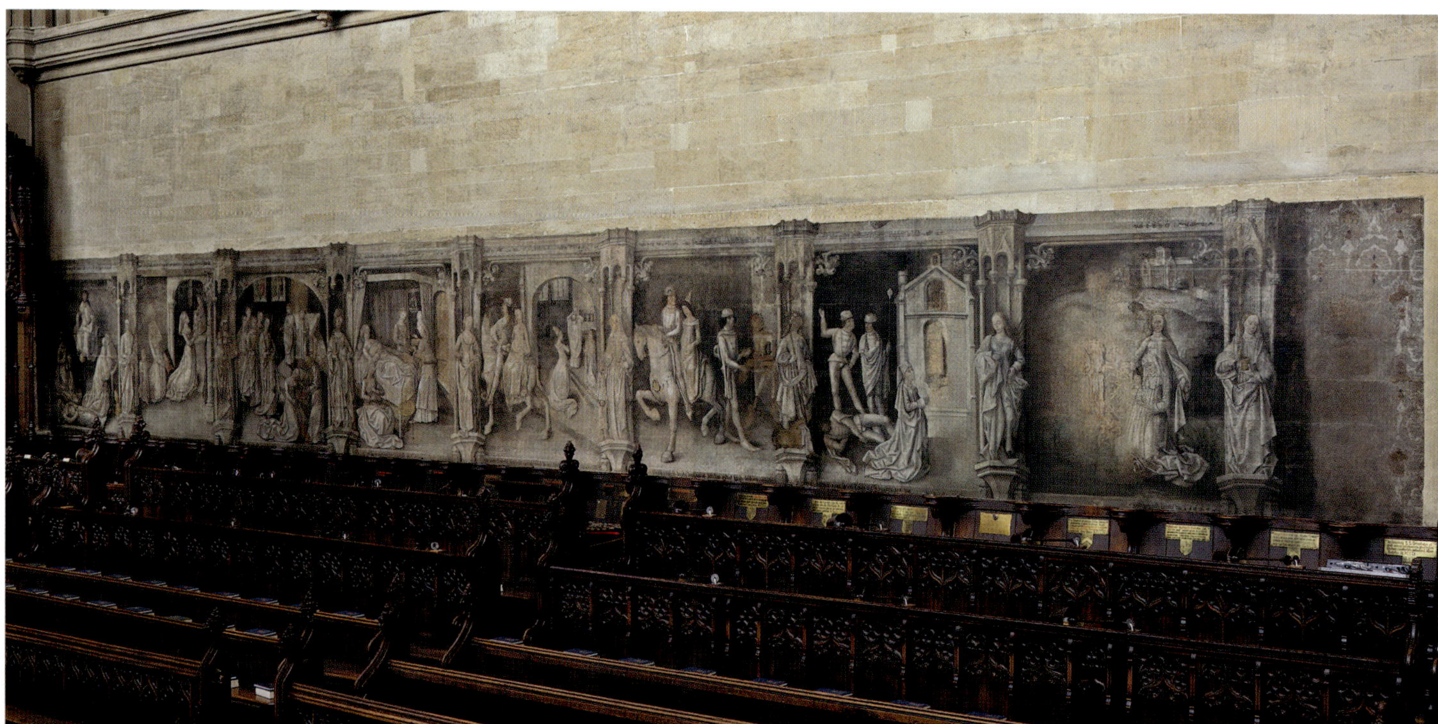

66 See Agnew in McConnell 1976, 120.

Henry VI's original plan would have lent the nave. The figures of saints standing on plinths within their niches are skilfully foreshortened to give the impression of being viewed from below, an illusionistic quality which is heightened by the use of a single imagined light source which illuminates the scheme from the west.[67] To complete this three-dimensional illusion a wide band of foliate ornament has been painted, running horizontally along the wall beneath the lower register (though now obscured by stalls) and vertically along the eastern edges of the scheme, in imitation of sumptuous damask hangings (see Figure 9).[68]

The subject matter of each miracle is announced by a Latin inscription which runs along the bottom of the scene, painted in black Gothic 'textura' script on a white ground (see Figures 40, 78 and 79). All but one of the surviving inscriptions make reference to one of two literary sources.[69] Eight of the scenes cite Jacobus de Voragine's *Legenda aurea* (or 'Legenda sanctorum', as it is called in the inscriptions), dated to *c.*1260. This compilation of saints' lives, a copy of which seems to have been in the possession of the College, was arranged according to the liturgical calendar and makes mention of numerous Marian miracles in its accounts of the Purification, Assumption, and Nativity of the Virgin.[70] A further 14 of the Eton miracles are derived from Vincent of Beauvais' *Speculum historiale* (*c.*1244) which, following an account of the Assumption, catalogues some 32 miracles attributed to the intercession of the Virgin.[71] Both these texts were well known, and were being printed by Caxton around the time the wall painting programme was commissioned – the *Legenda aurea* (or *Golden Legend*)

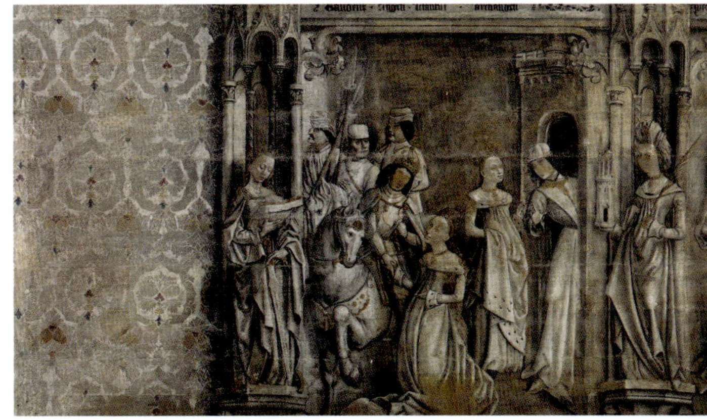

Right Fig. 9. South wall, scene 1, with fictive damask textile painted to the east.

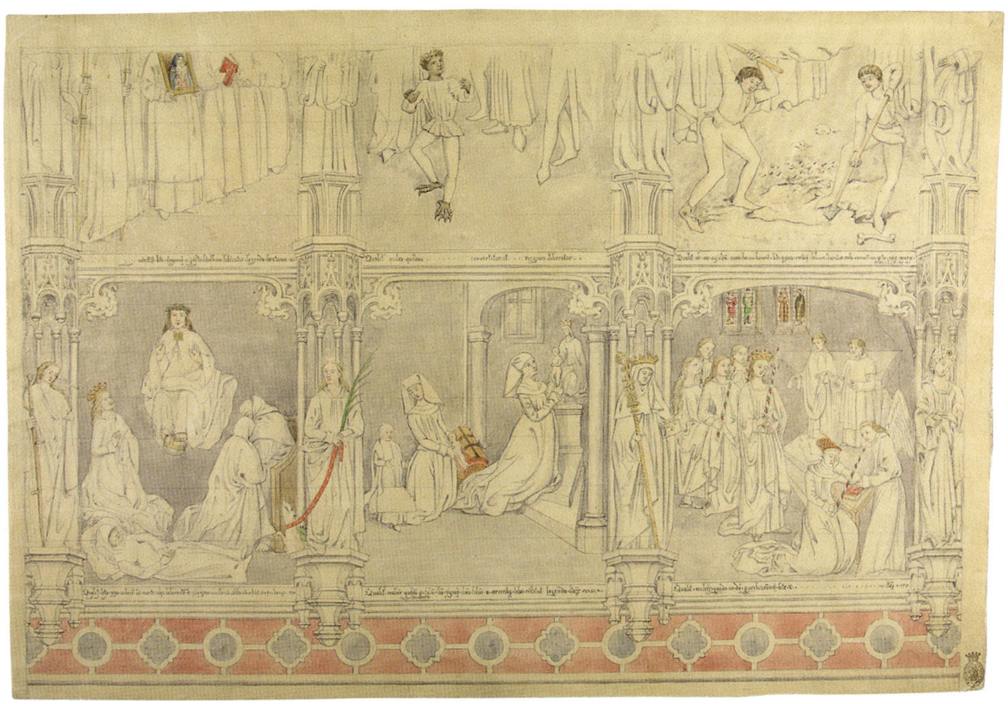

Fig. 8. Copy of the paintings at the west end of the chapel's north wall, made by R.H. Essex in 1847, showing part of the paintings' now missing upper register.

67 Martindale 1995, 137; Gill 2003, 173.
68 For discussion of the style of the hangings, see chapter 4 below. The painting of fictive draperies at dado level was common practice in ecclesiastical contexts; see Gill 2002, 199, on the use of painted brocade textiles and cloths of honour to denote a sanctified space.
69 The inscription beneath scene 1 on the upper register of the south wall, the 'Assumption of the Virgin', does not cite a literary source, but is thought to be taken from the Roman Breviary's Office for the Assumption; see James 1907, 20.
70 See Gill 2003, 183. The work is listed in an inventory of books at Eton for 1465; see Noad 1997, 39, citing James 1920.
71 Gill 2003, 183.

Fig. 10. *The Miracles of the Virgin:* table of the mural programme's subject matter.

SOUTH SIDE

(East: left)

	I	1	II	2	III	3	IV	4	V	5	VI	6	VII	7	VIII	8	IX
A	Archangel Gabriel	The Assumption of the Virgin	Evangelist /Church Father	Miracle of the Jew at the Virgin's funeral	St Ambrose or Luke?	Miracle of Theophilus	Evangelist /Church Father	Miracle of St John of Damascus and his hand	St Augustine or John?	Miracle of the columns at Constantinople	St Jerome or Matthew	Miracle of the youth betrothed to the Virgin's image	Evangelist /Church Father	Miracle of the Mass of St Bonnet	St Jerome or Mark?	Miracle of the Jew of Bourges	St Gregory ?
B		← *The Legend of the Empress falsely accused* →															
B	St Catherine	The Emperor's departure; his brother imprisoned	St Barbara	The Empress is accused of infidelity and banished	St Apollonia	The Empress is rescued by a knight	St Agnes	The Empress is accused of infanticide and banished	St Ursula	The Empress sees the Virgin in a vision	St Dorothy	The Empress heals the knight's brother	St Cecilia	The Empress heals her brother-in-law	St Juliana	The Empress takes the veil	St Winifred

NORTH SIDE

(East: right)

	IX	8	VIII	7	VII	6	VI	5	V	4	IV	3	III	2	II	1	I
A	Prophet	Miracle of Mount St Angelo	Prophet	Miracle of the Devil disguised as a steward	Prophet	Miracle of the dead monk and the rose	Prophet	Miracle of the sick clerk	Prophet	Unidentified scene with a knight	Prophet	Miracle of the pious painter	Prophet	Miracle of the blaspheming gambler	Prophet	Miracle of Ebbo the thief ?	The Virgin?
B	St Sidwell	Miracle of the woman dying unconfessed	St Martha	Miracle of the image held hostage	St Etheldreda	Miracle of the candle	St Mary of Egypt	Miracle of the Jewess delivered by the Virgin	St Agatha	Amoras' wife is delivered by the Virgin	St Elizabeth of Hungary	Amoras sells his wife to the Devil	St Margaret	Miracle of the wounded image	Unidentified (new)	Miracle of Mont St Michel	St Mary Magdalene

Note: Figures and scenes are numbered from east to west*; scenes and figures highlighted in red vary from James' original identifications, those in grey no longer survive.*

Right Fig. 11. North wall, scene 3, the legend of Amoras who sells his wife to the Devil.
Below Fig. 12. North wall, scene 3, detail of Amoras' head.

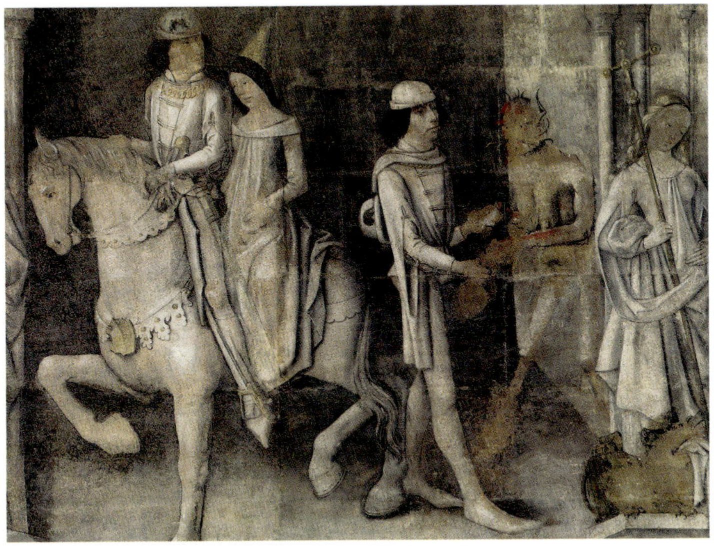

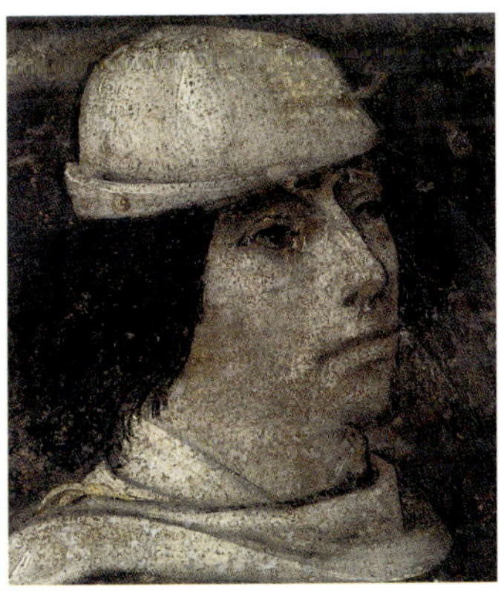

in both Latin and English – and it is reasonable to suppose that Waynflete, being an enthusiastic supporter of the new printing press, owned copies of both.[72]

The rationale behind the selection of the miracles depicted at Eton and the figures with which they are interspersed continues to provoke discussion. Our understanding of the iconographic programme has evolved considerably since M.R. James first published his exposition of the scheme in the 1890s.[73] As a result of the cleaning and restoration of the paintings undertaken by Pauline Plummer in the 1960s and 70s, it is now possible to make out much more of the original scheme than was visible to James, who relied heavily upon comparison with a derivative scheme of wall painting commissioned by Prior Silkstede for the Lady Chapel at Winchester (*c*.1500) for clues as to the subject matter of the missing elements at Eton.[74] Large areas of the lower register that previously lay obscured have now been recovered from beneath layers of darkened varnish and overpaint,[75] and a revised catalogue of the subject matter, based on much recent scholarship on the paintings, can now be proposed (Figure 10 and see the Catalogue, p.93). With the exception of the 'Amoras' legend, which occupies two bays of the lower register of the north wall, and the protracted recitation of the story of 'The Empress falsely accused', which takes up the entire lower register on the south, each miracle story is recounted in a single scene. Many of the scenes depict different moments in the same story simultaneously, with the result that in several cases the same character is portrayed more than once.[76] In the first of the 'Amoras' scenes on the north wall, for example (scene 3), Amoras can be seen on the right making a pact with the Devil, while on the left of the same scene he is shown riding away with his unsuspecting wife (Figures 11 and 12). The configuration of this scene and others reveals that the images on both walls are intended to be read from east to west.[77]

72 Davis 1993, 90-2. Indeed, Caxton's vernacular version of the *Speculum historiale* was the earliest illustrated book to be printed in England (see Hind 1935, 708); Maxwell Lyte 1911, 85-6, observes that the *Speculum historiale* had already gone through three printed editions by 1479.

73 James 1895b.

74 On the Winchester paintings, see James 1907; James & Tristram 1929, 13-37; Park & Welford 1993, 133-4.

75 In particular bays 4 and 5 on each side; see chapter 5 below on the paintings' physical history.

76 See Gill 2003, 186-7 on this narrative technique.

77 The numbering system adhered to in this study reflects this and, as such, departs from the nomenclature employed by James for the north wall paintings in his study of 1907 (which works from left to right). It is, however, in keeping with the system employed by him in his later publication with Tristram (James & Tristram 1929). Throughout the present study, figures are numbered I-IX and scenes are numbered 1-8, running from east to west.

The Miracles of the Virgin

The *Miracles of the Virgin* cycle portrayed at Eton is almost certainly the most extensive surviving programme of its type in English art.[78] While the general subject matter of the scheme is unsurprising, given the dedication of Eton College, the rationale for the choice and sequence of the miracles depicted remains elusive. The upper register of miracles, of which only the westernmost scene on the south wall survives, is known to us only through the drawings of R.H. Essex, who was commissioned in 1847 to copy the already partially obliterated murals prior to the installation of new stall canopies.[79] The only obvious sense of order to the scheme as revealed in these drawings is of a gender-based hierarchy.[80] With the exception of the 'Assumption', which was depicted in a position of prominence at the east end of the upper register on the south wall, the remaining scenes in the upper register on both walls seem to have represented a diverse range of miracles of which men were the subject. The intervening saint figures are also thought to have been male. In the lower registers, conversely, the figures and the subjects of the miracles are entirely female. With the exception of the 'Assumption', all the episodes portrayed relate to miracles performed by the Virgin following her death. While there does not appear to be any chronological sequence to these episodes, it has been suggested that those on the south wall are set in the period of the Roman Empire and Early Church, whereas those on the north wall find their action in more recent times – a division visually undermined by the fact that the protagonists in almost all of the scenes are depicted wearing fifteenth-century costume.[81] In the 24 miracles depicted at Eton, however, no single theme predominates. Certainly there is some emphasis on the intercessory benefits of venerating Marian images, a subject which occupies no fewer than five of the mural scenes.[82] In the now lost upper register on the north wall, the 'Miracle of Mount St Angelo' (scene 8) recounts how

Fig. 13. North wall, scene 2, the 'Miracle of the wounded image'.

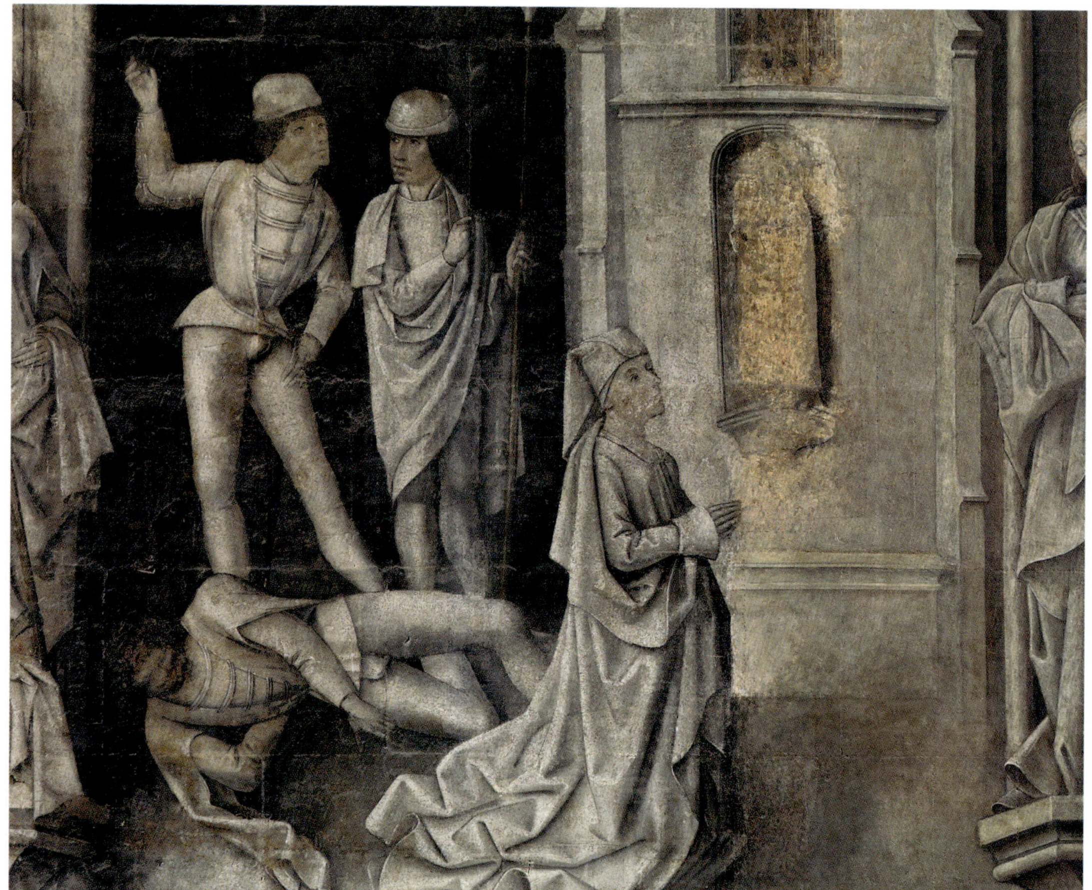

78 Gill 2003, 182; see also chapter 3 below for discussion of other Marian cycles from this period.
79 Regrettably the fitting of the new canopies was to result in still further destruction of the murals; see chapter 5 below on the paintings' physical history.
80 Martindale 1995, 142, discusses this gender-based division; Gill 2003, 184-5, observes that the miracles are not recounted according to the chronology of either of the cited literary sources. On the choice of miracles see also Noad 1997, 7.
81 For these observations see Gill 2003, 186.
82 The miracles on the north wall include those of Mount St Angelo, the pious painter, the image taken hostage, and the wounded image, and on the south, the youth betrothed to the Virgin's image.

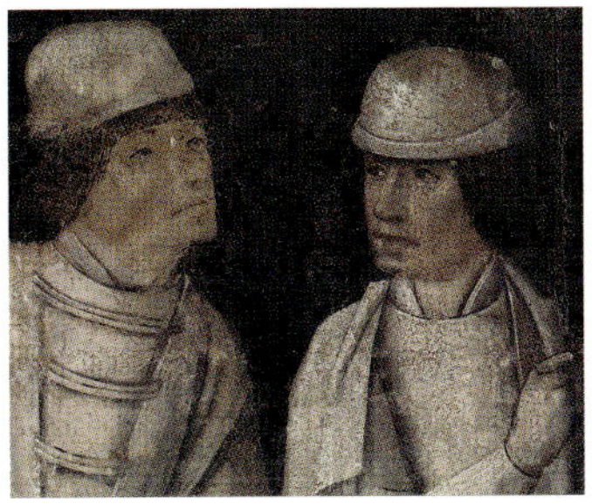

Above Fig. 14. North wall, scene 2, detail.
Right Fig. 15. North wall, scene 1, the 'Miracle of Mont St Michel', detail showing the Virgin sheltering the mother and her new-born child.

Pope Gregory processed carrying an image of the Virgin when the country was beset by plague. Further east, in the 'Miracle of the pious painter' (scene 3), the Virgin intervenes to save a man who, having been commissioned to paint her image on a church, is caused to fall from his scaffold by the Devil. The punishment for desecrating an image of the Virgin was made plain for all to see in the 'Miracle of the wounded image' (north wall, lower register, scene 2), in which a soldier, having ridiculed a pious woman for her devotion to a statue of the Virgin and Child, throws a stone at the effigy, whereupon the statue bleeds and the soldier drops down dead (Figures 13 and 14). Tales such as these would only have heightened expectations of the rewards of venerating Eton's own statue of the Virgin.[83]

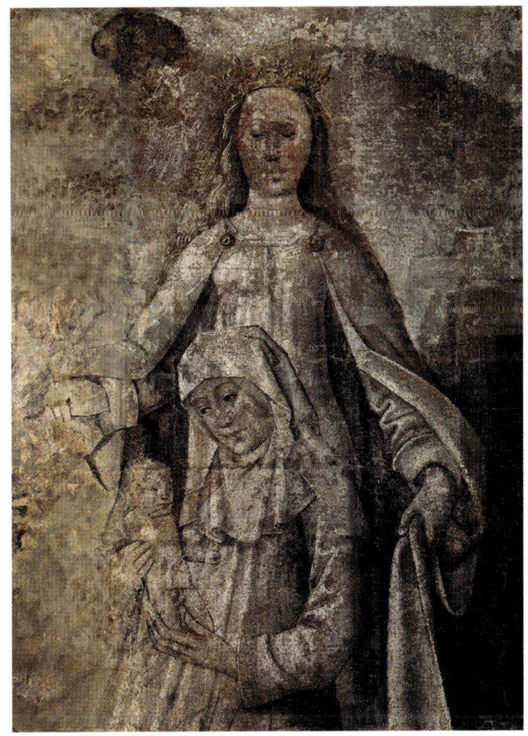

But the overarching message of the mural programme – at once reassuring and inspiring to its viewers – was surely that even the most undeserving sinner could be redeemed through devotion to the Virgin.[84] Her compassion towards a shamed woman who finds herself pregnant outside of wedlock is given vivid expression in the popular legend of the 'Miracle of Mont St Michel', depicted in a prominent position at the east end of the north wall (lower register, scene 1) (Figure 15). The miracle recounts the story of the expectant woman who had come on pilgrimage to the shrine in the early eleventh century. The legend goes that, as the woman was making her way across the sands toward the abbey, a sudden storm blew in the tide. In her desperate efforts to reach the safety of the shore, she went into labour and was consumed by the rising waters. The Virgin, whose own purity was unsurpassed, took pity on her and held back the waters with the folds of her great mantle until the woman was safely delivered of a son.[85] The intervention of the Virgin as celestial midwife – particularly among those women who were illicitly pregnant – was a common theme among contemporary miracle collections.[86] Indeed, as we see

83 Gill 2003, 188.
84 Duffy 1992, 187.
85 See Smith 2005, *passim*, who discusses how this miracle was contemporaneously attributed to both the Virgin and St Michael.
86 See Smith 2005, 773-4, who cites the ten birthing scenes which featured in the fourteenth-century *Miracles de Nostre Dame par personages*. Smith suggests that the Virgin's association with pregnancy and childbirth was further evoked by popular medieval Marian relics such as vials of the Virgin's milk and her girdle. See also Karras 1988.

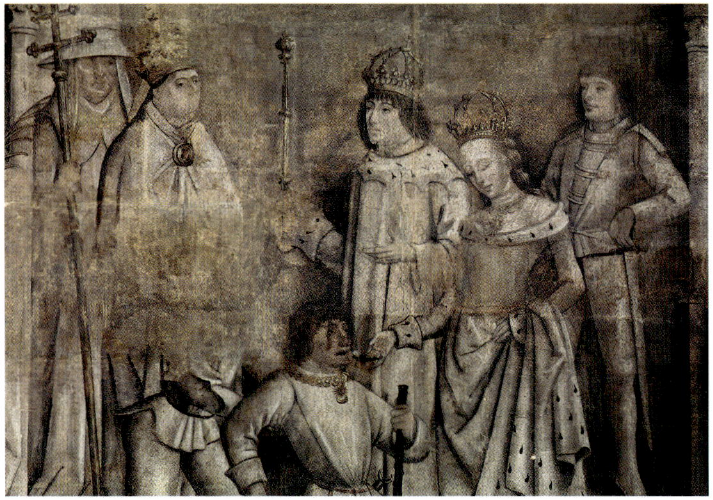

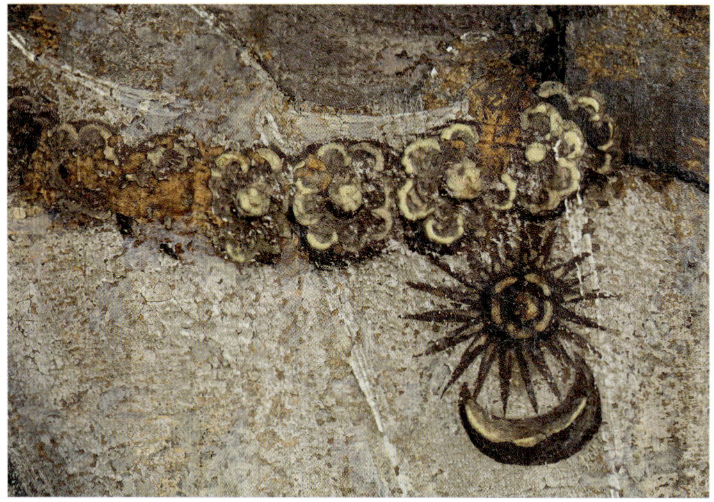

Left Fig. 16. South wall, scene 7, the Empress heals her brother-in-law.
Right Fig. 17. South wall, scene 7, detail showing the brother-in-law's *rose-en-soleil* pendant.

further along the wall, even a penitent Jewess could be found deserving of her intervention (lower register, scene 5).

One of the most widely-known Marian miracle stories of its time, the legend of 'the Empress falsely accused' occupies the whole of the south wall's lower register (Figure 16).[87] To summarise, an Empress is maliciously charged with infidelity by her brother-in-law and condemned to death, only to be rescued by a knight who is unaware of her true identity. The knight's brother, whose advances she spurns, frames the Empress for the murder of the child in her care and she is banished to a remote island. The Virgin appears to the Empress in a dream, revealing to her a miraculous plant that cures leprosy. Having cured and extracted confessions from the men who have falsely accused her, she renounces the world and enters a nunnery. Commissioned during the Wars of the Roses, this depiction of a popular courtly tale of 'gullible rulers, corrupt brothers, wronged queens and murdered nephews' must, observes Martindale, have found tremendous resonance with its audience.[88] Indeed, Pamela Tudor-Craig draws our attention to the distinctive pendant which hangs from the livery collar worn by the Emperor's wicked brother (scene 6), which would seem to combine the Yorkist *rose-en-soleil* with an upturned crescent moon (Figure 17). This heraldic

87 The story featured in a wide variety of vernacular versions, including Chaucer's *The Man of Law's Tale*, Middle English collections of saints' lives and the later fifteenth-century *Le Roman de Bon Florence*; see Gill 2003, 188.
88 See Martindale 1995, 147-9.

symbol was sometimes used to denote the status of a second son and as such, suggests Tudor-Craig, the pendant may be an allusion to the treacherous usurper Richard III.[89] If this detail of costume was, as has been suggested, a surreptitious declaration of anti-Yorkist sentiment by an institution whose founder had been murdered by the Yorkist regime, then it serves as a useful *terminus post quem* for the paintings of the south wall, inferring their execution sometime between 1485 and 1487 (that is to say, after Richard III's death and prior to the coronation of his niece as Henry VII's queen).

Fig. 18. South wall, scene 1, detail showing the deliberately obliterated face and livery collar of the Empress's brother-in-law.

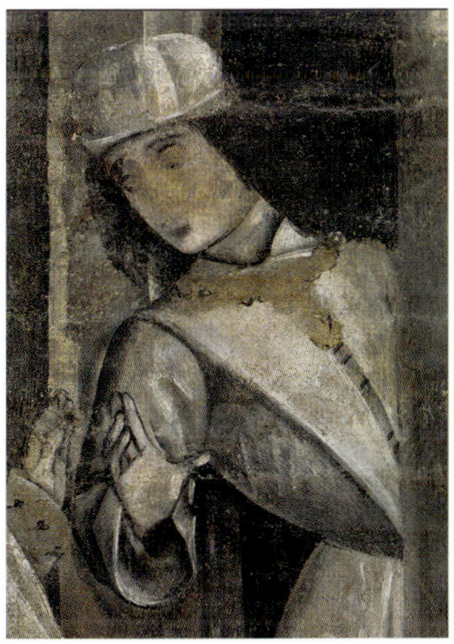

Of course, the symbolism of the pendant may equally have been intended to evoke the sun rays and crescent moon traditionally associated with the Virgin of the Assumption who, through the intercession of the Empress, redeemed the repentant sinner. If the allegory of Yorkist rehabilitation is pursued still further, it may be suggested not only that the wicked brother-in-law was intended for Richard III, but also that the Empress was meant to represent Elizabeth of York, through whose marriage to Henry VII the houses of York and Lancaster were at last reconciled.[90] Given that the lower register of the south walls was probably among the last elements of the mural cycle to be completed, it is not beyond the realms of possibility that other individual miracle scenes originally intended for the south wall's lower register were, at the last minute, replaced with a politically more apposite legend. The portrayal of these figures certainly seems to have provoked a strong reaction amongst some of their viewers – almost all of the faces of the Emperor, his brother and the Empress, and the livery collars worn by them, seem to have been deliberately defaced (Figure 18).

The Standing Figures

In the standing saints at Eton we see represented the heavenly host of prophets, Evangelists, Doctors of the Church and virgin martyrs who, according to St Jerome, accompanied the Virgin at her Assumption.[91] While only two of these figures survive from the scheme's upper register, it seems reasonably certain, based on the evidence of the drawings made by Essex, that the two easternmost figures in the upper register were the Virgin (on the north) and the Archangel Gabriel (on the south), together forming an Annunciation.[92] James proposed that the remaining eight male figures in the upper register on the south wall represented the four Evangelists (Sts Matthew, Mark, Luke and John) interspersed with the four Doctors of the Church (Sts Ambrose, Augustine, Jerome and

89 Tudor-Craig 1973, 21; also Martindale 1995, 147-9. Though Richard III was not a second son, he succeeded his older brother, Edward IV, as king. On livery collars more generally, see Knowles 2002; also Norris 1999, 406, 461.
90 See Anderson 1989, 28-31.
91 This astute observation is made by Williamson 2000, 366.
92 James & Tristram 1929, 17. While there is no evidence at all for the lost Virgin figure, Essex's drawing clearly show a figure with a sceptre on the south. The representation of the Annunciation across an opening seems to have been quite common and particularly associated with the transition from the nave to the chancel; see Gill 2002, 223-4, who cites the painting of the Annunciation (*c.*1450-1500) on the chancel arch at Great Hockham in Norfolk, and the depiction of Gabriel and the Virgin Annunciate on the easternmost wall posts of the great angel roof (*c.*1445) at St Mary's, Bury St Edmunds. See also Gill 2003, 179, and Binski & Park 1986, 34.

Gregory). Although surviving mural parallels for these figures are scarce,[93] the four Evangelists and four Doctors were certainly popular subjects on pulpits and painted rood screens in England in the later fifteenth century.[94] Fresh examination of the two surviving upper register figures on the south wall at Eton, however, prompts some revision of the exact configuration of these figures.[95] Figure VIII, described by James as St Gregory 'wearing a mutilated papal tiara',[96] is today quite visibly a tonsured figure dressed in monastic robes and holding a scroll and a staff, a couched lion at his feet, and most probably therefore represents Saint Jerome (Figure 19).[97] Likewise Figure IX, dressed in what would appear to be the regalia of a bishop or a pope, is certainly not St John as previously identified, and most probably depicts St Gregory (Figure 20).[98] There is, however, no cause to challenge James's suggestion that the figures recorded by Essex in the upper register of the north wall, all of whom are shown robed and holding long curling scrolls, were prophets.[99] Indeed, such an arrangement would accord with the theological tradition that the north side of a church was associated with the Old Testament and the south with the New.[100]

The improved clarity of the paintings following their conservation has made it possible to revise with some certainty the identities of the surviving female saint figures in the lower registers of the paintings,[101] though here the juxtaposition between the north and south walls is less readily apparent. While all those represented on the south – Sts Catherine, Barbara, Apollonia, Agnes, Ursula, Dorothy, Cecilia, Juliana and Winifred – seem to belong to the category of virgin martyrs,[102] those on the north – reading east to west, Sts Mary Magdalene,

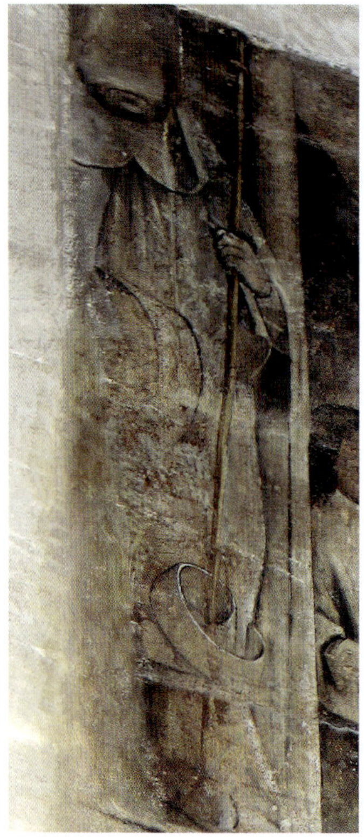

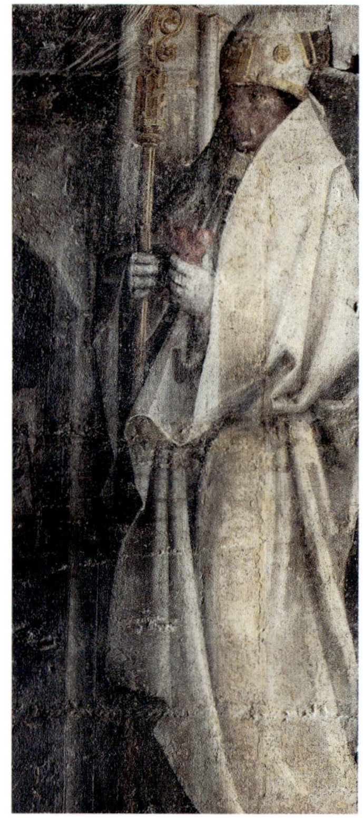

Left Fig. 19. South wall, upper register, figure VIII, possibly St Jerome.
Right Fig. 20. South wall, upper register, figure IX, possibly St Gregory.

93 Gill 2003, 179, cites a wall painting of *c.*1470 featuring the four Doctors at St Gregory's, Norwich; see also Tudor-Craig 1992, 116.

94 See Alexander 1994, on the pulpit and rood screen at Castle Acre in Norfolk, *c.*1445, and contemporary English iconography of the four Doctors more generally; also Gill 2003, 179, and 2002, 296-7, who cites, in addition, the Erpingham reredos in Norwich Cathedral (*c.*1500).

95 James (James & Tristram 1929, 18) suggested that while the Evangelists appeared in their usual biblical order, the Doctors were arranged in chronological sequence, thus St Matthew, St Ambrose, St Mark, St Augustine, St Jerome, St Luke, St Gregory and St John. He also postulates that the Evangelists' signs are depicted alongside the Doctors, rather than with their usual owners, a fashion for which he asserts there was some precedent.

96 James & Tristram 1929, 18, 22.

97 On the depiction of St Jerome with his lion, see Alexander 1994, 203.

98 Noad 1997, 9, has suggested that this figure represents St Augustine, presumably on the basis that he wears the pallium and holds the crozier of a bishop. This acknowledged, the style of the sumptuous cope is much longer than that usually worn by bishops and may be intended to represent a papal mantum.

99 James & Tristram 1929, 18.

100 See Gill 2002, 225, and 2003, 179, who cites a hierarchically comparable programme of wall painting at Friskney in Lincolnshire (*c.*1400-10), where four prophets are depicted on the north wall and four Doctors on the south. She suggests that such distinctions between north and south tend to occur especially in iconographically sophisticated schemes where there is evidence of clerical involvement.

101 The identities of the female saints, which have until now been based almost exclusively on the scholarship of James (James & Tristram 1929, 18-19), have most recently been subject to revision by Anderson 1989, 17-26.

102 See Kidd 1987, 16.

Margaret, Elizabeth of Hungary, Agatha, Mary of Egypt, Etheldreda, Martha and Sidwell – form a rather less homogenous group, though again virgin martyrs do feature.[103] This emphasis on Roman martyrs echoes the iconographic preoccupations of the large number of painted rood screens which survive from the second half of the fifteenth century.[104] The inclusion of St Mary Magdalene and St Catherine in a prominent position at the east end of the scheme, on the north and south walls respectively (Figures 21 and 22), is quite obviously an acknowledgement of these saints' particular importance to Eton's royal founder and episcopal patron. Henry VI's particular affinity with St Catherine, the patron saint of learning, is repeatedly evoked in illuminated royal manuscripts showing the saint interceding with the Virgin on the king's behalf,[105] and in 1447-8 a great image of the saint was brought from London to the new church at Eton, presumably at the king's behest.[106] Not only had Henry presented the College with a relic of the saint, but there was also an altar in the nave dedicated to her.[107] Of Waynflete's allegiance to his own patronal saint, Mary Magdalene, no further explanation is required.[108]

Left Fig. 21. North wall, figure I, St Mary Magdalene.
Right Fig. 22. South wall, figure I, St Catherine.

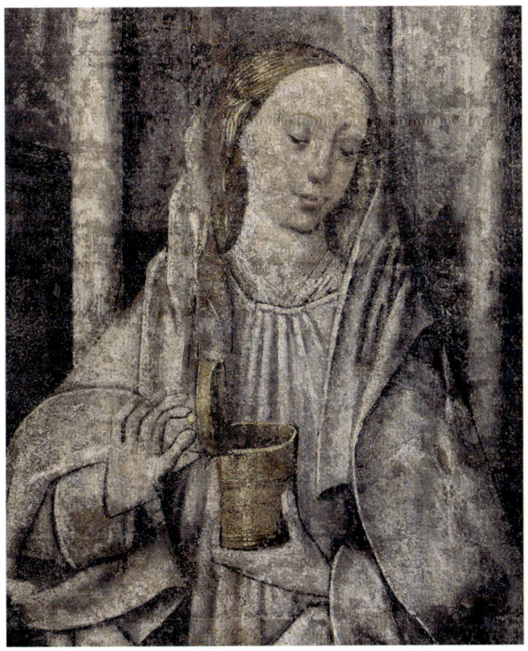

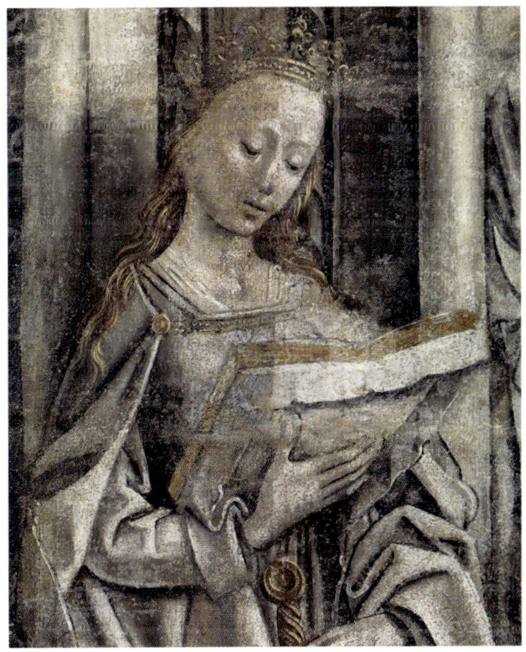

Of the less frequently invoked female saints that feature in the Eton scheme, the presence of St Elizabeth of Hungary (Figure 23) on the north wall, depicted holding two crowns and clothing an infant standing at her knee, may be linked to the fact that she was the patroness of Edward IV's sister, Elizabeth of York,[109] while St Etheldreda and St Winifred are known to have been especially venerated by Henry VII's mother, Margaret Beaufort.[110]A more obscure choice lies in the figure of St Sidwell, who hides in the shadows at the far west end of the north wall (Figure 24). Depicted with a scythe around her neck, St Sidwell (also known by the name Sativola) was, according to the legend, murdered by

103 Saint II on the north wall was completely lost when a new organ was inserted in the 1600s, and an entirely new, and deliberately unidentified, saint was inserted by Pauline Plummer in the 1970s (pers. comm.). Anderson 1989, 17, evokes a programme of *Virgo inter virgines*; on this iconographic theme, which was particularly prominent in late fifteenth-century Netherlandish art, see Weed 2002.

104 Duffy 1990, 175-6. Indeed, 12 of the 18 female saints identified at Eton feature among the most popular saints depicted on rood screens in the counties of Norfolk, Suffolk and Devon in this period, see Gill 2003, 180 (who cites Duffy 1990, 180).

105 See, for example, the miniature in which St Catherine supports Henry VI before the Virgin and Child, in the king's psalter (London, BL, MS Cotton Dom. A. XVII, f.75*r*); on the psalter, see Backhouse 2005. See also Eton's first seal (Fig. 3 above), in which a crowned female, possibly Catherine, kneels in veneration of the Virgin.

106 Gill 2003, 180, citing Colvin 1963, 284, n.3.

107 Maxwell Lyte 1911, 90.

108 See chapter 1 above on Waynflete's devotion to Mary Magdalene and foundation of Magdalen College at Oxford.

109 The revised identification of this figure, previously identified by James as St Radegund, is offered by Anderson 1989, 19, who observes that the saint can also be seen standing behind the queen in the Henry VII window in the chapel of St Anthony in Padua in Antwerp Cathedral. The window, which dates from 1503, is reputed to have been a gift from the English monarch in celebration of a lucrative trade agreement with the Burgundian duke, Philip the Fair; see Helbig 1968, 21-35, and figs 2 and 7.

110 Anderson 1989, 21. Margaret was, of course, the wife of Henry VI's half-brother, Edmund Tudor.

haymakers at the instigation of her jealous stepmother, her remains being buried outside of the city of Exeter. It is surely significant that this is one of only two known depictions of the saint outside the West Country, the other being in the programme of stained glass in the ante-chapel of All Souls College, Oxford (*c*.1441).[111] It is thought that Sidwell's appearance at both sites stems from their links with Roger Keys, a canon and later archdeacon and precentor of Exeter Cathedral, who was employed by Henry VI to oversee building projects at both of these new foundations. College accounts attest that Keys served as master of the works at Eton between 1448 and 1450, during which time he also served as chaplain to Henry VI, and it is conceivable that, following his death in 1477, Waynflete regarded the inclusion of Keys' patronal saint in the college wall paintings as a fitting tribute to one held in such high esteem by the king.[112]

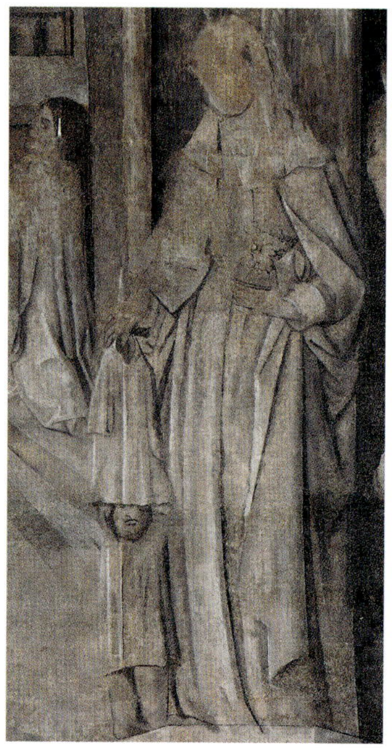

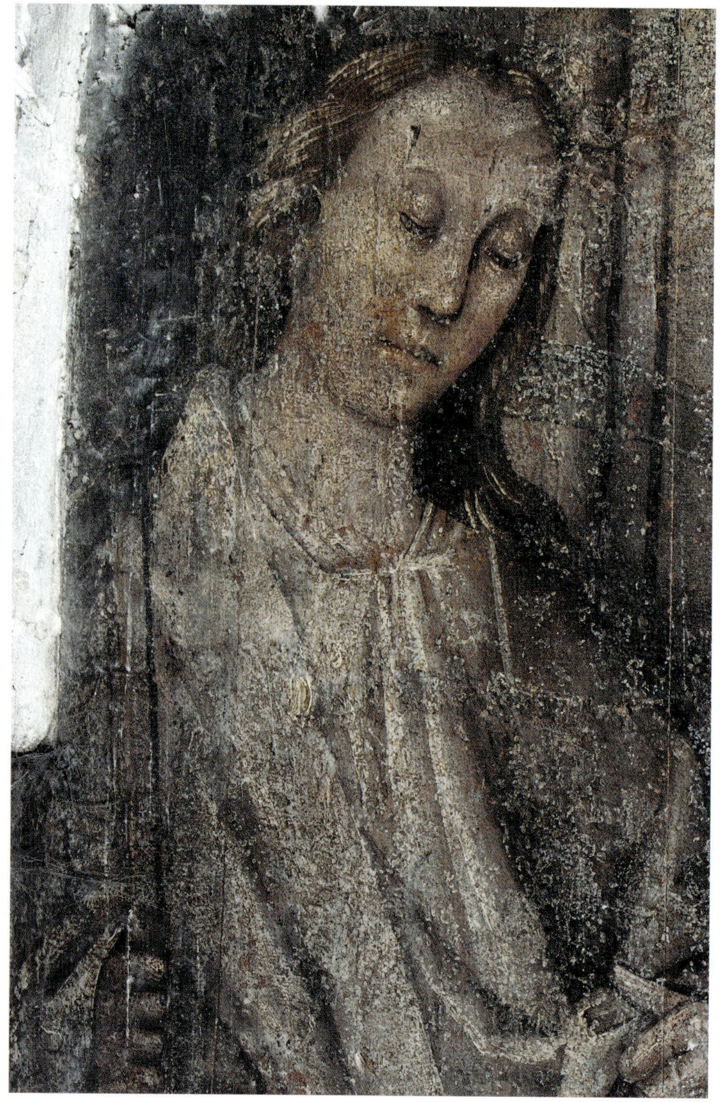

Left Fig. 23. North wall, figure IV, St Elizabeth of Hungary; she has been only recently identified by the crowns she holds and the small child she is clothing.
Right Fig. 24. North wall, figure IX, St Sidwell.

111 On St Sidwell see Hutchinson 1949, 34-7; Swanton 1986, 21; Marks 1993, 63; also Orme 2000, 235 and Gill 2002, 482-7.

112 On Roger Keys, see Colvin 1963, 280; also *Burke's Peerage and Baronetage*, 107th edition, vol.2, 2147. Hutchinson 1949, 35, draws our attention to a painted rood screen in the church of Whimple, just outside Exeter, the advowson of which was given by Henry VI to Eton College; here the king and St Sidwell are depicted side by side; on the relationship between St Sidwell and Henry VI, see also Rose-Troup 1933.

3. Devotion at Eton and beyond

Reconstructing the ritual space in which the Eton miracle paintings were originally viewed is especially problematic.[113] When we enter the chapel today, there is no sense of the nave for which these paintings were commissioned. Stripped of their upper register, the remaining scenes appear to hover, devoid of an architectural context or any obvious liturgical function. What did Waynflete's nave look like and how was it used? For a start we must mentally remove the monumental organ screen which now divides the chapel from the ante-chapel. This is a much later addition, inserted in 1881-2, and deprives us of any sense of the massive original connecting archway and the resulting impression of openness and space. Once it was clear that Henry VI's ambitious plans for the church could not be fulfilled, it became necessary to carve a nave for the use of the parish out of the existing choir. As we have seen, the ante-chapel on its own was considered insufficiently capacious, and accounts attest that in 1475 Waynflete commissioned Walter Nicholl of Southwark to construct a 'pulpitum', or choir screen, to be erected three bays to the east of the present organ loft.[114] While Henry VI's scheme had envisaged an impressive stone screen some 4m (12ft) thick, Nicholl's screen was evidently a far less substantial timber structure, most probably quite transparent in the manner of a rood screen, making it possible for those in the nave to follow the liturgy being performed in the choir.[115] Modelled on its western side on the rood screen in Winchester College chapel, and on its eastern face on the screen in the chapel of the London college of St Thomas of Acre, the structure not only comprised a rood screen and loft but quite probably also housed the organ.[116] The Crucifixion, flanked by the Virgin and St John the Baptist, would, as a matter of course, have formed the focus of the rood loft, but there is apparently no record of the imagery with which the lower panels were decorated, nor of its iconographical relationship with the wall paintings. Williamson's

113 The term 'ritual space' is borrowed from Williamson 2000, who explores the iconographical and liturgical context of the wall paintings.

114 Willis & Clark 1886, 409, cite ECR 38/309; the contract, which is dated 16 August 1475, was for a rood loft and choir stalls to be completed by the feast of the Assumption in 1477, for which Nicholl was to be paid the sum of 100 marks.

115 Martindale 1971, 189-93.

116 Martindale 1971, 191, n.6. The Winchester screen does not survive, having been torn down, like that at Eton, in the early 1570s.

suggestion that the rood screen at Eton may have featured the 12 Apostles, who are otherwise missing from the imagery of the nave, is certainly logical, viewed in the context of similarly decorated fifteenth-century screens surviving in East Anglia.[117] Nor should we neglect to consider the immense stained glass windows that surmounted the wall paintings and which undoubtedly formed an important element of the nave's hagiographic programme. In the absence of any surviving physical evidence, our knowledge of the glazing programme commissioned by Waynflete must be confined to the realms of conjecture. It seems likely, however, that in these vast panels of glass a still more expansive heavenly host found representation.[118]

With the demolition of these windows and Nicholl's rood screen during the Reformation, and the refashioning of the choir that ensued, the parochial nave of Eton's church was destroyed, and along with it any real understanding of how the wall paintings might have functioned within it.[119] Wilson has suggested that the choice of a muted, grisaille palette for the wall paintings was, in part, born of a concern not to distract from other highly coloured and three-dimensional imagery located elsewhere in the church.[120] As discussed, the rood screen would have been painted, and both the College rolls and private wills attest to the presence of a gilded statue of 'Our Lady of Eton' that stood in a tabernacle in the centre of the nave, adorned with costly textiles, gold rings and other precious gifts bestowed by pilgrims to the church.[121] Other statues of the Virgin are reported to have stood in the south porch and at the entrance to the choir,[122] and scenes from the saint's life, including an Annunciation featuring a large-scale depiction of her emblem 'le lyle potte', featured in the chancel's great east window.[123] Entries in the audit rolls suggest that the Assumption was also represented on a large scale in the choir, though in what form is not clear.[124] The foundation was also a repository for numerous Marian relics – among them a piece of the Virgin's thumb, a vial of her milk and a lock of her hair – along with those of other saints, many of whom (including the Evangelists, the four Doctors, St Catherine and St Winifred) were depicted in the wall paintings.[125] Many of these relics had been bestowed by Henry VI himself; in securing unparalleled indulgences for those coming to the church on the feast of the Assumption, the king clearly aspired to establish at Eton an unrivalled centre of popular pilgrimage.[126] The paintings commissioned to adorn the nave of Henry's foundation served to underline the corporeal presence of the Virgin at Eton, and her miraculous healing and intercessory powers. The depiction of the saints standing in their niches, many of whom were

117 See Williamson 2000, 368; also Duffy 1992, 157-9.
118 Williamson 2000, 368, has suggested that images of 12 prophets, made for Eton's old parish church in 1445-6, would have been translated to the new church in the 1470s. Some indication of Waynflete's iconographic preferences can be deduced from the programme of stained glass he commissioned around the same time for the collegiate church at Tattershall, which seems broadly to echo the iconographic choices he made at Eton; see Marks 1979, 145-6.
119 An entry in the bursar's account book records that the choir screen was dismantled in 1570; see Willis & Clark 1886, 443. Subsequent entries suggest that any surviving fragments of stained glass were removed from the chapel by around 1606-7.
120 Wilson 2003, 351.
121 Maxwell Lyte 1911, 91 and n.8; also Williamson 2000, 362.
122 Maxwell Lyte 1911, 91-2 and ns 1 and 2.
123 Maxwell Lyte 1911, 92, and n.3; also Willis & Clark 1886, 408-9.
124 See entries in the audit rolls for 1479-80, 1484-5 and 1488-9, in Maxwell Lyte 1911, 91 and n.7.
125 See Williamson 2000, 362 (citing chapel inventories in James 1920), 402-3 (inventory for 1465) and 404-5 (inventories for the early sixteenth century).
126 Spencer 1990, 29, records that Henry VI granted the College two annual fairs and a weekly market to help cater for pilgrims.

reputed to have been present at the Assumption of the Virgin, evoked the simultaneous presence of a much wider company of holy intermediaries.[127]

Our understanding of how the wall paintings might have functioned in relation to the liturgy performed in the church is greatly illuminated by Williamson's exploration of the roughly contemporary Eton Choirbook (*c.*1505).[128] The congregation of the chapel was prescribed by the College statutes formulated under Henry VI: while the Provost, Fellows, scholars and their master were allotted seats within the choir, the fee-paying 'commensal' schoolboys, almsmen and ancillary staff of the foundation worshipped alongside the parishioners in the nave.[129] Of the numerous daily religious offices observed in the College's church, we know that two were certainly celebrated in the nave. Vespers were said here daily, except on feast days, by 10 Fellows, and at dusk 16 choristers and their instructor processed into the church and sang an antiphon to the Virgin before her image in the nave.[130] It has been observed that the timing of the office, at the end of the working day, would have enabled lay attendance at the service. During Lent and on the vigils of feasts, of which there were around 50, the scholars of the College were also required to attend. A growing contingent of pilgrims would also have been present. The celebration of the Marian *Salve* ceremony in the nave of the church was thus both a public and a corporate act of devotion.[131] The words of the liturgy sung during these offices not only invoked the intercessory powers of the saints, several of whom were depicted in the paintings (St Mary Magdalene and St Catherine, certainly), but also made reference to the working of miracles. Indeed it would seem that Robert Wylkynson, who composed the *Salve regina* for performance at Eton on the feast of the Assumption, drew heavily on the *Golden Legend*, like the originator of the wall painting cycle.[132] The rewards for participating in such devotions to the Virgin were made plain for all to see on the walls around them, the murals serving to underline the validity and potency of the acts of worship performed in the nave.[133]

Given the potentially broad social spectrum of the congregation at Eton, Waynflete's mural programme was required to function on several levels. It was surely not by coincidence that the subjects of the miracle paintings included men and women, the young and old, the poor and the noble, devout pilgrims and hopeless sinners. Certainly these scenes would have served as powerful visual *exempla* to the illiterate parishioner attending Mass or listening to sermons in the church. Indeed, Gill has demonstrated that many of the stories depicted at Eton would have been familiar to the

127 As recounted in the *Golden Legend*; this astute observation is made by Williamson 2000, 366.
128 Williamson 2000; on the Choirbook, see also Marks & Williamson 2003, 165.
129 Martindale 1995, 135.
130 Williamson 2000, 360.
131 The celebration of the *Salve* ceremony in a public devotional space seems to have been received practice at this time; see Williamson 2000, 360-1; also Skinner 2004, 170-1, for examples of similar *Salve* ceremonies.
132 Wylkynson was a lay clerk at Eton in the 1490s and instructor of the choristers from 1500 to 1515; see Williamson 2000, 368-9.
133 Williamson 2000, 371; Skinner 2004, 176; also Duffy 1992, 17, with reference to the depiction of the celebration of Candlemas in the paintings.

uneducated layman through the oral dissemination of vernacular saints' lives and romance tales.[134] Numerous popular versions of the story of the Empress seem to have been in circulation around this time, including Chaucer's *The Man of Law's Tale* and the late fifteenth-century *Roman de Bon Florence*, while the story of Amoras selling his wife to the Devil, which is depicted across two scenes on the north wall, features in the sermon for the feast of the Assumption in the fifteenth-century vernacular homily the *Speculum sacerdotale*.[135] The presence of a Latin inscription beneath each of the scenes, however, presupposes a degree of literacy amongst at least a portion of the paintings' audience. Indeed, it would seem that these inscriptions, which serve not only to describe the scene but also to cite the literary sources of the legends from which these miraculous episodes were drawn, were intended to provoke further study and reflection among those who were in a position to consult the necessary texts.[136]

The significance of these hagiographic choices is best considered in the wider devotional context of England on the eve of the Reformation. When Waynflete commissioned the wall paintings for the nave, the cult of the Virgin – celebrating Mary's exceptional status as Mother of God and supreme intercessor – lay at the heart of the Roman Catholic faith. Indeed, recent scholarship has demonstrated that England took up devotion to the Virgin with exceptional zeal from as early as the late seventh century.[137] By the fifteenth century, Marian feasts and offices dominated the devotional calendar,[138] and images of the Virgin proliferated, many becoming the focus of pilgrimage. Prayers such as the *Ave Maria* and *Salve regina* were clearly well known even among the illiterate,[139] and collections of Marian miracle stories enjoyed popularity not only among those who could read Latin, but also – through vernacular versions and sermon *exempla* – a much less exclusive social group.[140] Visual representations of the Virgin's miracles abound in art surviving from the Middle Ages.[141] Illuminated manuscripts dating from the fourteenth century, such as the Queen Mary's Psalter (*c*.1310-20, British Library, Royal MS. 2 B. vii), the Taymouth Hours (*c*.1325, British Library, Yates Thompson 13), the Luttrell Psalter (*c*.1325-35, British Library Add. MS 42130), the Smithfield Decretals (*c*.1330-40, British Library, Royal MS. 10 E.iv), and the Carew Poyntz Hours (*c*.1360, Fitzwilliam, MS 48), feature numerous illustrations of the Virgin's intercessory powers.[142] In sculpture, a depiction of the Assumption marks the beginning of the magnificent, though now badly mutilated, miracle cycle in the Lady Chapel at Ely Cathedral (*c*.1335-53),[143] while the popular tale of Theophilus features on the marble reredos of

134 See Gill 2003, 187-9, who also remarks that five of the miracles depicted at Eton are featured in the *South English Legendary*.

135 This point is flagged by Williamson 2000, 365; see Weatherly 1936, 189-91.

136 Martindale 1995, 143. Gill 2003, 187, draws parallels with the late medieval wall paintings in the chapel of the Guild of the Holy Cross at Stratford-upon-Avon, which featured textual inscriptions drawn from amongst others the Vulgate, Lydgate's *Dance of Death*, and Caxton's *Golden Legend*; see also Davidson 1988.

137 See Williams Boyarin 2010, 1-7. On the celebration of Marian devotions in England during the Anglo-Saxon period, see Edgren 1993, 25-8; also Clayton 1990 and Rubin 2009, 105-12, 182-8, on the emergence of a monastic Marian literary tradition.

138 The Purification (2 February), the Annunciation (25 March), the Visitation (2 July), and the Assumption (15 August), were certainly observed in England as early as the end of the seventh century (see Williams Boyarin 2010, 2). Later on, the Nativity (8 September) and the Immaculate Conception (8 December) were also marked.

139 See Morgan 1991, 73-5. Indeed, a work published *c*.1400, entitled *Instructions for a Devout and Literate Layman*, reveals how ceaseless devotions to the Virgin might punctuate the daily round of the layman; see Morgan 1993, 40-1, and n.14.

140 See Edgren 1993, 52-3; these collections drew on a much earlier literary tradition of *Mariales;* see Gill 2003, 183; also Rubin 2009, 239-42. On vernacular Anglo-Norman and Middle English treatments of Marian legends, see also Morgan 1993, 36, and Williams Boyarin 2010, 13-16.

141 See Edgren 1993, 164-7, for a survey of Marian miracles depicted in early medieval French and English monumental art, and 172-5 for English and continental illuminated manuscripts; also Kidd 1987, 7-14. Glover 2007, 344, n.8, draws attention to one very early example of this pictorial miracle tradition: a linen garment dating from the twelfth century, woven with miracles of the Virgin, that was presented to Winchester Cathedral by Henry of Blois.

142 James & Tristram 1929, 16; also James 1895a, appendix; also Morgan 1993, 45; on the Luttrell Psalter, see Camille 1998, 138. A far more exhaustive list of manuscripts can be found in Glover 2007, 354.

143 See James 1895a.

*c.*1340 at Beverley Minster, Yorkshire.[144] Only a handful of Marian miracles depicted in stained glass seem to have survived the iconoclasm of the sixteenth century. In the east window of the north choir aisle of Lincoln Cathedral, dating from *c.*1220-30, the legends of Theophilus and the Jew of Bourges are both depicted, and a little later the same two miracles are portrayed in the choir at Canterbury.[145] Further depictions of the Virgin's miracles are also recorded in the glazing of the church of St Denis in York.[146] Three of the Virgin's miracles – the Theophilus legend, the miracle of the Jew of Bourges, and the healing of the sick clerk – featured in stained glass and paintings which formerly adorned the abbey church of Bury St Edmund's.[147] While extant contemporary wall paintings depicting the miracles of the Virgin are few and fragmentary, this of course is not to say that such schemes did not once exist. A survey of the surviving material suggests, however, that Marian mural schemes were for the most part concerned with the Virgin's life rather than her posthumous miracles.[148] The earliest surviving mural treatment of Marian miracles was recently rediscovered in the chapel of St Mary de Castro in the Agricola Tower at Chester Castle.[149] The scheme, which dates from the reign of Henry III, features the legends of Theophilus, the Mass of St Bonnet, Ebbo the thief and the Jew of Bourges. Later, the Theophilus legend and the miracle of the Jew of Bourges again found representation in a mural of *c.*1330 at Chalfont St Giles in Buckinghamshire.[150]

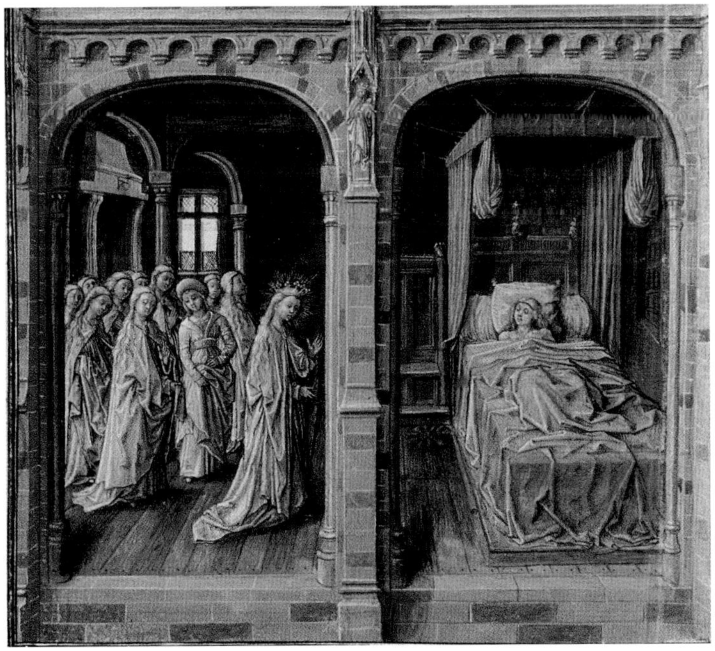

Fig. 25. 'The Miracle of the Dying Girl' from *Les Miracles de Nostre Dame*, *c.*1456, compiled by Jean Miélot and illuminated by Tavernier's workshop (Bibliothèque nationale, Paris, MS Fr.9199, f.16*v*).

Enthusiasm for this type of Marian iconography appears, however, to have waned somewhat after the middle of the fourteenth century, both in England and on the Continent.[151] In manuscripts dating from the fifteenth century, illustrations of the Virgin's miracles seem to have been confined to dedicated miracle collections, of which the most representative example is perhaps the *Miracles de Nostre Dame* (*c.*1456) (Figure 25) compiled by Jean Miélot, secretary to Philip the Good, Duke of Burgundy.[152] This work, which contains some 70 grisaille miniatures by Jean Tavernier, displays obvious affinities with the wall paintings at Eton, not least in its narrative technique of depicting multiple 'moments' from the miracles it illustrates.[153] Of works published in

144 Tracy 1987, 428, cited in Edgren 1993, 167, n.486. On the popular Theophilus legend, which is believed to be eastern in origin, see Fryer 1935.

145 Edgren 1993, 167; also Marks 1987, 140.

146 Edgren 1993, 167; James & Tristram 1929, 16.

147 It is not completely clear whether the paintings were on the walls or on panels; see James 1895c, 120-90, 143, 190; Tristram 1950, 373, 516; Cather *et al.* 2000, 77 and n.15; also Glover 2007, 345.

148 See, e.g., the fourteenth-century mural schemes at Broughton (Oxon), Chalgrove (Oxon) and Croughton (Northants); Morgan 1993, 40, n.11.

149 See Cather *et al.* 2000.

150 Note that Tristram (1955, 150-1) misidentified the Theophilus episode as the 'Miracle of the youth who became betrothed to the Virgin'.

151 Edgren 1993, 165-6, 173.

152 The Bodleian Library's Douce MS 374 and Bibliothèque Nationale, Paris, MS 9199 are two of several copies of this book; see Kidd 1987, 12-13; also Glover 2007, 354.

153 These works are treated in some detail in the following chapter.

England, only a single collection of Marian miracles seems to have emerged around this time, *The Myracles of Oure Lady* published by Wynkyn de Worde in 1496.[154] The gradual decline in representations of Marian miracles in late medieval manuscripts was mirrored in monumental art. In contrast with preceding centuries, no parish wall paintings and few sculptural schemes depicting the miracles of the Virgin survive from the fifteenth century.[155] Most surviving late medieval Marian schemes seem instead to have shown either scenes from the Virgin's life, such as those dating from the mid-fifteenth century in the church at Willingham, Cambridgeshire, or new and more fashionable devotional themes, such as the *Five Joys of the Virgin* depicted in the deanery at Durham (*c.*1475-80) (Figure 26).[156] Indeed, apart from the eight scenes preserved on the south wall of Eton's chapel, only one other English pictorial scheme of the legend of the Empress falsely accused survives, in a near contemporary scheme of wooden bosses in the Bauchan Chapel in Norwich Cathedral (*c.*1460-75).[157] Here depictions of the Assumption and Coronation of the Virgin are accompanied by 32 scenes from the Empress's tale. Other individual Marian miracles, such as the Jew of Bourges, Theophilus and the miracle of Mont St Michel, are depicted on bosses dating from *c.*1425-30 in the cloister of the cathedral.[158] While our impression of England's mural tradition in the years preceding the Reformation is of course unavoidably skewed, such an extensive exposition of the miracles of the Virgin as is found at Eton, with the derivative scheme of *c.*1500 commissioned by Prior Silkstede for the Lady Chapel at Winchester Cathedral (see Figures 33 and 34),[159] appears to have been exceptional among monumental art in northern Europe in the later medieval period.

It is important not to lose sight of the fact that the wall paintings in the nave formed part of a far broader programme of imagery, both pictorial and liturgical, of which the focus was the sculpted image of the Virgin that stood in the nave.[160] Indeed, the paintings of the miracles, and in particular the five scenes which explore stories describing the miraculous powers of Marian images, were surely intended to evoke the salvific potential of such cult statues.[161] Though Eton never became the impor-

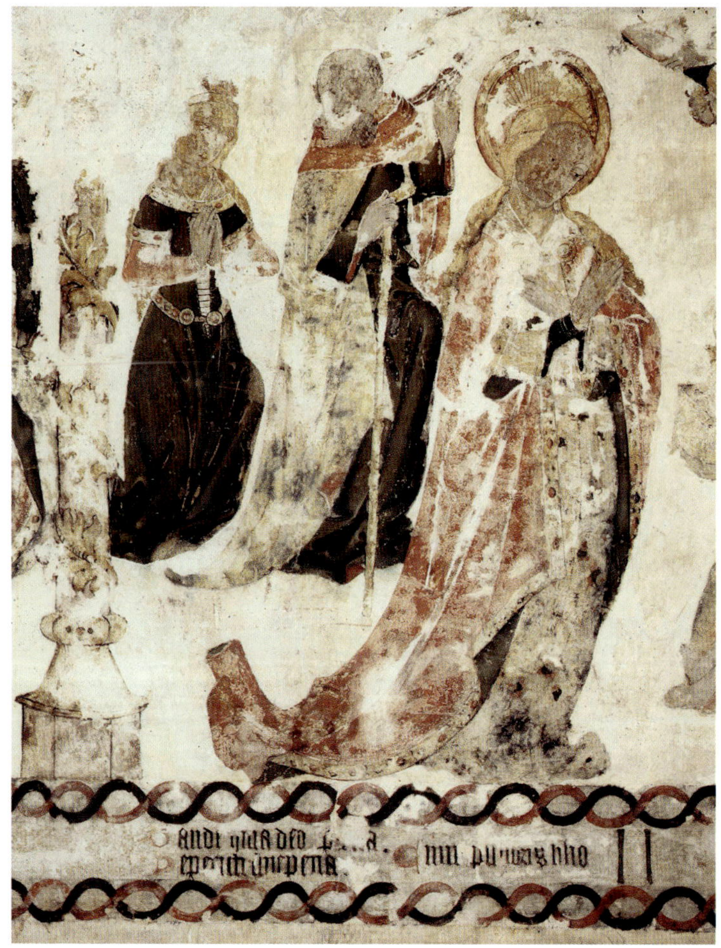

Fig. 26. Detail of a wall painting scheme depicting the *Five Joys of the Virgin* in the deanery at Durham, Northumberland, *c.*1475-80.

154 Glover 2007, 346.
155 Gill 2003, 182, 188, draws attention to the body of Marian miracle murals which survive in Finland from this period; see Edgren 1993, 66-155, on the late fifteenth-century mural schemes at Hattula and Lohja.
156 Gill 2003, 182; for the Durham deanery scheme, see Park 1993; also Graves & Rollason 2010.
157 On the Bauchan Chapel bosses see Whittingham 1981; also James 1930 and Rose 1996.
158 Nichols 2002, 115-16.
159 See James & Tristram 1929, 14-15; also Park & Welford 1993, 133-4. Thomas Silkstede was prior at Winchester 1498-1524.
160 Glover 2007, 343-4; also Williamson 2000, 360-2, 380.
161 Gill 2002, 202.

tant centre of international pilgrimage that Henry VI had hoped, the royal foundation did attract a good number of worshippers who came to venerate its sumptuous patronal statue. Pewter and silver badges depicting the Assumption of the Virgin, which survive from the middle of the fifteenth century, commemorate pilgrimages to Our Lady of Eton and attest to the shrine's popularity up until Eton's fall from royal favour in the 1460s.[162] And at the turn of the sixteenth century, after Eton's fortunes had revived, 'The Blessed Mary of the Assumption' at Eton is included, alongside the more prestigious shrines of Our Lady of Walsingham and Our Lady Undercroft at Canterbury, in a list of some 34 shrines in southern England favoured by Henry VII's queen, Elizabeth of York.[163]

In the standing saint figures painted on the walls of the nave, Waynflete's scheme vividly portrayed the wider host of saints who had accompanied the Virgin at her Assumption and who would intercede with her and her son, on behalf of the faithful who came to show them due reverence. Alongside miracle collections, the *Lives of the Saints* were among the most widely reproduced works to emerge from the new printing presses at the end of the fifteenth century. Indeed, the reading and recitation of popular verse lives, and the performance of plays based on these stories, seems to have permeated lay piety in the fifteenth and sixteenth centuries.[164] According to the *Golden Legend* – the compilation of saints' lives from which several of the episodes depicted in the Eton wall paintings were drawn – the cult of saints was a means of honouring God, for '...who that doth honour to saints, he honoureth him specially which hath sanctified them'.[165] Literary evidence attests to the growing attraction, in particular, of the legends of the virgin martyrs, a trend that is reflected in the preponderance of this group in the surviving lower register of the Eton wall paintings. Indeed, Eamon Duffy's study of painted rood screens surviving from this period reveals that, alongside the Apostles, Evangelists and Doctors of the Church, the virgin martyrs were among the most frequently depicted groups of figures.[166] Duffy ventures that, rather than advocating these chaste women as models for virginal living (and all the impracticalities which that might imply for the laywoman), they were instead invoked for their exceptional intercessory powers.[167] And like their male counterparts, these saints were invoked for assistance not only in attenuating the perils of purgatory, but also in navigating the more mundane afflictions of the present world, whether toothache, leprosy or the pains of childbirth.[168]

Several scholars have made reference to the female saints depicted at Eton as an example of the 'Virgo inter

162 See Spencer 1990, 29-30 and figs 58 and 64; also Spencer 1998, 148-50.
163 Spencer 1990, 29, citing Nicolas 1830, 3-4.
164 Duffy 1992, 165 and n.33; also Duffy 1990 on the cult of female saints in fifteenth- and sixteenth-century England.
165 Duffy 1992, 169, citing the *Golden Legend*.
166 Duffy 1992, 171-3.
167 Duffy 1992, 175-7.
168 See Duffy 1992, 179-80, on Sts Barbara and Catherine, both famed for their special power to intercede in childbirth, and St Apollonia, who was renowned for her power to relieve toothache.

virgines' genre made popular in southern Netherlandish painting of the later fifteenth century.[169] Most recently, Stanley Weed has explored depictions of this devotional theme and its origins in Germany and the Low Countries. His research suggests that the iconography, which usually comprised the Virgin accompanied by a stock group of Early Christian martyrs,[170] evolved out of earlier devotions to the 'virgines capitales', a collection of four virgin martyrs (Sts Barbara, Catherine, Dorothy and Margaret), in late fourteenth-century Germany.[171] By the late fifteenth century, the iconography of the 'Virgo inter virgines' seems to have migrated to Flanders, and in particular Bruges, where it entered mass artistic production in both painted and printed formats.[172] The primary audience for this imagery was clearly intended to be female. These holy women were venerated not only for their individual intercessory powers, but also for their collective purity and their status as brides of Christ.[173] Contemporary 'courtesy books' (or books of manners), many of which were written by men for the instruction of their wives and daughters, cited the virgin martyrs as exemplars of humility, obedience and chaste living and, despite their virginal status, these saints seem to have been popularly regarded as apposite models for the laywoman at all social levels.[174] Examination of late medieval wills reveals that, in their benefaction of parish churches, English laywomen certainly tended to favour these female saints,[175] and indeed, Edward IV's sister, Margaret of York, is known to have been particularly devoted to Sts Anne, Barbara, Catherine, Margaret and Agnes.[176] Evolving concepts of female sanctity meant that marriage was no longer seen as an impediment to chaste living and, inspired by the example of such holy women, even married women and mothers – such as Elizabeth of Hungary who herself finds representation in the paintings at Eton – were able to achieve canonisation.[177]

Though lacking contemporary parallel for their format or extent, the wall paintings in the chapel at Eton have been shown in their content at least to be thoroughly representative of late medieval devotional preoccupations, drawing on established hagiographic traditions. This said, the nave scheme is undeniably theologically backward-looking in its exhaustive depiction of Marian miracles, and it is interesting to consider what provoked Waynflete to commission such a programme. The miracles depicted at Eton emphasise the benefits of certain devotional practices, in particular the veneration of images of the Virgin, and by overtly referencing the literary sources of the episodes depicted, the author of the mural programme sought to underline the miracles' authority. As Glover observes, the mural

169 See, in particular, Anderson 1989, 17; also Noad 1997, 9 and Gill 2002, 201-02.
170 Weed 2002, 7 and chapter 5 *passim*.
171 See Weed 2002, 4-5 and chapters 2 and 3.
172 Weed 2002, 7; Weed's thesis includes an exhaustive catalogue of paintings depicting this devotional theme.
173 Weed 2002, 157.
174 See Weed 2002, 10, 154-5, and 300-12. Caxton published a *Book of Curtesye*, based upon an early fifteenth-century French text, in 1487; see Duffy 1992, 78; see also Bornstein 1983 and Nicholls 1985 on this popular literary genre.
175 French 1998.
176 Weed 2002, 301.
177 Weed 2002, 302-03.

cycle in the nave 'described and defended the Marian devotions celebrated at Eton'.[178] In the decades preceding Henry VI's foundation of his new college at Eton, such devotional practices had come under repeated attack from reforming groups such as the Lollards. Wycliffe, in whose teachings the Lollard movement found its roots, had been critical of apocryphal Marian miracles not founded in Scripture.[179] While Wycliffe had in fact acknowledged the place of devotional images in instructing the illiterate layman, Lollards, citing the Ten Commandments as their authority, rejected the veneration of images as idolatrous, and proclaimed their belief 'ayenst wurshipping of ymagis seing that we shall wurship no stokkis [wood] ne stonys ne nothing made or graven with mannys hand of no lykenesse of thingis in heven ne erth'.[180] The publication of the *Twelve Conclusions of the Lollards* in 1395 marked the most coherent and forceful expression of these accusations of false idolatry, and Gill observes that in 1405 Archbishop Arundel was moved to reaffirm the devotional belief which originated in the seventh act of the Nicene Council of 786 that reverence ('dulia' or 'latria') was due to images of the Virgin, saints and angels. This could be expressed either through kissing them or burning candles before them.[181] Lollards continued to protest that devotional reverence should be reserved for God alone and particularly resented the tendency to treat such 'dead idols' as if they were alive, urging instead that the faithful should redirect their attentions, both emotional and economic, towards 'quicke ymagis of God, þat ben pore folc'.[182] For this reason, the practice of pilgrimage was similarly disdained. At his trial in 1429 in Norwich, John Pyrye confessed that he thought that money squandered on 'worthless pilgrimages' should be spent on poor people who were the real living images of Christ.[183]

Following the Lollard rising of 1414, centred on Henry V's previously trusted supporter Sir Anthony Oldcastle, the investigation and persecution of heresy became a far better co-ordinated effort between ecclesiastical and secular authorities.[184] The severest penalties were imposed on those charged with holding heretical beliefs. Episcopal collegiate foundations seem to have been at the forefront of attempts to, as Aston puts it, 'educate heresy out of existence'.[185] As early as 1427, Richard Fleming, the Bishop of Lincoln, had obtained a charter for the foundation of Lincoln College, Oxford, as a kind of counter-Wycliffite seminary aimed at the extermination of heresy, and in 1448, Queen's College at Cambridge was similarly proclaimed to have been founded 'for the extirpation of heresies and errors, the increase of the faith and the enhancement and support of the clergy'.[186] The eradication of heresy had

178 Glover 2007, 356.
179 Glover 2007, 346.
180 John Tanner of Steventon, 1491, cited by Kamerick 2002, 23; on the Lollard heresy more generally, see Kamerick 2002, 22-7. On the Lollards' rejection of image worship, see Aston 1984, 143-59.
181 Gill 2002, 196.
182 Unnamed Lollard tract cited by Kamerick 2002, 24. See also Aston 1993, 23-4, and Thomson 1965, 126, on the Lollards' rejection of image worship and pilgrimage.
183 John Pyrye, cited by Kamerick 2002, 25. Similar sentiments were voiced by William Emayn at his trial in the same year; see Aston 1984, 143.
184 Aston 1993, 80-2.
185 Aston 1993, 85.
186 Aston 1993, 86; also Thomson 1965, 212-13, who cites similar concerns to eradicate heresy in the foundation charters of All Souls College and Corpus Christi College, Oxford, and at St Catherine's Hall and Christ's College, Cambridge.

certainly been a prime motivating factor for Henry VI when he founded both Eton and King's College in the 1440s, and in 1458 a clause was added to the statutes of both institutions requiring Fellows of these colleges to foreswear the heresies of Wycliffe and Pecock.[187] It is surely significant that this amendment was made at the instigation of Eton's former Provost, William Waynflete. In 1457 Waynflete had himself participated in the trial for heresy of Reginald Pecock, Bishop of Chichester and a member of Henry VI's Privy Council.[188] And in refounding, in the following year, St Mary Magdalen Hall as Magdalen College, Waynflete created an educational establishment expressly intended to stem the propagation of such heresies in academic circles.[189]

Far removed from these learned centres of theology, fifteenth-century English preachers seem not only to have extolled the orthodox belief that images were permitted as an important visual aid to devotion, but also positively encouraged their audiences to consider these images as animate embodiments of the saints they represented.[190] Late medieval sermon *exempla* and saints' legends, in particular the Marian miracles, were pervaded with stories about holy images performing miraculous deeds, in which the non-believers who seek to defile them are either converted or struck down dead. Indeed, such a tale is depicted on the north wall at Eton in the 'Miracle of the wounded image' which recounts 'How the image of the Blessed Virgin and Child, struck by the faithless, bleeds'.[191] In the figure of the devout woman who kneels before the statue of the Virgin and Child and the lifeless body of the soldier to her side, this episode simultaneously depicts the appropriate veneration of such holy images and the retribution that will be meted out against the faithless who seek to denigrate them. The power of holy images, and in particular of images of the Virgin, to steer the faithful towards Christian living was further portrayed in the 'Miracle of the youth betrothed to the Virgin's image' on the south wall of the nave.[192] Amid the ongoing contemporary debate surrounding the validity of image-based devotions, Waynflete plainly sought, in his wall painting programme at Eton, to reinforce the validity of traditional Marian beliefs and devotional practices. As Glover points out, the paintings not only reinforced belief in the Virgin as supreme intercessor, but they also emphasised the importance of image worship as a means of accessing the Virgin's intercessory powers.[193] The dearth of comparable iconographic schemes dating from the close of the fifteenth century is testament both to the theological specificity of the Eton mural programme and to the rapid subsequent demise of the devotional beliefs it sought to promote and defend.

187 Glover 2007, 347, citing Heywood & Wright 1850, 619.
188 Aston 1993, 83, 86-8; also Aston 1984, 181-7. Pecock, who sought to convince the Lollards of their errors with regard to image worship and pilgrimage, wrote in the vernacular and based his arguments on Scripture and logic; it was principally for his attack on the notion of ecclesiastical infallibility that he was ultimately condemned.
189 Glover 2007, 347.
190 See Owst 1961, 145-6, on pre-Reformation preaching in England; also Kamerick 2002, 54-60, on images in sermon *exempla*. Kamerick 2002, 63, also points out the distinction drawn in saints' *Lives* between pagans who worshipped idols and the Christian faithful who venerated holy images.
191 Both Gill 2003, 184, and Glover 2007, 356, point out that the word 'Qualiter', which opens many of the inscriptions at Eton, was frequently used in the context of medieval preaching.
192 The legend recounts how a young man, who was devoted to the Virgin, placed his ring on a statue of the Virgin. When the youth later decided to marry, the statue refused to relinquish the ring, reminding him that he was already betrothed to her, upon which the youth abandoned his worldly attachments and became a monk.
193 Glover 2007, 349.

4. Style and the influence of the Netherlands

If the paintings commissioned by Waynflete for Henry VI's new church at Eton were theologically backward-looking, stylistically they were quite the opposite. Indeed, in their format, palette and figurative style, the murals in the nave represent the cutting edge of courtly fashion in England in the last quarter of the fifteenth century. While no specific model for the painting programme has yet been identified, the paintings' affinity with contemporary Netherlandish art is universally acknowledged.[194] This influence is evident not only in the treatment of the human form, but also in details of costume, such as the elaborate 'hennin' headdresses worn by several of the women on the north wall.[195] Whether the artists were 'Flemish', as has so often been asserted, or just English painters emulating this fashionable style is, in the absence of more elucidating records, impossible to say. The College audit rolls offer frustratingly little evidence as to the identities of the painters employed on the scheme, and the nationalities of those few individuals who are singled out for mention are ambiguous. The peculiarly un-English sounding 'Lodovico Palmer', who is twice mentioned in relation to the paintings, might well be an anglicised form of Lodovico *da Palma*,[196] and it does not take a huge leap of the imagination to arrive at Martindale's hypothesis that 'Willelmi Baker' might have been 'Villem Becker' of Bruges.[197]

Certainly we know that, in the second half of the fifteenth century, England saw an influx of artists from the Burgundian Netherlands, many of whom quickly secured patronage at court.[198] At this time, England and the Continent were bound not only by a mutual language and shared faith, but also by their commercial interdependence.[199] The weaving towns of Bruges, Ypres and Ghent were almost completely dependent upon English wool for their trade, while English merchants relied upon the Flemish network of banking and credit for their own prosperity.[200] The marriage in 1468

194 See, among others, Tristram in James & Tristram 1929, 42-3; Martindale 1995, 137; also Noad 1997.

195 E.g. in the first scene of the Amoras legend (scene N3) and the miracle of the candle (scene N6), for which see Norris 1999, 445-8, and Cunnington & Cunnington 1969, 159-64; see also Chrisman 1995 on contemporary costume more generally. The 'butterfly' form of the hennin, worn in the Candlemas scene was, according to Noad 1997, 8, a more anglicised version of the headdress.

196 A suggestion made by Tudor-Craig 1973, 2.

197 See Martindale 1995, 149; also Kidd 1987, 27, who notes that several artists by the name 'de Bakker' were working in Brussels in the later fifteenth century.

198 See Gill 2003, 191, for an exhaustive list of panel paintings and manuscripts executed for British patrons, including Edward IV's sister, Margaret of York. Also Lindley 1993, 807.

199 See Barron 1995.

200 Barron 1995, 2-6.

of Charles the Bold, Duke of Burgundy, to Edward IV's sister Margaret of York was an event attended by a large number of the English court and served to cement these cultural and economic allegiances.[201] Indeed, when Edward fled England during the political turmoil of 1470-1, it was in Bruges that he sought sanctuary. Noad observes that Edward's host there was the renowned bibliophile Louis de Gruuthuse and that, upon his return to England, the king assembled a library of lavish Bruges-produced manuscripts.[202] Patrons of Netherlandish painting and manuscripts were also prominent among Edward's family and courtiers, in particular the queen and her brother, Anthony Woodville, Lord Rivers.[203] Coincidentally, the Woodvilles were also major benefactors of Eton College and in 1475 Rivers endowed a daily Mass and annual obit for himself and the royal family.[204] During this period Flemish manufactured goods, including high-quality textiles, tapestries, monumental brasses, illuminated manuscripts and printed books, flooded into England.[205] Documents also attest that immigrant Flemish painters, sculptors, carvers and glaziers were engaged on an increasing number of England's most prestigious artistic and architectural commissions.[206] We know that John Utynam, the glazier contracted in 1446 by Henry VI to make coloured glass for the windows of the old parish church at Eton, was Flemish, and that some 40 years later – around the time the wall paintings were being executed in the nave of the new church – it was Flemish glaziers again who were called upon to commemorate Edward IV and his family in the royal window at Canterbury Cathedral.[207] In 1477-9 two sculptors from the Low Countries, Dirike van Grove and Giles van Castell, were awarded the contract for carving the figurative elements of the new choir screen in St George's Chapel, Edward IV's sumptuous new foundation at Windsor.[208] More significantly, however, Bishop Waynflete engaged Flemish sculptors to undertake his monumental Great Screen in Winchester Cathedral (*c.*1476), and commissioned an 'immigrant carver', Walter Nicholl, in 1475 to make the choir stalls and rood loft for the new church at Eton.[209]

While there is no concrete evidence for the nationality of the painters engaged by Waynflete to execute the wall paintings at Eton, the affinity of the female figures, in particular, with the 'Early Netherlandish' painting style is striking.[210] The women's long flowing hair and distinctive facial characteristics, with high foreheads and heavily lidded eyes held in a graceful downward gaze, correspond entirely with the style pioneered by the likes of Jan van Eyck (*c.*1395-1441) and his followers. The same is true of the figures' attenuated bodies, which are enveloped in heavy draperies falling in voluminous,

201 Kidd 1987, 24, cites the example of Sir John Donne who, while in Bruges for the royal wedding, commissioned the painter Hans Memling to make a triptych for him (the *Donne Triptych*, *c.*1478, National Gallery, London); also Sir Edward Bonkil, Provost of the Collegiate Chapel of the Holy Trinity in Edinburgh, who commissioned Hugo van der Goes to paint an altarpiece for his chapel at Holyrood (the *Holy Trinity*, *c.*1478, National Galleries of Scotland).

202 Noad 1997, 6. De Gruuthuse evidently visited England frequently, and in 1472 Edward IV made him Earl of Winchester. On the royal library in England in the reigns of Henry VI and Edward VI, see Stratford 1994 and Backhouse 1987.

203 See Backhouse 1987, 29-31. On English patronage of Flemish painters in the later fifteenth century, see also Tudor-Craig 1973, 6.

204 Noad 1997, 6.

205 See Barron 1995, 9-12, 16, who observes that in 1480-1 alone some 900 books were imported into London by merchants from the Low Countries; also Childs 2010, 37-8, on the large numbers of painted cloths and panels imported in the later fifteenth century.

206 See Barron 1995, 16-17, who details many such artistic commissions from the fifteenth century; also Stone 1972, 212-13; Lindley 1993, 806-7; and Gill 2003, 190-1.

207 See Gill 2003, 191; also Marks 1993, 206, who cites a complaint by the London Glaziers Company in 1474 against some 28 immigrant craftsmen practising their trade in the City. On these disputes, see also Lindley 1993, 807, n.70.

208 See Lindley 1993, 807; also James 1933.

209 On the Winchester screen, see Lindley 1993, 806-7; on Walter Nicholl, see Willis & Clark 1886, 409; also Harvey 1984, 216; but also Davis 1993, 115, who challenges the latter's assertion that Nicholl was a foreigner.

210 See Tudor-Craig 1973, 28; also Agnew in McConnell 1976, 129-30; also Gill 2003, 189.

angular folds. The artist responsible for the majority of the north wall scenes at Eton, whose style art historians have likened to the later work of Rogier van der Weyden (*c.*1399-1464) and Dieric Bouts (*c.*1415-75), displays a particular preoccupation with architectural settings. The action of almost all of these episodes is depicted in or around an interior space, only sparsely populated by the protagonists of the tales they portray. The overall mood, as Noad has observed, is one of contemplation, with almost every scene focusing on the figure of a woman kneeling in prayer.[211] In the scenes on the south wall, by contrast, which have been compared with the work of the Ghent artist Hugo van der Goes (*c.*1440-82), it is the figures that take centre stage. Any sense of spatial depth is destroyed by the throng of animated actors that crowd at the front of the pictoral frame, sometimes even encroaching beyond it.[212] The stylistic dissimilarities between the north and south wall paintings have been the subject of much discussion, and earlier scholars such as Tristram and Rickert concluded that, while the north wall murals must have been the work of a Flemish master, the south wall was most probably the work of a less-accomplished English assistant.[213] More recently Peter Kidd has proposed that a third hand may have been responsible for the most westerly scene on the south wall (scene s8), presumably the last section of the cycle to have been painted.[214] Indeed, the better preserved faces of the female saints at the far western end of the scheme permit more specific comparison with contemporary Flemish works of art. The face of St Sidwell on the north wall (see Figure 24) is close in style to that of the Virgin in Bouts' *Virgin and Child* of *c.*1470 (Figure 27). The women share the same gently inclined head and lowered gaze. Their eyes, defined by fine arched brows, are hooded, with lids almost closed, their lips together in a full, unsmiling mouth. The hair is softly waved, with individual sinuous strands picked out in golden yellow. St Winifred on the south wall, with her slightly higher hair line and more pronounced eyelids, displays closer affinities with the Virgin in van der Goes' *Portinari Altarpiece* (*c.*1474-8) (Figures 28 and 29).[215]

Left to right
Fig. 27. Dieric Bouts, *Virgin and Child*, *c.*1470 (Städel Museum, Frankfurt am Main).
Fig. 28. Hugo van der Goes, *Portinari Altarpiece*, *c.*1474-8 (Uffizi Gallery, Florence).
Fig. 29. St Winifred, south wall, figure IX.

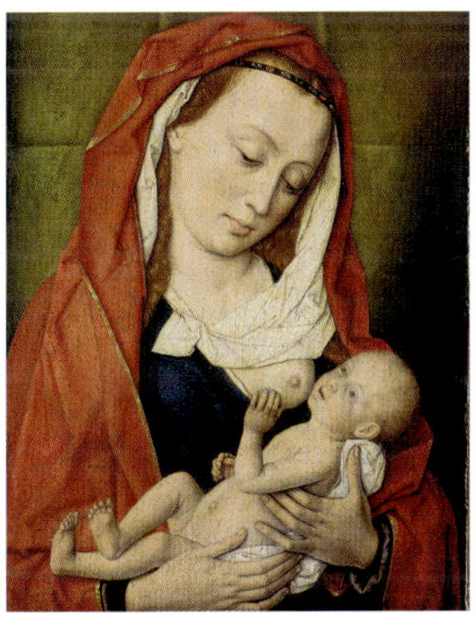

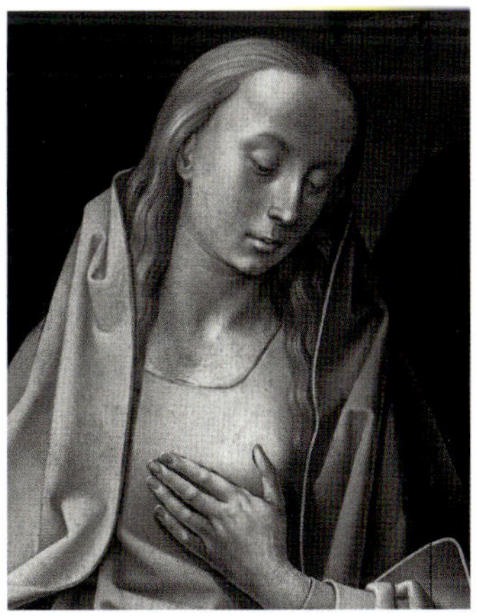

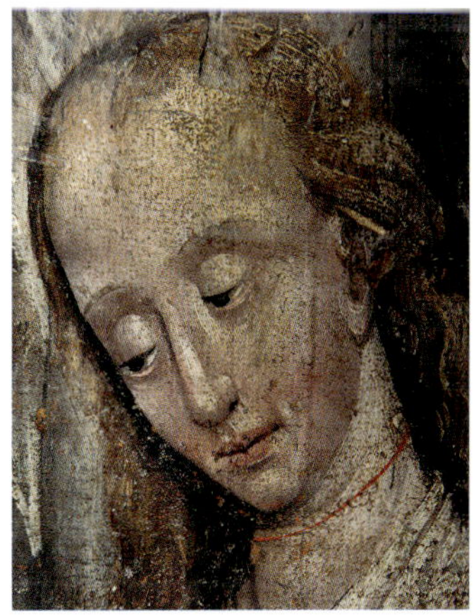

211 Noad 1997, 16.
212 Gill 2003, 189-90.
213 Tristram in James & Tristram 1929, 43; Rickert 1965, 191-2; see also Lindley 1993, 806; Martindale 1995, 137; and Alexander 1975, 59.
214 Kidd 1987, 28.
215 The figure of the woman dying unconfessed in scene N8 is also very close in form and style to that of the dying Virgin painted by van der Goes in 1481-2 (a panel now in the Groeningemuseum in Bruges); see Dhanens 1998, 334.

Some of the closest stylistic parallels for the female figures at Eton are, however, to be found much nearer to home and in a medium other than painting. The sculpted figure of the Virgin believed to have come from Waynflete's Great Screen at Winchester Cathedral, which is dated to about 1476 and attributed to the Dutch sculptor Adriaen von Wesel, shares the same facial features and calm, downward gaze common to so many of the Eton saints (Figure 30).[216] With her high forehead and smoothly curved eyebrows, she bears perhaps the closest resemblance to St Agatha (figure V on the north wall) and St Winifred (figure IX on the south). Examination of other surviving female torsos from the Winchester screen, in particular the fragmentary figure of a queen (fragment no.236), reveals a broad similarity in the treatment of draperies,[217] and in the screen's surviving northernmost spandrel (Figure 31), St Elizabeth is depicted wearing the same type of turban

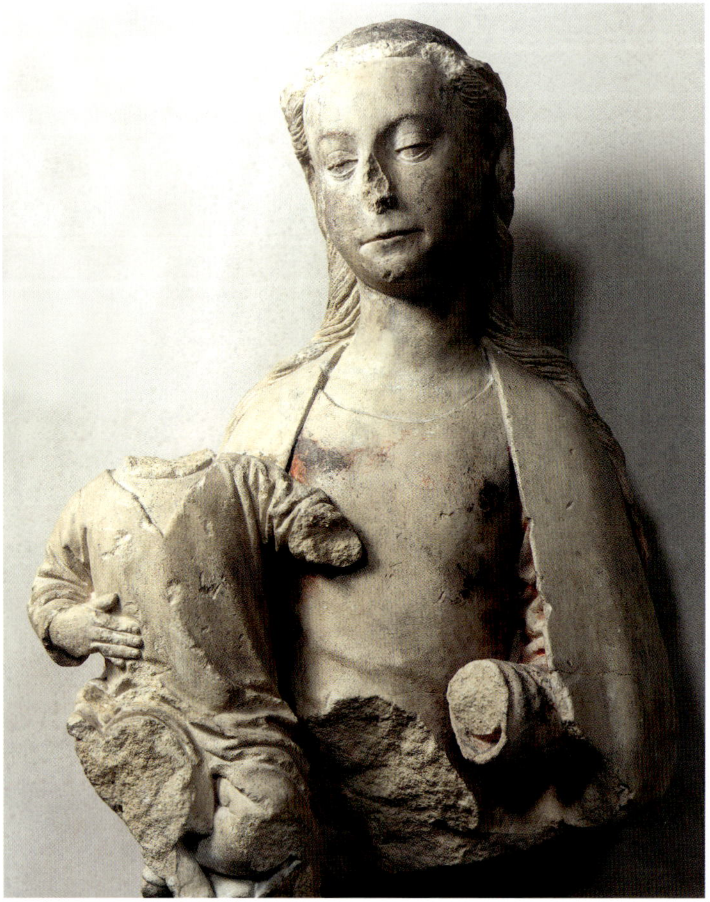

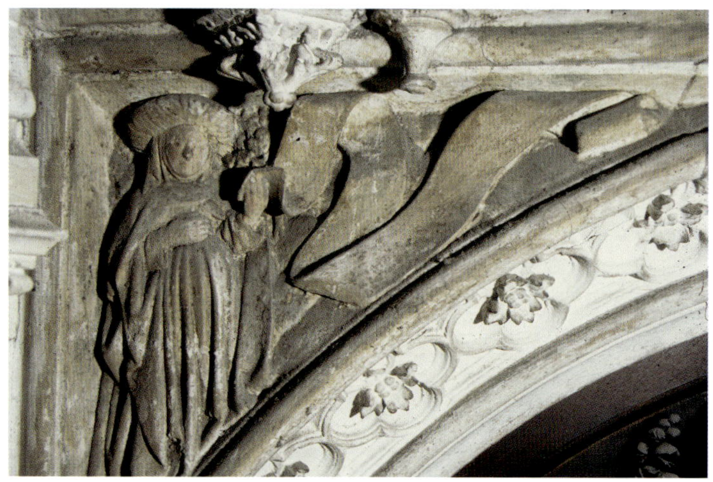

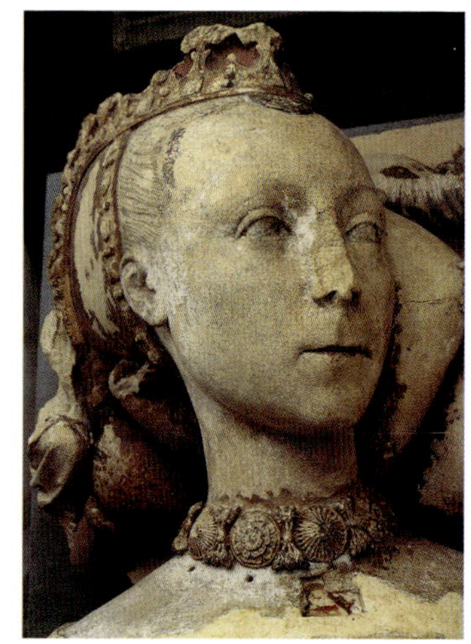

Left to right
Fig. 30. Virgin and Child, from the Great Screen, Winchester Cathedral, *c.*1476.
Fig. 31. Great Screen, Winchester Cathedral, *c.*1476; the surviving northern spandrel, featuring St Elizabeth.
Fig. 32. Funerary effigy of Joan Nevill, *c.*1470-80, Fitzalan chapel, Arundel Castle (reproduced from Brodrick & Darrah 1986).

216 See Lindley 1993; also Tudor-Craig 1973, 28, who perhaps first drew this comparison.
217 See Lindley 1989, figures 5, 6 and 7, for examples of female draperies from the Winchester screen.

worn by three of the Eton figures, including one of the attendants in the 'Miracle of the Jewess' (scene 5 on the north wall).[218] In their portrayal of the female form, both schemes display strong stylistic similarities with the closely contemporary funerary effigy of Joan Nevill (wife of William Fitzalan, a close confidant of Bishop Waynflete) in the family chapel at Arundel (*c.*1470-80) (Figure 32).[219]

Numerous less well-known survivals of late fifteenth-century English sculpture in wood, stone and alabaster evoke the same fashionable figurative style.[220] Indeed, in their subdued palette and artful deployment of shadow, the paintings seem to some extent to have been deliberately intended to emulate sculpture, which is paradoxical given that medieval statuary was almost always enlivened with colour. The genre of grisaille painting, which it has been suggested found its roots in the Lenten observance of covering images,[221] was becoming increasingly fashionable across a wide range of media. Altar hangings, such as the well-known *Parement de Narbonne* (*c.*1370, Musée du Louvre, Paris), painted in black ink on white silk, were perhaps the earliest examples of this practice, which continued late into the fifteenth century.[222] The 1466 inventory of the London church of St Stephen's, Coleman Street, details the provision of similar Lenten cloths painted with monochrome, two-dimensional images of the statues they were designed to conceal.[223] Similar considerations started to influence the production of altar panels, the outer wings of which were closed during Lent to conceal all but their grisaille outer images. Several such panels were produced in Flanders in the early fifteenth century, among the most famous being van Eyck's *Dresden Triptych* (*c.*1430-1, Staatliche Kunstsammlungen, Dresden), which features a monochrome Annunciation on its closed exterior wings, and his *Ghent Altarpiece* (*c.*1432, Ghent Cathedral), which is decorated with grisaille representations of St John the Baptist and St John the Evangelist.[224] It was an aesthetic which, having shed its original liturgical associations, was perpetuated not only by panel painters, but also by manuscript illuminators, stained glass painters and – as we have seen at Eton – those working on walls.[225]

It is surely significant that some of the most extensive examples of grisaille painting from this period are to be found in illustrated *Books of Hours* featuring miracles of the Virgin. One such work, dating from around 1450 and produced for Philip the Good, Duke of Burgundy (The Hague, Koninklijke Bibliotheek, MS 76), features no fewer than 150 black and white miniatures by the illuminator Jean le Tavernier.[226] In 1456, two further volumes recounting *Les Miracles de Nostre Dame* were compiled by the duke's secretary, Jean Miélot, and

218 The others being St Mary of Egypt and St Barbara. See Tudor-Craig 1973, cat. entries 7 and 40.

219 See Lindley 1993, 804-5; neither the identity nor the nationality of the sculptor is, however, known.

220 See Tudor-Craig 1973, cat. entries 4, 6, 7, 25 and 50 which, for their similarities of form and/or treatment of draperies, she compares to the Eton wall paintings. On late fifteenth-century sculpture from Flanders and Brabant, see Stone 1972, 225; also Woods 2007.

221 Teasdale Smith 1959, *passim*.

222 Teasdale Smith 1959, 43-6; also Nash 2008, 266-7.

223 See Woods 2007, 137.

224 Teasdale Smith 1959, 48-9.

225 Teasdale Smith 1959, 51; Nash 2008, 266-7. For more detailed discussion of the use of grisaille by Netherlandish panel painters, see Noad 1997, 13-15, 17-18. One example that is particularly close in format to the Eton scheme is a late fifteenth-century panel painting in the Grand Séminaire at Bruges featuring Margaret of York's step-daughter, Archduchess Mary of Burgundy; composed of two registers, the figurative scenes are enclosed within fictive stonework niches with textual citations running beneath (see Martens 1992, 69). For examples of grisaille in contemporary Flemish stained glass and manuscripts, see Heck *et al.* 2003.

226 See Nash 2008, 266-8; also Noad 1997, 21.

illustrated in grisaille by Tavernier's workshop (Paris, Bibliothèque nationale, MS Fr.9199 and Oxford, Bodleian Library, MS Douce 374).[227] Many of the miracles depicted in these works are among those featured on the walls at Eton, and bear some resemblance to them in limited elements of composition and style (see Figure 25).[228] As Noad observes, it is not improbable that Netherlandish grisaille manuscripts in a style more closely comparable to the wall paintings at Eton were in circulation at the English court in the last quarter of the fifteenth century, or even that such a volume was in the possession of Bishop Waynflete and served as a source of inspiration for the scheme.[229] Indeed, it has been argued by both Gill and Glover that slight discrepancies between the miracle scenes depicted at Eton and the texts they purport to illustrate indicate that the artists almost certainly drew on existing visual models for the scheme.[230]

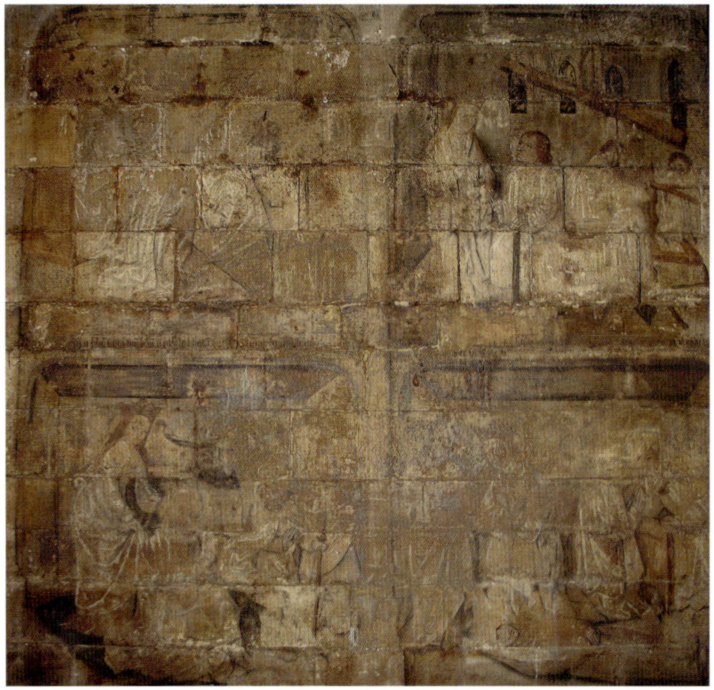

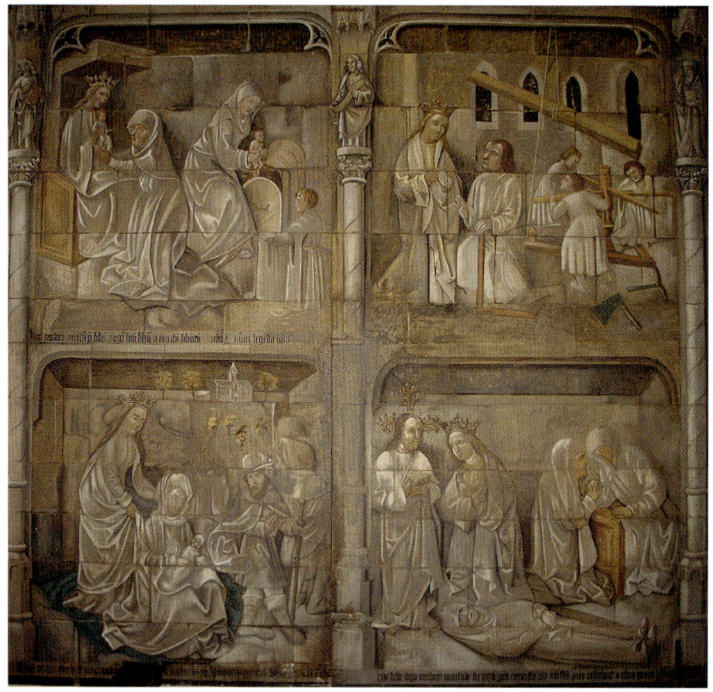

Left Fig. 33. Detail from *The Miracles of the Virgin*, c.1500, Lady Chapel, Winchester Cathedral.
Right Fig. 34. Reconstruction of this area by E.W. Tristram.

227 Noad 1997, 21-3; and see also 24-7 for numerous other manuscripts with which Noad draws parallels.
228 See Laborde 1929; plate XV (Douce 374, fol.37, the miracle of Mont St Michel), plate XXI (MS Fr.9199, fol.2, the miracle of Amoras), plate XXV (MS Fr.9199, fol.7, the miracle of the candle), also plate XXXIV (MS Fr.9199, fol.16*v.*, the miracle of the dying girl) which, although not depicted at Eton, displays similarities in its micro-architectural setting, the treatment of the bed and the composition of the group of female saints, to scenes 5 and 6 on the chapel's north wall. On the comparison of these works with the Eton wall paintings, see also Gill 2003, 194.
229 Noad 1997, 20-1, 26-7. Noad also observes (25) that the grisaille genre was a particular favourite with Margaret of York, Edward IV's sister.
230 In the legend of Amoras, for example, whereas at Eton the devout wife is depicted kneeling attentively in prayer, in the *Golden Legend* it is described how the woman fell asleep before the altar; see Glover 2007, 349-55. Also Gill 2002, 107-8 and Gill 2003, 194-9, who cites the example of the miracle of the candle (scene N6), in which the 'messenger' featured in the text is here replaced by an angel.

Left to right
Fig. 35. St Margaret, early sixteenth-century wall painting in St Peter's church, Cassington, Oxfordshire.
Fig. 36. Princess Cecily, daughter of Edward IV, from the royal window in the north transept of Canterbury Cathedral, *c.*1482-7 (Burrell Collection, Glasgow Museums).

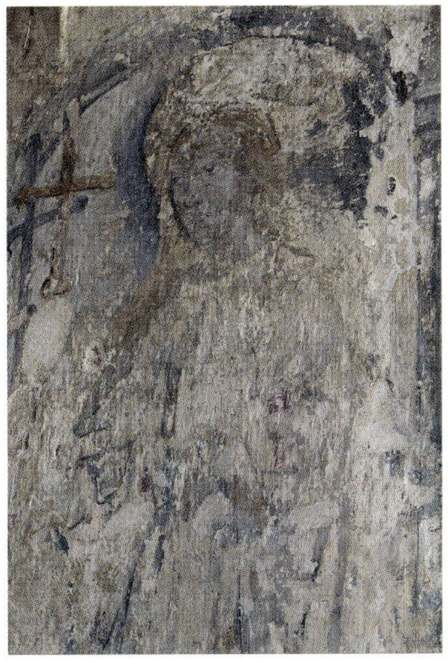

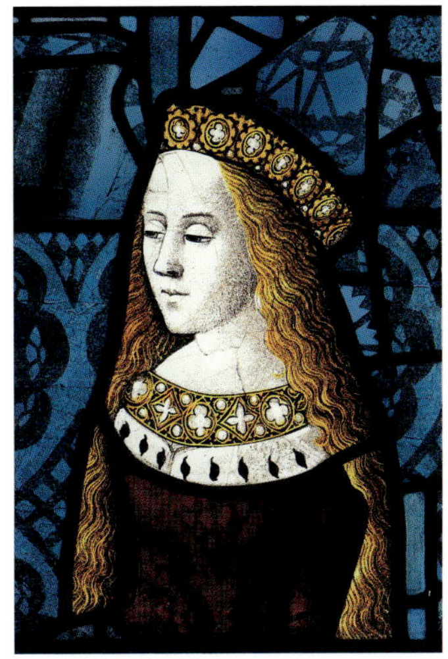

While there do not appear to be many precedents for the use of grisaille in English illuminated manuscripts of this period,[231] there is an increasing body of evidence that this device found popularity in monumental art forms, though none of the known examples appear to pre-date the Eton scheme. The mural scheme in the Lady Chapel at Winchester, which dates from *c.*1500 and is derived from that at Eton, was also executed in a predominantly monochrome palette, with touches of colour used to enliven elements of the composition (Figures 33 and 34). In the 1520s, figures of Edward the Confessor and Abbot Islip, standing beneath canopies on pedestals not dissimilar to those at Eton, were painted in the upper chamber of the Jesus Chapel in Westminster Abbey.[232] Tristram alludes to another pair of saints of *c.*1500 in Canterbury Cathedral that were executed in a monochrome palette of black and white.[233] A further pair of early sixteenth-century monochrome saints standing beneath fictive canopies, believed to represent St Catherine and St Margaret, adorns window jambs in the nave of St Peter's church, Cassington, Oxfordshire (Figure 35).[234] Gill draws our attention to two rather less well-known figurative schemes of this type, painted in imitation of statuary, the first a depiction of the Virgin and Child in the chantry chapel of John Clopton (d.1495) at Long Melford, Suffolk, and another of St Urith, which formerly adorned the church of Mells, Somerset.[235] Though surviving examples are far fewer, grisaille was evidently a technique also employed in narrative mural cycles. Semi-grisaille scenes depicting the Nativity, the Trinity and 'Noli me tangere' survive on masonry blocks from the chapel of St Mark's Hospital in Bristol (*c.*1510) (see Figure 80) and a much deteriorated early sixteenth-century cycle comprising six episodes from the life of St Catherine is preserved in the north aisle of St Peter's church, Raunds, Northamptonshire.[236] Comparable examples of the technique can be found on contemporary painted choir screens in the churches of Ashton, Bridford and Buckland-in-

231 Gill 2003, 192, citing Scott 1996, II, 372.
232 Croft-Murray 1962, 13, and plates 3 and 4.
233 Tristram in James & Tristram 1929, 42. Though he does not mention the location of these paintings, it seems likely that they may be the same seated bishop figures mentioned by Croft-Murray (1962, 13). Said to represent St Gregory the Great and St Augustine, they are painted on concave wooden panels that are thought to have originally formed part of the underside of an organ loft; see also Gostling 1825, 251.
234 Gill has observed that these paintings display a sophisticated shadow treatment which bears comparison with the device used in the paintings at Eton; Gill 2003, 178, 193; also Long 1972, 93.
235 On the Long Melford painting, see Parker 1873, 128-9. See also Gill 2003, 193, who makes reference (178) to a surviving series of coloured figures depicted standing on fictive pedestals between the windows in the Guild Chapel at Stratford-upon-Avon (post-1496).
236 For Bristol, see Gill 2003, 193; for Raunds, see Howe 2005, 24-5, 28, 30; like the Eton paintings, these narrative scenes are depicted within micro-architectural niches, some of which feature windows with lattice quarries.

the-Moor, Devon,[237] and in glazing programmes such as that depicting Edward IV and his family in the north transept of Canterbury Cathedral (*c.*1482-7) (Figure 36).[238] Commissioned at almost exactly the same time as the Eton programme, this window exploits many of the same painterly techniques that characterise the College wall paintings, including subdued grisaille flesh tones with elements such as crowns and long golden hair picked out in vibrant yellow.

The format of the Eton murals, painted in emulation of carved historiated panels divided by columns bearing canopied figures, is one that proliferates in northern European art in the later fifteenth century. Some of the closest parallels are to be found in contemporary woodwork. The retable from the high altar of the church of St Mary and John the Evangelist in Bad Segeberg (north Germany), which dates from around 1515, epitomises this genre. Like the Eton paintings, the narrative scenes are ranged in two registers, each contained within an ornately worked micro-architectural niche. On the columns between each niche, an individual figure stands on a pedestal beneath a canopy, and along the bottom of each scene runs an inscription in Latin.[239] A similar oak panel, depicting scenes from the life of St Colombe, survives in the church in Deerlijk, western Flanders (*c.*1535) (Figure 37).[240] Kim Woods' invaluable recent survey details countless analogous works among the vast corpus of Netherlandish sculpture imported into England in the fifteenth and early sixteenth centuries.[241] Reaching its apogee in the extravagant carved stone choir screens of cathedrals such as Amiens and Chartres (*c.*1530),[242] this was a decorative vocabulary which surpassed the boundaries of material and scale, flourishing simultaneously in both two- and three-dimensional art forms.

Fig. 37. Altarpiece depicting scenes from the Life of St Colombe, *c.*1535, Deerlijk, western Flanders.

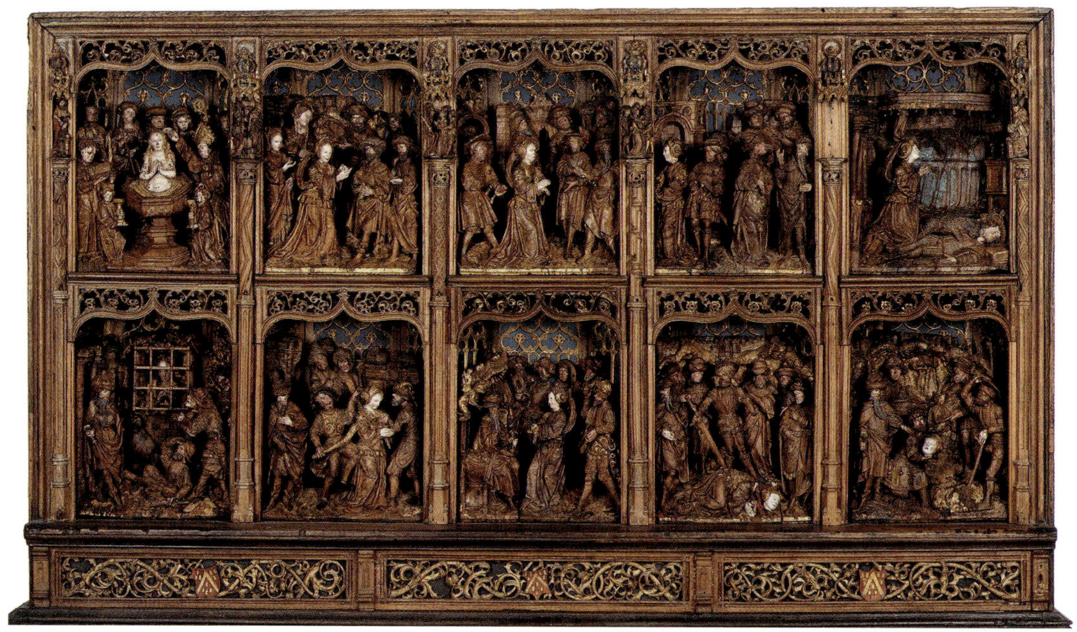

237 See Gill 2003, 193, for these and other contemporary examples of grisaille in English panel painting; Glasscoe 1987, writing on the Ashton screen, observes that the figures holding scrolls of Latin text seem to be derived from late medieval block-book illustration such as those found in *Biblia pauperum*.

238 Tudor-Craig 1973, 18, cat. no.32. For examples of grisaille windows on the Continent, see Nash 2008, 95, including those in the church of the Charterhouse of Miraflores, Burgos, undertaken by the Brussels-based glass painter Nicolas Rombouts in 1480-4.

239 See Kahsnitz 2006, fig.39.

240 See Woods 2007, 63, fig.23.

241 Woods 2007.

242 Croft-Murray 1962, 13.

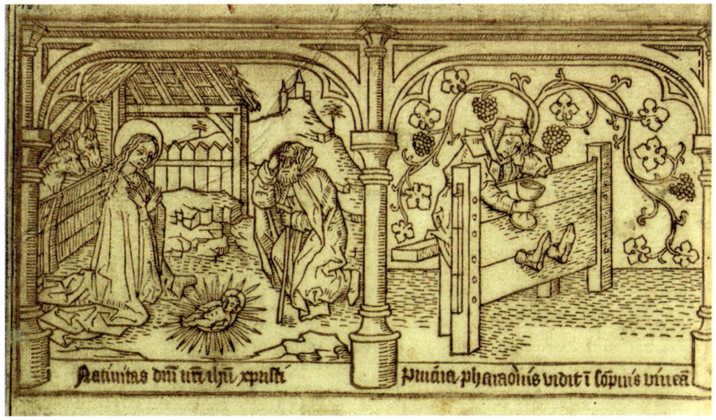

Fig. 38. 'The Nativity' and 'The dream of Pharaoh's butler', from *Speculum humanae salvationis*, Dutch block book, *c.*1470-5, fol. 20*v*. (Bayerische Staatsbibliothek).

The configuration of the Eton wall paintings certainly finds resonance in contemporary Flemish tapestries, such as those made to hang in the choir of La Chaise-Dieu in Auvergne (France).[243] Animated scenes from the lives of the Virgin and Christ are played out beneath fictive micro-architectural canopies, with Latin texts running both above and beneath the action. A similar set of hangings was given by Canon Hugues le Coq to the collegiate church of Notre-Dame in Beaune in 1500.[244] Designed in 1474, they also comprise a narrative of the life of the Virgin, depicted within an arcade of niches. It is widely believed that the designs for such hangings were based on the format of contemporary Netherlandish block books. Indeed, numerous parallels for the micro-architectural format of the Eton murals can be found in mid to late fifteenth-century woodcuts such as those in the *Speculum humanae salvationis*, a Dutch publication of *c.*1470-5 (Figure 38),[245] and an edition of the *Canticum canticorum* printed in the Netherlands in around 1470.[246] Furthermore, some of the closest stylistic parallels for the script used for the texts beneath the scenes at Eton can be found in early editions of the *Ars moriendi*, dating from *c.*1450 onwards (Figures 39 and 40),[247] and the *Ars memorandi*, a southern German work of about 1470.[248] Interestingly, both of these books feature a small dragon-like line-filler motif that is identical to that used in the inscription above scene 8 on the south wall at Eton.

While the use of printed books as models cannot be proved at Eton, Gill has argued that woodcuts almost certainly influenced the composition of other later fifteenth-century wall paintings in England, such as the schemes depicting *Death and the Gallant*, formerly in the Hungerford Chapel in Salisbury Cathedral, and the *Dance of Death* in the chapel of the Guild of the Holy Cross in Stratford-upon-Avon.[249] Many of the typological models upon which contemporary stained glass cycles were based undoubtedly originated from block books.[250] It was from such a work that the iconography of the glazing programme at Tattershall College, also commissioned by William Waynflete, seems to have

243 Heck *et al.* 2003, 394-6.
244 Heck *et al.* 2003, 395; also Nash 2008, 249-50.
245 Hind 1935, 245-6 and fig.102; also Parshall 2009, 73.
246 Hind 1935, 243-5, fig.101.
247 Hind 1935, 229, fig.96; see also Duffy 1992, plates 117-19.
248 Hind 1935, 254 and fig.106.
249 Gill 2003, 195; also Gill 2002, 275 and 407 on Stratford-upon-Avon; and 409 on Salisbury.
250 See, e.g. Gill 2002, 296 and n.157, on the late fifteenth-century cycle of glass at Great Malvern Abbey which was, in part, derived from a block-book version of the *Biblia pauperum*.

been derived.[251] Anderson, citing the Eton paintings' 'heavy black defining strokes, strong highlights…, spatial distortions, vertical compartmentalization, and … grisaille palette with localized colour', goes so far as to suggest that the painters responsible for the scheme may have been engaged on the project as an adjunct to their primary vocation as glass painters.[252] Although there is little evidence to support this proposition, it is true that glass painters, like wall painters, were accustomed to painting on a large scale and, in many cities, belonged to the same guilds.[253] Anderson draws specific parallels between the Eton paintings and the early sixteenth-century programme of stained glass in the church at Fairford, Gloucestershire, which was executed by Flemish glass painters and also derived, at least in part, from the contemporary block book, the *Biblia pauperum*.[254] Certainly, there are some striking stylistic similarities, not least in the semi-grisaille palette and the depiction of saints on pedestals beneath ornate micro-architectural canopies (Figure 41).[255] In both schemes, the representation of these standing saints drew on a long-established hagiographic tradition, serving not only to imbue the narrative programme with spiritual authority but also to inspire reverence towards it.

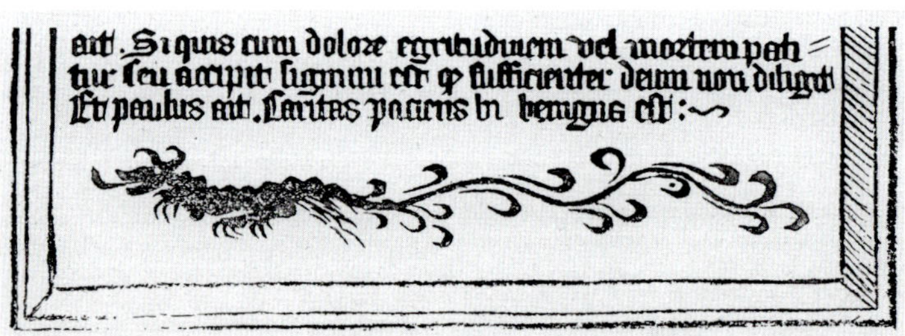

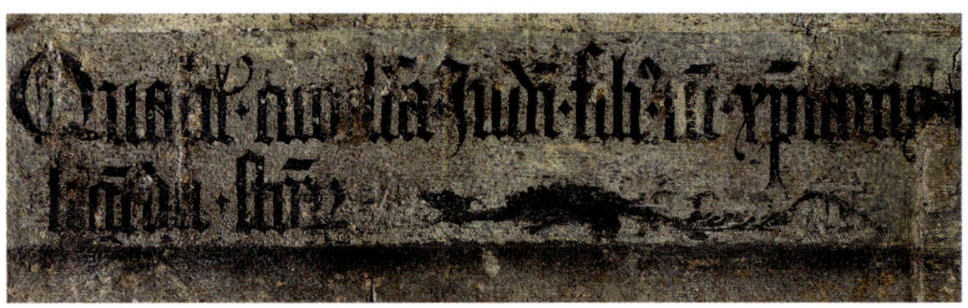

Adornment with sumptuous textiles, whether real or painted, was another means through which devotional gravitas could be conferred on a sacred space or object. Though now obscured from view, an elaborate fictive damask is depicted all the way along the bottom of the wall paintings at Eton. Parts are still visible in the broad vertical bands that border the scheme at its eastern end, where it adjoined the rood screen (see Figure 9). The painted damask evokes a highly fashionable stylised 'pomegranate' motif combined with acanthus leaves, executed in white on a grey ground – perhaps in imitation of silver – with touches of golden yellow, deep red and blue. Luxurious and costly 'tissues' of this type, woven with raised loops of gold and silver thread, were imported to England in the fifteenth century from

Fig. 39. Line-filler motif from the block book *Ars moriendi*, *c.*1450 (reproduced from Hind 1935).
Fig. 40. Line-filler motif similar to that in the *Ars moriendi*, from the inscription above scene 8 on the south wall at Eton.

251 See chapter 1 above; also Marks 1979, 145, 150-2 and plates LI and LII; also Davis 1993, 101; also Noad 1997, 11.
252 Anderson 1989, 3-4.
253 On guilds, see Blair & Ramsay 1991, 277-8; also Anderson 1989, 8, who points out that from the mid-fifteenth century, Flemish glass painters were incorporated into the painters' guild of St Luke. Harvey 1975, 163-4, 168, suggests that glaziers were often reliant on painters for their designs. Interestingly, however, the painter of the panel representing four kings in St George's Chapel, Windsor (*c.*1493) seems to have derived his design from glazing, to the extent that figures are depicted against a ground imitating glass quarries; see Marks 1993, 55-7.
254 Anderson 1989, 4-6 and n.8; see also Wayment 1984, 12, 85-6, 94-6, and, most recently, Brown & MacDonald 1997, 49-70, 93-9.
255 Even in some of the more specific details, the affinity of these schemes is undeniable; see for example the figure of Emperor Nero, depicted among the 'Persecutors of the Faith' in Fairford's north nave clerestory (window nII), who sports a sash inscribed with Latin text very similar to that worn by the Emperor's henchman in scenes s2 and s3 of the Empress legend at Eton.

Fig. 41. Window depicting the four Doctors of the Church, *c.*1510-15, in the south nave aisle, St Mary's church, Fairford, Gloucestershire.

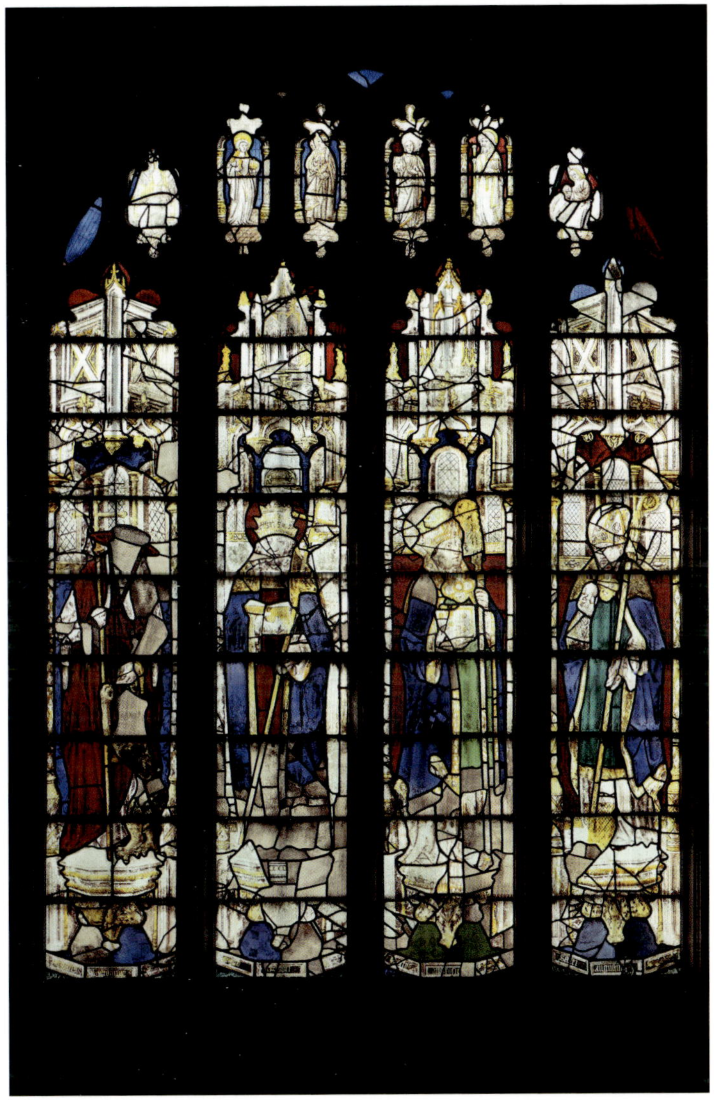

Italy and Spain; many such items are detailed in the inventories of Henry VI's wardrobe.[256] By the 1470s brocaded velvet 'cloths of gold' decorated with pomegranate motifs were at the height of their popularity,[257] and fragments of textiles closely comparable with the Eton wall paintings survive in various collections. Among the finest examples are the brocaded velvet cloth of estate held by the Victoria & Albert Museum, London (Figure 42),[258] and a mid-fifteenth-century cope in Durham Cathedral.[259] With its connotations of fertility, regality and immortality, the pomegranate was particularly suited to an iconographical scheme centred on the Virgin.[260] Indeed, ornate damask cloths of this type are frequently depicted suspended behind the Virgin and Child in fifteenth-century Netherlandish panel paintings, such as Bout's *Virgin and Child with Saints Peter and Paul* (*c.*1460) (Figure 43).[261] In English wall painting too, sumptuous imitation brocades, such as the one to the north of the altar of Elsfield church, Oxfordshire, were being used to denote sanctified spaces and 'cloths of honour' depicted behind both fictive and real statues of saints.[262] Surviving fragments suggest that the lavishly decorated chantry chapel of Sir Henry Vernon at Tong, Shropshire, which can be dated to about 1510-15, was painted to appear as though entirely draped with hangings of fine silk damask similar in style to those

256 Monnas 1998, 64-5.
257 Monnas 2008, 258-9; also Monnas 1998, 69; by the early sixteenth century, textiles decorated with these designs were no longer deemed fashionable for dress and were used only for ecclesiastical vestments and furnishings (termed 'churchework').
258 Though dated to 1606, this cloth of estate is believed to have been made from older fabric and has a design typical of the 1470s, see Monnas 2008, 261, fig.290; for other examples of this type, see Monnas 1998, figs 3 and 8 (accession numbers 81-1892, T.111-1910). See also the Fayrey Pall in Marks & Williamson 2003, cat. no.349. For further comparative examples from Italy and Spain, see Geijer 1979, figs 44 and 49.
259 Monnas 2008, 135, fig.144.
260 On the symbolism of the pomegranate motif in textiles, see Monnas 2008, 218-19.
261 On the depiction of such textiles in fifteenth- and sixteenth-century Netherlandish painting, see Monnas 2008, 121-48.
262 Gill 2002, 199-202.

depicted at Eton (Figure 44).[263] What is more, evidence suggests that the imagery formerly in the niches of the Tong tomb screen related to the life of the Virgin. The Vernons' historic dealings with Eton College (to which they supplied lead from their Derbyshire mines), and Sir Henry's close affinity with the royal household, make it entirely plausible that he was familiar with the chapel paintings and sought in some small way to emulate them. Whatever Vernon's motivation, he demonstrated in his iconographic choices at Tong that, some 30 years on, paintings of this type remained both fashionable and impressive.

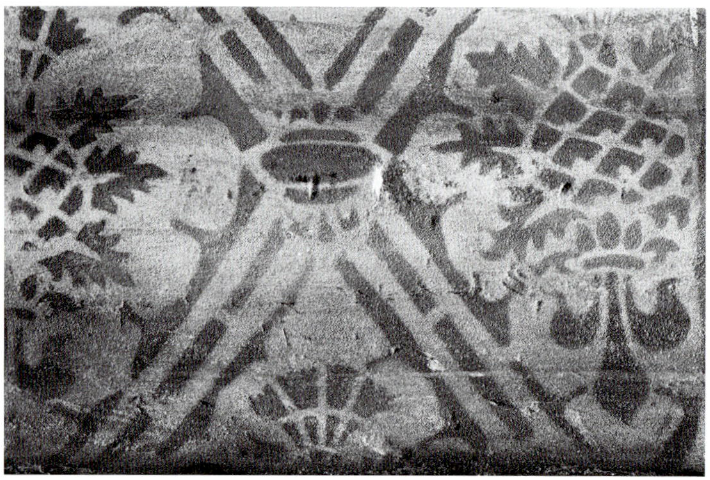

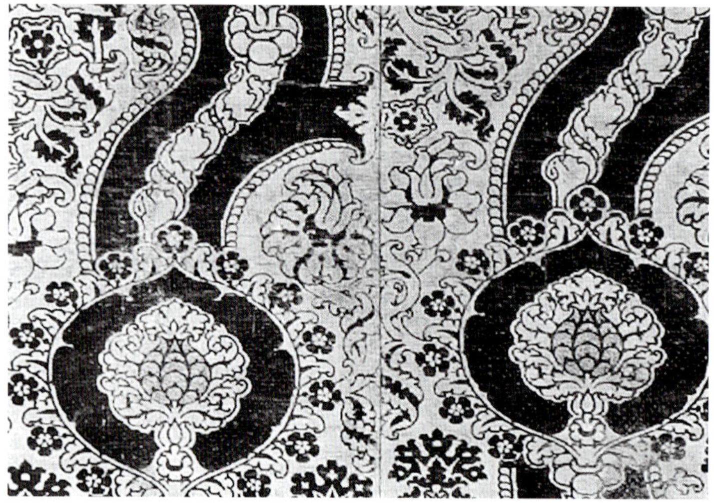

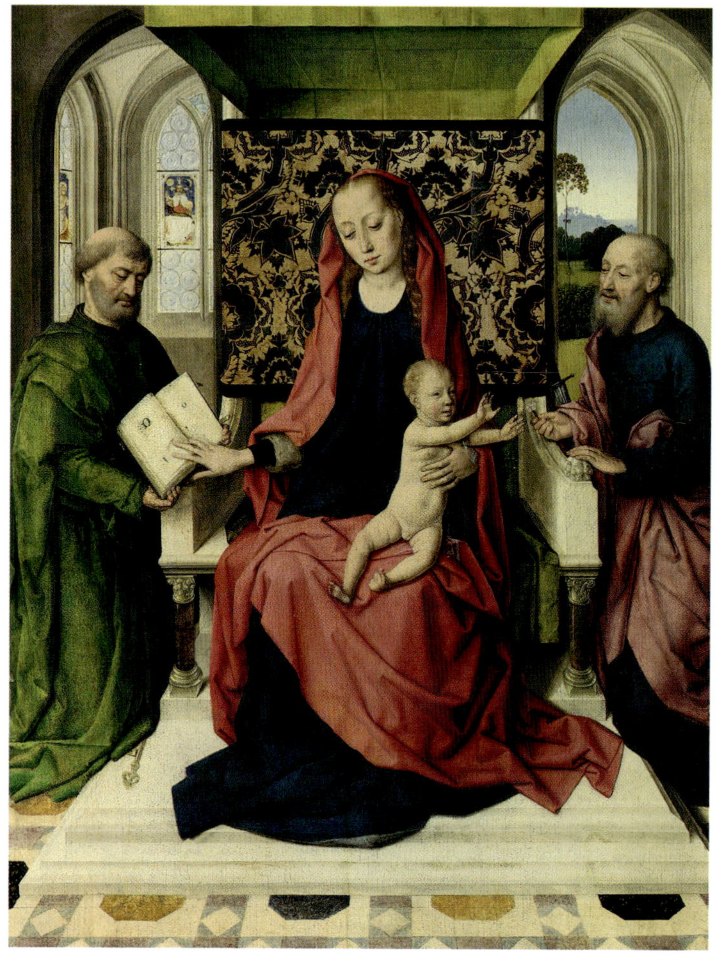

Clockwise from top
Fig. 42. Detail of a cloth of estate made of brocaded velvet, Italian, *c.*1470s (Victoria & Albert Museum, acc. no. 142-1869).
Fig. 43. Dieric Bouts, *Virgin and Child with Saints Peter and Paul*, *c.*1460 (National Gallery, London).
Fig. 44. Detail of fictive damask hangings painted on the walls of the chantry chapel of Sir Henry Vernon at Tong, Shropshire, *c.*1510-15.

263 Gilderdale Scott 2005, 70-3.

5. The physical history of the paintings

Appreciation of Eton's *Miracle* cycle was to be short-lived. Just 60 years after its completion, Edward VI acceded to the throne, and with him a new Protestant regime. In July 1547, under the protectorate of Edward Seymour, the Privy Council ordered bishops to remove all superstitious images from their churches. While received scholarship suggests that, despite these directives, the wall paintings escaped malicious damage until the accession of Elizabeth I,[264] more recent research suggests that the *Miracles* may have been the subject of unwelcome attention much earlier.[265] An entry in the College bursar's records for 27 September 1547 mentions what would seem to be an order that, in some part of the church, paintings should be whitewashed and overpainted with passages from the Scriptures.[266] There is, however, no definitive evidence that these entries refer to the nave wall paintings, and indeed it seems far more likely that they apply to texts painted around the high altar.[267] In any case, with the succession of Mary Tudor in 1553 and the temporary restoration of Catholicism, these texts were ordered to be removed.[268] James conjectures that it was during Mary's reign that the fictive textile hanging, which runs beneath the lower register of the paintings and borders the scheme along at its eastern ends, was updated with a more fashionable treatment evoking geometrical panels of coloured marble inlay (Figure 45).[269] When Elizabeth I acceded to the throne in 1558, Protestantism returned to England. In 1560 the College accounts record a payment of 6*s.* 8*d.* to the College barber for 'wypinge oute the imagery worke vppon the walles in the Churche' in accordance with recent injunctions against 'paintings of counterfeit miracles'. There can be little doubt that this entry refers to Waynflete's paintings in the nave.[270] In the following year, a similar fate befell the 'Tabernacle of stone in ye bodie of the Church' that had housed the cult statue of Our Lady of Eton.[271] The rood screen was definitively removed in 1570, after which time 'pues' (pews) seem

264 E.g. James & Tristram 1929, 5; see also Gill 2003, 174.

265 See Williamson 2000, 375.

266 Williamson cites ECR 62/38 (bursar's book 1544-53), f.105*r*, under the heading 'Custus solucionum forinsecarum': 'Solut Crooke pictori pro templo depingendo ut conventus est ex pacto, xj li. x. s.'

267 See Willis & Clark 1886, 442.

268 Williamson 2000, 375, n.58, cites an entry in 1554 (ECR 62/3, 94*r*), recording that John Barbour was paid 10*s.* 8*d.* for 'blotting out the Scripture on the chirch walls', though again, there is no mention of the specific location of these texts. In 1557 the rood screen, which had likewise been demolished under Edward VI, was also reinstated; see ECR 62/3, 342, under the heading 'Custus Templi', … 'a roode and payntinge thereof, xlvij s. viij d.'

269 James & Tristram 1929, 4-5. This pattern was evidently visible on the north wall in the 1840s, when Essex made his drawings, and was certainly present on the south until its removal by Plummer. The incised lines used in setting out this design are still clearly visible over the fictive textiles located at the east end.

270 James & Tristram 1929, 5, citing ECR 62/3, 528 (1560-1); see also Maxwell Lyte 1911, 163. It is conceivable that 'the barber' was the same 'John Barbour' who was paid to whitewash the Scripture in the church in 1554 (see n.268, above).

271 For which 'Filde the Mason' was paid 5*s.*; see the bursar's account book 1561-2 (ECR 62/3, 553), cited by Willis & Clark 1886, 443.

to have been introduced in the chapel and a sounding-board installed over the pulpit.[272]

No further mention is made of alterations to the church until 1613-14, when the accounts record the installation of a new organ in the nave. James conjectures that the position of this must have been on the north wall where 'a portion of the painting was scraped off to the bare stone',[273] presumably in the area now occupied by Plummer's new female saint figure (Figure NII) (Figure 46 and Catalogue p.129).[274] James also observed that on the south side, towards the west end, a mural tablet had been affixed to the wall, resulting in the obliteration of the figure now identified as St Cecilia.[275] The precise date at which this may have occurred remains unclear. Sometime later in the seventeenth century, however, an entirely new scheme of wall painting in a 'classical style' comprising 'fluted pilasters with ornamented bases' seems to have been executed over Waynflete's murals.[276] Indeed, elements of this overpainting are clearly visible in photographs of the east end of the south wall taken prior to the conservation of the paintings in the 1960s (see Figure 45).

In 1700, under Provost Godolphin, significant modifications were planned to the arrangement of the church. The ante-chapel was enlarged to include the westernmost bay of the former nave, the walls of which were reportedly wainscoted up to the windows. A new organ loft was erected in the second bay from the west.[277] Reports suggest that some attempt was made to scrape off the paintings in these areas, but this proving too difficult a task, they were instead overpainted with layers of a reddish-brown and then white oil paint.[278] As a result, scenes 4 and 5 and the western portions of scene 3 were obliterated from the lower register of painting on both the north and south walls. The upper register

Fig. 45. Detail of the east end of the south wall in 1966, prior to Plummer's conservation, showing the fictive marble scheme painted over the original wall paintings in *c.*1550 and remnants of fluted pilasters painted over the figure of St Catherine in the seventeenth century.

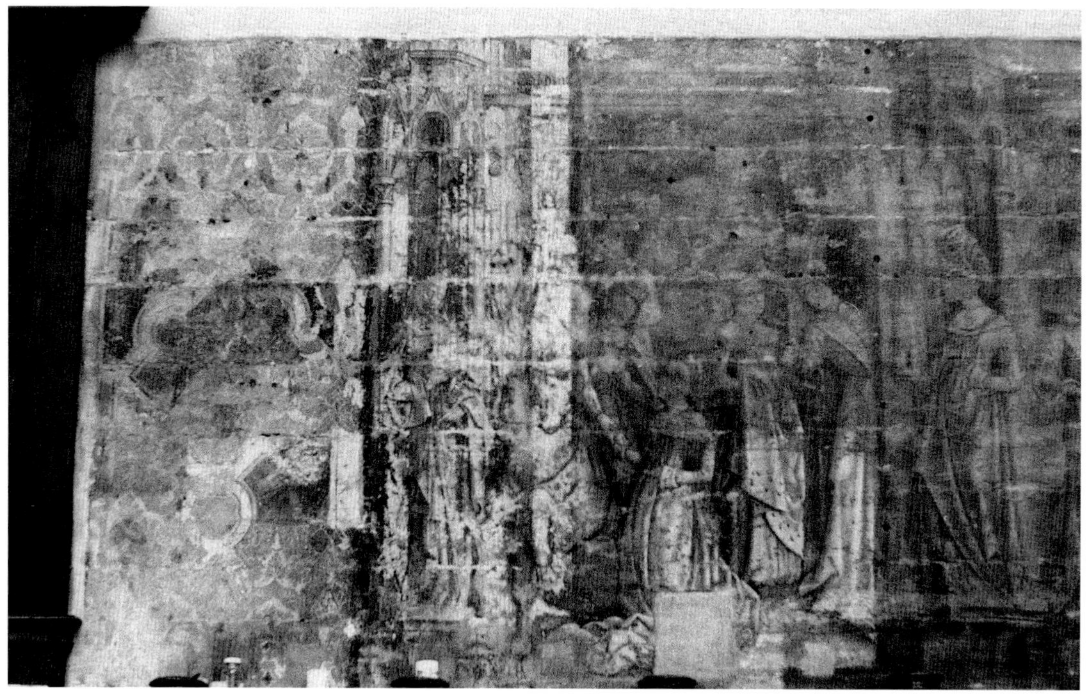

272 The records suggest that the original choir screen had been removed under Edward VI and replaced during Mary's reign; see Willis & Clark 1886, 442-3, who also draw attention to an entry in the bursar's account book for 1571-2 for monies paid 'to Harrye Woodell for…worke in the churche abowt the pews'. With some notable early exceptions, bench pews are generally thought to have been introduced into the nave of English churches in the fifteenth and sixteenth centuries. Prior to this, stone or wooden benches were sometimes provided around the base of the walls for the use of the aged or infirm; see Randall 1980, 56-7; also Cox 1916, 1-16 and Cox 1923, 103-15. While Walter Nicholl was contracted to provide the stalls in the choir at Eton in 1475 (see Willis & Clark 1886, 409), evidence for earlier seating arrangements in the nave is lacking, save for the observation that the fictive damask which runs along the lower edge of the *Miracles* scenes seems to have extended down behind the existing stalls to the original medieval floor level.

273 James & Tristram 1929, 5; also Willis & Clark 1886, 444.

274 See n.300, below.

275 While Tristram struggled to identify this figure, Anderson 1989, 25, has convincingly argued the case for the saint's identity; see also the Catalogue entry for this figure, p.114-15.

276 See James & Tristram 1929, 5; though also Agnew in McConnell 1976, 121, who states that they were in fact 'groups of reeded pilasters on tall bases, which were decorated with knotted ribbons', painted at intervals along the walls. A tracing of the lower part of one such pilaster was made by Pauline Plummer during her work on the scheme (pers. comm.), for details of which see below, p.64.

277 Willis & Clark 1886, 447-8.

278 Agnew in McConnell 1976, 122; Plummer 1986, 37.

seems to have been protected by the insertion at each end of the screen of a flight of stairs (the outline of which is indicated on Essex's original plan of the wall paintings).[279] At this time, the remainder of the chapel walls were also wainscoted up to the windows.[280]

Fig. 46. The north wall following its uncovering in the 1920s, showing the area of painting lost during the insertion of a new organ in the 1600s.

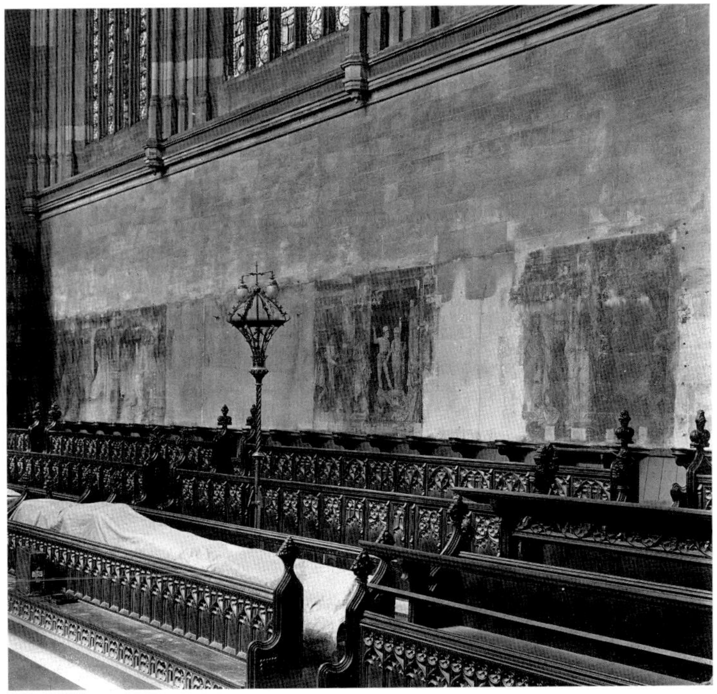

In May 1847 work was commenced to remodel the chapel interior anew.[281] The project, initiated by Provost Hodgson, was ambitious and far-reaching, involving not only the removal of the eighteenth-century wainscoting and the insertion of entirely new stalls, but also the installation of a new oak ceiling, the repositioning of the existing organ and its screen some 6-9m (20-30ft) towards the west, and the lowering, by about 60cm (2ft), of the floor 'to its original and ancient level'.[282] Soon after work had begun to strip out the old panelling, the medieval scheme of wall painting was revealed. The sensational story of how the clerk of works ordered his men to scrape the paintings from the masonry has been widely recited.[283] The devastation was only arrested by chance when, one afternoon, the Reverend John Wilder, a Fellow and later Vice-Provost of the College, happened to pay a visit to the site. By this time the top half of the upper register of paintings on both the north and south walls had already been destroyed, except for a small portion, still preserved today, in the far south-west corner. Evidently the public interest that ensued was not sufficient to prevent further destruction of the paintings.[284] Hodgson, while recognising their value as 'historical curiosities' and lamenting their partial destruction, considered the scenes unfit for the interior of an Anglican place of worship and insisted they be covered from view. Prince Albert, who visited Eton to view the new discovery, is reported to have entreated that some mechanism be devised whereby the paintings could be revealed for examination by interested parties, perhaps through hinged doors in the panelling, but such ideas evidently came to nothing.[285] By way of some small concession, the artist R.H. Essex was commissioned to make pencil drawings of the paintings before work continued with the planned refurbishment.[286] By 1849-50, the paintings were again obscured from view. Sixty neo-Gothic crocketed canopies were commissioned to surmount the new stalls, and

279 James 1895b, 94.
280 See Willis & Clark 1886, 447; also James & Tristram 1929, 5-6. It is thought that the wainscoting was designed by 'Mr Hopson the Joyner' and overseen by Matthew Bankes, variously referred to as the 'king's carpenter' and 'the Surveyor'. These new arrangements are visible in a drawing by Mackenzie published in Ackermann's *Eton* (see Willis & Clark 1886, 449, fig.35).
281 Willis & Clark 1886, 450-1.
282 *The Windsor & Eton Express*, 1 May 1847.
283 See Maxwell Lyte 1911, 471-2; also James & Tristram 1929, 6-13.
284 The paintings were, at this time, widely believed to be of Florentine authorship; see articles from *The Times*, *The Builder* and *The Windsor & Eton Express* cited in James & Tristram 1929, 7-8.
285 James & Tristram 1929, 8-9.
286 See James & Tristram 1929, 9. While evidently an architectural draughtsman of some standing, little is known of Richard Hamilton Essex (1802-55), save that between 1823 and 1837 he is listed as an associate of the Society of Painters in Water Colours, drawing among other buildings Magdalen College, Oxford, and Ely Cathedral. At the same time that Essex was working at Eton, three local young ladies, the Misses Eleanor, Georgiana and Charlotte Cust, were also granted permission to make drawings of the uncovered paintings, copies of which are held in the Print Room at Eton College. Interestingly these ladies were the aunts and a cousin, respectively, of the art historian and museum director Sir Lionel Cust (1859-1929) who was educated at Eton and subsequently published his own history of the College (Cust 1899).

the upper registers of the paintings – with the exception of the single remaining scene at the far west end of the south wall – were scraped off just above the line of their inscriptions.[287] Somewhat ironically, the lower registers of the murals were carefully covered with cloth so as to protect them from abrasion caused by contact with the new woodwork.[288]

The appearance of the first edition of Sir Henry Maxwell Lyte's *A History of Eton College* in 1875 seems to have rekindled public interest in these important wall paintings and, most importantly, captured the imagination of one Montague Rhodes James, who came to Eton as a boy the following year. While the paintings remained covered at this time, the insertion of a new organ screen in 1881-2 at the nave's west end required the two westernmost saints, St Winifred and St Sidwell, to be momentarily uncovered prior to being encased by the new masonry.[289] The appearance four years later of Willis and Clark's *The Architectural History of the University of Cambridge and of the Colleges of Cambridge and Eton*, which gave substantial treatment to the hidden wall paintings, excited further interest in the lost mural scheme.[290] In 1894 James, recently appointed Director of the Fitzwilliam Museum, presented a paper on the Eton wall paintings to the Cambridge Antiquarian Society, accompanied by an exhibition of Essex's drawings.[291] It was almost entirely due to the campaigning of James, who subsequently returned to Eton as Provost, that, on 28 August 1923, the wall paintings in the chapel were again exposed.[292] The celebrated wall painting conservator Professor E.W. Tristram was engaged to salvage the scheme. While no formal record of his treatment survives, it seems that he attempted to clean the paintings, particularly in those areas covered by historic layers of oil paint, and undertook a limited amount of reintegration where small losses obscured unhindered reading of the scenes.[293] Tristram also applied a wax coating to the paintings, no doubt in an attempt both to consolidate and to saturate (and thus enliven) the appearance of the paintings. For those sections in which large areas of the scheme had been irretrievably obscured or completely lost, Tristram painted conjectural reconstructions onto canvas. The canvases were marouflaged onto blockboard panels, which were suspended over the damaged paintings and screwed into the unpainted wall above, a narrow wooden cornice being used to conceal their exposed uppermost edge (Figure 47).[294]

After a short period of admiration, the advent of the Second World War saw the paintings covered once more, this time for their protection.[295] Bomb damage to the chapel's roof and glazing meant that the paintings, though relatively well concealed, were exposed to

287 Willis & Clark 1886, 451; see also woodcut opp. 450.

288 James & Tristram 1929, 10. An angry rebuke by the architect G.E. Street in the *Ecclesiologist* (April 1848) recounts the unhappy fate of the paintings: 'May I have some of your space to remonstrate against the iconoclastic feeling which can induce men to treat paintings so curiously discovered as these have been, in the manner in which the Eton authorities are now treating these precious relics? It having been decided that canopies should be formed for all the upper range of the new stalls, it was found that the upper part of these paintings would be visible over the said canopies, and to prevent so great a disfigurement to stalls and chapel, and perhaps to conceal the fact that they were covering up anything of the sort, they [the College] have actually scraped off all the paintings above a certain line, and the remainder are to be concealed, only to be discovered by a future age, when modern carpentry and joinery has lasted its time, and may have to give place to something else.'

289 Hussey 1923, 303. The incisions resulting from the later removal of this stonework remain visible today.

290 Willis & Clark 1886, 598ff.

291 See Pfaff 1980, 355. While the text of James' paper was printed in the *Proceedings of the Cambridge Antiquarian Society* in 1895 (James 1895b), Essex's drawings were not reproduced until the publication of James' monograph of 1907.

292 The offending stall canopies were given to Lancing College in 1926; see James & Tristram 1929, 11.

293 James (James & Tristram 1929, 12) recalls that Tristram and his assistant applied certain 'elixirs' to the paintings; the removal of overlying layers of oil paint seems to have been attempted using mechanical methods. Plummer 1976 notes that there were two small areas of opaque retouching on the westernmost scene of the north wall, and that a toned varnish had been painted over losses in dark areas to restore unity to the scheme.

294 These panels were installed on the north and south walls in 1927 and 1928 respectively; James & Tristram 1929, 13.

295 See Agnew in McConnell 1976, 124-5, who also observes that the paintings were coated with a protective layer of sodium silicate (water glass) during the subsequent repair of the chapel roof.

high levels of water ingress and particulate matter. Concerns for the deteriorating stability of the murals heightened and, in June 1960, Stephen Rees Jones, Head of the Courtauld Institute of Art's Scientific Department, undertook an assessment of their condition. Extensive areas of flaking could be observed below the wooden cornice and along the grid of the original mortar lines. The surface of the paintings, having been coated with wax by Tristram, was now obscured by a thick layer of air-borne dust and dirt, in addition to the discoloured historic varnish layers and remnants of overpainting that he had not been able to remove.[296] Following this assessment, the College commissioned a project to conserve the paintings, with Pauline Plummer working on the scheme intermittently between 1961 and 1975.

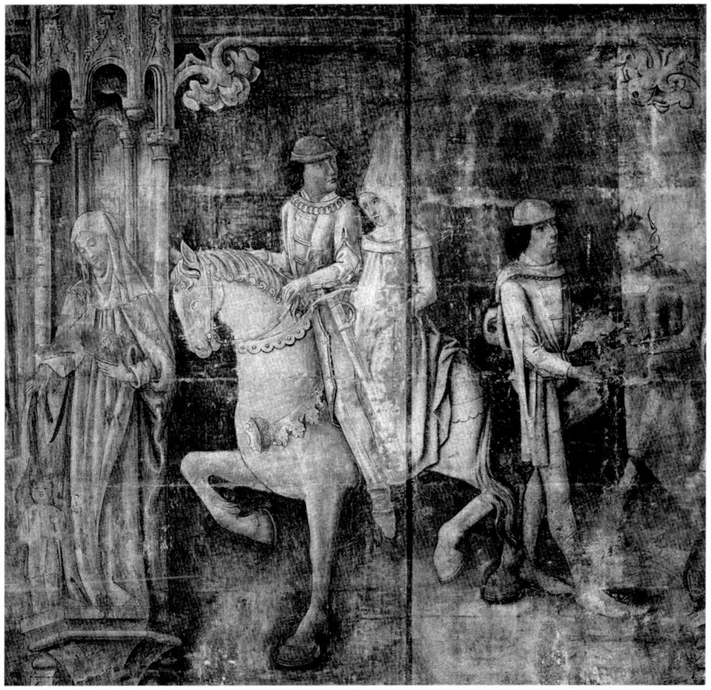

Fig. 47. Detail of the north wall, scene 3, as reconstructed by E.W. Tristram in the 1920s (after James & Tristram 1929, plate XV).

As well as stabilising the deteriorated paintings, Plummer did much to restore pictorial homogeneity to the scheme. Beginning on the north wall, Plummer fixed the extensive areas of flaking using polyvinyl acetate in industrial methylated spirit.[297] The paintings were simultaneously cleaned using a 'weak ammonium solution through white spirit'. Holes and losses in the stone were filled, many of them relating to the installation of stall canopies, and the surface polished with micro-crystalline polythene wax.[298] Reintegration of losses was undertaken on top of this layer using egg tempera, taking care not to cover any of the original paint layer. The fictive marble scheme was removed to reveal the original fictive textile border and, in March 1963, Tristram's reconstruction panels, which appeared discordantly dark in tone compared with the newly cleaned paintings, were removed. In these badly compromised areas, attempts were made to recover the original scheme from beneath the layers of oil paint associated with the insertion of the organ screen in the 1700s

296 Plummer 1986, 37.
297 These, and all subsequent details of Plummer's treatment, are taken from her report; see Plummer 1986, 37-8. A complete set of photographs was taken of the paintings before and after treatment, copies of which are held in the Conway Library at the Courtauld Institute of Art.
298 This product is known by the proprietary name of 'Renaissance Wax' (Plummer 1976); see Horie 1987, 88.

(Figures 48-50).[299] In the area between scenes 1 and 2 at the eastern end of the north wall – where, in 1613, an organ had been installed and the original masonry completely replaced – Plummer was commissioned to paint an entirely new figure (see lower register, figure NII in the Catalogue, pp.126-7).[300] A thin band of reconstructive painting was also undertaken along the upper edge of the paintings, to attenuate the raw transition between the severed murals and the bare wall. On the south wall, where much more of the seventeenth-century architectural scheme remained, uncovering proved more problematic and had to be undertaken mechanically.[301] While the first three scenes were varnished and retouched in egg tempera, in subsequent scenes reintegration was carried out using an acrylic emulsion.[302] At the conclusion of the project, both walls were cleaned (using deionised water on cotton wool) and again polished with micro-crystalline wax.

In November 2010 the wall paintings were subjected to a comprehensive scientific study of their original materials and technique by the present author, the findings of which form the basis of the following chapter.

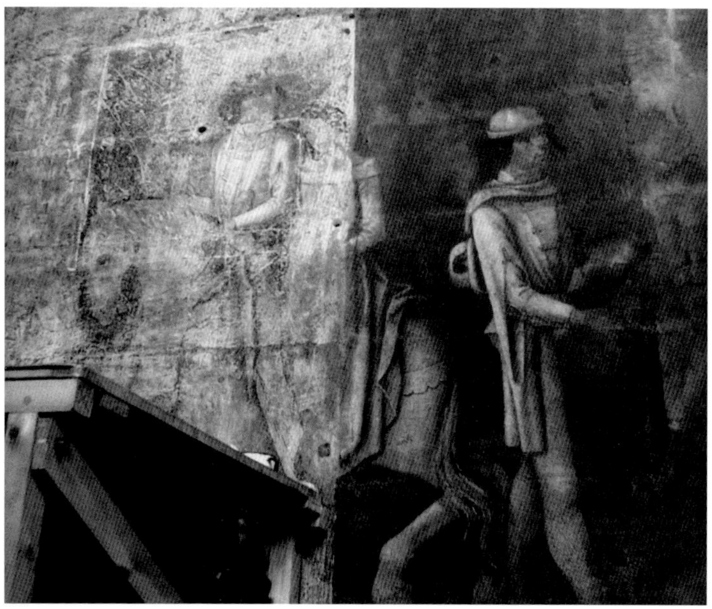

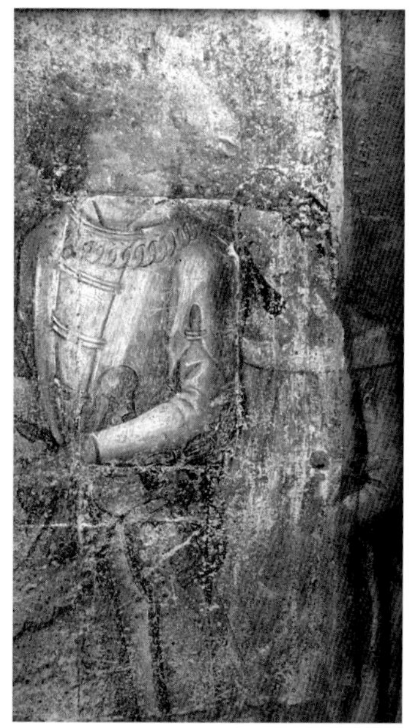

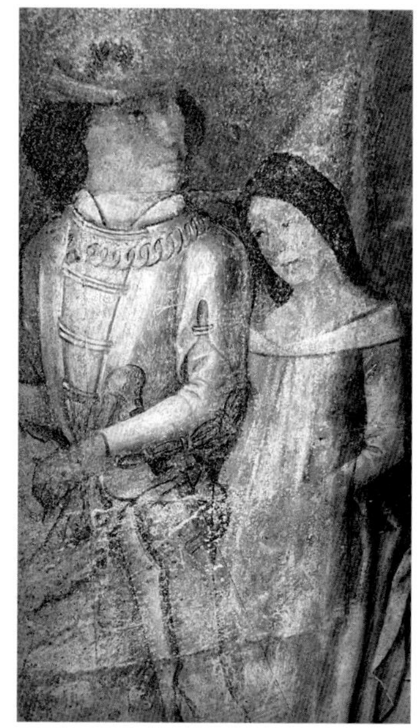

Left to right
Fig. 48. Detail of the north wall, scene 3, photographed by Plummer during the removal of historic oil paint that had been applied over the central sections of both walls during the course of the eighteenth century.
Fig. 49. North wall, scene 3 showing the condition of the scene in 1963 after the removal of surface dirt and the wax applied by Tristram.
Fig. 50. North wall, scene 3 showing this area following the removal of historic over-paint and the reintegration of losses.

299 Dimethyl formamide was used to remove the overpaint; see Plummer 1986, 38.

300 This area of new painting is denoted by a dotted line where it meets the original, and is signed and dated by Plummer. While Gill 2003, 175, has speculated that the figure represents St Veronica, Plummer asserts (pers. comm.) that the identity of this new saint was deliberately left elusive, lest the viewer believe that there were any original fragments of paint surviving in that area.

301 This work was undertaken using a heated scalpel in conjunction with dimethyl formamide on a swab (Plummer 1986, 38). Plummer states that she was unable to remove all of this scheme and that in some areas it was therefore painted out (Plummer 1976).

302 Plummer 1986, 38, records that these scenes were varnished with AW2 ™ in white spirit mixed with 5% cosmolloid wax. AW2™ is a proprietary ketone resin; see Feller & Curran 1975; also de la Rie & Shedrinsky 1989; and Horie 1987, 116-17.

6. Painting materials and technique

The superb quality of the paintings in the chapel at Eton, and their huge significance for our appreciation of medieval wall painting practices, has inspired numerous distinguished scholars to write about them since they were finally uncovered in 1923. Over the years, a hypothesis – based predominantly on visual observation – has evolved about the way in which the murals were painted. Pauline Plummer, who worked on the scheme on and off for some 14 years, knows the paintings perhaps better than anyone.[303] During this time she developed an intimate understanding of the ways in which the artists responsible for this vast scheme had worked, the materials they had used and the ways in which they had deployed them.[304] In her report on her work at Eton, she observed that, while the handling of the paint is similar throughout the scheme, 'it is safe to assume different designers for the two walls'.[305] She was also persuaded that the scheme was the product of workshop collaboration, with at least four distinct hands detectable in the surviving lower register.[306] Her observation that there is no obvious ground, 'except on the three westernmost bays of the south wall, where there is a thin red-brown ground', seemed moreover to suggest that a different workshop may have been responsible for this part of the scheme.[307]

Historically it seems to have been assumed that, owing to their divergent compositional styles, the north and south walls of the Eton chapel wall paintings were neither the work of the same artists, nor undertaken simultaneously. Margaret Rickert – believing the north wall to be superior both in execution and technique – concluded that while these scenes must have been the work of a Flemish master, the spatially less sophisticated south wall was most probably undertaken by a less-accomplished English artist, possibly an assistant.[308] In his seminal paper of 1995, however, Andrew Martindale challenged this supposition, asserting that the stylistic differences between the two walls suggested

303 See Plummer's report on the conservation of the paintings, Plummer 1986; also chapter 5 above on the physical history of the paintings.

304 See Plummer 1976, 2-4, and 1986, 36-7.

305 This theory was also expounded, somewhat earlier, by Tristram; see James & Tristram 1929, 43.

306 Plummer suggests that there are four distinct facial types 'if one compares the first figure…at the west end of the north wall with numbers two and three, seven and eight on that wall, … and on the south numbers one to seven with scene eight and niche figure nine'; Plummer 1976, 4.

307 Plummer 1986, 36.

308 Rickert 1965, 192; see also Lindley 1993, 806.

nothing more than 'the presence of two designers working in contrasted but near-contemporary styles – and within an agreed and unified architectural framework'.[309] Kidd, building on Plummer's observations, has proposed that an additional third hand was responsible for the two westernmost scenes on the south wall (scene 8 in both upper and lower registers) and it is possible, given the considerable surface area covered, that the number of artists actually deployed in executing the scheme was greater still.[310]

In commissioning the present research project, the current Provost has made it possible for the first time to subject the Eton wall paintings to rigorous scientific examination.[311] The paintings have been submitted to close visual inspection in diffuse, raking and ultraviolet illumination.[312] Evidence of the painting materials, and their application techniques and condition, have been documented. Examination of underdrawing and *pentimenti* was also undertaken using infrared photography.[313] Minute paint samples were taken following a systematic strategy to characterise the range of painting materials used and the ways in which they had been employed.[314] Particular attention was paid to the question of whether the widely discussed stylistic differences between the north and south wall paintings were corroborated by technical evidence of a difference in painting technique.[315] These investigations have not only furnished important new information, enabling us to place the Eton paintings more clearly in their contemporary technological context, but have also presented some unexpected conundrums.

Examination of the samples taken from the paintings indicates that, while stylistically divergent, scenes 1 to 7 on the north and south walls were painted in a broadly consistent manner, using predominantly identical painting materials. There are, nevertheless, sufficient differences in the materials employed, especially the binding media, to substantiate the hypothesis that these sections of the north and south walls were painted by different artists and/or workshops, and therefore possibly at different times. Furthermore, it would appear that the westernmost scenes on both the north

Left to right
Fig. 51. North wall, scene 8, detail of Christ.
Fig. 52. South wall, scene 8, detail of the Emperor's attendant.
Fig. 53. North wall, scene 8, detail of the Virgin.
Fig. 54. South wall, scene 8, detail of the Empress.

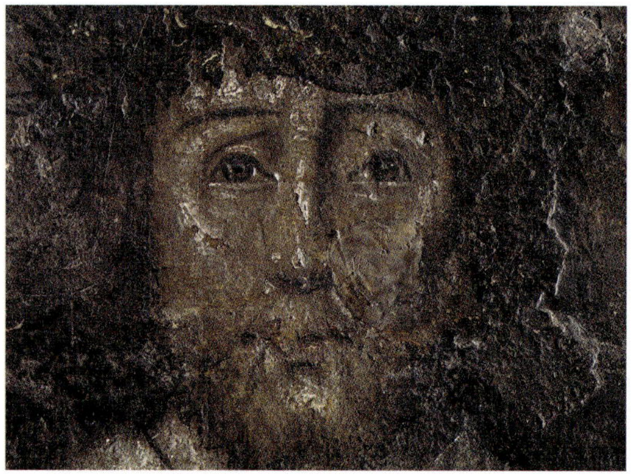

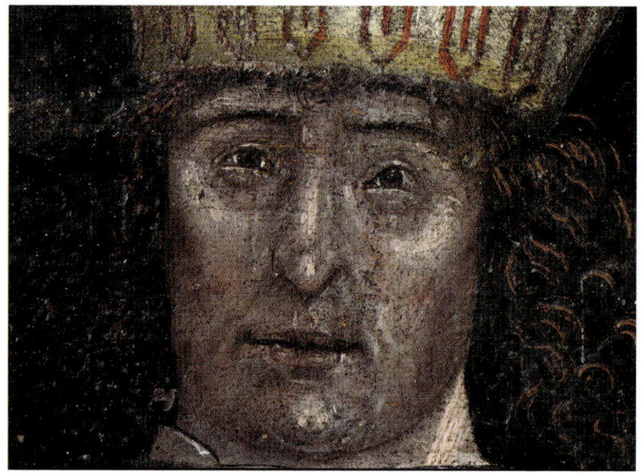

309 Martindale 1995, 137-42.
310 Kidd 1987, 28.
311 Dr John Mills at the National Gallery, London, seems to have undertaken some analysis of the paintings' binding medium during the course of Plummer's work, but no written report of his findings survives.
312 Peak emission at 365nm.
313 Infrared imaging was undertaken using a Nikon Coolpix 995 camera with the blocking filter removed, in conjunction with X-Nite filters (715nm, 830nm and 1000nm).
314 An overview of the analytical methodology and findings of these investigations can be found in the Appendix, p.167 ff.
315 On these stylistic differences, see chapter 4 above.

and south walls (and on the south in both upper and lower registers) were painted by a completely separate hand using a quite different technique. Not only do the painting materials and techniques employed in these three western scenes seem to be concordant with each other, but fresh comparison reveals compelling and previously undetected stylistic affinities. This is particularly noticeable when comparing the head of the Emperor's attendant on the south wall (scene S8) with that of Christ on the north wall (scene N8). They share the same flat-bottomed eyes and troubled brows, square jaws and pouting lips (Figures 51 and 52). Likewise, the Empress and the Virgin in these scenes share the same peculiarly-shaped, inanimate eyes and flat, oval-shaped face (Figures 53 and 54). The stylistic similarities between Sts Sidwell and Winifred (see Figures 24 and 29) have already been remarked upon, and there can be little doubt that both figures were completed by the same hand.[316]

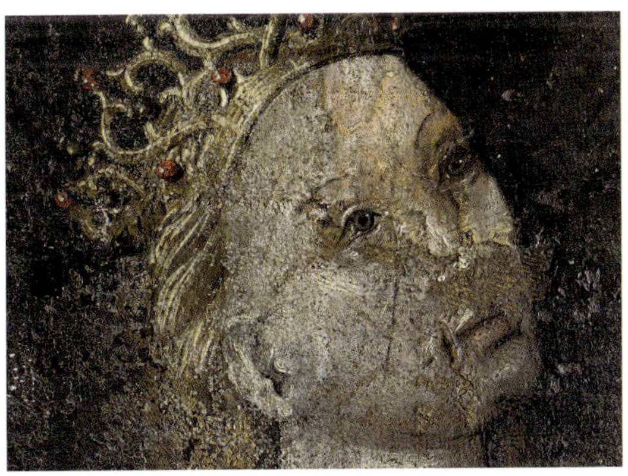

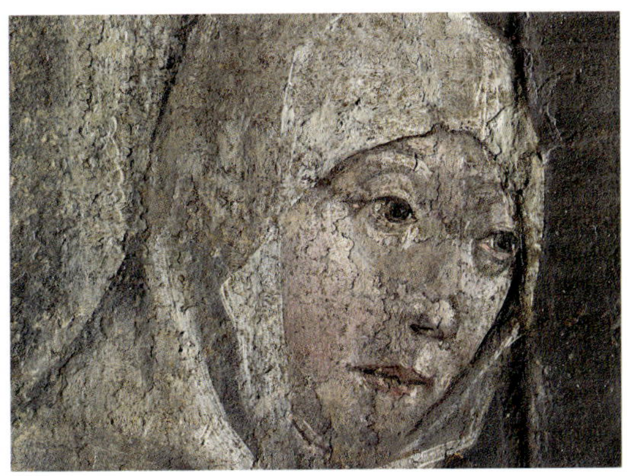

This new interpretation poses problems for our understanding of the paintings' execution. It might be supposed that, once the overall design of the programme was decided, the scheme would have been completed on one wall before proceeding to the other. Given that the scenes were meant to be read from east to west, it would also seem logical that they were painted in this order, starting with the uppermost scenes and then moving down to the lower register, thereby avoiding the risk of spoiling already completed work. Examination of the paint samples, however, almost certainly indicates that the north and south walls, despite their stylistic variances, were painted virtually simultaneously, starting at the east and progressing west. At the very least, the south wall must have been commenced before the north was completed, or *vice versa*. Moreover, the upper registers were evidently *not* completed before the lower scenes were begun; indeed, they seem to have been undertaken concurrently – an observation which surely has implications for the number of artists involved. The last scene and the standing saint at the western ends of each wall, in both the upper and lower registers, were undertaken by a different, third artist (or group of artists) in

316 See chapter 4 above.

a very different painting technique, and presumably at a slightly later date.[317] We can only conjecture as to the reasons behind this hiatus in Waynflete's ambitious painting project. It may have been that, with building work continuing on the new ante-chapel, access to the westernmost regions of the walls was obstructed. Or perhaps the break in technique reflects the moment at which Waynflete died and the initiative for completing the work fell to the College. Unfortunately, it is unlikely that we shall ever know.

Support

The accounts attest that the lower walls of what was intended to be the choir of Henry VI's new church were complete by the time of his deposition in 1461.[318] The paintings are undertaken on a combination of Taynton stone from Oxfordshire, a hard, medium-grained, oolitic limestone which is buff to pale orange in colour, and Huddleston stone, a grey- to cream-coloured fine-grained, magnesian limestone quarried in north Yorkshire.[319] In the king's 'Will' of *c.*1447-8, it was specifically stated that 'Yorkschyre' and 'Teynton' stone were to be used for the wall faces, with rubble infill of 'hard and durable heth ston and flynt' set in 'good and mighty mortar made with fine stone lyme and gravel sand'.[320] In fact, observes Maxwell Lyte, 'Teynton stone was used for the lower courses and some ornamental work, Hudleston stone for the main part of the walls up to the level of the transoms across the windows'.[321] Clearly the masons were painfully aware how quickly the Reigate stone they had used for earlier foundations at Eton deteriorated, since the document takes care to stipulate that 'neyther in the seid growndes ne walles schall in anywise be occupied Chalke Bryke ne Reygate stone otherwise y called Merstham stone'. While the ashlar, comprising long rectangular blocks, is mostly regularly coursed, both the width and depth of the blocks varies significantly, with the result that the depth of the masonry courses is not consistent.[322]

The outward-facing surface of each stone has been worked smooth with a broad flat chisel or 'bolster', so that almost no tool marks are evident. While the ashlars have clearly been joined with a lime mortar, there has been no systematic attempt to bring this mortar level with the masonry surface, or to smooth over the joints. A wide range of masons' marks is also evident on both painted and unpainted areas of wall in the former nave, with identical marks featuring on the north and south walls (Figures 55 and 56). While this has been suggested as evidence that these walls were not originally

317 It may be significant that in the College nominal roll for 1486 (ECR 61/NR/2) mention is made, in the third and fourth quarters, of 'Commons' (board and lodging) for Bridewell Senior and Junior, who – it has been postulated – may have been journeyman painters; see Anderson 1989, 12.
318 Martindale 1971, 186 and n.3.
319 On these varieties of stone, see Green 1992, 139, and Knoop and Jones 1938, respectively.
320 Salzman 1952, 83, 527. St George's Chapel in Windsor, built in the last quarter of the fifteenth century, was made almost exclusively from Taynton stone. See also Willis & Clark 1886, 367, 386, 395-401, 424-45, and Colvin 1963, 281, on the varieties of stone used at Eton.
321 Maxwell Lyte 1911, 50.
322 The depth of the courses varies between 140 and 320mm.

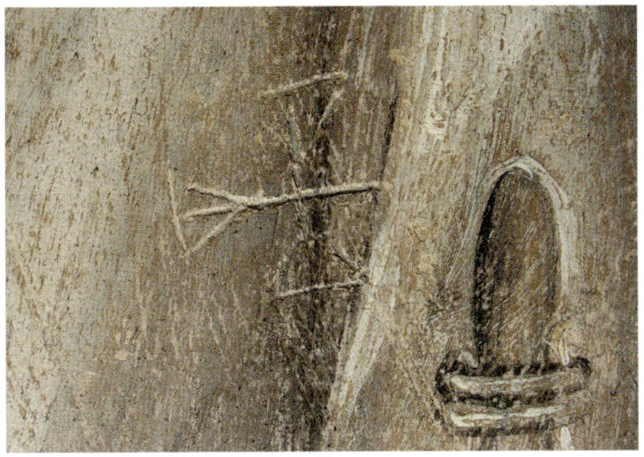
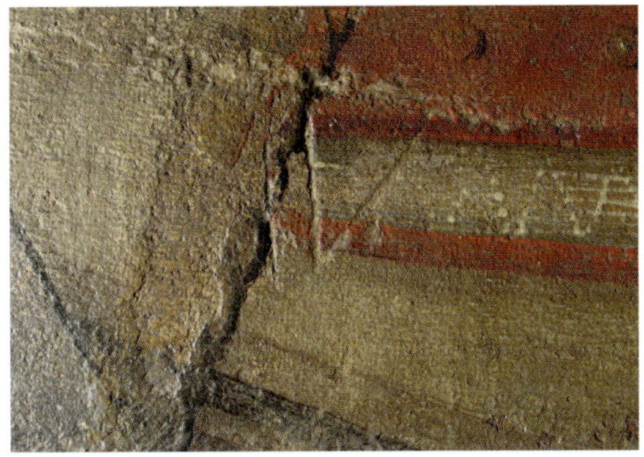

Figs 55 and 56. Two of a range of masons' marks identified on the north and south walls.

intended to be painted, it should be noted that similar masons' marks can be observed beneath important late thirteenth-century wall paintings in Westminster Abbey.[323] Indeed, it would appear that such marks were deliberately faced outwards to provide the foreman with a means of identifying the work of individual masons, who were paid on piece work.[324] Evidently no attempt was made in either building to disguise these marks prior to painting on the wall. Indeed, such a mark is visible even upon the face of St Margaret (figure nIII).

Sealants and grounds

Analysis of cross-sections taken from the north and south walls reveals that a range of sealants and ground layers was used to prime the limestone substrate prior to painting. This would have been done to prevent the medium in which the pigment was applied from being absorbed into the porous stone, thereby reducing the coherence and luminosity of the paint layer. Analysis reveals that in scenes of the south wall, a sealant comprising linseed oil combined with small amounts of red and white lead and a little calcium carbonate was applied to the stone (Figure 57). Lead-based pigments were well known for their siccative properties and would have been added in order to speed up the process of drying, whereas calcium carbonate was a cheap bulking material. A similarly translucent, though in some cases much thicker, medium-rich layer was applied beneath scenes 1-7 on the north wall, and analysis of a sample taken from the figure of St Martha (figure nVIII) indicates that, as well as oil, it may have contained a proteinaceous substance such as animal glue (Figure 58).[325] In many places this sealant is covered by a fine layer of lead white, occasionally mixed with a little carbon black. No such sealant system is, however, visible in scene 8 on either the north or south wall.[326] Instead, a thick ground of red lead mixed with lead and calcium carbonate white has been applied to the stone (Figures 59 and 60). Applied in two coats, the first of which contains a higher proportion of red lead, this thick cushioning layer would have had the

323 Plummer 1986, 36, ventures that the original intention must have been to plaster the walls, while Martindale 1995, n.15, recalls that Henry VI intended these flat expanses of wall to be covered with choir stall canopies. For Westminster Abbey, see Howe 2006, 96 and 101.

324 It is not, however, clear whether these marks were added by the quarry mason or the building mason; see Salzman 1952, 127-8.

325 Analysis of organic binding media using Fourier transform infrared spectroscopy (FTIR) and gas chromatography coupled with mass spectrometry (GC-MS) was undertaken by Dr Brian Singer at the University of Northumbria, see Singer 2011; due to the nature of the sample interrogated, it is not certain whether the glue replaced the oil, or whether a mixture of these media was employed.

326 It may be that unadulterated oil was brushed on the wall, and that no trace of this is now visible; histochemical tests for oils proved inconclusive.

dual function of priming the substrate and creating a smooth painting surface. This was then skimmed over with a finer grey ground layer, comprising lead white mixed with a little calcium carbonate and carbon black. It is interesting that the application of this red ground does not appear to have been universal, but rather confined to specific areas. In those places, for instance, where white draperies were to be depicted, only the pale grey ground was employed (see, for example, Appendix, sample 15).

A rather different and more localised red ground is in evidence in some areas of scenes 1-7 on the north and south walls. A thick layer of red lead mixed with large conglomerates of lead white was applied beneath the inscriptions on both walls, presumably to ensure a smooth surface upon which to paint the texts (see, for example, sample 31). A similar layer was applied beneath the brown-black hair of the dead iconoclast in the 'Miracle of the wounded image' (scene N2) (Figures 61 and 62) and the flesh of St Ursula's forehead (figure sV, sample 7). It may be that particular care was taken to create a smooth substrate under important features such as heads, but given that this layer does not seem to extend over the whole head in either instance, this seems unlikely. More probably it represents an area of unusually thick underdrawing.

Left to right; top
Fig. 57. South wall, scenes 1-7: the stone substrate was primed with a sealant comprising linseed oil, combined with small amounts of red and white lead and a little calcium carbonate (cross-section, sample 2, taken from the fictive textile, photographed at 100x).
Fig. 58. North wall, scenes 1-7: here the sealant layer is thicker than on the south wall and seems to comprise a mixture of oil and a proteinaceous substance such as animal glue (cross-section, sample 22, St Martha, photographed at 100x).

Left to right; bottom
Fig. 59. South wall, scene 8: a thick ground of red lead mixed with lead and calcium carbonate (cross-section, sample 14, imaged at 200x).
Fig. 60. South wall, scene 8: examined under UV illumination, it appears that this red ground was applied in two separate layers, comprising slightly different proportions of the same components (cross-section, sample 14, imaged under UV illumination at 200x).

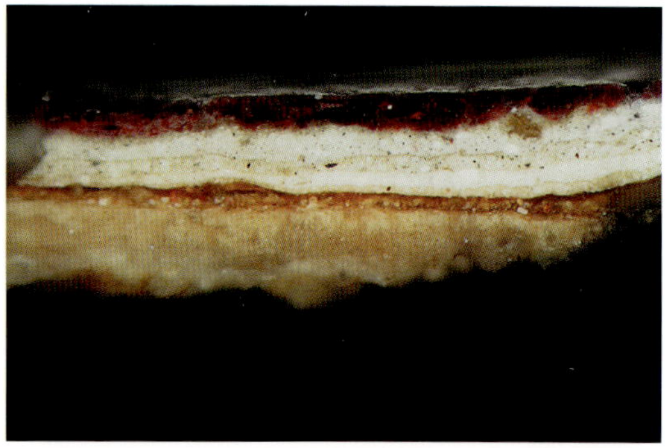

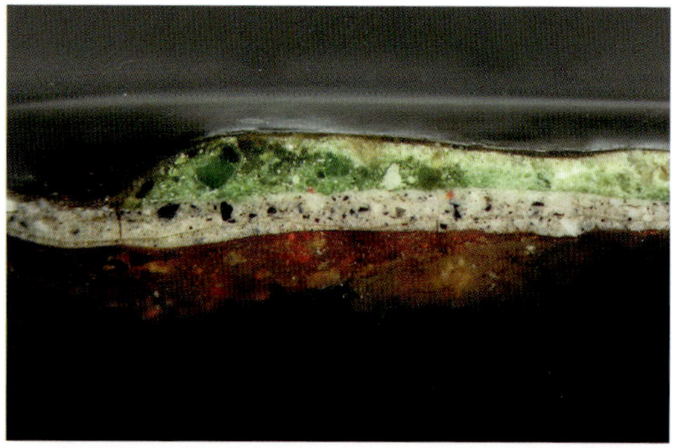

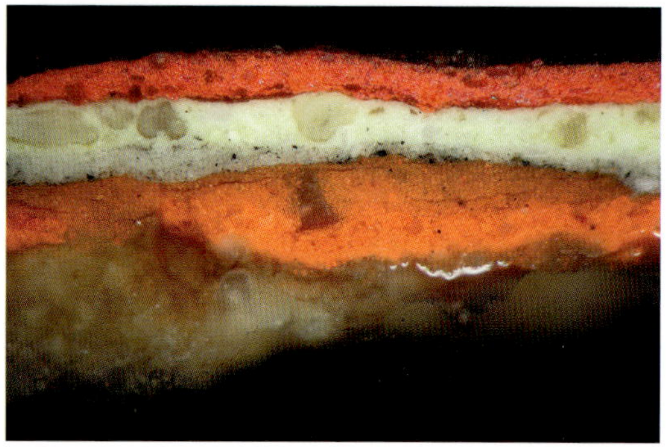

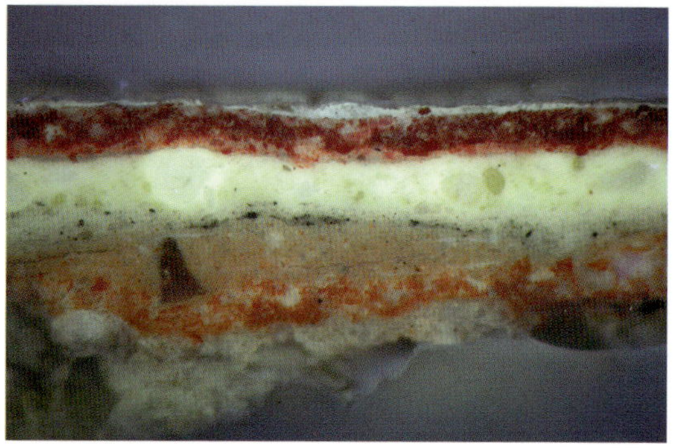

Preparatory techniques and underdrawing

The evidence for preparatory techniques relating to the original wall painting scheme is scant. Throughout all areas of the scheme, underdrawing appears to have been undertaken in red lead bound in oil. In scenes 1-7 on both walls, this has been executed on top of the sealant layer (see, for example, sample 24). In the westernmost scenes, where no sealant layer is evident, the underdrawing seems to have been executed directly onto the stone (see sample 15). Several of the female standing saints (notably figures nVI-IX and figure sIX) are scarred by long deep vertical incisions in the stonework, though these do not seem to relate in any way to the setting out of the original painting scheme. Indeed, they cut straight through the paint layer and seem rather to be associated with later modifications to the building fabric, possibly relating to the installation in the 1840s of stall canopies. Further incisions, though of a much less crude nature, can be discerned at the east end of the scheme on both walls, where fictive textiles are depicted. These circular markings, which appear to have been made with the aid of a pair of compasses or another instrument, clearly relate to the geometric scheme of fictive marble inlay which was painted over the original textile decoration in the mid-1550s.[327]

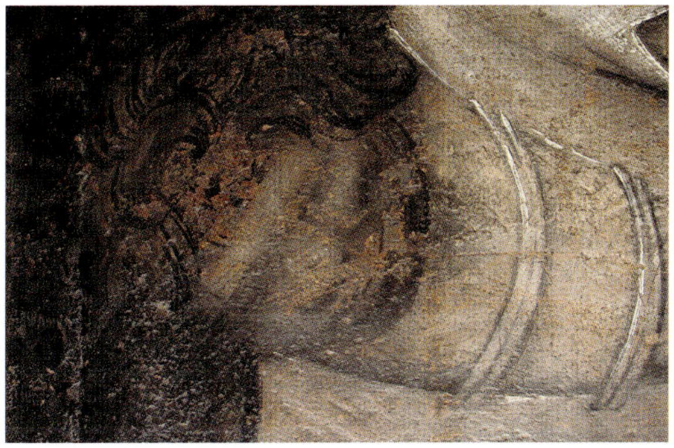

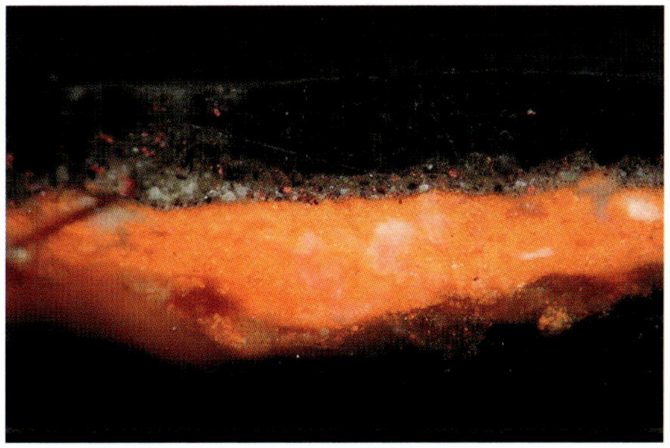

Left Fig. 61. North wall, scene 2, detail of the dead iconoclast in the 'Miracle of the wounded image'.
Right Fig. 62. North wall, scene 2: a thick layer of red lead mixed with large conglomerates of lead white was applied beneath the brown-black hair of the dead iconoclast (cross-section, sample 28, north wall, scene 2, imaged at 200x).

Binding media

Analysis of paint samples taken from the three distinct zones of painting (that is to say the north wall, the south wall and the westernmost scene on each wall) reveals that scenes 1-7 of the south wall of the scheme and the westerly scenes on both walls were undertaken using a medium of raw linseed oil.[328] In many areas a distinctive craquelure, caused by the deterioration of the oil film, is visible (Figure 63). Indeed, in many of the samples, lead soaps derived from the interaction of lead-based pigments and linseed oil are visible (this is especially evident in layers of the pigment lead-tin yellow; see samples 14, 20 and 23).[329] On the north wall, however, there

327 Most traces of this later scheme were removed by Plummer during her treatment of the paintings; see chapter 5 above.
328 FTIR and GC-MS analysis of the painting media was undertaken by Dr Brian Singer at the University of Northumbria.; see Singer 2011.
329 On this deterioration mechanism, see Higgitt *et al.* 2005.

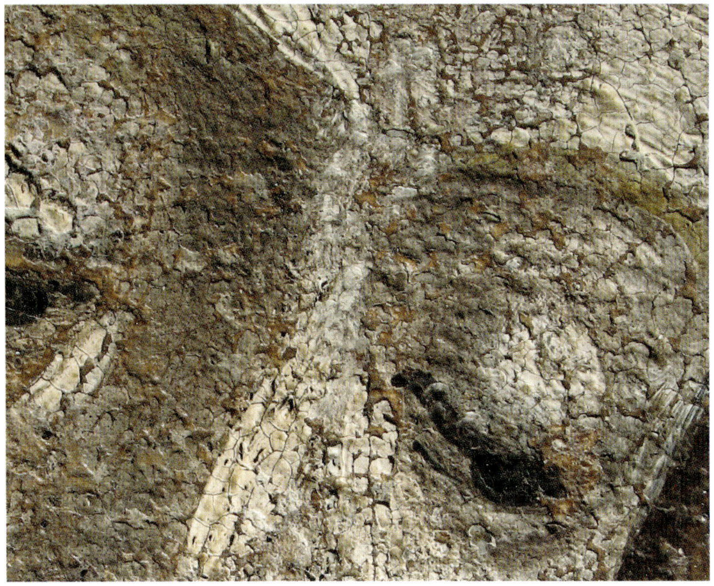

Left Fig. 63. South wall, figure 1, detail of St Catherine, showing the distinctive craquelure that is characteristic of oil-based painting techniques.

is good evidence to suggest that walnut oil was used.[330] It is not clear from the limited number of samples examined whether this binding medium was used throughout scenes 1-7 on the north wall, as an alternative to linseed, or just in localised areas. Walnut oil, which was more expensive than linseed, was probably employed because it was less likely to yellow on drying, making it a good choice for the depiction of white draperies. There is also some analytical evidence that a small amount of egg was used as a binder in one of the underlying paint layers.[331]

Pigments and paint stratigraphy

While much has been made of the fashionable monochrome palette of the Eton chapel wall paintings, close examination reveals that the impression of grisaille is significantly heightened by the extensive damage and deterioration sustained by the paintings during their lifetime. This is especially the case in areas where the limestone has been exposed through losses in the paint layer, lending the painting a buff-coloured cast which belies its original appearance. It is now clear from the examination of cross-sections that, far from comprising a palette confined to black and white, these murals were fashioned through the sophisticated deployment of a wide range of colours, including some of the most opulent and costly painting materials of their day. The range of pigments identified in the chapel paintings includes not only the obvious components – lead and calcium carbonate (lime) white and carbon black – but also indigo, a copper green, red lead, vermilion, a sumptuous madder lake,[332] iron oxide red and yellow, and considerable quantities of lead-tin yellow.[333] Most of these pigments receive mention in the College account roll of

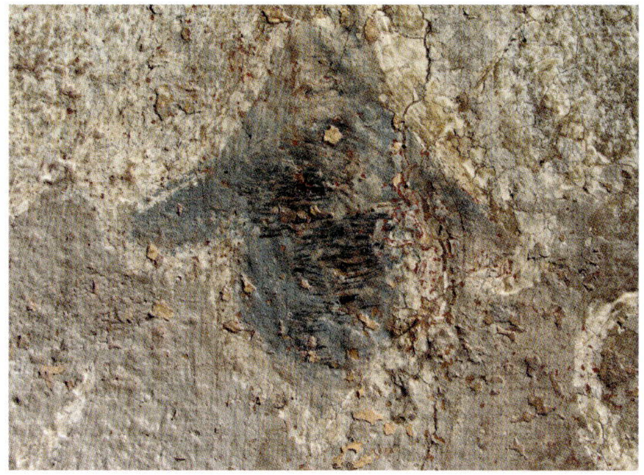

Fig. 64. South wall, fictive textile: indigo combined with lead white gives a bright opaque blue for the foliate buds, with shading applied on top in a rich translucent indigo glaze.

330 See Singer 2011, 13, 15. While the azelate to sebacate and azelate to suberate ratios in the sample suggest that the oil is most likely walnut, another possibility for the palmitate to stearate ratios obtained (2.7) is poppy seed oil mixed with linseed oil.

331 See Singer 2011, 10-11, 14; only a trace of the amino acids indicative of the presence of egg protein were recorded in the sample taken from this figure. Unfortunately, it was not possible to completely separate out the paint layers prior to analysis, and as a result it is not possible to tell from which layer this protein originates.

332 I am extremely grateful to Jo Kirby and Dr David Peggie of the National Gallery's Scientific Department for undertaking high-performance liquid chromatography (HPLC) on the organic colorants in the scheme. Scanning electron microscopy coupled with energy-dispersive x-ray (SEM-EDX) analysis of the lake, undertaken by the author, reveals that the dyestuff is precipitated onto a substrate of hydrated alumina; surprisingly high levels of sulphur, silicon, calcium and chlorine were also found to be present. Studies undertaken at the National Gallery suggest that a high sulphur content, in conjunction with the presence of proteins, is indicative of alkaline-based extraction of the lake from shearings of dyed wool; see Kirby *et al.* 2005. It is interesting to note that this seems to have been the principal method of madder lake preparation in this period (Kirby *et al.* 2005, 76-8).

333 There are two kinds of lead-tin yellow, types I and II. In this instance the type I variety (Pb_2SnO_4), which was more frequently used in northern European painting, seems to have been employed, though x-ray diffraction (XRD) analysis would be required to confirm this; see Kühn 1993.

1486-7 which details painting materials procured in association with the *picturam ecclesie*, namely 8 gallons of painter's oil, 1lb of varnish, 10lbs of red and white lead, 11lbs of English verdigris, 5lbs of ochre, 5lbs of vivianite and indigo, 9lbs of the 'tawny' colour called 'generall', ¾lb of vermilion, and ¾lb pure gold. Calcium carbonate white, carbon black, lead-tin yellow and the red lake are not, however, itemised.[334] Lime white and carbon black were cheap, readily-available materials and may well have been sourced more locally than the more costly, specialist pigments cited in this document. The missing lead-tin yellow and red lake may have been among the 'diuersis aliis coloribus' for which William Baker received payment of three shillings. But as Martindale has previously observed, the strange quantities cited in this account suggest that these pigments were not exclusively procured for use on the nave paintings – 11lbs of verdigris were certainly not required for the *Miracles* scheme and, as far as the surviving evidence shows, neither was any gold.[335]

Subtle hues and optical effects have been achieved by skilfully mixing and layering these pigments in ways that were designed to enhance or attenuate their covering power. For the fictive textile panels at the east end of the scheme, for example, the organic colorant indigo was combined with lead white to achieve a bright opaque blue for the foliate buds, with shading applied on top in a rich translucent indigo glaze (Figure 64).[336] The same brilliant copper green has been used on both the north and south walls to evoke foliage.[337] For the palm held by St Martha (figure nVIII), a succulent green glaze comprising the copper pigment mixed with a very small amount of lead white has been applied over the reflective light grey draperies of the saint's robe (see Figure 58). Pale citrus highlights, comprising the same green mixed with lead-tin yellow, have been laid on top. A virtually identical technique has been employed in scene 5 on the south wall, to evoke the various shades of the miraculous herb gathered by the marooned Empress (Figures 65 and 66). The same green glaze is also used, with red, to pick out the gems on the crown worn by the Virgin on the north wall.

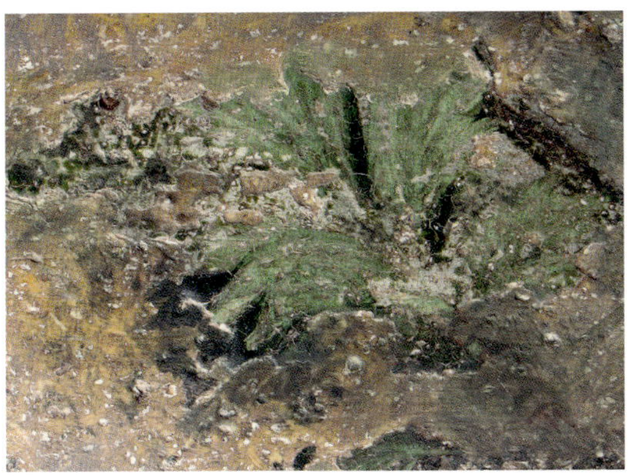

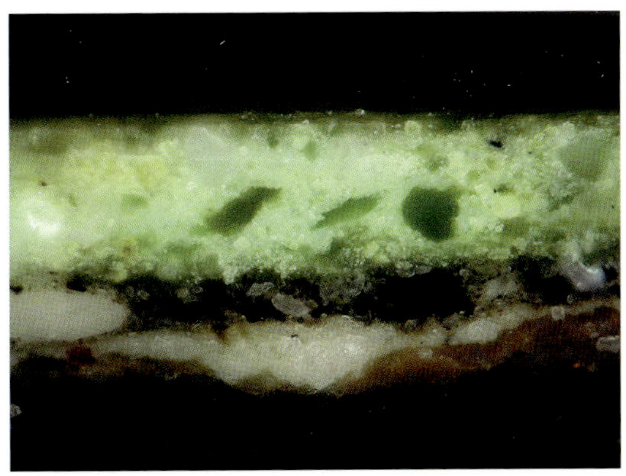

Left Fig. 65. South wall, scene 5: the miraculous green herb has been achieved using a copper green pigment mixed with a small amount of lead white, applied over an opaque grey underlayer.
Right Fig. 66. South wall, scene 5: cross section of the miraculous herb (sample 8, imaged at 500x)

334 Roll 22 (1486-7), ECR 61/AR/F/2, m2, cited by James (James & Tristram 1929, 3-4). On balance, it seems that the pigment 'generall' cited in the account roll does not refer to lead-tin yellow, but to some other much cheaper 'tawny colour'. On the confusing and evolving nomenclature for lead-tin yellow, see Kühn 1993, 93-4; also Howard 2003, 160. While the names 'massicot' and 'general' were purported by Haydocke (writing in 1598) to be interchangeable terms for lead-tin yellow, this theory would seem to be negated by the fact that, in some accounts, entries are made for the purchase of both. Indeed, Salzman 1952, 168-9, insists that the term 'generall' cited in the accounts for painting undertaken at Christ's College, Cambridge (1511) and at Westminster (1532) refers to 'a neutral colour used for outlines and shading' and that lead-tin yellow was the more expensive pigment referred to as 'mastecote'. This argument would seem to be supported by the price of the 'generall' in the Eton roll which, at only 4*d.* per lb, was significantly cheaper than the 'mastecote' bought at Westminster in 1532, at the cost of 2*s.* 8*d.* per lb.; see Howard 2003, 160.

335 Martindale 1995, 149-50.

336 A similar technique, using the organic colorant madder, was used for those buds picked out in red.

337 While this translucent pigment bears all of the characteristics of a copper resinate, microscopic and instrumental analysis have proved inconclusive. Unlike verdigris (copper acetate), which displays clear green-blue pleochroism, this pigment comprises amorphous glassy green fragments, with a low refractive index. Howard 2003, 93-5, notes, however, that verdigris in an oil medium, though difficult to distinguish under the microscope, was commonly used as a glaze in medieval English wall paintings. Van Eikema Hommes 2001 also suggests that the use of copper resinate on easel paintings has been overestimated, and that green glazes were more often made by combining verdigris with pre-polymerised linseed oil and a small amount of resin to improve its glazing properties.

Given the pronounced differences in style between the north and south walls of the mural scheme and their westernmost scenes, it is perhaps surprising that the artists who executed these paintings seem not only to have employed almost exactly the same range of pigments, but to have applied them in very similar stratigraphies. The ornately decorated hat worn by the Emperor's attendant in scene 8 on the south wall (see Figure 59, sample 14), for example, is achieved using the same technique as for the lead held by St Martha on the north (sample 23). In both cases, a pale grey underlayer comprising lead white and carbon black is overpainted with the same impasto layers of lead-tin yellow and a succulent bright red comprising vermilion mixed with a little madder lake and lead white. The same red lake is used to various effects in all three zones of the nave paintings. It is mixed with lead white to achieve the subtle dusky pink of St Paul's robes in the 'Miracle of the candle' (scene N6, sample 25), and the velvet cushion bearing the Empress's crown in scene 8 on the south wall (Figure 67). For the scarlet roses in St Dorothy's basket, the same lake is applied in an unctuous glaze over a reflective light grey ground, with bright pink highlights picked out using the lake mixed with vermilion and white lead (see sample 9). A very similar approach is used to model the cord around the waist of the Emperor's leprous brother in scene 7 of the 'Empress' legend (Figures 68 and 69). Some variation in materials and technique is, however, apparent between the north and south scenes in their treatment of hair. On the north wall, the long, loose tresses of the Virgin and the accompanying female martyrs are wrought with a simple undercoat of iron-oxide yellow, overlaid with impasto strands in lead-tin yellow (Figure 70 and sample 26). For the hair of the Empress on the south wall, lead-tin yellow is applied over a darker brown layer comprising a mixture of lead white, vermil-

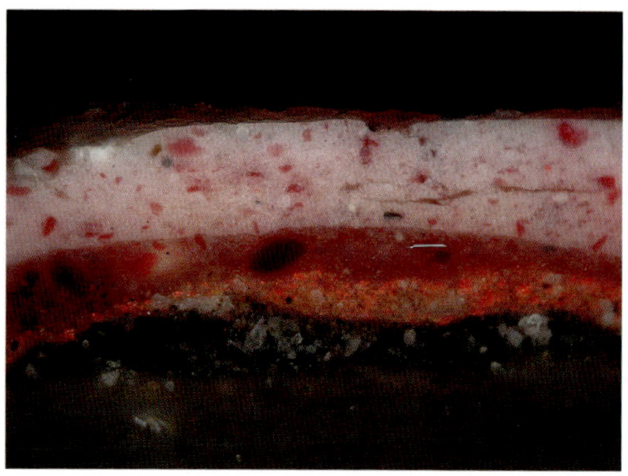

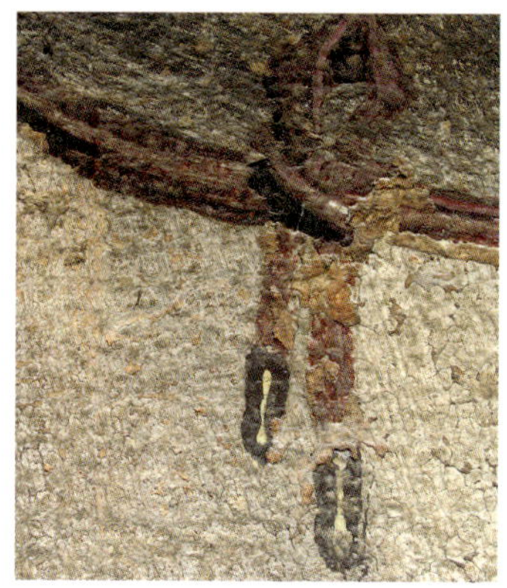

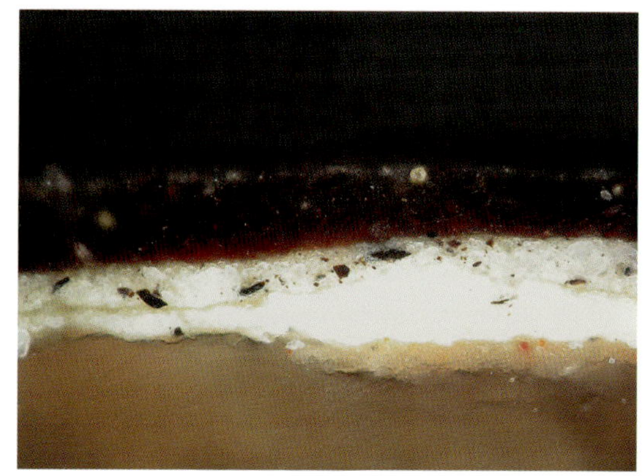

Left to right
Fig. 67. South wall, scene 8: for the velvet cushion bearing the Empress's crown, madder lake is mixed with lead white in varying proportions to achieve different hues of a sumptuous pink (cross-section, sample 18, imaged at 500x).
Fig. 68. South wall, scene 7: the cord around the waist of the Emperor's brother is modelled using the same lake as in scene 8, applied in an unctuous glaze over a reflective light grey ground.
Fig. 69. South wall, scene 7: cross-section of the cord round the brother's waist (sample 13, imaged at 500x).

Left to right
Fig. 70. North wall, figure III, detail of St Margaret's hair, which is achieved with a simple undercoat of iron oxide yellow, overlaid with impasto strands in lead-tin yellow.
Figs 71 and 72. North wall, scene 8, detail of the Virgin's crown and cross-section showing impasto highlights in lead-tin yellow applied over a ground of iron oxide yellow (sample 20, photographed at 500x).

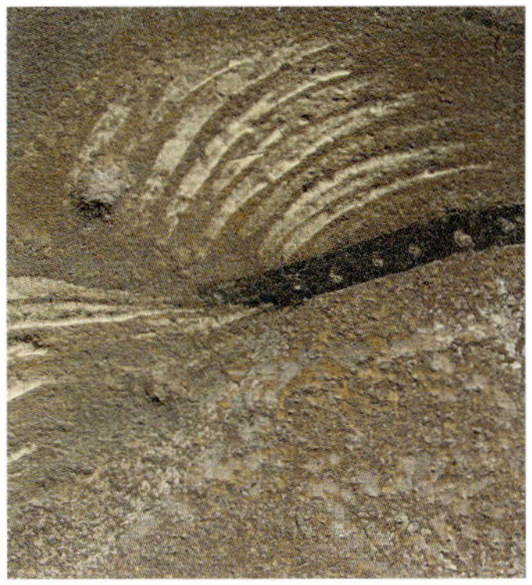

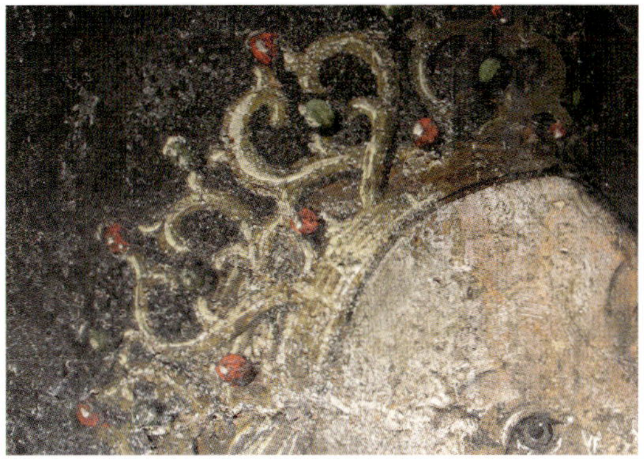

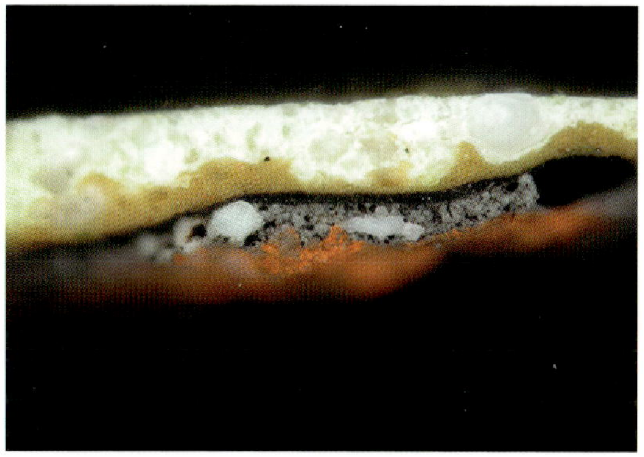

ion, carbon black, and lake inclusions (scene s6, sample 11). Crowns, jewellery and armour are treated in an identical manner (Figures 71 and 72), though the degree of impasto lead-tin yellow employed in the southern and western scenes is less restrained than on the north wall.

The sequence in which the painting of each scene was undertaken is unclear. Close examination of brushstrokes certainly suggests that the background field was painted in around the figures after their completion, while in most instances hands and the attributes held by them can be seen to have been painted in over draperies, backgrounds and architectural elements, suggesting that they were painted in last of all (Figure 73). Likewise, the foliate corbels which hang down from the corners of the architectural frame seem to have been painted in over the black background field. It is quite conceivable, given the evidence of contemporary painting practices, that the paintings were varnished soon after completion.[338] Plummer mentions a discoloured historic varnish layer which she removed from the paintings, and traces of a coating of this type, which fluoresce under UV illumination, are visible in the interstices of many of the cross-sections taken from the scheme.[339] While not conclusive, the fact that varnish is also itemised in the accounts pertaining to the paintings gives further support to this suggestion.[340]

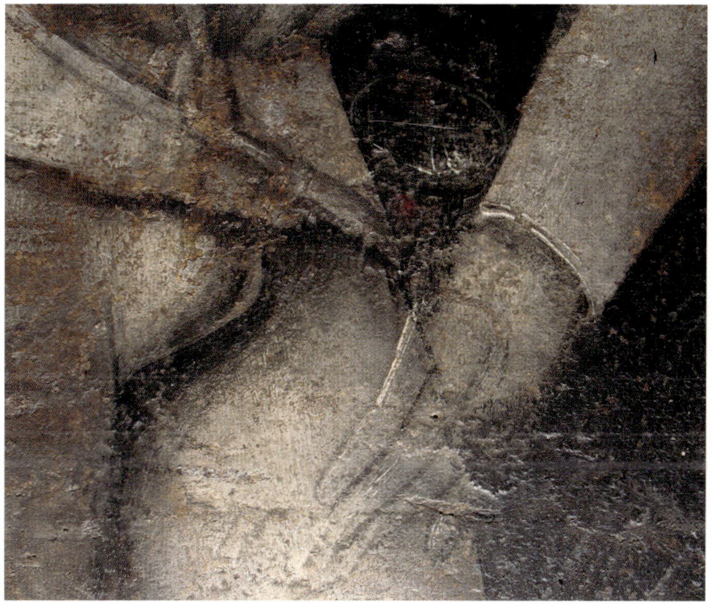

Fig. 73. North wall, scene 2, detail from the 'Miracle of the wounded image', showing that elements such as hands were painted in last, on top of the otherwise completed paint layer.

338 On the medieval practice of varnishing oil-based wall paintings see Howe 2006, 98-9, 107, 109.
339 See, for example, sample 14. Plummer 1986, 37-8, suggests that these might be nineteenth-century varnish layers, though it seems unlikely that the workmen who half obliterated the scheme would have taken the trouble to varnish it.
340 See chapter 1 above; though the amount of varnish mentioned is very small, it is possible that greater quantities had previously been purchased.

Modelling

While the pigments and application methods observed in the three phases of the chapel paintings are remarkably similar, differences are apparent in the way in which the paint is handled. Variations in approach to the modelling of draperies are among the most striking disparities. The mastery of the north wall artist is particularly evident in the 'Miracle of the wounded image' (scene N2), in which the kneeling woman's heavily crumpled gown is accomplished in two simple layers applied over a fluid red underdrawing. The cloth is evoked with a layer of pure lead white, and the definition of the folds achieved with a deft grey outline comprising lead white mixed with carbon black (Figure 74 and sample 24). The treatment of the draperies by the west-end artist is, by comparison, elaborate and somewhat laboured. Without recourse to outlines for definition, the artist attempts to model the cloth using three separate shades of grey, before applying two further layers of impasto highlights in lead white (Figure 75 and sample 15). The result is not only a far thicker paint layer, but an altogether heavier and less convincing painting style.

Similar disparities are evident in the treatment of flesh. The face of the woman in the 'Miracle of the wounded image' (scene N2) is rendered using a fine layer of lead white, modelled with subsequent additions in the palest pink (sample 29). This technique is in evidence throughout the main sections on the north and south walls, with highlights applied in fluid sweeping lines which accentuate the eye sockets, the brow and

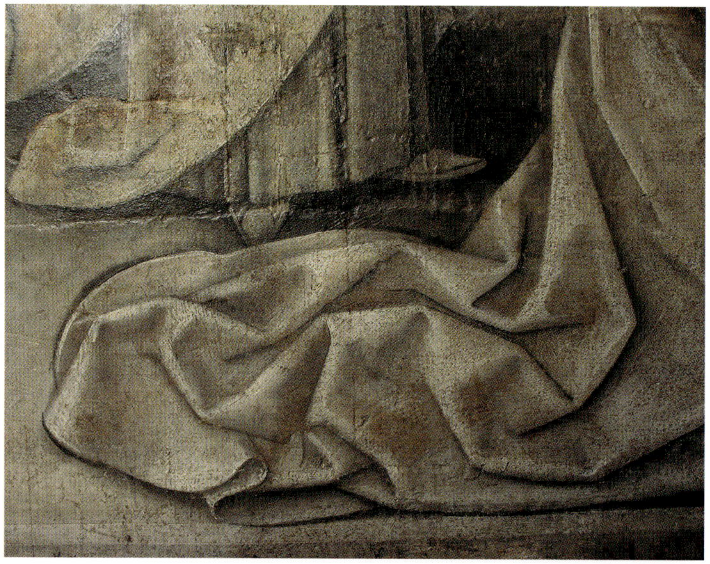

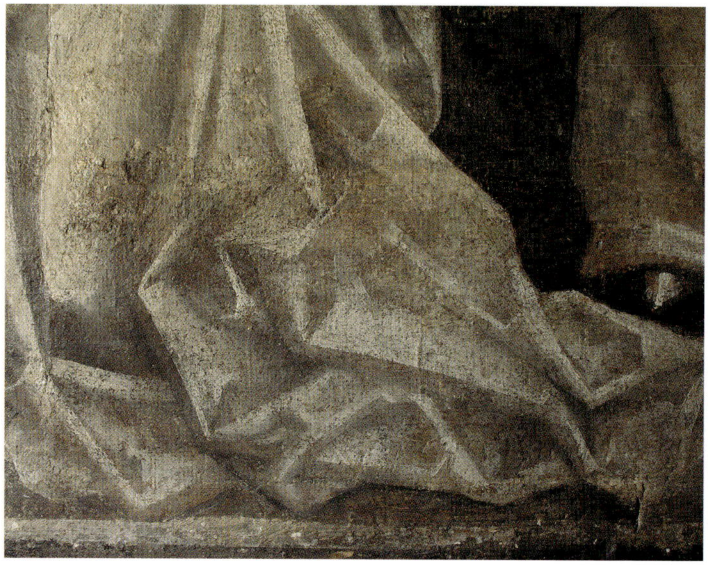

Top Fig. 74. North wall, scene 2, detail of the kneeling woman's draperies.
Bottom Fig. 75. South wall, scene 8, detail of the draperies of the kneeling Empress.

Left Fig. 76. South wall, scene 3, detail of the Empress, showing the fluid lines used to accentuate eye sockets, brow and the curve of the upper lip.
Right Fig. 77. South wall, scene 8, detail of the Emperor's hand, showing the very different treatment of flesh in the western scenes from that in the main sequence.

the curve of the upper lip (Figure 76). This contrasts dramatically with the treatment of flesh in the western scenes, where a dark greyish-pink base colour, comprising vermilion, red lake and carbon black in a lead white matrix, has been laid in, and impasto highlights in bright pink and white used to modulate the effect (Figure 77 and sample 19). The modelling is altogether more robust and vibrant, and some attempt has been made to blend the layers wet-in-wet. In contrast to the north and south wall artists, who use black for outlines, the painter responsible for the western scenes uses a more naturalistic brown to lend definition to elements such as hands, arms and faces. Indeed, save for the monochrome micro-architectural elements, there is little sense at all in these scenes of the grisaille palette which predominates elsewhere in the scheme. This visual imbalance, far from being the result of the deterioration of the less well-protected sections of the scheme over the years,[341] is quite clearly the result of a markedly different approach to painting at the outset.

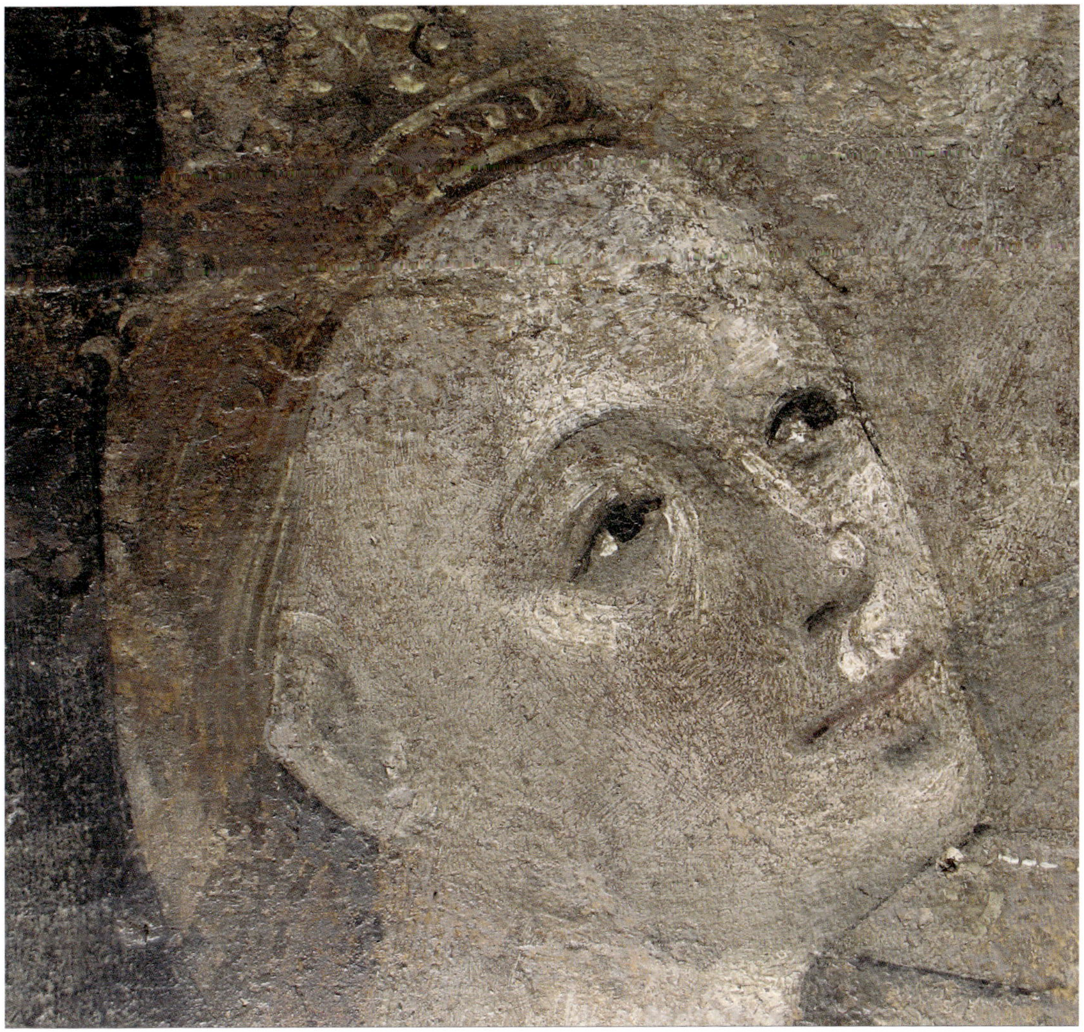

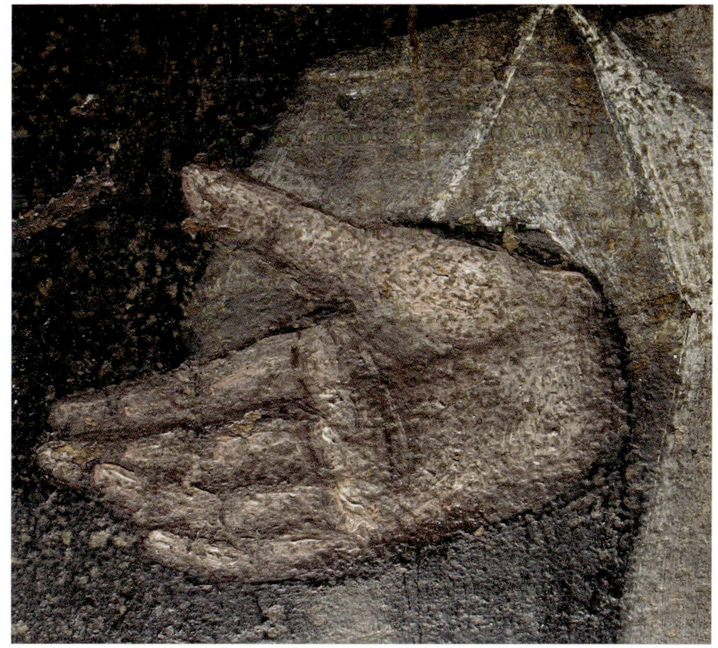

341 As suggested by for example, Plummer 1986, 36, and Gill 2003, 193.

Inscriptions

Similar discontinuities are evident in the inscriptions painted along the bottom of the *Miracle* scenes. Several different hands seem to have been involved in their execution. The style of script employed in the upper register of the north wall, for example, is more refined and elaborate than the solid and comparatively unadorned text used on the lower register of the same wall, and the same is broadly true on the south wall (Figures 78 and 79). It is perhaps significant, however, that despite these variations in writing style, the painting technique used to create the inscriptions is apparently identical on both walls. In each case a thick red ground layer comprising a mixture of red and white lead was used to smooth the substrate, prior to the application of a grey background colour (see, for example, sample 31). This layer, which was applied in two separate coats, comprised lead white with a little calcium carbonate and coarsely-ground carbon black. The text itself, which in places measures some 100µm thick, was undertaken in carbon black. Surprisingly, analysis of this black layer indicates the presence of relatively high proportions of copper. Black pigments were notoriously slow-drying when applied in oil, and this copper content may point to the introduction of visually imperceptible quantities of a copper-based pigment as a siccative.[342] While it is not possible to determine from the samples taken when, in relation to the figurative painting, the inscriptions were undertaken, the absence of any underlying paint layer suggests that they were broadly coterminous with the narrative scenes and were always intended to be part of the scheme. It is not, however, clear whether they were executed as the painting of the scenes progressed, or undertaken in a single campaign at the conclusion of the project.

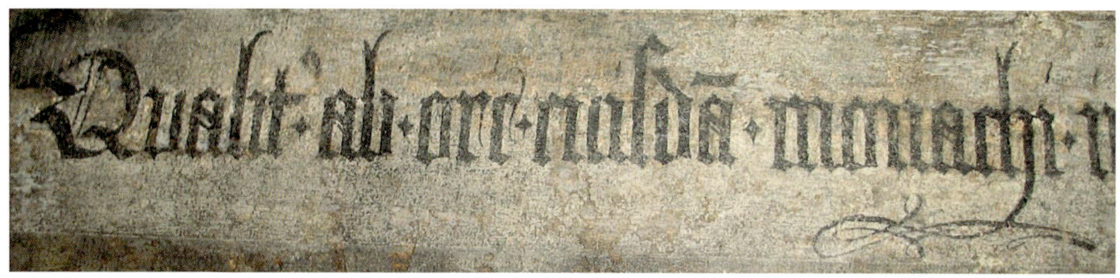

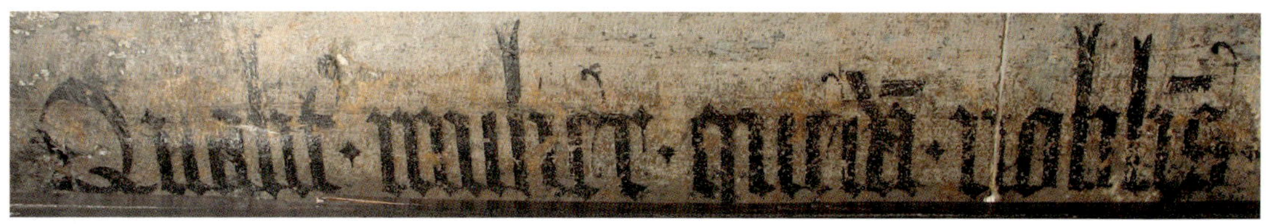

Top Fig. 78. North wall, upper register, scene 6, example of an inscription executed in a refined and elaborate style.
Bottom Fig. 79. North wall, lower register, scene 7, example of an inscription in a relatively simple and unadorned style.

342 Examination using SEM-EDX revealed that the copper lay in the matrix of the paint layer, not in the individual black pigment particles. Wider evidence for this hitherto little-known practice is discussed in further detail in the following chapter.

7. The technological significance of the paintings

> **Interesting discovery** – During the extensive repairs which are now going on at the venerable chapel attached to Eton College, a large number of fresco paintings have been discovered upon the removal of the oak panelling from the walls of the sacred edifice, which appear to have been executed by Florentine artists between 1440 and 1480…
> *The Times*, 17 July 1847

The technique of the wall paintings in the chapel at Eton College has been the subject of considerable debate since their discovery in 1847. The artist R.H. Essex, who was commissioned to make copies of the partially obliterated scheme, asserted that the paintings were not 'frescoes' as previously thought, but rather had been executed 'in distemper on the bare walls, without plaster of any kind'.[343] An article published in *The Windsor and Eton Express* in November of that year elaborated that the paintings 'are now pronounced by competent judges not to be frescoes, but oil paintings'. Further visual examination of the paintings following their uncovering in 1923 moved Sir Charles Holmes, then Director of the National Gallery, to speculate 'whether wax may not have been the principal ingredient in the medium used'.[344] Our understanding of English medieval painting practices has advanced considerably in recent years, enhanced by the scientific study of painting materials and their application methodologies.[345] The recent analysis of samples from the Eton chapel wall paintings has revealed the scheme to have been undertaken on an oil-primed substrate in a variety of organic media, using a range of pigments and sophisticated application methodologies which belie its muted appearance. Comparison of the murals' technique with other contemporary works of art, together with evidence afforded by documentary sources from the period, reveals the scheme to be wholly representative of painting practices in England and the rest of northern Europe around the end of the fifteenth century.

Late medieval artists' treatises are especially valuable in providing us with a technological context for

343 *The Builder*, vol.5, 1847. Injudicious use of the term 'frescoes' in relation to the scheme, most conspicuously by M.R. James in the title of his otherwise invaluable monograph on the paintings (James 1907), has engendered confusion about the way in which they were achieved. In true 'fresco' technique, paintings are executed on a fresh lime plaster, the carbonation of which serves to bind the pigments to the wall. Most recently, Martindale 1995, 136, and n.15, expressed surprise that the chapel walls were not plastered prior to painting, suggesting that this omission might be explained by 'some otherwise unrecorded need for urgency'.

344 Holmes 1923, 230, 235.

345 The National Gallery, London, established its own Scientific Department in 1934, as did the Courtauld Institute of Art. In 1985, the Courtauld Institute set up the first department dedicated to the conservation of wall paintings, incorporating the National Survey of English Medieval Wall Paintings; see Howard 2003, 1-3.

the Eton chapel wall paintings. Writing in around 1400, Cennino Cennini offers insight into contemporary painting techniques north of the Alps as well as in Italy.[346] Describing, in chapter 94 of his *Libro dell'Arte*, 'How you should work in oil on iron, on panel, and on stone', he remarks on the necessity of 'always sizing first'.[347] Elsewhere in his treatise, Cennini alludes to the practice of applying a preparatory linseed oil-based 'mordant' to walls as a precaution against moisture.[348] He is presumably referring in both instances to the practice of sealing the substrate prior to painting. Similar recommendations for sealing stone with an animal-glue size are made in the early fifteenth-century German artist's treatise known as the *Strasbourg Manuscript*.[349] At Eton, the porous limestone support was primed with linseed oil, combined with small amounts of red and white lead and a little calcium carbonate. The lead-based pigments, as we have seen, served as driers for the oil, while calcium carbonate was employed as a bulking material. An almost identical treatment has been observed in the slightly later scheme of wall painting that decorated the interior of a closet adjoining the chapel at St Mark's Hospital in Bristol (Figure 80).[350] Analysis of the three surviving fragments from this scheme, which have been dated to *c.*1510, reveals that the paintings were executed on a stone support that was sealed with two oil-based layers, the first mixed with chalk and calcium sulfate, and the second with a little lead white. A slightly different sealant, comprising an emulsion of linseed oil mixed with a little protein (possibly egg) and very similar to the mixture identified on the north wall at Eton, was used to seal the Caen limestone for the effigies of William Fitzalan and his wife Joan Nevill (*c.*1470-80) at Arundel (see Figure 32).[351] Analysis of statuary dating from between 1460 and 1480 on the west front of Exeter Cathedral reveals that a similar emulsion of oil and protein was used to seal the limestone there prior to the application of colour, and research suggests that oil and proteinaceous binders were employed, both on their own and in combination, as sealants for monumental statuary in cathedrals throughout northern Europe at this time.[352]

Written and material evidence attests that the application of organically-bound lead-based ground layers was, by this time, another well-established practice for painting on stone. Not only did such ground layers provide a smooth, compact surface upon which to paint, but they also furnished a highly reflective layer upon which more translucent glazes of colour could be layered to luminous effect. In the principal north and south wall scenes at Eton, a

Fig. 80. Detail of God the Father, from the *Trinity* depicted on one of three painted ashlar blocks from St Mark's Hospital, Bristol, *c.*1510.

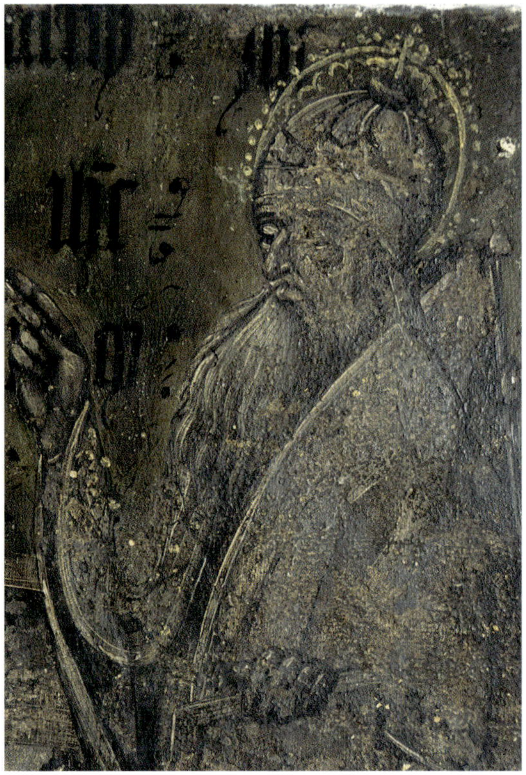

346 The edition cited here is that edited by Thompson (Cennini 1960). For the most up-to-date critique of this treatise, see Burns 2011. While Clarke 2001, 22-3, and Bomford *et al.* 1990, 2, posit that the *Libro dell'Arte* was written *c.*1390, the dating of this text is widely contested. Earlier editions by Merrifield and Herringham have dated the treatise to 1437 on the basis of an inscription at the end of the text.

347 Cennini 1960, 60; for the Italian ('… incollando sempre prima…') see Cennini 1982, 102. Whether the term 'incollando' refers to an oil-based sealant or, as Thompson seems to have translated, the glue-based size traditionally employed in the preparation of wooden panels, is not clear.

348 Cennini 1960, 120, chap. 175; for the Italian ('…abbi olio di lin seme cotto a modo di mordente… ma prima di questo olio o ver mordente be bogliente ne da' o con penello o con pezza sopra il ditto muro…') see Cennini 1982, 192-3.

349 See Strasbourg MS 1966, 61; on the manuscript, see Howard 2003, 19-20.

350 Gill & Howard 1997, 98-101.

351 Brodrick & Darrah 1986, 70, 74.

352 On Exeter, see Sinclair 1991, 119-20; for a survey of the European material see Rossi-Manaresi 2002; also Furlan *et al.* 1981.

very fine lead white layer was applied over the sealed limestone, whereas in the western scenes and beneath the inscriptions, the ground comprised a thick layer of red lead mixed with lead white. Variations on this technique are evident in the paintings from St Mark's Hospital, where a thick, opaque lead white ground was used, and on the Arundel effigies, which feature a pale pink ground comprising lead white mixed with a little red lead.[353] Similar layers comprising either lead white on its own or a mixture of red and lead white are also in evidence on the painted statuary surviving from the Great Screen at Winchester Cathedral (*c*.1476) (see Figure 30), as well as in the early fifteenth-century wall paintings in St Leonard's Chapel at Farleigh Hungerford Castle and in the mural of *c*.1480 depicting the *Legend of St Eustace* in Canterbury Cathedral.[354] That this practice was widespread in England by the end of the fifteenth century is further attested by surviving accounts for the purchase of painting materials. In 1473 at York Minster, for example, a staggering 319lb of lead white (compared with just 2lb of vermilion and ochre, 6lb of red lead and 12lb of verdigris and other colours) was purchased for painting the central tower.[355] The vast quantities involved indicate that the pigment was almost certainly being used as an overall painting ground.[356] Costed at between 2 and 3*d*. per lb in the Eton accounts for 1486-7, both white and red lead were sufficiently inexpensive to be used for this purpose.[357] Prescriptions in Paris guild regulations dating from 1391 indicate that, on the Continent too, the application of a lead white layer over a priming coat of oil was considered proper practice in the polychromy of stone sculpture.[358] Analysis of late fifteenth-century northern European panel paintings, such as Dieric Bouts' *Portrait of a Man*, (*c*.1462, National Gallery, London) and the work of his contemporaries, reveals that priming layers comprising organically bound lead-based pigments were usually also applied over the initial gesso ground on wood.[359] The practice persists in panel paintings produced in England in the sixteenth and seventeenth centuries.[360]

There is, by contrast, little evidence for the use of red lead for underdrawing as seems to have been the case at Eton. Given that the pigment was at this time only fractionally more expensive than red ochre, there was no reason to favour the latter on economic grounds. Preparatory drawings – many of which have never been analysed – were very commonly undertaken in red, though in apparent contrast to the underdrawing at Eton, these were almost always executed on top of the ground layer.[361] This technique was employed, for example, to set out the main compositional elements of the *Last Judgement* scene painted over the chancel arch at Holy

353 On St Mark's, see Gill & Howard 1997, 99; on Arundel, Brodrick & Darrah 1986, 70, 74.
354 On the Winchester figures, see Brodrick & Darrah 1989, 613-15; on the wall paintings, see Howard 2003, 128-9, 134, 178-9, 184; also Howard *et al.* 1998 and Hluvko 1991, 28.
355 Tatton-Brown 1989, 145.
356 Howard 2003, 176.
357 They were approximately five times cheaper than verdigris and six times cheaper than vermilion.
358 See Nash 2010, 154-5 and n.125.
359 Billinge *et al.* 1997, 20-4 and n.88.
360 See Jones 1995.
361 Howard 2003, 143.

Trinity church in Coventry (*c.*1435-60).[362] Underdrawing in an unidentified red has also been observed on the painted ashlar blocks from St Mark's, Bristol.[363] In other schemes, such as the Marian programme in the deanery at Durham (*c.*1470) (see Figure 26) and in the approximately contemporary *Legend of St Eustace* in Canterbury Cathedral, underdrawing is undertaken in what seems to be a brownish earth pigment.[364] Elsewhere, as in the early sixteenth-century semi-grisaille paintings in the north aisle of St Peter's, Raunds, Northamptonshire, the scheme is set out in carbon black.[365] Black also seems to have been the preferred colour for underdrawing in panel paintings executed in England and on the Continent around this time.[366] On balance, it seems that the choice of pigment was relatively unimportant and that such preparatory sketches were undertaken in whatever inexpensive colour the artist was accustomed to using or had to hand.

While organic binding media are known to have been used for wall painting in Europe from at least as early as the beginning of the ninth century,[367] the earliest confirmed use of oil in an English wall painting, at Canterbury Cathedral, dates from about 1130.[368] It was not however, considers Helen Howard, until the fourteenth century that such painting techniques, 'governed by concepts of luminosity and translucency', were really embraced in England.[369] After this date, an increasingly diverse range of organic binding media was deployed in an attempt to achieve more opulent and sophisticated optical effects. Linseed oil, which was perhaps the most commonly employed medium, has been identified not only at Eton, but in the near contemporary mural schemes at Farleigh Hungerford Castle, Holy Trinity church in Coventry, and St Mark's in Bristol.[370] The use of walnut oil, which has been identified in a sample from the green palm leaf held by St Martha on the north wall at Eton, is far less usual. Indeed, we know of only one other example of walnut oil used as a binder in English medieval wall painting – the somewhat earlier vine scroll motif in the tomb recess in the north-east transept of Rochester Cathedral, which is dated to around 1340.[371] Interestingly, as at Eton, the walnut oil is associated with a layer of copper green (verdigris). It is surely significant, given the almost unprecedented use of walnut oil at Eton and the scheme's strong Netherlandish connections, that walnut oil has been identified as a binding medium in numerous late fifteenth-century Netherlandish panel paintings.[372] In almost all of the instances cited, walnut oil – which is slower drying than linseed oil but less prone to yellowing – has been employed alongside linseed in specific areas, such as for white draperies or pale flesh tones, where particular

362 Howard 1996, 5.
363 Gill & Howard 1997, 99.
364 See Howard 2003, 146; also Allardyce *et al.* 1983, 8, and Allardyce 1984, 125, on Durham and Canterbury respectively.
365 Howe 2005, 42.
366 See Jones 1995, 231 and 235; also Billinge *et al.* 1997, 25.
367 See, for example, the wall paintings of *c.*800 at Müstair, Switzerland; Mairinger & Schreiner 1986, 196.
368 Cather & Howard 1994.
369 Howard 2003, 6, 202.
370 Howard 2003, 120; also Howard *et al.* 1998, 60; Howard 1996, 7-9; and Gill & Howard 1997, 99.
371 Rickerby 1988, 11; also Howard 2003, 89-90, 131.
372 See Billinge *et al.* 1997, 40-1, 53-5; also Nash 2008, 206, for examples. Howard 2003, 89-90, suggests that there was a similar preference for walnut oil in Italian easel painting until the sixteenth century.

brightness was required. Indeed, in her recent survey of the accounts of the dukes of Burgundy in the late fourteenth and early fifteenth centuries, Nash observes that walnut oil was employed at the ducal court to the exclusion of all others.[373] Whether the 'olei pictorum' cited in the closing accounts at Eton refers to linseed or walnut oil, we cannot know, but we do have evidence from contemporary English customs accounts that both 'lynsed oleum' and specially prepared 'peyntures oyle' were being imported into London from the Low Countries throughout the fifteenth century.[374]

Fig. 81. Detail of St John the Baptist, from the *Last Judgement* scene painted over the chancel arch at Holy Trinity church in Coventry, *c*.1435-60.

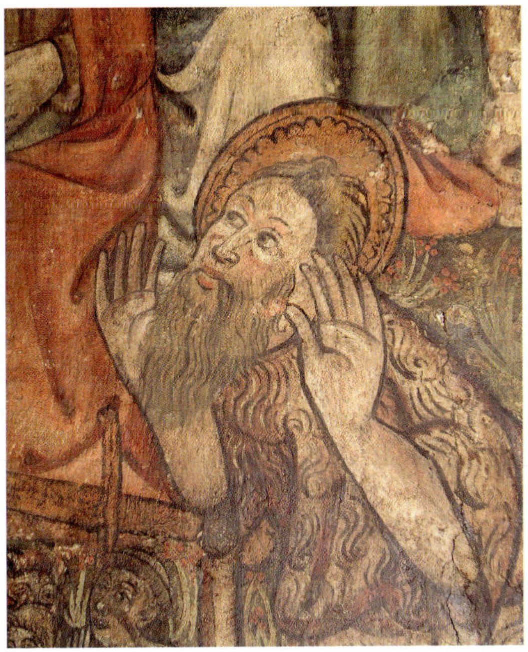

Increasingly, it seems, oil was combined with other organic media in pursuit of more refined optical effects.[375] We have evidence for such manipulation of materials on the north wall at Eton, where oil appears to have been combined with animal glue and possibly egg in some of the lower paint layers.[376] Egg was apparently also combined with linseed oil in the polychromatic treatment of sculpture for Waynflete's Great Screen at Winchester.[377] At Arundel too, an emulsion of linseed oil and egg was used for the subordinate paint layers, while the final paint layers were applied in unadulterated oil. By manipulating the painting technique in this way, it was possible to ensure both a durable substrate and optimal luminosity in the uppermost paint layers.[378] Similar discrimination has also been observed in the Holy Trinity *Last Judgement* painting (Figure 81), where egg was used on its own to apply a layer of red lead, and was also mixed with oil in a red lake glaze, and on the fifteenth-century statuary on the west front of Exeter Cathedral, where linseed oil and egg have been identified both separately and in an emulsion.[379] Netherlandish panel painters working in this period display a similarly sophisticated understanding of binding media, exploiting their working properties to spectacular effect. Egg tempera, which was faster drying and provided more opaque coverage, was frequently employed for the coloured underlayers between the priming and uppermost oil-bound paint layers.[380] What is striking is that exactly the same painting techniques were being employed by artists working on panels, statuary and walls and, by extrapolation, it seems highly likely that at least some artists were adept at working on a variety of these different substrates.

The broad palette employed in the Eton chapel murals is wholly representative of painting materials employed both in England and on the Continent around the end of the fifteenth century. Of the

373 Nash 2010, 157 and table 18, cites accounts for the period 1375-1419.

374 Childs 2010, 35-6. I am most grateful to Jo Kirby for this information.

375 See Howard 2003, 202; proteinaceous media were, for example, often used to apply copper blues, not only because the colour of these pigments appears more brilliant in proteinaceous binders (there is a greater difference in their relative refractive indices than with oil), but possibly also because proteinaceous media were known to inhibit the degradation of the pigment that can occur through its interaction with oil.

376 See sample 22 in the Appendix.

377 See Brodrick & Darrah 1989.

378 Brodrick & Darrah 1986, 70 and 80.

379 On Coventry, see Howard 1996, 7-9; on Exeter, see Sinclair 1991, 124-5.

380 See Billinge *et al.* 1997, 41; also Nash 2008, 205-7, and Jones 1995, 237.

pigments identified, indigo, verdigris, red and white lead, ochres, red lakes and vermilion receive regular mention in purchase accounts and customs records surviving from the period.[381] It is interesting that carbon black and calcium carbonate white, which are consistently identified in analyses of late medieval painting schemes, are often absent from these records. Presumably these materials, being cheap and easily sourced, were not purchased from the same specialist merchants as the more expensive pigments and dyes. Indeed, in many instances the artists may have made these pigments themselves. One of the most puzzling technical discoveries thrown up during the analysis of the paintings at Eton is the detection of significant levels of copper in the black paint employed for the inscriptions. Almost all of the blacks used as pigments in medieval wall painting were formed by the pyrolysis of organic matter; none of these naturally contain copper, and it seems unlikely that it could have been introduced during the making of the pigment.[382] Carbon black, significant quantities of which were employed in the Eton chapel scheme, dries poorly, however, and analysis of Lucas Cranach the Elder's *Portrait of a Man, probably John Feige* (*c.*1524), which portrays the sitter wearing an ornately embellished black tunic against a dark background, has revealed that a little verdigris was added to the lamp black as a siccative (Figure 82).[383] Azurite is also reported to have been used in this way. Traces of the costly blue pigment were identified mixed with carbon black on the Great Cross (*c.*1395-1404), also known as the *Well of Moses*, at the Chartreuse de Champmol built for Duke Philip the Bold just outside the Burgundian capital of Dijon.[384] Red lakes, like carbon black, dried particularly slowly when bound in oil, and close inspection of northern European panel paintings from the later fifteenth century reveals that glazes of lakes and copper greens were often blotted, using a cloth or even the fingers, to reduce the thickness of the glaze and thus its drying time.[385] Van Eyck has been observed to have used his fingers to blot the green paint of the robe worn by Arnolfini's wife in his celebrated *Arnolfini Portrait* (*c.*1434, National Gallery, London), and the presence of fingerprints

Fig. 82. Lucas Cranach the Elder, *Portrait of a Man, probably Johann Feige, c.*1524 (National Gallery, London).

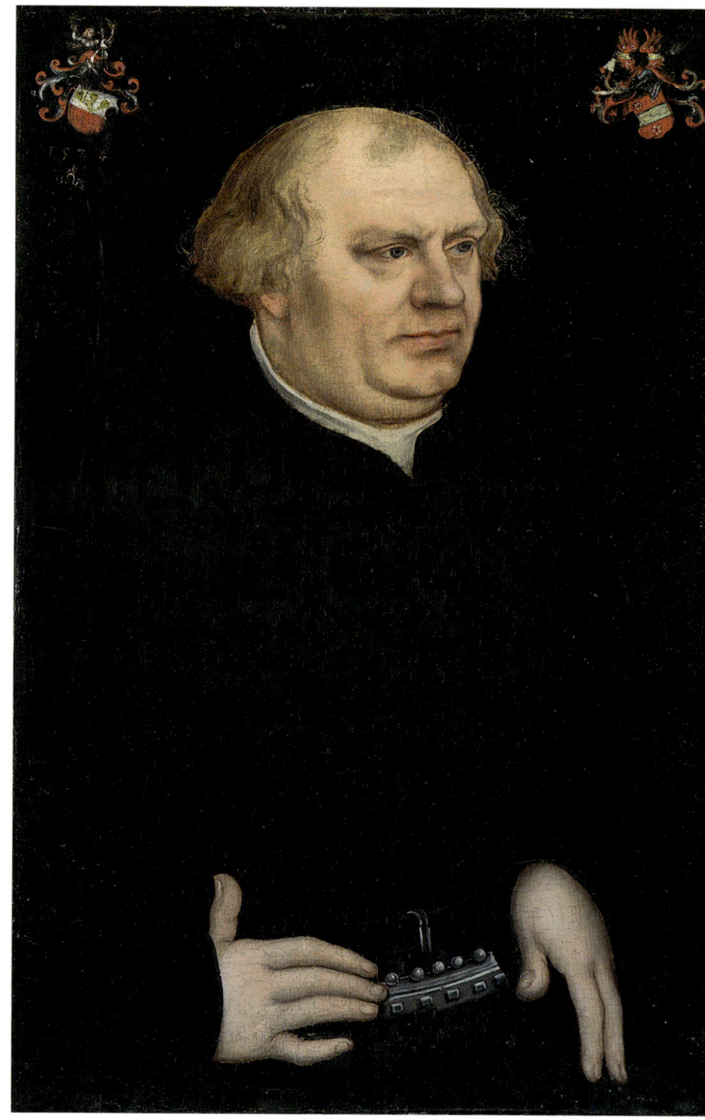

381 See, for example, Kirby 2010 on the trade in painters' materials in sixteenth-century London; also Nash 2010, 157, on the accounts of the duchy of Burgundy for the period *c.*1375-1419.

382 Howard 2003, 187; also Winter 1983. It is interesting, however, that a black paint comprising copper oxide was used to paint glass in this period. The paint, which is referred to as 'geet' or 'arnement' in contemporary English accounts, comprised a mixture of the copper (or lead) oxide mixed with glass as a flux, and a binder such as gum arabic, urine, vinegar or wine; see Marks 1993, 34.

383 Billinge *et al.* 1997, 42.

384 This pigment admixture was used for the niches of the pillar against which the prophets are set and for the lining of robes; see Nash 2010, 157, and n.135, citing Demailly *et al.* 2001, vol.1, 145, sample 49.

385 Nash 2008, 208; also Billinge *et al.* 1997, 42.

suggests that a similar technique was used on the north wall of the Eton wall paintings to attenuate the black background of the 'Amoras' legend.

It is particularly interesting that a range of pigments closely comparable with those identified in the paintings at Eton was employed in the polychromy of Waynflete's Great Screen at Winchester (*c.*1476), and in the funerary effigies of his close associate William Fitzalan and his wife at Arundel (*c.*1470-80).[386] The only notable disparity between the materials employed in these three schemes is the absence, at Eton, of any traces of gilding or the costly blue mineral azurite. Instead, the organic colorant indigo was employed for the details of the fictive textile on the north and south walls. Indigo features regularly in wall painting schemes of the period, and has been identified on the fragments of painted ashlar from the scheme at St Mark's, Bristol (*c.*1510), as well as on the recently uncovered painting in Eton's Head Master's Chambers (*c.*1520).[387] Blue pigment derived from indigo was also employed on projects as diverse as the sophisticated Marian mural scheme of *c.*1470 in the deanery at Durham (see Figure 26), the fifteenth-century polychromy on the statuary on the west front of Exeter Cathedral, and on a painted wooden figure of Christ from the chapel of St Anthony in Cartmel Fell, Cumbria.[388] While the best quality of this intense blue dye was obtained from the plant *Indigofera tinctoria* L., native to India, a more common and affordable source in the later Middle Ages was the European plant woad (*Isatis tinctoria* L.)[389] Though grown in England, woad was also imported from as early as the thirteenth century.[390] By the fifteenth century, specialist production was centred on the German town of Erfurt and the region around Toulouse in France, with vast quantities being imported into London and Southampton to meet the needs of the cloth-dying industry.[391] In 1480-1 alone, 5,108 bales of 'southern' woad, 56 pipes of Toulouse woad and 18 vats of Cologne woad are recorded entering the capital. Unfortunately, it is not possible to identify the source from which the indigo pigment used in the chapel at Eton was prepared, but it seems likely that most of the indigo deployed in painting schemes at this time was derived from its more readily available European source.[392] While the colorant specified in the Eton accounts – blew yende – suggests that we are dealing with the superior Indian dye, it seems that this term had become generic, regardless of the true source.[393] That the indigo used at Eton has not suffered fading is probably due to the fact that the scheme has spent much of its life obscured from view, rather than to the pigment's superior quality.

Madder lake, derived from the roots of the plant

386 See Brodrick & Darrah 1989 and 1986 respectively.
387 See Brodrick & Darrah 1989, and Gill & Howard 1997, 99-101. On the painting in the Head Master's Chambers at Eton, see Part II below.
388 See Howard 2003, 60, 63; also Howard 1988; Sinclair 1991, 123; Sinclair 1992, 10 and Behrens 1982, 133, on Durham, Exeter and Cartmel respectively.
389 See Howard 2003, 57-64.
390 See Kirby 2010, 342; also Howard 2003, 57-8.
391 Childs 2010, 34.
392 Indigo prepared as a painting pigment (*ynde*) is frequently cited in customs accounts for ships bound from the Netherlands; see Childs 2010, tables 1 and 2.
393 Howard 2003, 58-9. The same term is used in accounts relating to the painting of the central tower vault at York Minster in 1472, and in Scottish treasury accounts of 1502 pertaining to the painting of ceilings; see Gee 1984, 13.

Rubia tinctorum L., is another organic colorant that has been identified at Eton. Like woad, madder was used as a dye for cloth, and although it could be grown in England, customs accounts attest that it was imported continuously from the Netherlands.[394] Zeeland, in particular, was celebrated for the quality of its madder, and regulations issued in the city of Reymerswaal in 1480 indicate that the production of the dye was closely regulated.[395] Red lakes were, of course, notoriously expensive. While madder lakes were far cheaper than lakes prepared from scale insects, their orange-red colour being considered less desirable than the crimsons of kermes or cochineal lakes, they had the advantage of being less susceptible to photodegredation.[396] By the later Middle Ages, red lakes for painting were commonly extracted from dyed cloth clippings. The colorant was extracted by boiling the shearings with an aqueous alkali, such as lye (potassium carbonate), and alum (potassium aluminium sulfate), which reacted to form a precipitate of hydrated alumina onto which the dye would attach.[397] Indeed, pioneering analysis undertaken at the National Gallery, London, suggests that alkaline extraction from dyed wool may have been the principal method of madder lake preparation in this period.[398] It is precisely this process – against which Cennino Cennini advises – which seems to have been used to produce the madder employed at Eton.[399] Analysis of other medieval lakes reveals that a mixture of cloth shearings was often used, resulting in a pigment comprising more than one kind of dyestuff.[400] A combination of madder and the more expensive colorant kermes has, for example, been identified in the robe of the courtier in the Parisian panel painting of *St Giles and the Hind* (*c*.1500) (Figure 83),[401] and at Eton itself, in the slightly later paintings of *c*.1520 in the Head Master's Chambers, recent analysis has identified an admixture of madder and brazilwood in the tunic of one of the boys.[402] It is frustrating that so few of the lakes identified in English medieval wall paintings have been subjected to instrumental analysis. Only two other much earlier instances of the use of madder have, as yet, been verified: in the scheme of *c*.1300 in the Ante-Reliquary Chapel in Norwich Cathedral, and in the similarly dated paintings in the feretory of St Alban's Abbey.[403] Red lakes became increasingly popular in the later Middle Ages and their use is evident in the fifteenth-century mural schemes in St Leonard's Chapel at Farleigh Hungerford Castle and on the chancel arch at Holy Trinity, Coventry, as well as in the sculptural polychromy from the Winchester screen, the Fitzalan effigies at Arundel, and on the west front at Exeter Cathedral.[404] A great deal more analytical evidence exists for panel paintings. In a technical

Fig. 83. Master of St Giles, *St Giles and the Hind*, detail, *c*.1500 (National Gallery, London).

394 See Childs 2010, 34, who notes that in 1480-1, imports of madder to London by aliens numbered some 239 bales, valued at £479. See also Howard 2003, 111-12.

395 See Kirby & White 1996, 656.

396 See Howard 2003, 113, citing Burmester & Krekel's analysis (1998, 102) of fifteenth- and sixteenth-century pharmacy price lists. On the photostability of madder lakes, see Kirby *et al.* 2006, 240-1.

397 Howard 2003, 114-15; see also Kirby *et al.* 2005; the process is also discussed at length by Nash 2010, 143.

398 See Kirby *et al.* 2005, 76-8; in those cases where madder dyestuff was identified, high levels of sulphur and protein were indicative of the dissolution of the wool caused by more aggressive alkaline extraction treatments.

399 In chapter 44 of his *Libro dell'Arte*, Cennini counsels his reader against using lakes made from cloth shearings, and to use only the lake which is made from gum (which Thompson suggests refers to the resinous secretions of insects). For analysis of the Eton lake, see chapter 6 above.

400 Howard 2003, 115.

401 Kirby & White 1996, 67-8.

402 See Part II below, citing HPLC analysis by Jo Kirby and David Peggie (National Gallery).

403 Howard 2003, 115-16.

404 For the mural schemes, see Howard *et al.* 1998, 60, and Howard 1996, 5; in both cases preliminary examination suggests that the pigment may be madder. On Winchester, see Brodrick & Darrah 1989; on Arundel, see Brodrick & Darrah 1986; and on Exeter, see Sinclair 1991, 122, who also details the use of lakes on the painted portal at Lausanne Cathedral and on the west front at Wells.

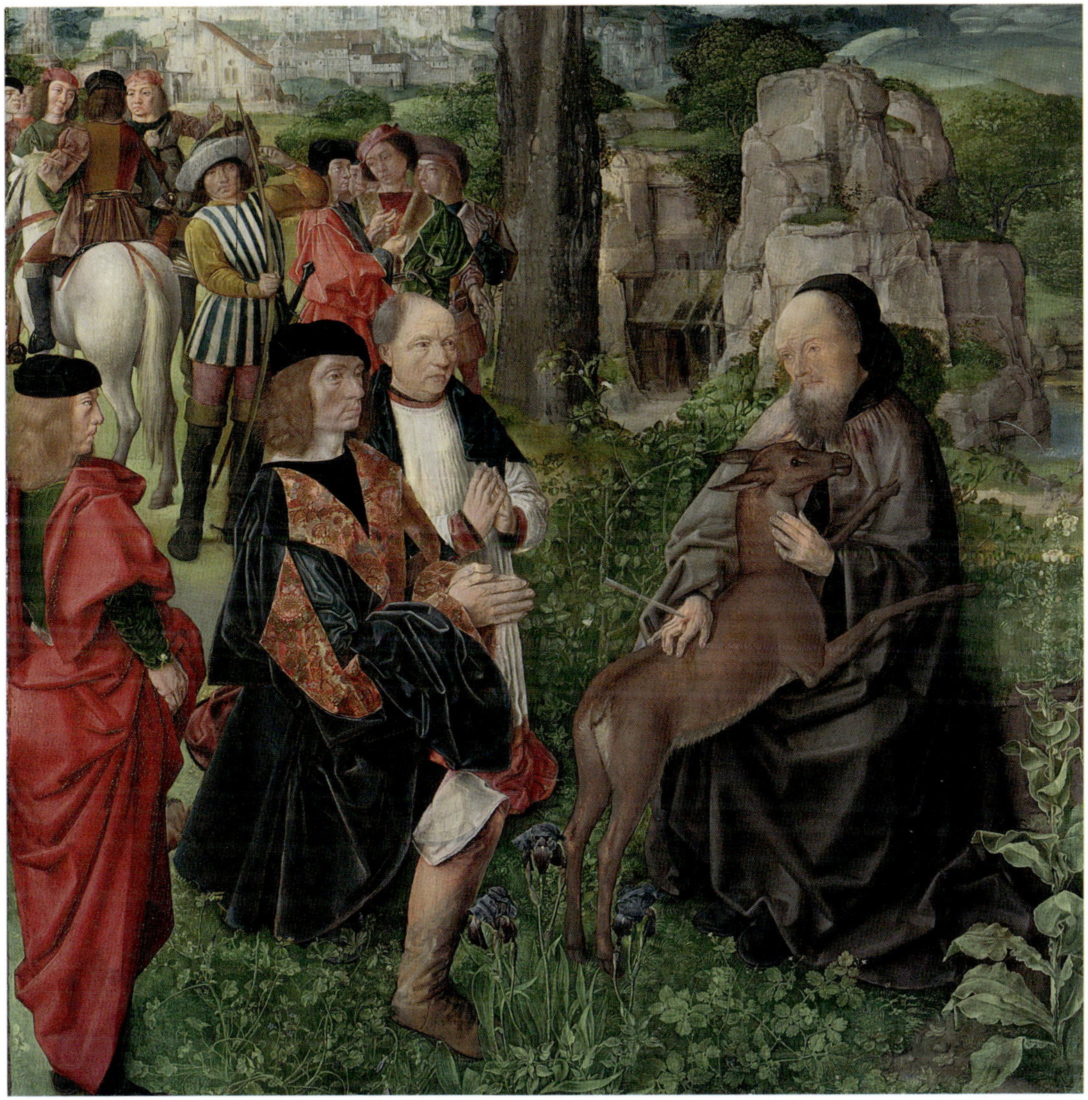

survey of northern European panel painting dating from between 1400 and 1600, Kirby and White discovered that madder was by far the most widely employed red lake, particularly in Germany, the Netherlands and Flanders.[405] As in the Eton paintings, the lake was usually applied as a translucent glaze over a brightly reflective underlayer of lead white, sometimes mixed with a little carbon black, or else over an opaque pink layer comprising a mixture of the same lake, and sometimes vermilion, with lead white.[406]

Among the most unusual pigments identified at Eton is lead-tin yellow. It seems strange that this pigment, which was used so extensively in the paintings to highlight such elements as hair, jewellery, crowns and armour, does not feature in the account roll for 1486-7.[407] Research by Howard reveals that few instances of the use of lead-tin yellow have been confirmed in English medieval wall painting.[408] Interestingly, almost all of the examples cited – including the murals in St Leonard's Chapel, Farleigh Hungerford, in the presbytery at St Alban's Abbey and those at St Mark's, Bristol – date from the fifteenth and early sixteenth centuries.[409] Evidently, however, lead-tin yellow was used in continental mural schemes; Kühn cites fifteenth-century schemes in Ghent, Nivelles and Freiberg (Saxony),[410] and two Swedish examples have been cited, dating from around

405 Lakes derived from scale insect dyestuffs were by contrast favoured in Italy; see Kirby & White 1996; also Howard 2003, 122.

406 See Billinge *et al.* 1997, 38.

407 On balance, it seems that the pigment 'generall' cited in the account roll does not refer to lead-tin yellow, but to some other, much cheaper, unspecified 'tawny colour'. On the confusing and evolving nomenclature for this pigment, see n.334 in chapter 6 above.

408 Howard 2003, 161-2.

409 'Type I' lead-tin oxide has been identified at Farleigh Hungerford using XRD analysis; see Howard *et al.* 1998, 62. For St Alban's and St Mark's, see Perry 1998, 6, and Gill & Howard 1997, 99, respectively. Howard also reports that preliminary identification of the pigment has also been made by Jo Darrah in an early fifteenth-century wall painting in the south choir aisle of Lichfield Cathedral.

410 Kühn 1993, 99-111.

1500.[411] Traces of lead-tin yellow have also been found on sculptural polychromy of the period in both England and on the Continent, including the west front statuary at Exeter and the late fifteenth-century effigies at Arundel where, as at Eton, the pigment was used to highlight elements such as hair.[412] It was also used by Jean Malouel for the polychromy of Sluter's Great Cross (*c.*1395-1404) at Champmol. Analysis reveals that here, as at Eton, the pigment was mixed with verdigris to achieve a range of green hues.[413] A similar deployment of lead-tin yellow mixed with verdigris and lead white has been noted in the foliage and landscapes of Early Netherlandish paintings, often applied as an underlayer beneath a glaze of copper resinate.[414] Indeed, lead-tin yellow, a recipe for which appears in the sixteenth-century *Traktaat om kleuren te bereiden* (Plantin-Moretus Museum, Antwerp, MS 253), seems to have enjoyed far greater popularity as a material for use in panel painting.[415] The fine particle size of the pigment meant that a relatively small amount of binding medium, usually oil, was required to apply it. The result was a densely opaque and bulky paint that held its shape beautifully, enabling the execution of exquisite impasto effects.[416] The imitation of gold brocade and cloth of gold, which Nash considers to be 'a distinctive feature of the Netherlandish painter's repertoire', relied heavily upon these properties.[417] Though working on a far larger scale, the artists responsible for the paintings in the chapel at Eton exploited the qualities of lead-tin yellow to similar effect.

While technically among the most sophisticated schemes of their day, the wall paintings commissioned by Bishop Waynflete to adorn Henry VI's new church at Eton have revealed themselves in their painting materials and methods to be wholly representative of their time, reflecting the complexity and versatility of late medieval oil-based painting techniques. Not only do the materials and application methodologies observed in the *Miracles* scenes bear comparison with those employed in other English wall painting schemes of the later fifteenth century, but they also display particularly close affinities with contemporary polychromed sculpture, such as the painted choir screen commissioned by Waynflete for Winchester Cathedral. Indeed, the analysis of Eton's wall paintings has afforded valuable new insights into the similarity of painting practices among those working on walls, statuary and panels. Moreover, the unexpected identification of walnut oil in the Eton chapel murals, together with the widespread use of madder lake and lead-tin yellow, provides compelling new evidence that the influence of Netherlandish artists on painting practices in England in the late fifteenth century was not only stylistic, but also technological.

411 Nord & Tronner 2000, 99.
412 For Exeter and Arundel, see Sinclair 1991, 123-4 and 1992, 10, and Brodrick & Darrah 1986 respectively; for continental material, see Kühn 1993, 106.
413 Nash 2010, 151-2.
414 Kühn 1993, 94; also Billinge *et al.* 1997, 40.
415 The process involved calcinating 3lb of lead with 2lb of tin, followed by the addition of minium (red lead) and further heating for 12 hours. This recipe appears to have been for the 'type I' variety of the pigment (Pb_2SnO_4), more commonly used in northern European painting (see Billinge *et al.* 1997, 14-15 and n.45); it seems that references to the preparation of this pigment were relatively uncommon, possibly because lead-tin oxides were historically produced in association with ceramic glazes. See also Kühn 1993, 89-91.
416 For these observations, see Nash 2008, 208-9.
417 Nash 2008, 208-9, cites the example of the brocade robe worn by St Donatian in van Eyck's *Van der Paele Madonna* (1436, Groeningemuseum, Bruges). See also Jones 1995, for similar examples in panel paintings executed by English artists in the fifteenth and sixteenth centuries.

8. Conclusions

So much more of the chapel wall paintings at Eton are visible to us today than when M.R. James uncovered and wrote about the scheme in the 1920s. This is thanks, in no small measure, to the assiduous and painstaking work of Pauline Plummer in eliminating centuries of limewash, overpaint, dirt and varnish which previously obscured large areas of the paintings. Their removal has restored the readability of the scheme and, with it, our ability to contemplate the function of the paintings within Henry VI's new church at Eton. It is hoped that, in bringing together the last nine decades of scholarship on the paintings, the present work will serve to enhance further our perception of the scheme's significance.

What has become apparent in the course of this study is that, in William Waynflete, the king found a loyal and staunch supporter of his new foundation, and one who shared completely and profoundly his vision of a centre for Marian devotion. While Henry's own plans for the walls upon which the murals were ultimately executed were undoubtedly quite different, there can be little doubt that Eton's founder would have approved of such a monumental display of his patron's intercessory powers. Written accounts make clear that it was Waynflete who subvented and controlled the programme of building at Eton following the king's demise, and while it cannot be proven that he was personally responsible for the design of the scheme of *Miracles* in the new nave, there is ample circumstantial evidence for his influence upon the choice of subject matter for this iconographically complex programme. The paintings which Waynflete commissioned to adorn the nave of Henry's church served to underline the miraculous healing and intercessory powers of the Virgin and, as such, were intimately and inextricably linked to the Marian liturgy celebrated daily in its nave. The depiction, alongside the miracles, of a host of standing saints in niches evoked the simultaneous presence of a much wider company of holy intermediaries, many of whom were reputed to have been present at the Virgin's Assumption. Most significantly, in a period which saw the rise of heretical attacks upon the 'wurshipping of ymagis', many of the miraculous episodes depicted on the walls at Eton portrayed the benefits of such devotional practices as a means of accessing the Virgin's intercessory powers.

If the cycle of miracles depicted in Eton's nave seems, in the context of other contemporary devotional schemes, theologically somewhat backward-looking, stylistically they reveal themselves to be quite the opposite. In their format, palette and style, the paintings represent the cutting edge of courtly fashion in England in the last quarter of the fifteenth century. While enquiry yields no extant model for either the range or extent of the miracles depicted at Eton, there is undoubtedly precedent for the format in which these scenes are represented. Indeed, this type of compartmentalised narrative sequence, set within micro-architectural niches interspersed by canopied figures of standing saints, proliferates among commissions in the period, from painting and manuscripts, to block books and tapestries, stained glass and statuary. The use of grisaille has also been shown to have become increasingly fashionable in this period across a broad range of media, but perhaps most significantly for the paintings at Eton, in northern European illuminated manuscripts recounting the *Miracles of the Virgin*. There is increasing, if fragmentary, evidence to show that this continental trend was perpetuated in contemporary English wall painting schemes, particularly those depicting standing saints in imitation of statuary. There is no doubt that, in their attenuated figurative style and distinctive female facial characteristics, the paintings in the chapel at Eton betray the growing influence of Netherlandish artists in England in the later fifteenth century, and it is surely of no little significance that Bishop Waynflete engaged Flemish sculptors and carvers to undertake the work not only for the Great Screen at Winchester, but also for the choir stalls and screen in the new church at Eton.

While, frustratingly, it has not been possible to throw any new light on either the identity or nationalities of the painters responsible for the Eton murals, some clarification of the dating of the scheme does seem to have emerged. There is now evidence, in the new fragment of account rolls discovered at Eton in the 1980s, that painting of some sort was being undertaken in the College from as early as 1477, and it seems that at least some element of the *Miracles* scheme was complete by 1483, when the enigmatic 'Lodovico Palmer' received payment for washing the paintings in the nave. And if, as has been suggested, the pendant worn by the Emperor's treacherous brother on the south wall of the nave was indeed a surreptitious declaration of anti-Yorkist sentiment, then this would seem to imply that this part of the scheme, at least, was executed sometime between 1485 and 1487 (after Richard III's death and prior to the coronation of Henry VII's Yorkist queen). Certainly, all such work seems to have been completed soon after Waynflete's death, since a concluding account for artists' materials and labour is recorded in the College accounts for the year 1486/7.

The recent technical examination of the wall paintings at Eton seems to corroborate the long-held belief that scenes 1 to 7 on the north and south walls were painted by different artists and/or workshops. What has also become clear in the course of this investigation, however, is that the paintings were not executed in the manner traditionally supposed, with the north wall painted in its entirety before the south was commenced. Indeed, fresh evaluation of the programme's style and painting technique reveals that a different set of painters, using a very different technique and probably at a different point in time, was almost certainly responsible for the most westerly scenes on both the north and south walls in both upper and lower registers. Whether these scenes were painted before or after the main stretch of scenes (nos 1-7) on either wall cannot be proven, though it seems reasonable to suppose that the paintings were executed in the manner in which they were intended to be read, that is from east to west, and that these four scenes were painted at a later date, possibly after Waynflete's death, when responsibility for the paintings' completion fell to the College.

Scientific analysis of samples from the paintings in the nave has revealed the scheme to have been undertaken on a predominantly oil-primed substrate in a variety of organic media, using a range of pigments and sophisticated application methodologies which reflect the complexity and versatility of late medieval oil-based painting techniques. Comparison of the murals' technique with other contemporary works of art, together with evidence afforded by documentary sources from the period, reveals the scheme to be wholly representative of painting practices in England around the end of the fifteenth century. Not only do the materials and application methodologies observed in the *Miracles* scenes bear comparison with those employed in other late fifteenth-century English wall painting schemes, but they also display particularly close technological affinities with polychromed sculpture and painted panels commissioned around this time. Whether native or immigrant, the painters Waynflete enlisted to work in the chapel at Eton were clearly not only highly accomplished but also well acquainted with the latest developments in painting practices on the Continent. The identification of madder in the wall paintings, quite possibly derived from dyed wool clippings, is particularly telling, since madder obtained from this source was by far the most commonly employed lake in fifteenth-century northern European panel paintings. The discovery that walnut oil was employed as a medium on the north wall of the murals – which, with one earlier exception, is unprecedented in English medieval wall paintings – and the extensive use of lead-tin yellow throughout the scheme, provide similarly compelling evidence for the scheme's technical affinity with Netherlandish painting at the close of the fifteenth century. If anything, the murals in the chapel of Eton College have been revealed to be even more extraordinary than James might have imagined when he first caught a glimpse of them 130 years ago.

Catalogue

Figures are numbered I-IX; scenes are numbered 1-8, running **east to west**.[1] Some of the framing figures depicting saints and prophets are shown in two successive illustrations; their descriptions are also repeated on the relevant pages.

The following descriptions are based on those of M.R. James (James 1907 and James & Tristram 1929). At the time that R.H. Essex made the copies upon which James based his original identifications, some of the scenes and their inscriptions were obscured by covering layers of paint. As a result of Plummer's conservation of the scheme in the 1960s and '70s, much more is now visible and the following descriptions have been updated, based on more recent scholarship.[2] The Latin inscriptions belonging to each scene are transcribed as they appear today.[3]

1 The narrative scenes depicted on the walls of the chapel were intended to be read from east to west, and the numbering system adhered to in this study reflects this. As such, it departs from the nomenclature employed by James for the north wall paintings in his study of 1907 (which goes from left to right), but is in keeping with the system employed by him in his later publication with Tristram (James & Tristram 1929).

2 See, in particular, Anderson 1989 and Gill 2003.

3 The inscriptions were very kindly transcribed anew by Dr Christopher de Hamel (Gaylord Donnelley Fellow Librarian, Corpus Christi College, Cambridge). It should be noted that, in some instances, these new transcriptions vary greatly from what James originally suggested. Regrettably, it is not possible to discern which elements of James's transcriptions were made from text that was clearly visible to him, and which were the result of an educated guess. Conversely, some elements which were legible in James's day now appear badly abraded. For completeness, James's original transcriptions are provided in footnotes.

South wall, upper register

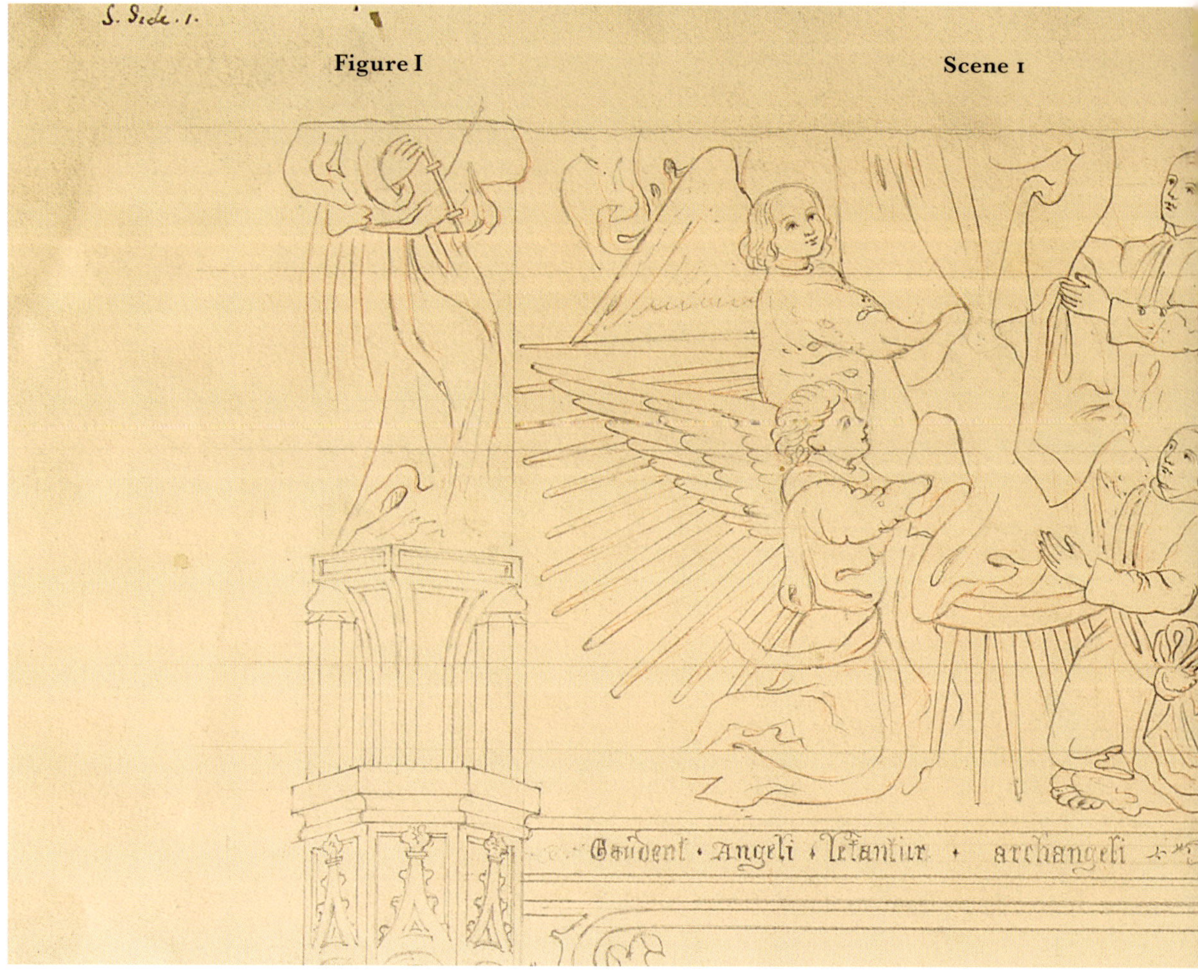

With the exception of figures VIII and IX, and scene 8, the upper register is entirely lost and known only from the drawings made by Essex.

Figure I | Archangel Gabriel (lost)
The lower part of a figure dressed in long robes, holding a sceptre; most probably the Archangel Gabriel as part of an 'Annunciation', with the accompanying figure of the Virgin depicted in the corresponding location on the north wall.

Scene 1 | The Assumption of the Virgin (lost)
The lower portion of the Virgin's draped figure (centre) is depicted within a mandorla of radiating sun rays; beneath her feet is what appears to be an upturned crescent-shaped moon – an allusion, no doubt, to the Book of Revelation (12:1, 'And a great sign appeared in Heaven: a woman clothed with the sun, and the moon under her feet').[4] The Virgin is supported on either side by a pair of angels; the draperies of what may be a fifth angel are visible at top left. Based on the Cust lithograph of this scene, James suggests that there may originally have been three angels on either side.[5]
INSCRIPTION: Gaudent. Angeli. letantur. archangeli [6]

Figure II | Evangelist or Church Father (lost)
The lower portion of a draped figure; James suggests this was one of the four Evangelists depicted in sequence along the upper register of the south wall, possibly St Matthew.[7]

Scene 2 | The Miracle of the Jew at the Virgin's funeral (lost)
In this well-known episode from the *Golden Legend*, the Virgin's funeral procession was disrupted by a disrespectful Jewish priest; when he attempted to overturn the bier, however, his hands stuck fast to it and withered. Only when he confessed his faith to St Peter were his hands released and healed. Here, on the left, the Apostle St John carries a palm branch in his left hand and a book in a bag-binding in his right; another Apostle (St Peter?) follows, also holding a book. Between these figures is a section of ringed pole, which forms part of the Virgin's bier. The figure of the disruptive Jewish priest is depicted twice: on the far right he is shown drawing his sword; at the bottom he is shown fallen to the ground, stretching up with his left arm, his sword and cap (or helmet) at his side.
INSCRIPTION: Jude[us]. q[ui] dam. feretru[m]. b[eat]e. v[ir] g[in]is. tange[n]s. g[ra]ci. petri. p[er]cu[ta]tur. &. ab. ra[m]ie. liberatur. *vi[n]c[entius]. li[br]o. 8º c[apitul]o 77º* [8]

Figure III | St Ambrose or St Luke (lost)
The lower part of a draped figure holding a scroll, with a small ox at his feet. While an ox was the symbol of St Luke, James suggests that the figure represents St Ambrose, one of the four Doctors of the Church. St Ambrose is sometimes depicted with an ox because of his commentary on the writings of the Evangelist.[9]

Scene 3 | The Miracle of Theophilus (lost)
According to this most famous of the Virgin's miracles, Theophilus, a lay official of the church of Adana in Cilicia, was ousted from office by an incoming bishop.[10] In his annoyance Theophilus sought out a Jewish magician who introduced him to the Devil. Theophilus made a pact with the Devil, who promised to restore him to his former position if he denied Christ and the Virgin. Once reinstated, Theophilus repented of this bargain and spent all of his time praying to the Virgin to deliver him. Eventually, the Virgin wrested the contract from the Devil and returned it to Theophilus, who, in the presence of the assembled church, confessed his sin and shortly afterwards died. Here the Devil, represented on the left of the scene with a hairy body and cloven foot, takes the hand of Theophilus, dressed in a robe and cape. It seems likely that the figure on the right of the scene was a second representation of

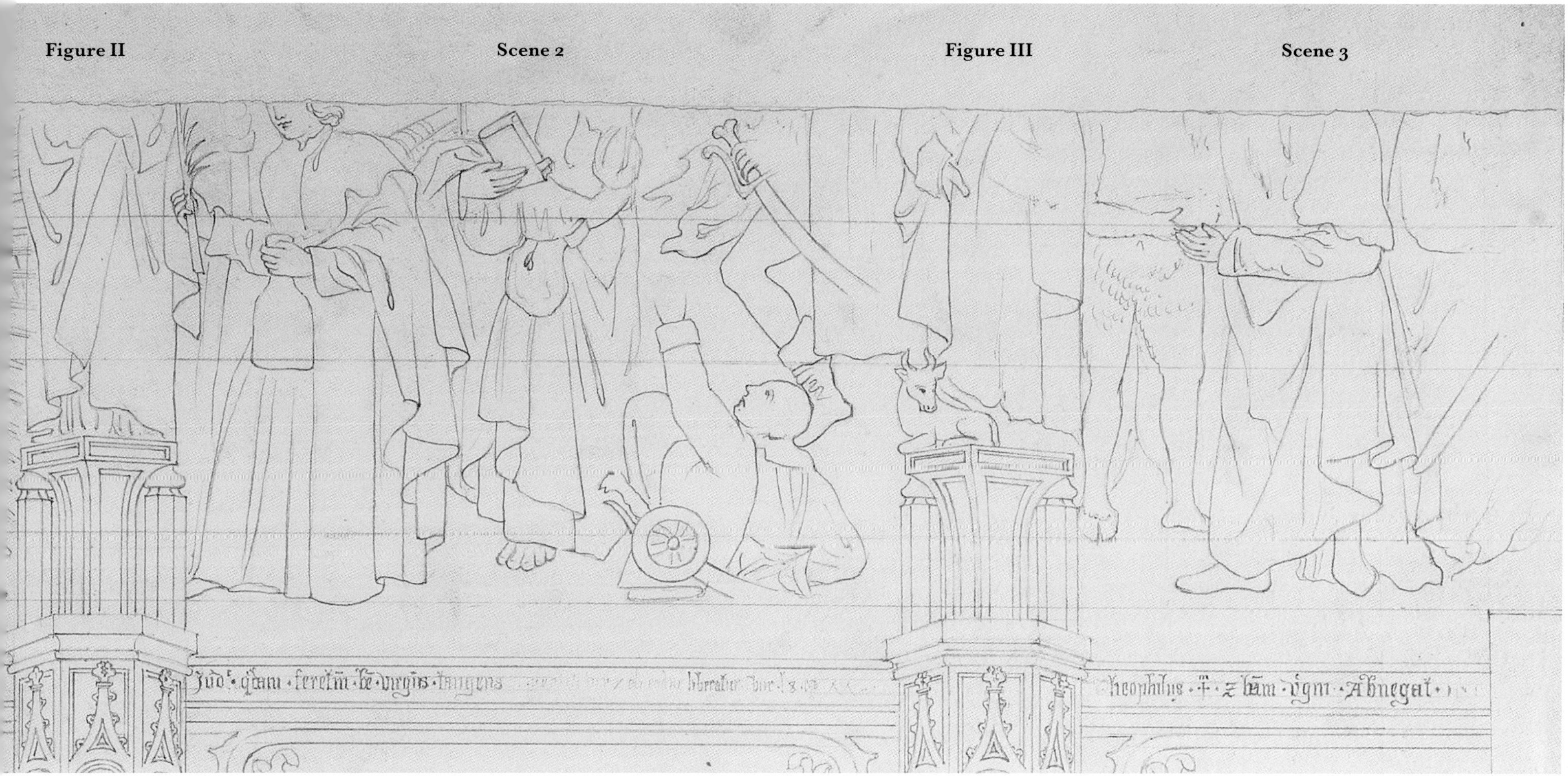

Theophilus, possibly receiving the contract back from the Virgin. Unfortunately, this part of the painting was obliterated during the insertion of a new organ loft in around 1700.[11]
INSCRIPTION: Theophilus. x[pistu]m. &. b[eat]am. v[ir]gi[n]em. abnegans. p[r]ius (?). ductus. per […] *vi[n]ce ntius li[br]o 22° ca[pitul]o 69°* [12]

4 Identical imagery of the Virgin standing on a crescent within a mandorla features on surviving pilgrim badges dating from the end of the fifteenth century and commemorating the feast of the Assumption at Eton; see Spencer 1990, 29-30, and 1998, 148-9.
5 James & Tristram 1929, 19.
6 James 1907, 20, transcribed this as: *Gaudant . Angeli . letantur . Archangeli*, and identified it as coming from the Roman Breviary's Office for the Assumption.
7 James & Tristram 1929, 19
8 James transcribes this as *Judeus . quidam . feretrum beate virginis . tangens.* <   > *credidit liberator. Vinc. Libro 8° Ca° 77.* He suggested that, throughout the scheme, book 8 was referenced in error (instead of book 7), when referring to Vincent of Beauvais' *Speculum historiale.* Recent enquiry reveals, however, this was not in fact the case, and that book 8 is correct.
9 James & Tristram 1929, 19.
10 The depictions of this story in contemporary stained glass, sculpture and manuscript illuminations are numerous; see chapter 3 above; also Gill 2003, 188; and Glover 2007, 345.
11 See chapter 5 above on the paintings' physical history.
12 James transcribes this as: *Theophilus . christum . et . beatam . virginem abnegat…* (he notes that the rest of the inscription is missing, but that the source was probably the *Legenda sanctorum* 131, 9).

Figure IV | Evangelist or Church Father (lost)
This figure was obliterated by the insertion of stairs to the new organ loft; James suggests that the figure may have represented the Evangelist St Mark.[13]

Scene 4 | The Miracle of St John of Damascus and his hand (lost)
St John was a trusted confident of the Umayyad caliph in Damascus, but an enemy forged a treasonable letter to the court of Constantinople in his name, and he was condemned to have his right hand cut off and nailed up in the marketplace. It was restored to him by the Virgin. On the left of this scene, St John kneels with his right hand on a block, behind which another figure stands, with only their draperies visible. To the right, two robed figures stand facing one another, possibly in a depiction of the Virgin restoring St John's hand to him.[14]
INSCRIPTION: Dam[ascenus ....]ta. per. be[ata]m. v[irginem. ... ex]hibata. et: *v[incentius]. l[ibro 18°] c[apitul]o 103* [15]

Figure V | St Augustine or St John the Evangelist (lost)
The lower portion of a robed figure holding a scroll; the figure appears also to hold some kind of bowl and has a bird sitting at its feet. James identifies this figure as St Augustine, on the basis that the bird may be an eagle, the symbol of John the Evangelist, on whose works St Augustine commented.[16]

Scene 5 | The Miracle of the columns at Constantinople (lost)
A basilica dedicated to the Virgin was being built at Constantinople. To the architect's despair, the columns brought to adorn it were so heavy that they could not be raised. The Virgin appeared to him and told him to engage three schoolboys to help him and, as a result of their ingenuity, the columns were successfully lifted. On the left, the architect is represented in a gown tied at the waist with a girdle and with a cloak draped over his left shoulder. His hands are raised in wonder as he witnesses the boys, on the right, raising a heavy column with the aid of a windlass. The three boys are dressed in tunics, over which two of them wear gowns, and knee-high boots.[17] Their caps and a school satchel are strewn on the ground. It seems probable that the Virgin was depicted in the missing upper section of the scene.
INSCRIPTION: M[irac]ulo in l... summa elevitare (?) sublimate ... *lege[nda]. san[ctorum]* [18]

13 James & Tristram 1929, 20.
14 A similar scene, depicted in reverse, appears among a derivative series of Marian miracles commissioned by Prior Silkstede for the Lady Chapel at Winchester (*c.*1500); see James & Tristram 1929, especially 20-1.
15 James transcribes this as: *...dam(asceni) ... ta per beatam virginem ... Vinc.* (probable source: *Speculum historiale*, vii, 104-5; see n.8 above).
16 James & Tristram 1929, 18. The presence of this bird may equally allude to St Gregory, who was often depicted with a dove.
17 It is interesting to compare the costumes of these schoolboys with the similar attire of the scholars depicted in the painting of *c.*1520 in the Headmaster's Chambers; see Part II below.
18 James transcribes this as: *Qualiter* . ... *per beatam* <*virginem*> (probable source: *Speculum historiale*, vii, 81; see n.8 above).

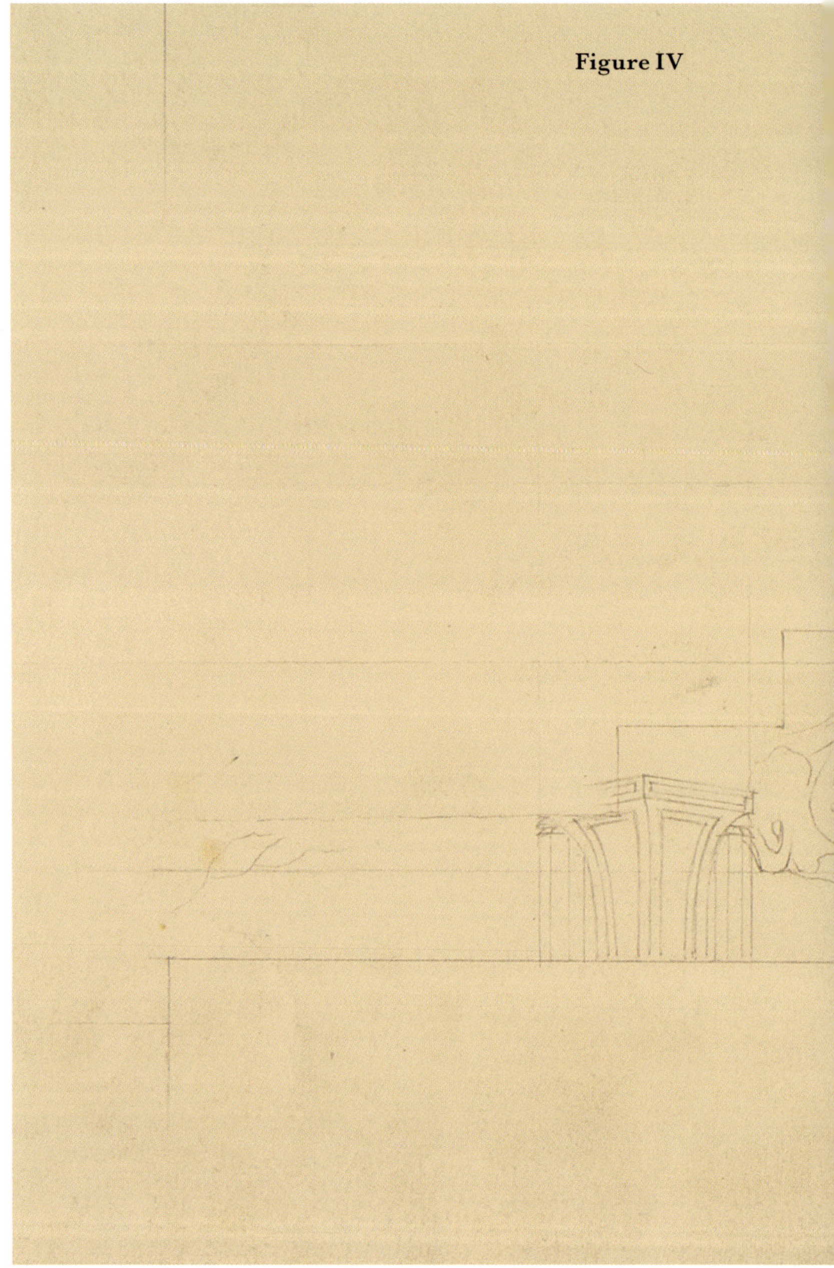
Figure IV

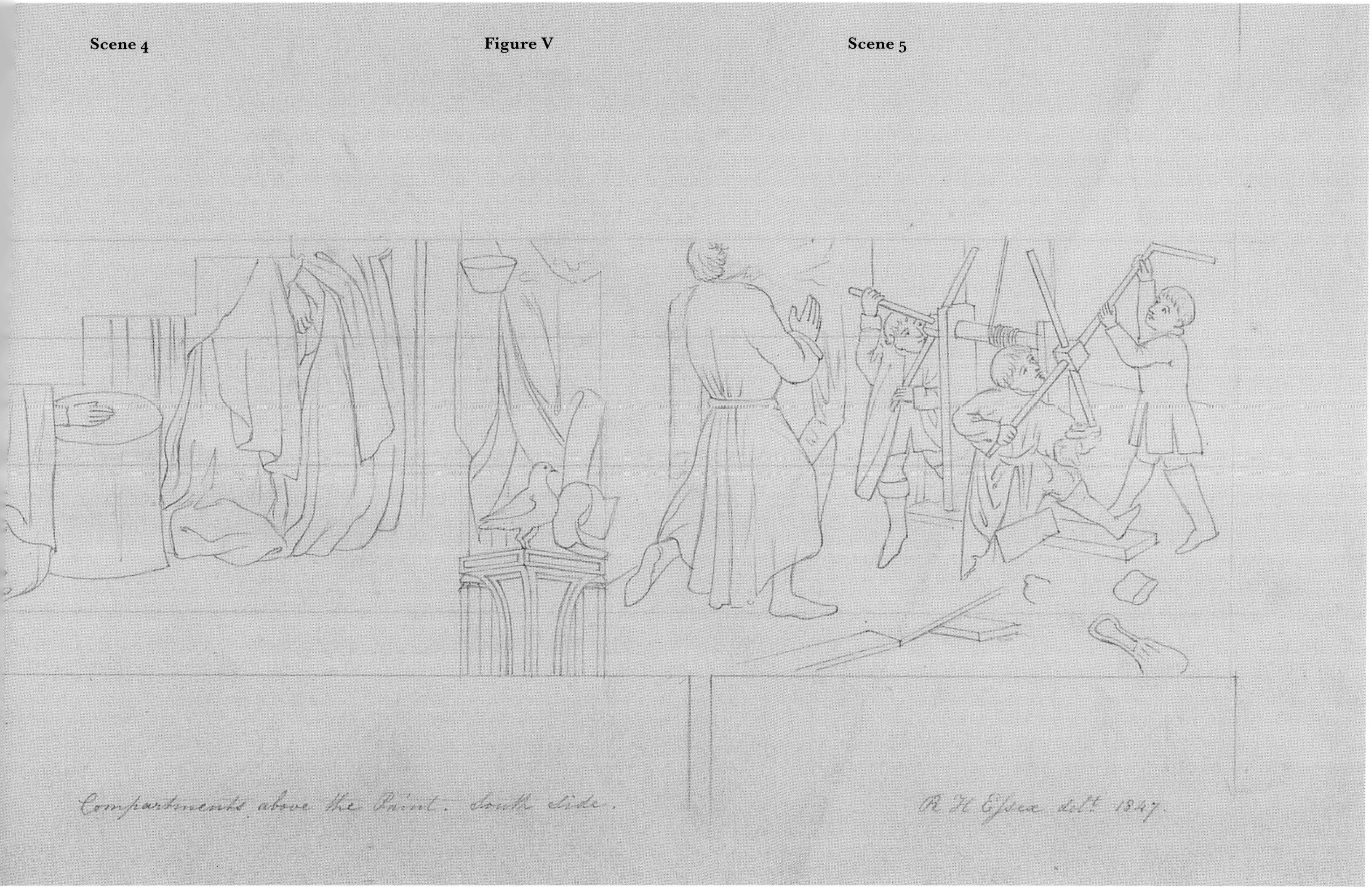
Scene 4
Figure V
Scene 5
Compartments above the Point. South Side.
R H Essex delt 1847.

Figure VI | St Jerome or St Matthew (lost)
The lower portion of a draped figure holding a scroll, with an angel kneeling at its feet; James identifies the figure as St Jerome, though the angel may equally allude to St Matthew, the Evangelist whose symbol this is.[19]

Scene 6 | The Miracle of the youth betrothed to the Virgin's image (lost)
A young man who was devoted to the Virgin placed his ring on the finger of a statue of the saint. When the youth later decided to marry, the statue reminded him that he was already betrothed, so he left his bride-to-be and became a monk.[20] On the left of the Eton scene is the base of a pedestal decorated with gothic tracery, upon which the statue presumably stood. To the right of this, two robed figures can be seen kneeling, possibly the youth and the girl he wishes to marry. He wears a girdle with a fashionable *gypcière* (or purse), and his over-gown has hanging sleeves. On the right of the scene, two figures face right, one holding a staff; this possibly depicts the youth becoming a monk.
INSCRIPTION: Qualiter. iuvenis. quida[m]. b[ea]te. v[ir]ginis. ymagine[m]. anulo. desponsavit. et. secus. renunciavit. *vinc[entius]. libro. 8°. c[apitul]o 87.* [21]

Figure VII | Evangelist or Church Father (lost)
The lower portion of a draped figure holding a scroll; identified by James as St Luke.[22]

Scene 7 | The Miracle of the Mass of St Bonnet (lost)
St Bonnet, Bishop of Clermont-Ferrand, remaining in his church after the services of the day, was surprised by the entry of the Virgin and a company of saints. The Virgin commanded him to celebrate Mass and presented him with a vestment, which was long preserved at Clermont. The lost scene at Eton, as recorded by Essex, depicts two moments from this episode. On the left, the bishop stands on the plinth of an altar in the act of celebrating Mass. On the right, a figure swathed in draperies (St Bonnet?) seems to receive the vestment from the Virgin (James suggests she might have been depicted above, appearing to him in the air).
INSCRIPTION: Qualiter. b[ea]ta. v[ir]go. s[an]c[t]o. Bonito. Al[ver]ne[n]si. ep[iscop]o. post. missar[um]. solemnia. veste[m]. celeste[m]. tradiderat. *vinc[entius]. li[br]o. 8. ca[pitulo] 97.* [23]

Figure VIII | St Jerome or St Mark (?)
One of only two standing saints to have survived from the upper register of the painting scheme, this figure appears to be dressed in monastic robes. Holding a scroll and a staff, it may well represent St Jerome. The couched lion, which is visible at his feet here in Essex's drawing but is barely discernible on the wall itself (see p.101), may refer to the saint's time in the wilderness, in the course of which he is reputed to have removed a thorn from the paw of a lion. James was inclined to identify this figure as St Gregory, but there is now no sign of the mutilated tiara upon which he based this identification.[24] The lion is, of course, also the symbol of the Evangelist St Mark.

19 James & Tristram 1929, 18, 21; this is based on the argument that St Jerome commented on the writings of St Matthew.
20 This miracle story, derived from the *Speculum historiale*, is thought to be a Christianised form of the legend told by William of Malmesbury (*Gesta regum*, ii, 205) in which a youth who puts his ring on the finger of a statue of Venus is haunted by the goddess, until he is freed from the contract by a wizard.
21 James transcribes this as: *Qualiter . imaginem . quidam . beate . virgins . annulo . desponsauit . et . <mundo> . renunciavit . Vinc. li° . 8° . ca° . 87°.*
22 James & Tristram 1929, 22.
23 James transcribes this as: *Qualiter . beata . virgo . sancto . Bonito . alvernensi . episcopo . post-missarum . solemnia . vestem . celestem . tradiderat (? – it) . Vinc. li° . 8° . ca° . 97°*
24 James & Tristram 1929, 18, 22.

Figure VI

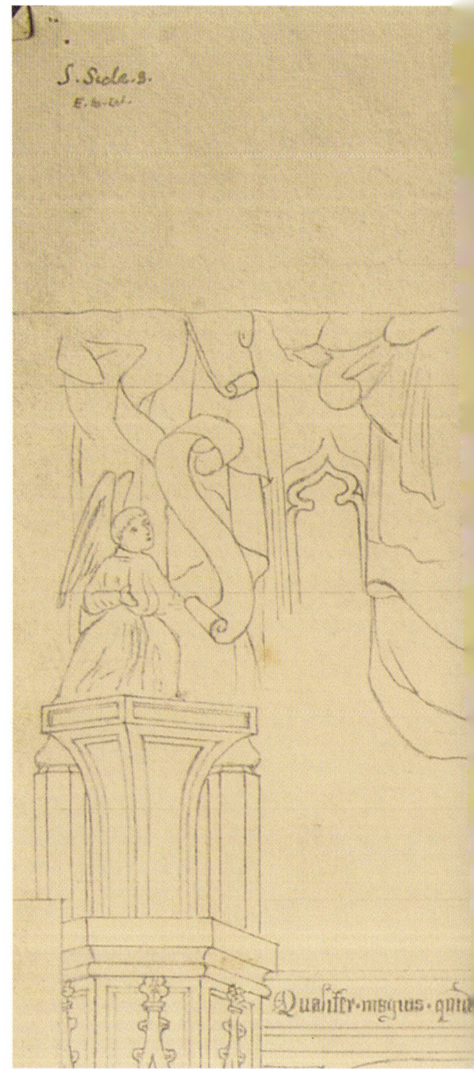

Scene 6 **Figure VII** **Scene 7** **Figure VIII**

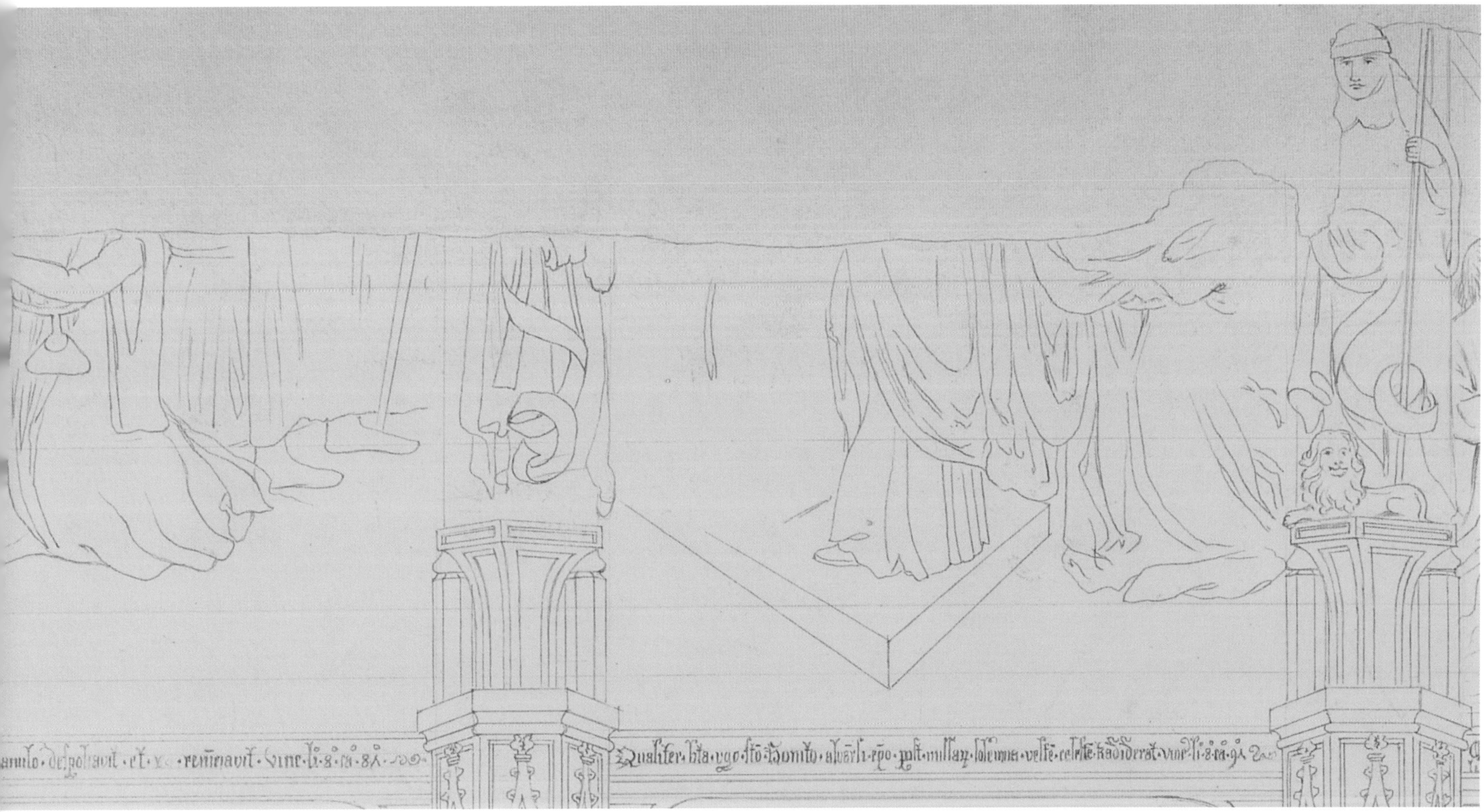

Figure VIII | St Jerome or St Mark (?)
One of only two standing saints to have survived from the upper register of the painting scheme, this figure appears to be dressed in monastic robes. Holding a scroll and a staff, it may well represent St Jerome. The couched lion, which is visible at his feet in Essex's drawing (see p.99) but is no longer discernible here, may make reference to the saint's time in the wilderness, in the course of which he is reputed to have removed a thorn from the paw of a lion. James was inclined to identify this figure as St Gregory, but there is now no sign of the mutilated tiara upon which he based this identification.[25] The lion is, of course, also the symbol of the Evangelist St Mark.

Scene 8 | The Miracle of the Jew of Bourges
The only miracle scene to survive from the upper register, and perhaps the most famous of the Virgin miracles after that of Theophilus, this episode is widely reproduced in late medieval works of art. The story recounts how a Jewish boy, attending church at Easter with his Christian friends, was overwhelmed by the beauty of the liturgy and partook of communion. His father, disgusted, cast him into an oven, but the boy was protected by the Virgin and survived unscathed. While the boy converted to Christianity, his father was in turn cast into the oven and perished. On the left of the Eton scene, a priest administers the Eucharist to four youths kneeling before an altar. On the right-hand side, the Virgin (whose face has been obliterated) reaches out to the boy, visible through the oven door.

INSCRIPTION: Qualiter. cuiusda[m]. Jud[e]i. fili[us]. cu[m]. xp[ist]ianis. co[mm] uni[on]e[m]. recipie[n]s. a. crudeli. p[at]re. i[n]. furnace[m]. inectus. a b[ea]tam. v[ir]gi[n] e[m]. ab. incendio. [con]servatur. *lege[n]da. s[anc]to[rum]* [26]

Figure IX | St Gregory (?)
Dressed in what would appear to be the regalia of a bishop, this figure, which is preserved in its entirety, most probably depicts St Gregory. While the figure wears a mitre and holds a crozier in his right hand, his splendid white gown, trimmed with sumptuous golden brocade, is much longer than the cope usually worn by bishops, and probably represents the papal mantum. In his left hand he seems to hold a small red book. James, working from Essex's drawings, interpreted this figure as St John, but there seems to be little substantiation for this supposition.[27]

25 James & Tristram 1929, 18, 22.
26 James transcribes this as: *Qualiter . cuiusdam . Judei . filius . cum . christianis . communionem . accipiens . a . crudeli . patre . in . fornacem . projicitus . per . beatam virginem . ab . (incendio . liberator) (l.2), legenda . sanctorum .* (probable source: *Legenda sanctorum*, 119, 5).
27 James & Tristram 1929, 23.

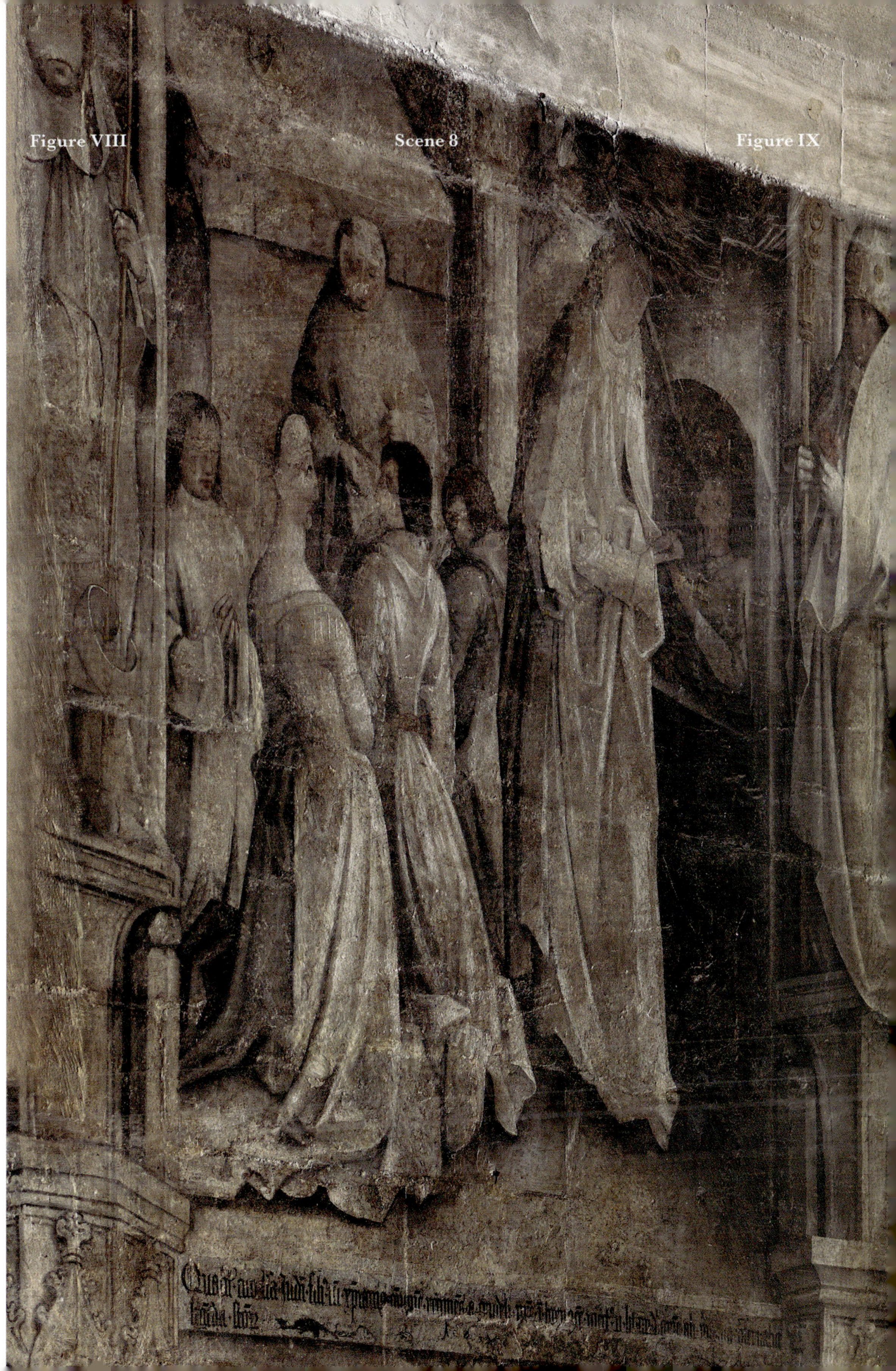
Figure VIII
Scene 8
Figure IX

South wall, lower register

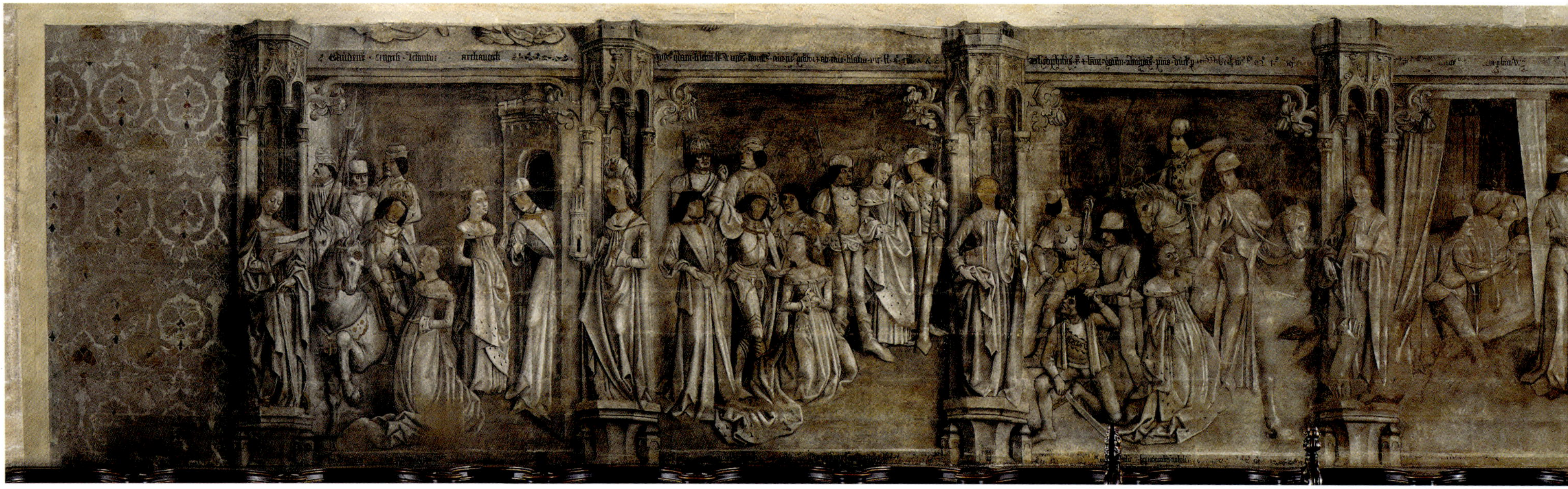

Scenes 1-8 | The Legend of the Empress falsely accused
All eight scenes of the lower register on the south wall are dedicated to the legend of 'The Empress falsely accused', as recounted by Vincent of Beauvais in his *Speculum historiale* (vii, 90-92).[28] The legend, in which the Virgin comes to the aid of the much maligned Empress, is eloquently summarised by James and it is useful to reproduce his account here.[29]

An Emperor of Rome going on pilgrimage committed his realm to the care of his chaste and beautiful wife, and in particular commended to her his younger brother. After the Emperor's departure, the brother tried to persuade the Empress, of whom he was passionately enamoured, to be unfaithful to her husband. She indignantly refused, and imprisoned him in a tower. After five years the Emperor returned. The brother entreated to be released before his arrival, and the Empress yielded. Immediately on the return of the Emperor, the brother accused the Empress of infidelity and treason. The enraged husband smote her on the face when she came to greet him, and bade his guards take her into the forest and slay her there.

When they were on the point of killing her, a noble knight with his train came by and rescued her, and took her to his castle, in ignorance of her rank, which she continued to keep secret. She took service as nurse to the king's infant son. Here again she was persecuted by the addresses of the knight's brother, whom she repulsed. He plotted her ruin, stole into her chamber at night, cut the throat of his nephew, and left the bloody knife in the hand of the sleeping Empress. When the murder was discovered, her guilt seemed clear, and the wicked brother urged that she should be put to death; but the merciful knight decided to spare her, and put her on board of an outgoing ship. Here again her beauty tempted the captain and sailors to offer her violence. Eventually they marooned her on a rocky islet. Here, as she slept, the Virgin appeared to her and told her that her troubles were nearing their end, and showed her a herb that grew in profusion on the island, the juice of which would cure leprosy. She gathered a store of it, and next day was taken off the rock by a passing ship. When she reached the mainland she proclaimed herself able to cure lepers, and the fame of her spread far and wide. Nowhere was she recognised for what she was.

After a time she came to the castle of the knight who had befriended her, and found that his wicked brother had become a leper. She was asked to heal him, and consented to do so if he would confess all his misdeeds. She warned him that nothing short of complete confession would allow the herb to operate. His brother, the knight, also urged him to confess even any offence against himself, promising him free pardon. Hereupon he made full confession of his conspiracy against the nurse and murder of the child, and was healed. Still unrecognised, the Empress eventually reached Rome, and here again the Emperor's brother, the fountain-head of all the trouble, had

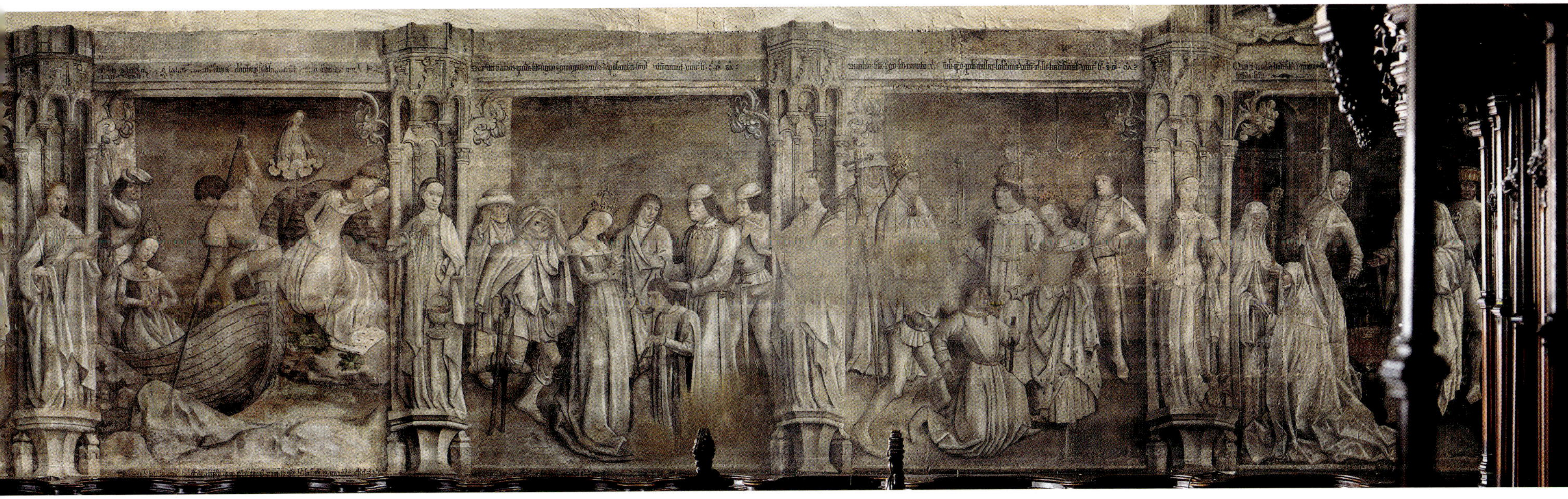

contracted leprosy. The Empress said that if he was to be healed, it must be done upon full confession, and in the presence of the Pope and Cardinals. There was again hesitation, followed at last by an avowal. The Empress then revealed her identity, but refused to return to her former life. She had vowed, in the time of her trouble, perpetual chastity; so she took the veil and entered a religious house.

As in the upper register, these eight lower scenes are interspersed by nine standing figures, this time all female saints, many of whom were martyrs.

28 The legend, which appears frequently in medieval literature, does not appear to have enjoyed similar popularity in art, the only other contemporary cycle being that depicted in the roof bosses of the Bauchun Chapel in Norwich Cathedral (see James 1907), a scheme commissioned by William Eckyngton and dating to *c.*1460-75.
29 James & Tristram 1929, 23-4.

Figure I | St Catherine
St Catherine, patron saint of learning and object of Henry VI's special devotion, is depicted crowned. She holds an open book in her right hand and supports a down-turned sword with her left. A small section of the wheel of her martyrdom is visible to the right of her feet.

Scene 1 | The Emperor's departure; his brother is imprisoned
The crowned figure of the Emperor, clad in armour and mounted on a white horse, takes the hand of the kneeling Empress as he bids her farewell. She is also crowned and wears a robe of ermine. Behind the Emperor are two mounted attendants and a third servant dressed in a turban. On the right of the scene the Empress is shown incarcerating in a tower her lecherous brother-in-law, who sports a fashionable long gown and cap. Note that the faces of all three figures seem to have been deliberately damaged. INSCRIPTION: hic. D[e]votus. [impera]tor. peregrinaturus. uxo[…..] [30]

Figure II | St Barbara
St Barbara, wearing a turban headdress of a style that became fashionable after the fall of Constantinople to the Turks in 1453,[31] holds a palm and a two-storeyed polygonal tower, representing the tower in which she was incarcerated by her father. Her face, like those of the Emperor and Empress, has been obliterated.

30 James transcribes this as: *hic . devotus . imperator . peregrinaturus . vxori . <sue valedicit . Vinc . li . 8°. ca° . 92°>*
31 Norris 1999, 444.

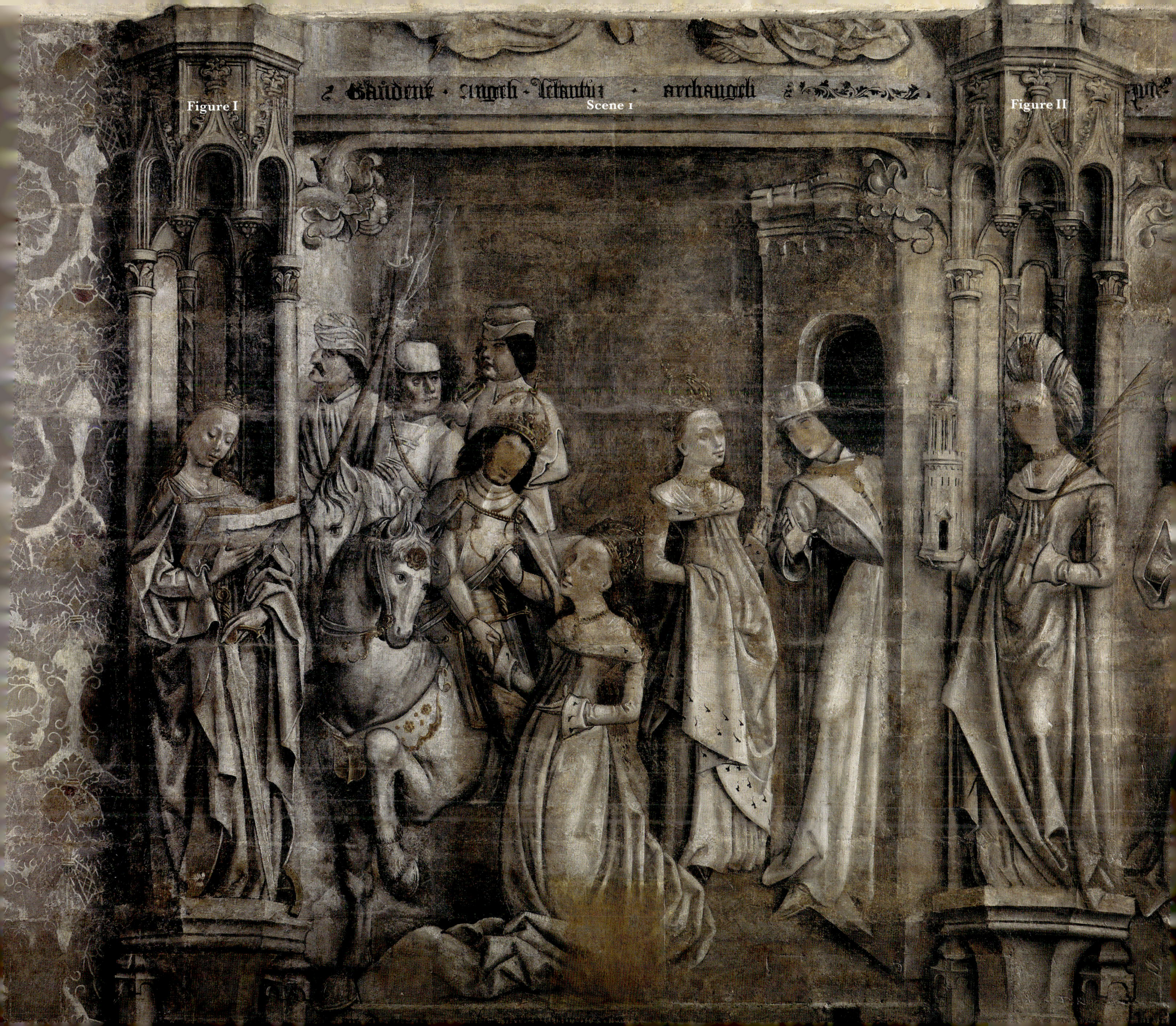
Figure I
Scene 1
Figure II

Figure II | St Barbara
St Barbara, wearing a turban headdress of a style that became fashionable after the fall of Constantinople to the Turks in 1453,[32] holds a palm and a two-storeyed polygonal tower, representing the tower in which she was incarcerated by her father. Her face, like those of the Emperor and Empress, has been obliterated.

Scene 2 | The Empress is accused of infidelity and banished
Flanked on the left by his brother, the Emperor (centre) raises his clenched right fist, ready to strike the kneeling Empress. Behind this group stand three attendants; the one behind the Empress raises his hand as if to remonstrate. Again, the faces of all the key players have been deliberately disfigured. On the right-hand side of the scene, the weeping Empress is led away between two guards holding javelins. The guard on the left wears a tunic decorated with scallops, the other sports a cross-belt emblazoned with the letters 'AMALE'.
INSCRIPTION: hic. rediens. [imperato]r. accusatu[m]. falso. sibi. u[xori. ju]bet. [in si]lva[m]. deduci. et. decaptitari. *vince[n]tius. li[bro]. 8°. ca[pitulo 90]* [33]

Figure III | St Apollonia
St Apollonia, her long hair bound in a fillet, is depicted holding a closed book under her right arm and a pair of tongs containing a tooth in her left. According to the *Golden Legend*, the saint was one of a group of virgin martyrs attacked in Alexandria during a local uprising against the Christians; her torture included having all of her teeth violently pulled out.

32 Norris 1999, 444.
33 James transcribes this as: *hic . rediens. Imperator . accusatam. Falso . sibi . vxorem . jubet . in . silvam . deduci . et . decapitari . Vincentius . li . 8° . cap*

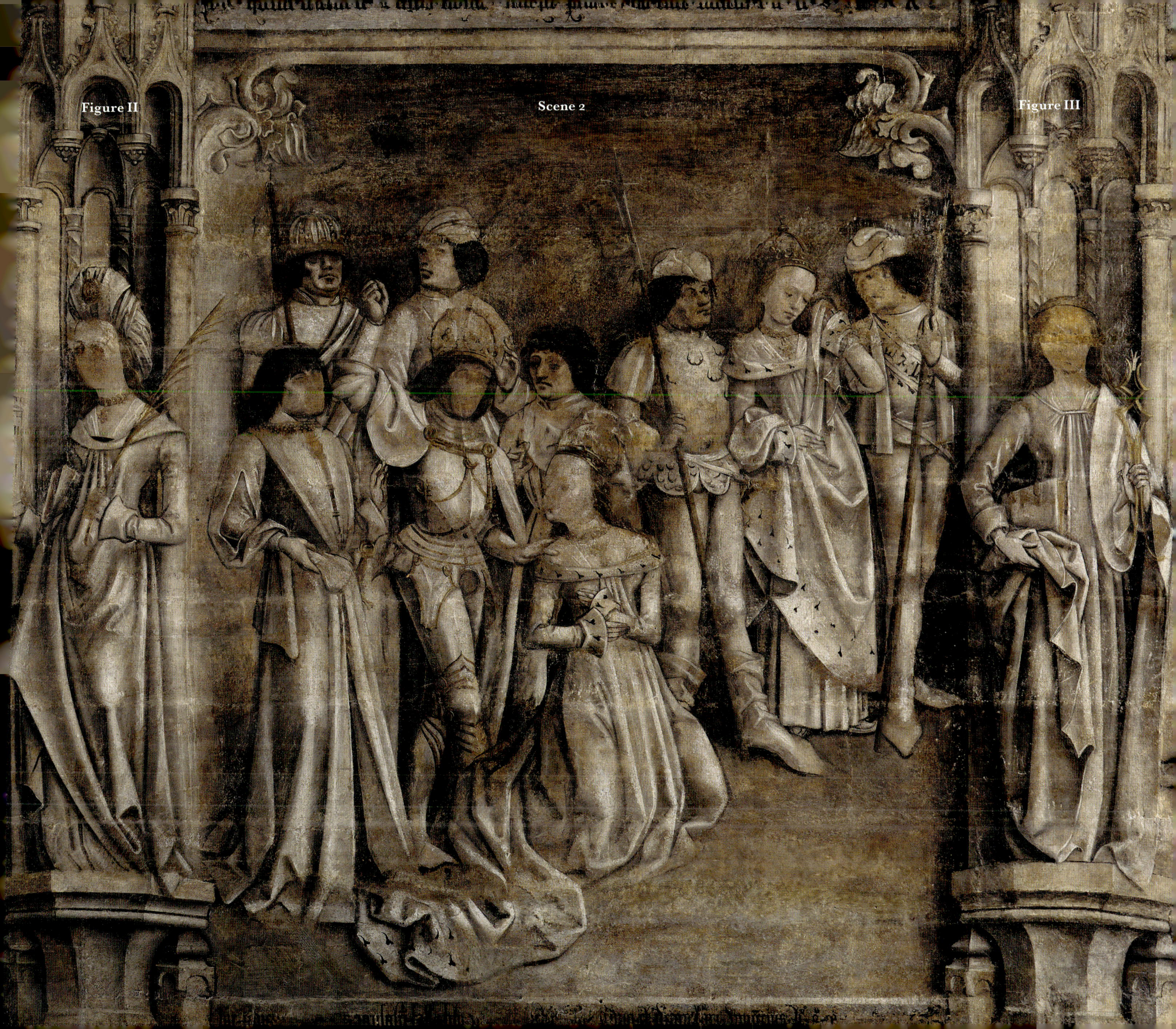
Figure II
Scene 2
Figure III

Figure III | St Apollonia
St Apollonia, her long hair bound in a fillet, is depicted holding a closed book under her right arm and a pair of tongs containing a tooth in her left. According to the *Golden Legend*, the saint was one of a group of virgin martyrs attacked in Alexandria during a local uprising against the Christians; her torture included having all of her teeth violently pulled out.

Scene 3 | The Empress is rescued by a knight
On the left the guard with the cross-belt, kneeling, is about to be stabbed by one of the knight's attendants. Above, his accomplice in the scalloped tunic comes under attack from a man on horseback (centre), armed with a bow. Below him, the Empress, kneeling towards the right, takes the hand of the mounted knight.
INSCRIPTION: [....] liberatur. a. sup[er]vienientes. nobiles ... *V[incentius. libr]o. 8º. ca[pitulo] 90* [34]

Figure IV | St Agnes
This saint was badly obscured at the time James was writing, and he suggested that it might have been St Agatha.[35] More recent scholarship in the light of the figure's much improved appearance suggests, however, that she is in fact St Agnes, the younger sister of St Clare of Assisi and abbess of the Poor Ladies at Assisi. The saint is identified by the ring of Christ she holds between her right thumb and forefinger, the book she holds in her left hand and the lamb that jumps up at her knees.[36]

34 James transcribes this as: ... *hic* .... *supervenientes . nobiles* . ...
35 James & Tristram 1929, 25.
36 Anderson 1989, 23.

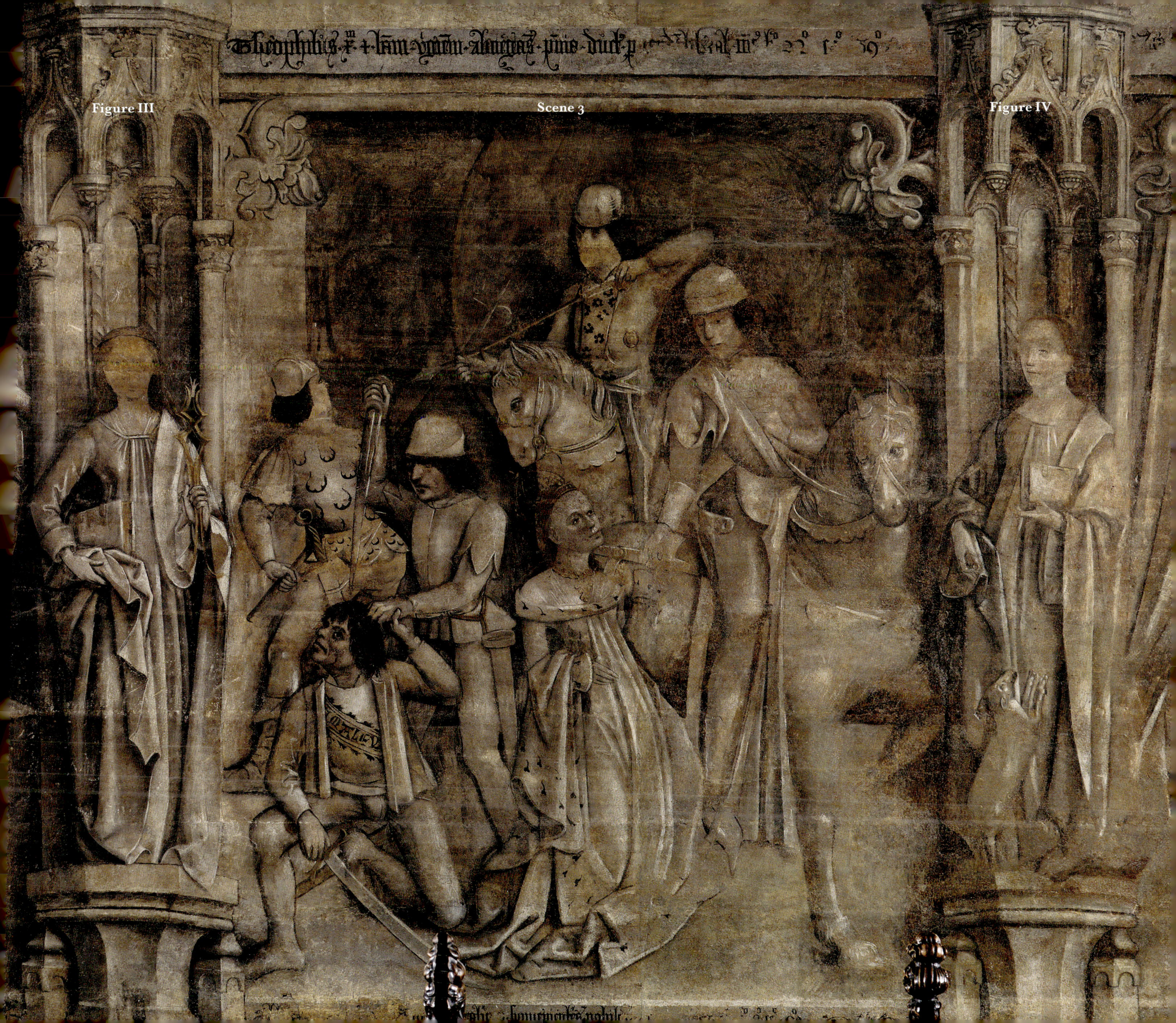
Figure III
Scene 3
Figure IV

Figure IV | St Agnes

This saint was badly obscured at the time James was writing, and he suggested that it might have been St Agatha.[37] More recent scholarship in the light of the figure's much improved appearance suggests, however, that she is in fact St Agnes, the younger sister of St Clare of Assisi and abbess of the Poor Ladies at Assisi. The saint is identified by the ring of Christ she holds between her right thumb and forefinger, the book she holds in her left hand and the lamb that jumps up at her knees.[38]

Scene 4 | The Empress is accused of infanticide and banished

This scene was completely obscured when Essex was making his copies, and only faintly visible to James in the 1920s. On the left side of the scene, the Empress lies asleep in her curtained bed, while the knight's brother slits the throat of the child sleeping at her side. On the right the knight, dressed in a long gown tied with a girdle bearing a purse, and wearing a fine collar, confronts the Empress, who is led away between two guards wearing moustaches and turbans.

INSCRIPTION: [lost] [39]

Figure V | St Ursula

St Ursula, crowned, stands holding an open book in her left hand and an arrow, the instrument of her martyrdom, in her right.

37 James & Tristram 1929, 25.
38 Anderson 1989, 23.
39 Not transcribed by James.

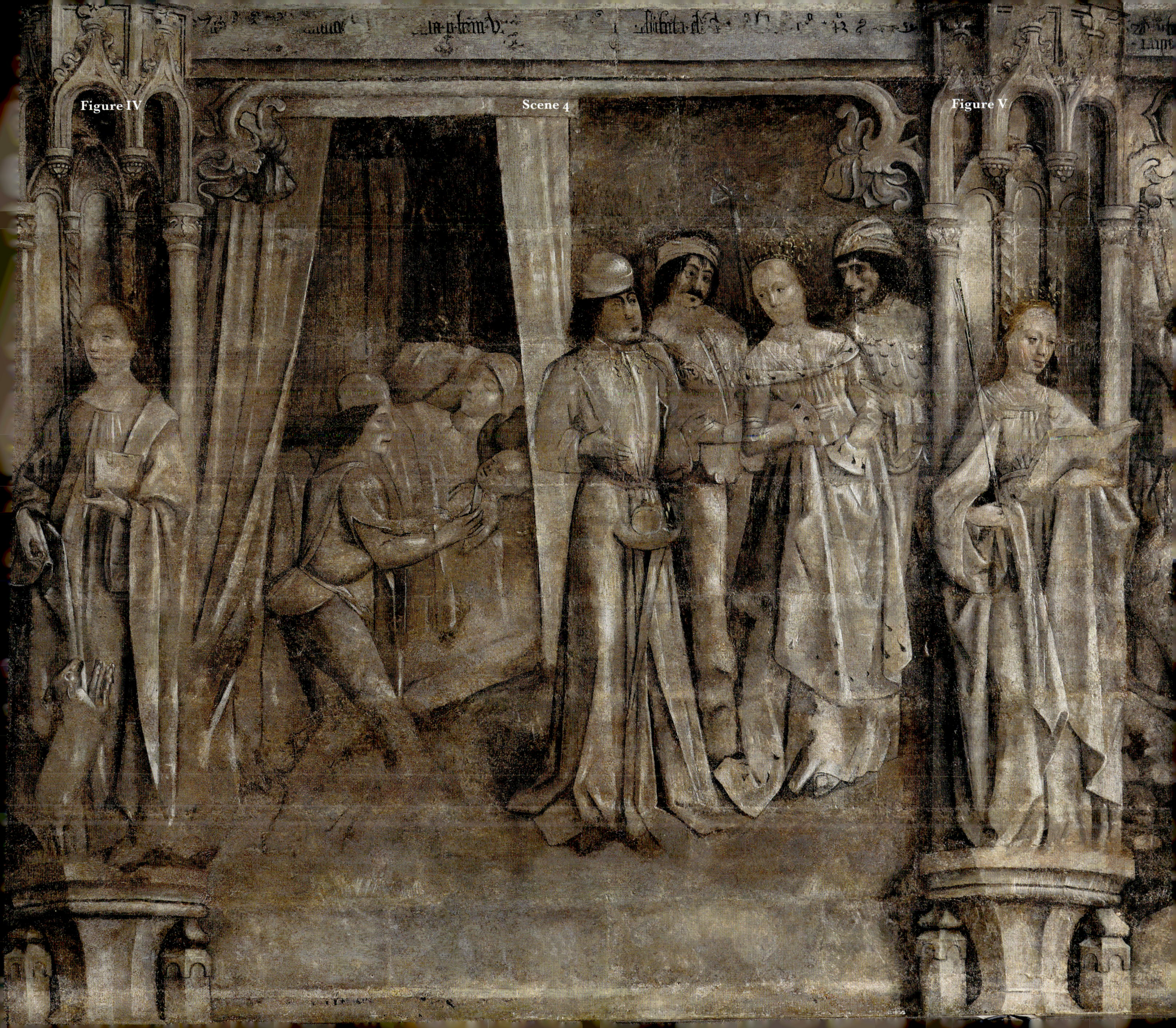
Figure IV
Scene 4
Figure V

Figure V | St Ursula
St Ursula, crowned, stands holding an open book in her left hand and an arrow, the instrument of her martyrdom, in her right.

Scene 5 | The Empress sees the Virgin in a vision
Obscured in 1848 when Essex was making his copies, only the right-hand side of this scene was visible to James in the 1920s. On the left, the crowned Empress kneels in a small wooden boat which is being steered, at either end, by two men wielding long oars. On the right, the Empress is shown asleep on a small rocky island. The Virgin, depicted in miniature as if floating on a cloud, appears to the Empress in a dream. Clumps of the miraculous green herb grow in the foreground.
INSCRIPTION: [...............] *v[in]c[entius. libr]o. 8°. ca[pitulo 90]*[40]

Figure VI | St Dorothy
St Dorothy (Dorothea) of Caesarea, another virgin martyr, is depicted holding a basket of red flowers in her left hand and a single flower in her right. The flowers refer to the legend of her martyrdom, in which an angel delivered a basket of fruit and flowers to one of her persecutors after she was beheaded.

40 Not transcribed by James.

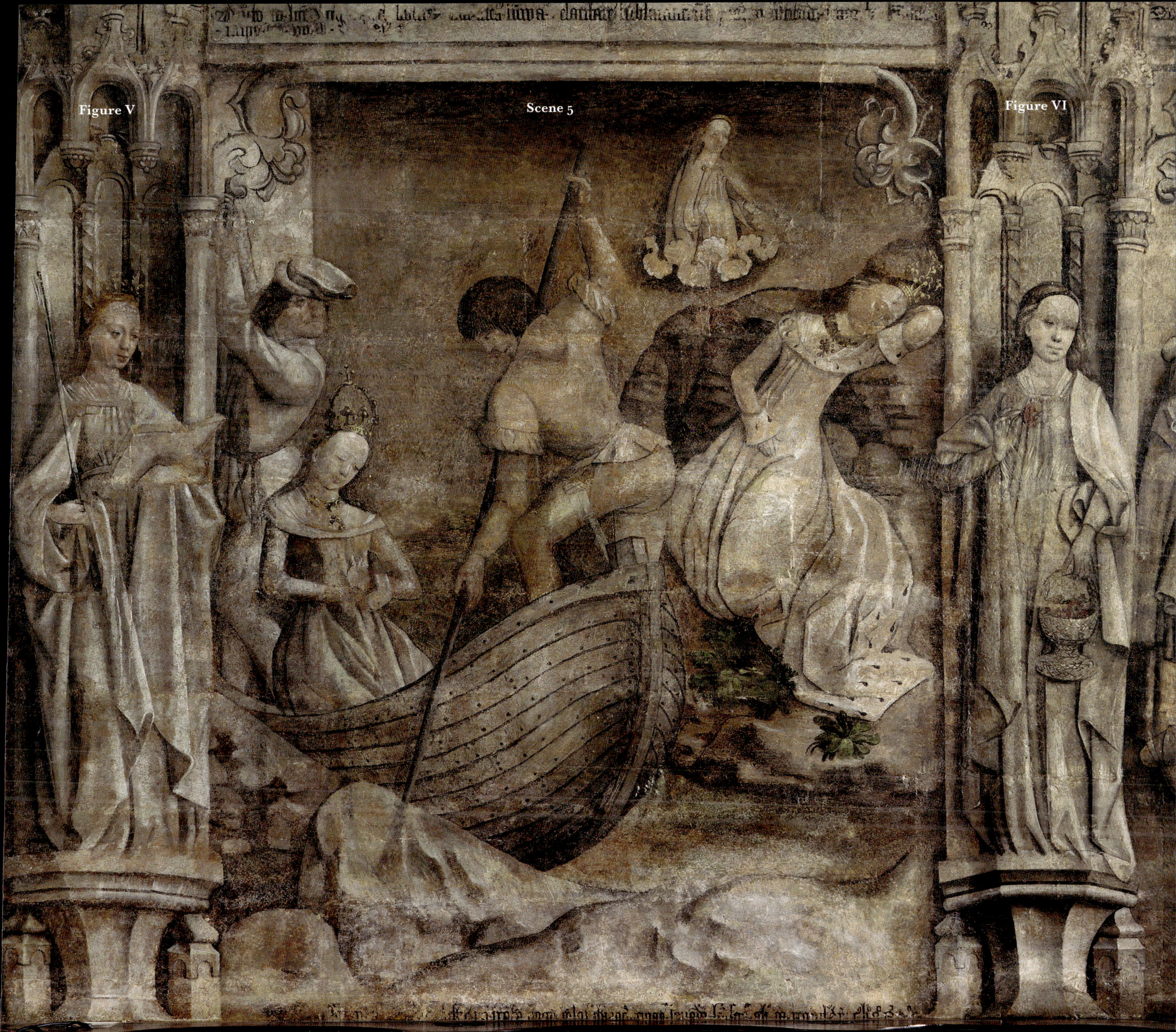
Figure V
Scene 5
Figure VI

Figure VI | St Dorothy
St Dorothy (Dorothea) of Caesarea, another virgin martyr, is depicted holding a basket of red flowers in her left hand and a single flower in her right. The flowers refer to the legend of her martyrdom, in which an angel delivered a basket of fruit and flowers to one of her persecutors after she was beheaded.

Scene 6 | The Empress heals the knight's brother
On the left two lepers approach the Empress, the foremost supporting his right leg on a crutch as he motions to remove his cap. To the right of them, the Empress administers the miraculous herb to the knight's kneeling brother. The knight, dressed as before, faces the Empress and lays a hand on his brother's head. He is flanked on either side by two armed attendants. The masonry in the lower right-hand corner of the scene has been replaced, perhaps following the removal of a memorial tablet that had previously been inserted in the wall.
INSCRIPTION: [..........] sui. filium. [......] [41]

Figure VII | St Cecilia
For a long while the identity of this saint proved elusive. Essex's original drawing showed her wearing what James describes as 'a striped close cap', with a palm in her left hand and a closed book in her right. James's rationale for identifying the figure as St Lucy is not, however, clear.[42] Indeed, subsequent examination of the paintings themselves led James to conclude that the presence of the book was doubtful.[43] Recent scholarship proposes that this badly obliterated figure might, in fact, represent the virgin martyr St Cecilia. Anderson suggests that the striped band which encircles the saint's head is not part of a cap, since her hair is visible at the crown, and might instead be a stylised representation of the floral garland given to Cecilia and her martyred husband, Valerian, by an angel.[44] Comparison with a near contemporary depiction of the saint on the rood screen in St Mary's church at North Elmham, Norfolk, suggests that she may have held a second wreath in her right hand.[45]

41 James transcribes as: ... *Vincent . li° . 8° . cap*
42 James 1907, 12.
43 James & Tristram 1929, 25.
44 See Anderson 1989, 25.
45 For which see Duffy 1992, 171 and pl.68.

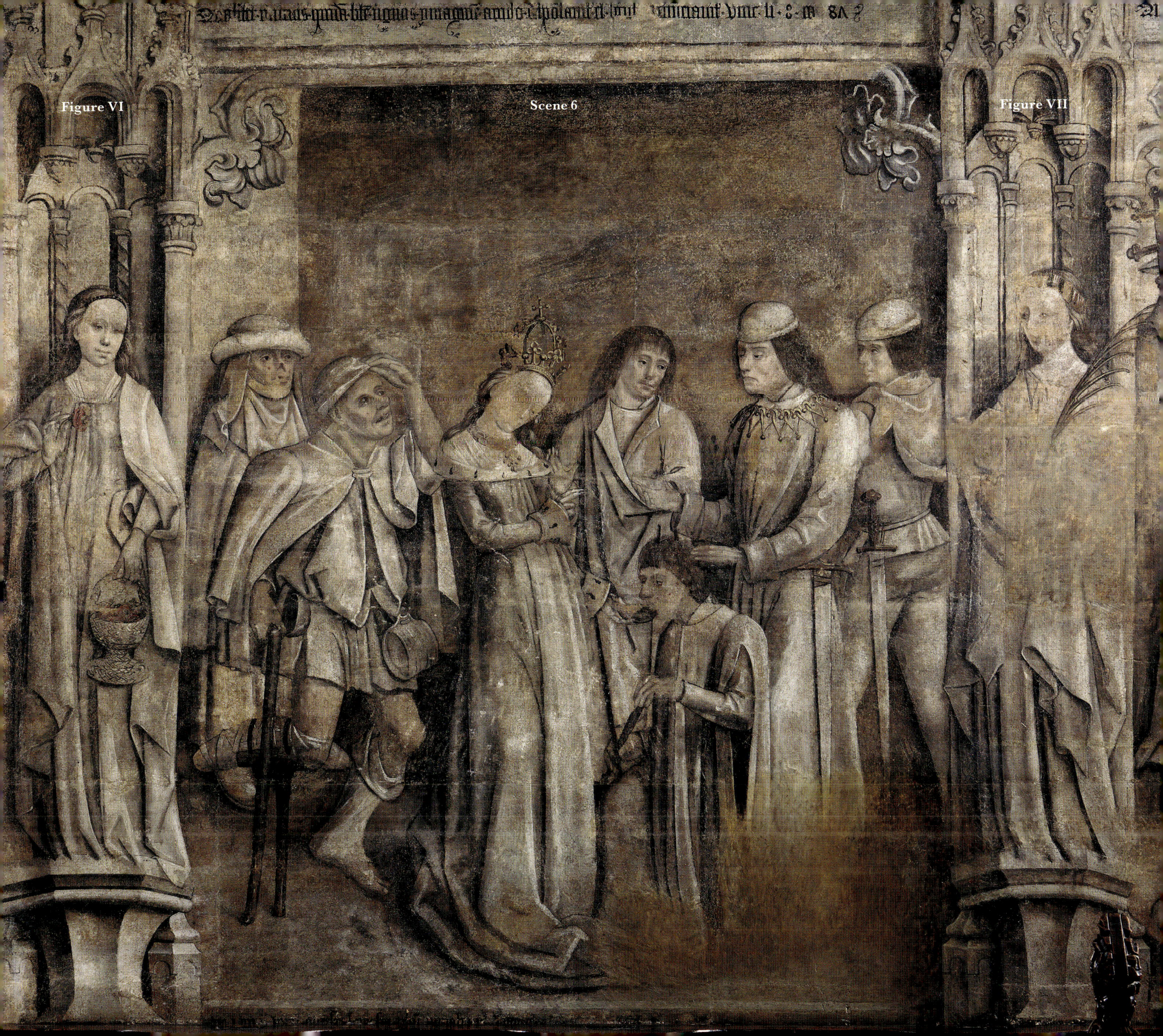
Figure VI
Scene 6
Figure VII

Figure VII | St Cecilia
For a long while the identity of this saint proved elusive. Essex's original drawing showed her wearing what James describes as 'a striped close cap', with a palm in her left hand and a closed book in her right. James's rationale for identifying the figure as St Lucy is not, however, clear.[46] Indeed, subsequent examination of the paintings themselves led James to conclude that the presence of the book was doubtful.[47] Recent scholarship proposes that this badly obliterated figure might, in fact, represent the virgin martyr St Cecilia. Anderson suggests that the striped band which encircles the saint's head is not part of a cap, since her hair is visible at the crown, and might instead be a stylised representation of the floral garland given to Cecilia and her martyred husband, Valerian, by an angel.[48] Comparison with a near contemporary depiction of the saint on the rood screen in St Mary's church in North Elmham, Norfolk, suggests that she may have held a second wreath in her right hand.[49]

Scene 7 | The Empress heals her brother-in-law
On the left a cardinal, identified by his broad hat, holds the pope's double-crossed staff. To the right of him stands the pope, in tiara and cope. In front of the pope is a squire, the upper half of the figure obliterated, who supports from behind the Emperor's brother. The latter kneels, centre, clutching a staff, and drinks from the glass dish proffered by the Empress, to the right. To the left of her the Emperor, holding a sceptre, observes the scene. A page, armed with a sword, stands on the far right.
INSCRIPTION: Hic. [imp] erator. [….]us. reconciliatio[n] em. intime. [..]antat. […] Deinde. […]. fratre[m]. suu[m]. […] [50]

Figure VIII | St Juliana
The fourth-century martyr St Juliana, dressed in a close-fitting ermine bodice, holds a chain in her left hand, to which is attached the small winged devil at her feet. It has been suggested that she holds a book in her left hand, but this area is badly effaced.[51]

46 James 1907, 12.
47 James & Tristram 1929, 25.
48 See Anderson 1989, 25.
49 For which see Duffy 1992, 171 and pl.68.
50 James transcribes this as: *hic . imperator . ipsam . (imperatricem?) <falso . accusatam> . agnoscit . et . reconciliacionem . intime . exoptat . postquam . viderit . fratrem . suum . scelus . suum . confessum . esse . vinc . li° . 8° . ca° . 9° .*
51 James & Tristram 1929, 26.

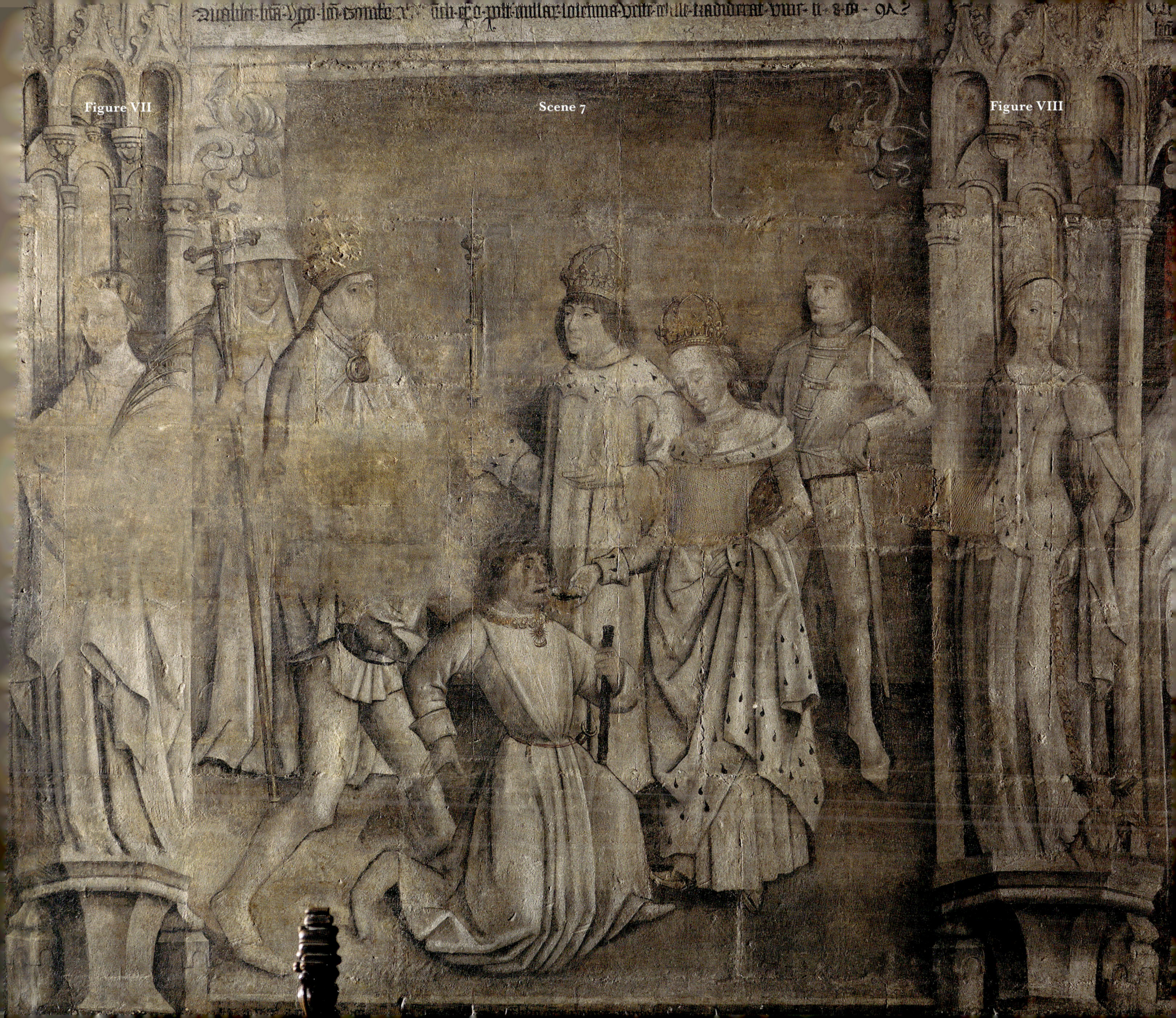
Figure VII
Scene 7
Figure VIII

Figure VIII | St Juliana
The fourth-century martyr St Juliana, dressed in a close-fitting ermine bodice, holds a chain in her left hand, to which is attached the small winged devil at her feet. It has been suggested that she holds a book in her left hand, but this area is badly effaced.[52]

Scene 8 | The Empress takes the veil
This is the concluding scene of the Empress legend. On the left of the scene, in a curtained doorway, stands an abbess holding a crozier; she touches hands with the Empress, who kneels before her, dressed in an identical white habit. The nun standing behind the Empress was identified by James as an observer,[53] yet the way in which she turns back to glance at the Emperor and points down to the crown, abandoned on a cushion, would seem to indicate that this figure is in fact the Empress herself, renouncing the world. To the right of the cushion stands the entreating Emperor, the sceptre of his worldly office in his hand. He is supported behind by a page wearing an unusually ornate cap, girt with a sword and bearing what would appear to be a large circular shield.
INSCRIPTION: hic [.........] [54]

Figure IX | St Winifred
Originally identified by James as St Agnes,[55] this last of the female saints on the south wall is now widely accepted as the Welsh noblewoman St Winifred. Holding a sword in her right hand and cradling the blade in her left with her skirts, she displays a fine red incision around her neck, showing where her head was severed and miraculously restored. It is appropriate to the legend of the Empress that Winifred was also associated with curing leprosy.[56]

52 James & Tristram 1929, 26.
53 James & Tristram 1929, 26.
54 James transcribes this as: *hic . eadem . imperatrix . marito . suo . et . mundo . renuncians . monachali . veste . velata . castitatem . servare . deo . et . beate . virgini . decernit . vinc . li° . 8° . ca. 90°*
55 James 1907, 12.
56 See Anderson 1989, 26 and n.29, which cites an eighteenth-century account of the miraculous cure of ‘the blind, lepers and other diseased persons’ who partook of the waters of St Winifred’s holy well.

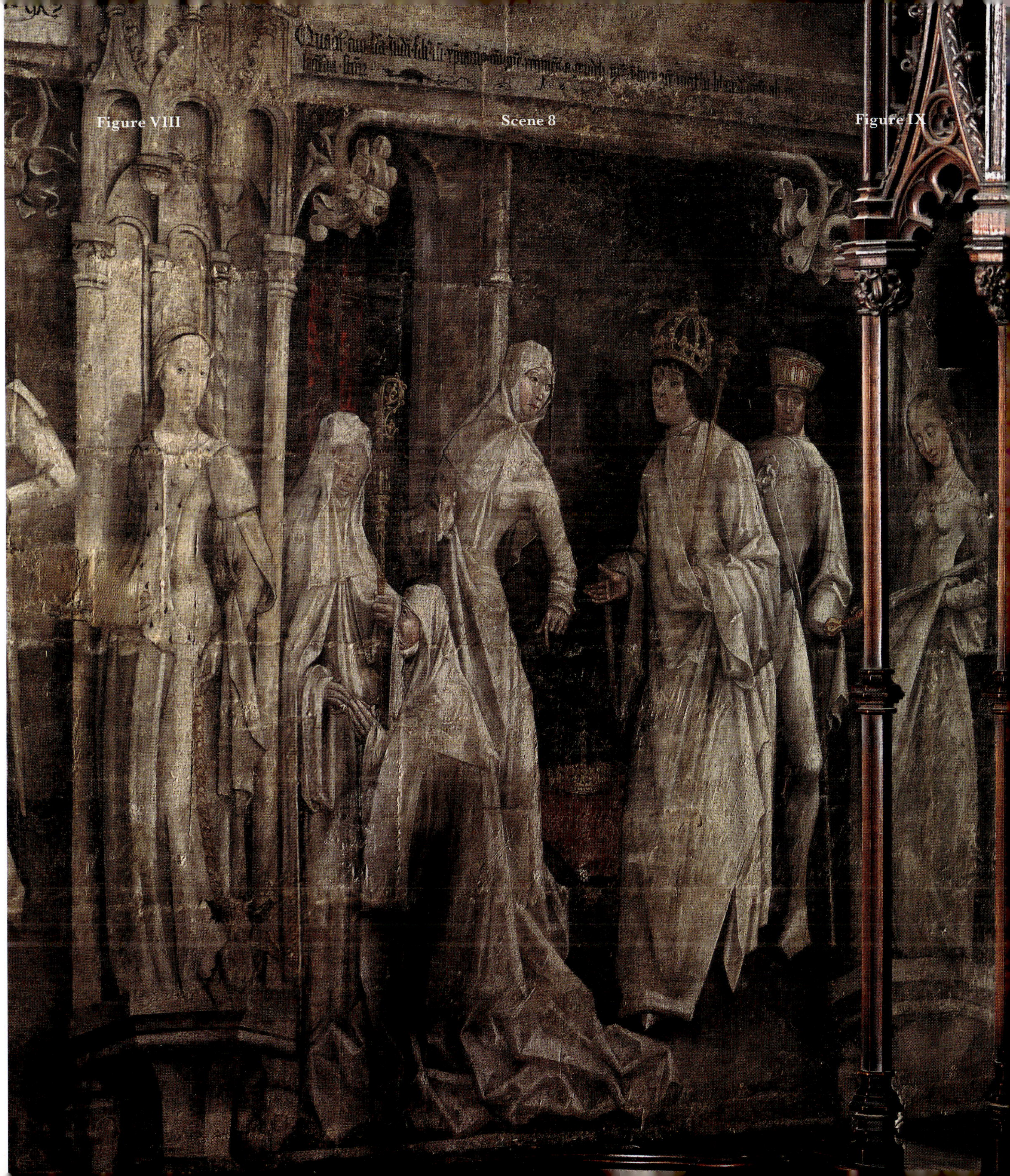
Figure VIII
Scene 8
Figure IX

North wall, upper register

The upper register is entirely lost, and known only from the drawings made by Essex.

Figure I | The Virgin (lost)
No trace of this figure remained by the time Essex came to make his copies of the paintings. It is supposed by James to have been the figure of the Virgin of the Annunciation, with the announcing Gabriel occupying the corresponding location on the south wall.[57]

Scene 1 | The Miracle of Ebbo the thief (?) (lost)
This scene was also completely obliterated before Essex was able to record it. Some vestiges of the inscription suggest it may have depicted the story of Ebbo the thief, as recounted by Vincent of Beauvais in his *Speculum historiale* (vi, 116).[58] When Ebbo, who was devoted to the Virgin, was captured and hanged, the Virgin is reputed to have supported him alive on the gallows for many days before he was eventually set free.
INSCRIPTION: [...............] *vinc[entius]. li[br]o. 8°. ii. 6.* [59]

Figure II | A prophet (lost)
In the absence of any drawings, this figure is assumed by James to have been one of nine prophets depicted in the upper register.

Scene 2 | The Miracle of the blaspheming gambler (lost)
A gambler who blasphemed against the Virgin was struck dead. Of this already obliterated scene, only the bottom left-hand corner was visible to Essex. On the left, in the foreground, the gambler lies dead, his cap fallen to the ground. Above him is the lower half of a gowned figure and, to the right of him, the corner of a table.
INSCRIPTION: Qualit[er]. lusor. quidam. ad. tessaras. x[pistu]m. &. matre[m]. s[uu]m. blasphemando. subito. & [...] [60]

Figure III | A prophet (lost)
The lower part of a robed figure holding a scroll; thought by James to have been a prophet.

Scene 3 | The Miracle of the pious painter (lost)
In this legend, a painter was commissioned to portray the Virgin triumphing over the Devil on the façade of the local church. The Devil appeared to the painter and entreated him not to make him appear so ugly; when the painter refused, the Devil upset the scaffold upon which he was working, but the Virgin in his picture stretched out her hand and stopped him from falling. All that remained when Essex made his copies were the bottom of the draperies and the feet of two figures (bottom left), and the figure of the painter holding a ladder, with another ladder or scaffold depicted behind him.
INSCRIPTION: Qualiter. pictor. [..... a. d]iabolo iniecta. relentus. est. &. ab. insultis. diab[o]li. liberat[us]. *vinc[entius]. li[bro] 8°. ca[pitul]o. 104.*[61]

Scene 3 Figure III

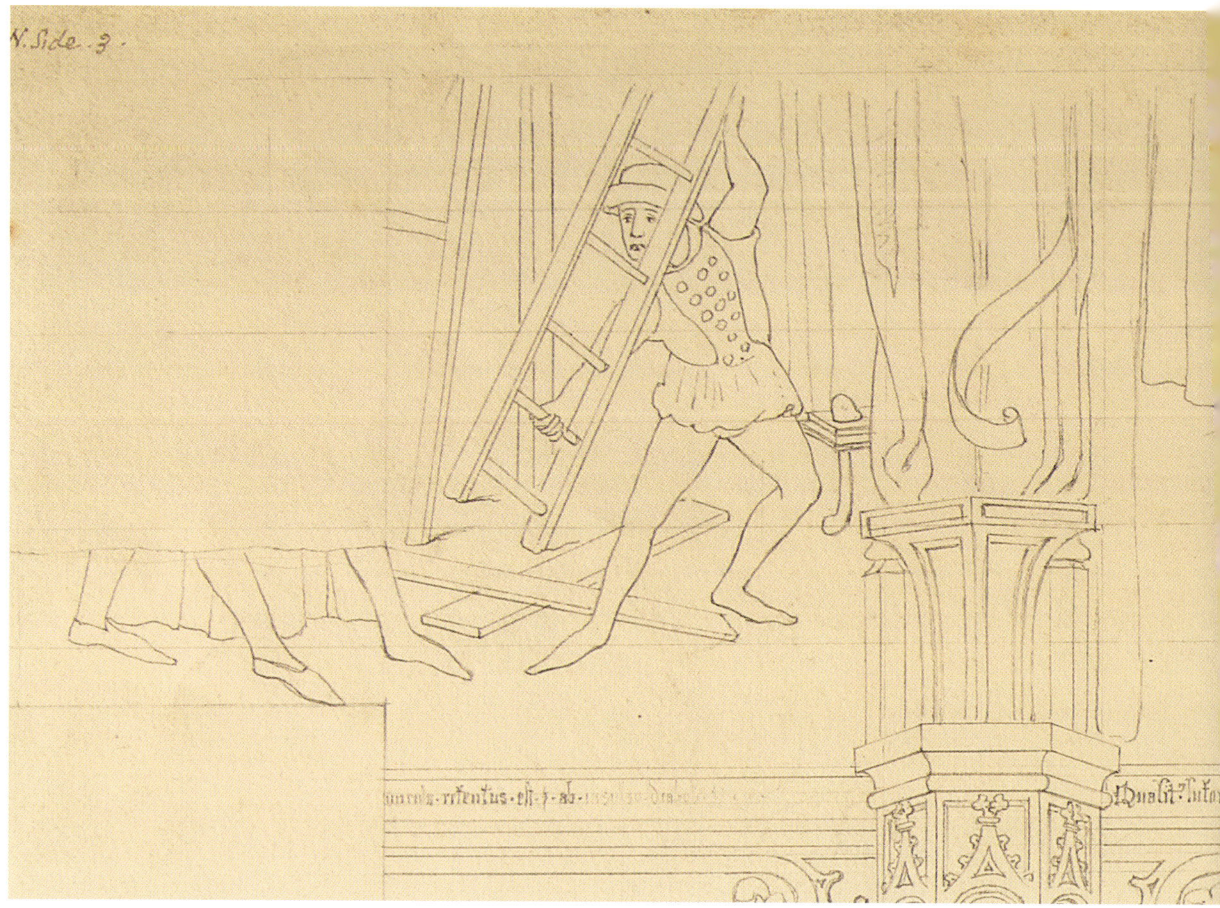

57 James & Tristram 1929, 26.
58 James & Tristram 1929, 26.
59 James transcribes this as: ...*erat. Vinc. Li° . 8° . c. ... 6°.*
60 James transcribes this as: *qualiter . lusor . quidam . ad . tessaras . christum . ....* *<hor>rida . morte de functus est* (probable source: *Speculum historiale*, vii, 104b; see n.8 above).
61 James transcribes this as: ... *retentus . est . et . ab . insidiis . diaboli . <liberatus> . vinc° . li° . 8° . ?....* (probable source: *Speculum historiale*, vii, 104a; see n.8 above).

Scene 2 Figure II Scene 1 Figure I

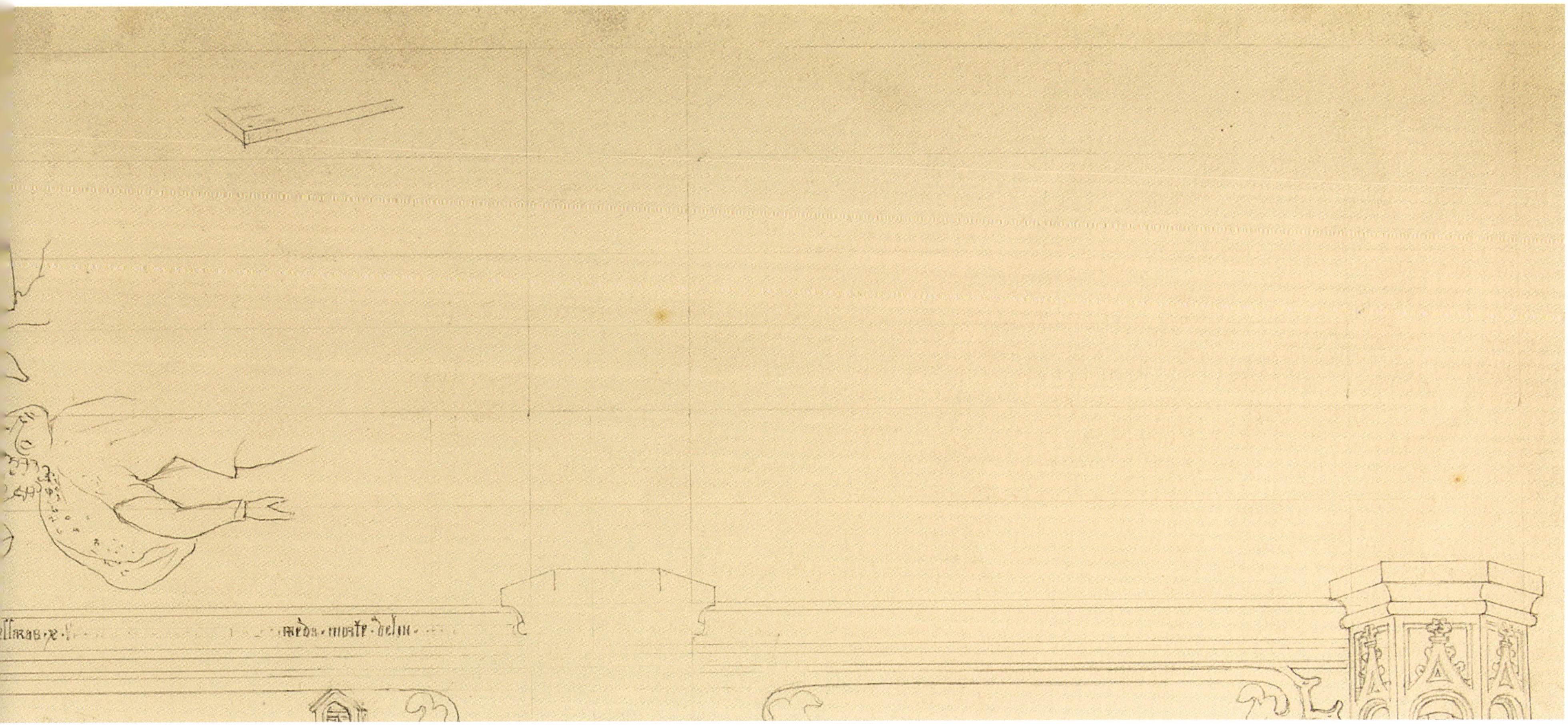

Figure IV | A prophet (lost)
Figure completely lost, only the pedestal remained for Essex to capture; presumed by James to be another prophet figure, holding a scroll.

Scene 4 | Unidentified scene with a knight (lost)
The subject of this scene has baffled scholars. In the bottom left corner, Essex shows two knights dressed in plate armour; the knight on the left is laid on his back and about to be slain by the other's sword. Behind these two, the legs of two more knights can be discerned. On the right of the scene are the legs of two or three further figures dressed in hose, one of whom holds a bundle of arrows. James makes three suggestions for the possible subject matter,[62] the first being the story recounted by Vincent of Beauvais (*Speculum historiale*, vii, 102-03) of a knight who protected a girl because she was named Mary, and who was later saved by the Virgin when he fell in a tournament. The second is an episode from the *Golden Legend* (131, 2) in which a knight on his way to a tournament stopped to say the office of the Virgin. On arriving late he found that someone in his shape had come forward and defeated all competitors. The third (and perhaps least convincing) suggestion proffered is the legend of St George who, raised from the dead by the Virgin, was despatched to kill the Emperor Julian (as recounted in the *Golden Legend*, 30).
INSCRIPTION: Qualit[er]. In.. [....] iaco[bus? ....]. *vin[centius libr]o [.]º [..] 8* [63]

Figure V | A prophet (lost)
The lower part of a robed figure holding a scroll; thought by James to have been a prophet.

Scene 5 | The Miracle of the sick clerk (lost)
In the episode recounted by Vincent of Beauvais (*Speculum historiale*, vii, 84), a clerk devoted to the Virgin fell ill, and she came to him and cured him with her milk. In Essex's drawing, the draperies of a bed are depicted, and a locked chest at its foot. The figure in the bed raises his hands in astonishment, presumably at the apparition of the Virgin above him. A pair of figures in draperies, the heads of which have been lost, are depicted on either side of the bed.
INSCRIPTION: Qualit[er]. quidam. [...]. b[eat]e. v[ir]ginis. multa. devota. ipsa. lac. infu[n]des. hi [?...][64]

62 James & Tristram 1929, 27.
63 None of the inscription was decipherable to either Essex or James.
64 None of the inscription was visible to either Essex or James.

Scene 5

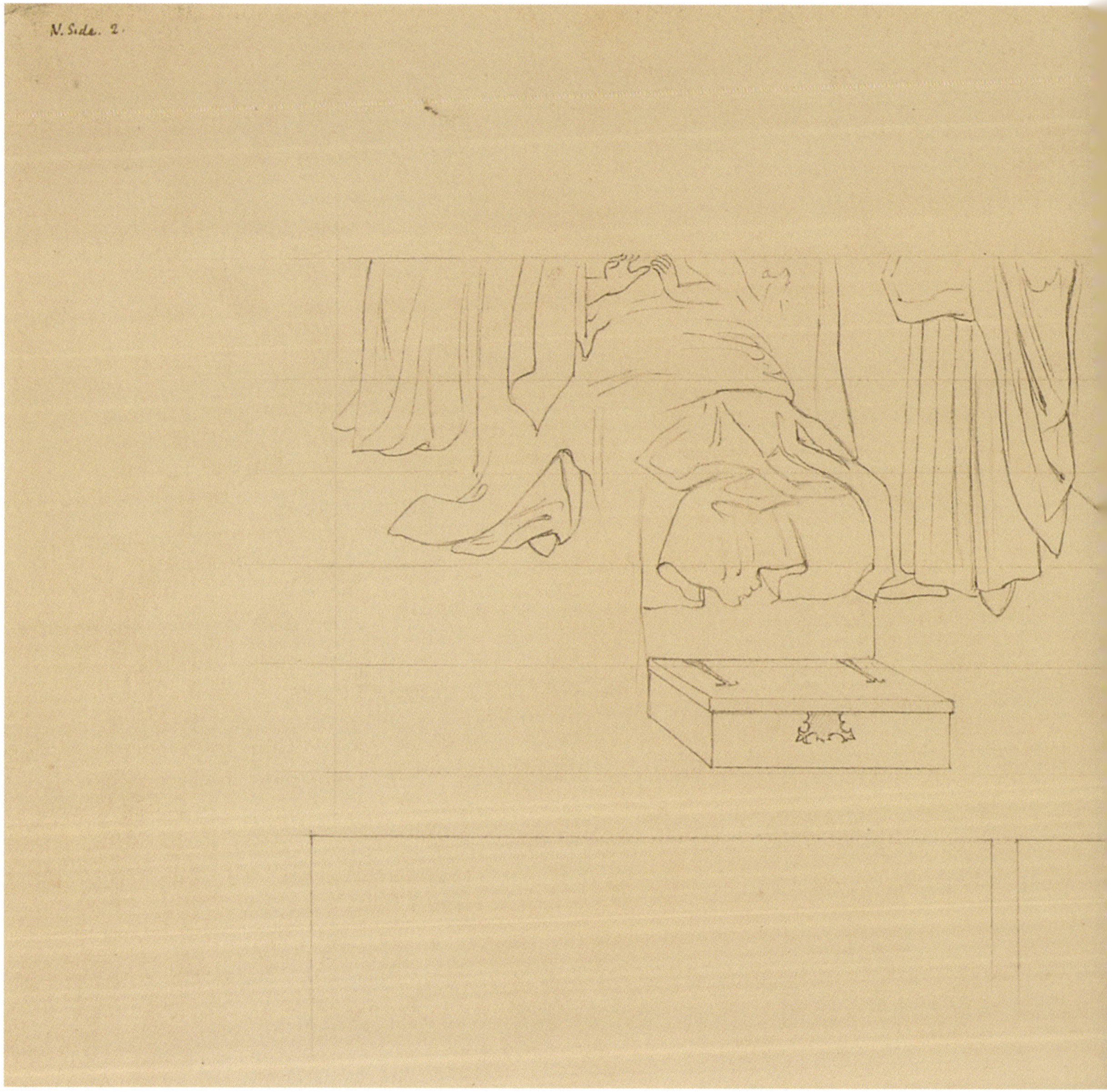

Figure V

Scene 4

Figure IV

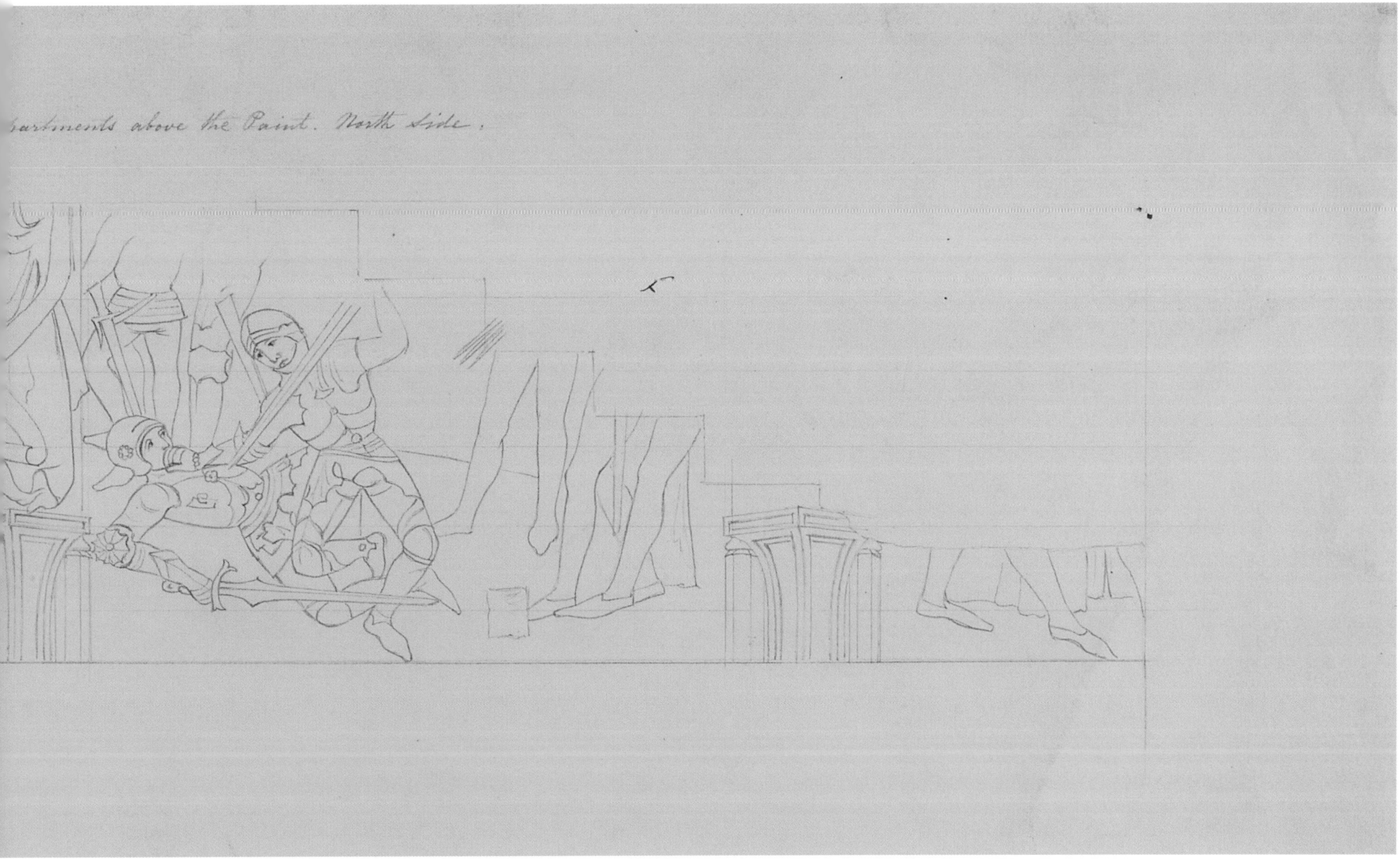

Figure VI | A prophet (lost)
The lower part of a robed figure, probably a prophet, holding a scroll which is elaborately curled.

Scene 6 | The Miracle of the dead monk and the rose (lost)
This story, recounted by Vincent of Beauvais, tells of a monk who constantly recited psalms, of which the initial letters formed the words 'Ave Maria'; after his death, flowers grew out of his eyes, ears and tongue. Here, in the foreground, two men in tunics dig a grave, and bones lie about. Behind are the feet and lower draperies of monastic figures, gathered around the monk's bier.[65]
INSCRIPTION: Qualit[er]. ab. ore. cuiusda[m]. monachi. in. honore. b[ea]te. v[ir]ginis. certos. psalmos. dice[n]tis. rosa. excrevit. inscripta. ave. maria. *vinc[entius]. li[br]° 8° ca[pitul]o 116.*[66]

Figure VII | A prophet (lost)
The lower part of a robed figure with scroll, thought to have been a prophet.

Scene 7 | The Miracle of the Devil disguised as a steward (lost)
Vincent of Beauvais recounts the story of a knight, devoted to the Virgin, who had in his employ a wicked steward. A holy man he captured told him that his steward was the Devil in disguise, and made the Devil assume his true form. The Devil confessed that, had the knight not been so devoted to the Virgin, he would have strangled him. In Essex's drawing the steward, dressed in a short tunic, with human head and clawed hands and feet, stands in the foreground to the left; behind him are the lower portions of what are supposed to have been (left to right) the holy man (in a long robe), an attendant, the knight (in a shorter gown), and another attendant, armed with sword.[67]
INSCRIPTION: Qualit[er]. miles. q[u]ida[m]. spoliis. et. furto. deditus. per. b[eat]am. v[ir]gine[m]. convertitur. et. a. p[er]iculis. magnis. liberatur. *lege[n]da. s[anc]to[rum]*[68]

Figure VIII | A prophet (lost)
The lower part of a robed figure, presumed to be a prophet, holding a scroll in both hands.

Figure IX **Scene 8** **Figure VIII**

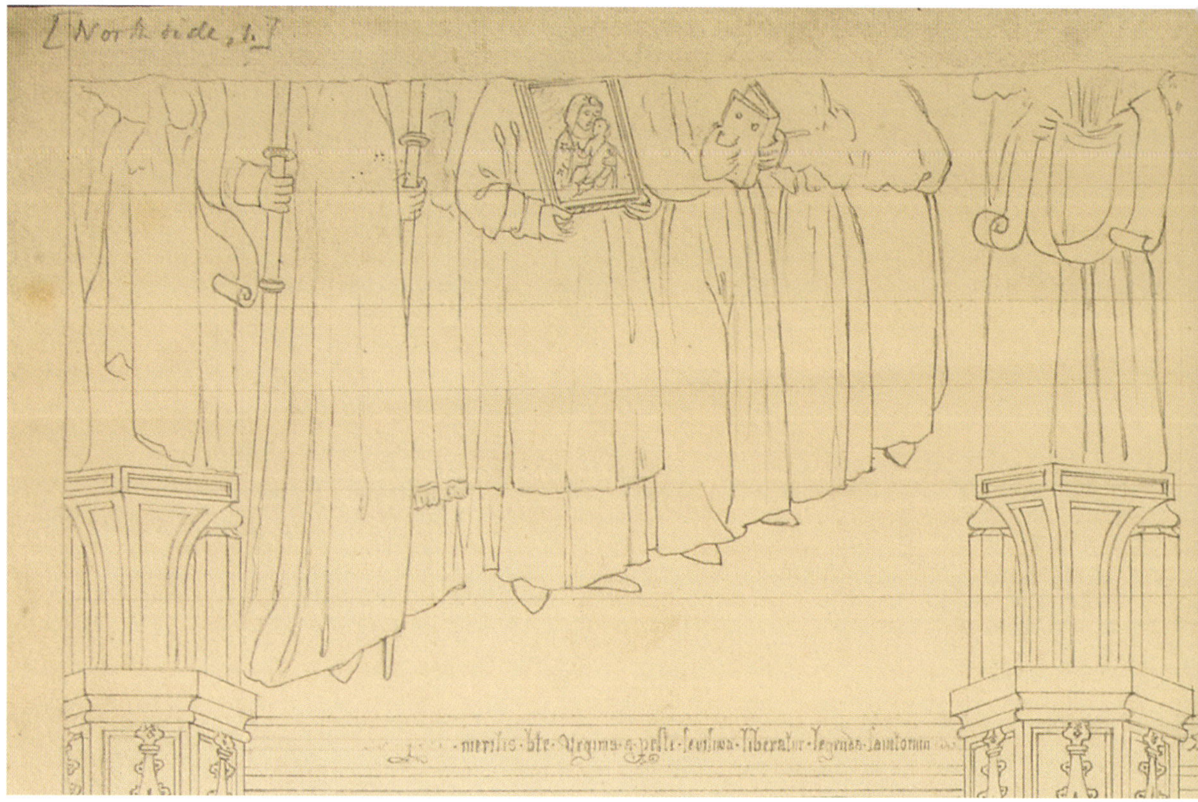

Scene 8 | The Miracle of Mount St Angelo (lost)
This episode, which is probably taken from the legend of St Gregory, recounts how the pope, in a time of plague, carried in procession a picture of the Virgin, painted by St Luke. He had a vision of St Michael on the Mount St Angelo, sheathing his sword, and heard angels singing 'Regina caeli'. In this depiction of the story, six vested clerics process from left to right. The first two figures (reading from left to right) are shown holding staffs, each with two projecting rings; the third – presumably Gregory, dressed in a cope – holds a framed picture of the Virgin and Child; the fourth holds a book; the fifth and sixth appear, from Essex's drawing, to be empty-handed.
INSCRIPTION: Qualiter. roman[us]. p[o]p[u]lus. meritis. b[ea]te. v[ir]ginis. a. peste. sev[er]issima. liberatur. *legenda. sanctorum.*[69]

Figure IX | A prophet (lost)
The lower part of a robed figure, presumed to be a prophet, holding a scroll.

Scene 7 **Figure VII** **Scene 6** **Figure VI**

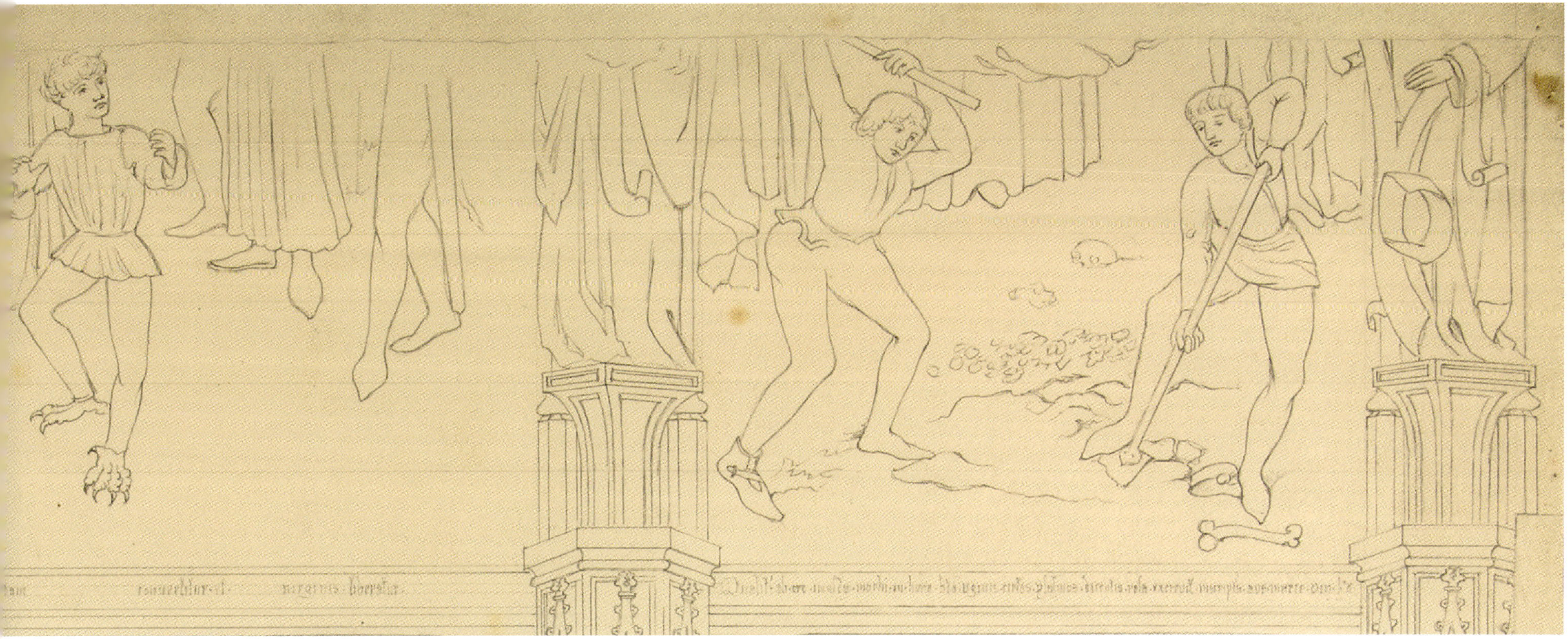

65 James & Tristram 1929, 28; James draws our attention to a similar scene in the scheme in the Lady Chapel at Winchester Cathedral.

66 James transcribes this as: *Qualiter . ab. ore . cuiusdam . monachi . in . honorem . beate . virginis . certos . psalmos . dicentis . rosa . excreuit . inscripta . ave . maria . Vinc . li° . 8°* (probable source: *Speculum historiale*, vii, 116b; see n.8 above).

67 James & Tristram 1929, 28; a similar scene is depicted in the Winchester scheme.

68 James transcribes this as: *Qualiter . miles . quidam . …. convertitur . et . … virginis . liberator …* (probable source: *Speculum historiale*, vii, 101; see n.8 above).

69 James transcribes this as: …. *meritis . beate . virginis . a . peste . sevissima . liberator . legenda . sanctorum* (probable source: *Golden Legend*, 46).

North wall, lower register

Figure I | St Mary Magdalene
Based on Essex's drawings, in which the attribute of the saint is not visible, James originally identified this figure as St Christina, a view which he later modified, having inspected the paintings.[70] St Mary Magdalene is represented holding a lidded jar of ointment.

Scene 1 | The Miracle of Mont St Michel
The legend, recounted by Vincent of Beauvais, tells how a woman on pilgrimage to the mount was trapped by the incoming tide and went into labour. Protected from the waters by the Virgin's cloak, the woman was safely delivered of a son before completing her pilgrimage.[71] The left-hand portion of this scene was entirely effaced by the insertion of an organ in *c.*1613-14 and very little of what survived was visible to Essex owing to layers of overpaint, which have since been removed. On the right, the crowned figure of the Virgin folds her cloak around the kneeling figure of a woman cradling a newborn baby. Green water swells about the woman's feet; the cruciform church of St Michael's is visible above in the distance. While the large area of loss on the left-hand side of the scene has been reintegrated by Plummer, no attempt has been made to reconstruct the figures of the two fellow pilgrims who bore witness to this miracle, faint traces of whose figures can still be discerned.[72]
INSCRIPTION: [….. lim]in[a. prop]erantibus. a. p[er]iculis. liberavit. *vinc[entius] li[bro] 8°. ca[pitul]o. 86.*[73]

Figure II | Unidentified female saint figure (new)
The figure which originally occupied this position was completely lost during the installation of a new organ in the early seventeenth century. The current image, which was painted in the early 1970s by Pauline Plummer as part of her restoration of the wall paintings, was deliberately not identified by an attribute, lest this should imply that some traces of the original figure had been salvaged. James originally conjectured that this position was occupied by a depiction of St Osith or St Winifred,[74] though the latter has since been identified at the west end of the south wall. A reconstruction panel, painted by Tristram in the 1920s, suggested that the missing figure might in fact have been St Agatha, but this saint has also since been identified elsewhere in the scheme (see figure V on the north wall, below) and Tristram's reconstruction has been removed.

70 James 1907, 18; James & Tristram 1929, 29.
71 On the Mont St Michel miracle, see Smith 2005.
72 James draws our attention to a similar scene in the derivative Marian miracle cycle at Winchester Cathedral (*c.*1500), in which the pilgrims remain visible; see James & Tristram 1929, 28-9.
73 James transcribes this as … *pari .* …. *eam . spectantibus . a . periculis . liberauit . Vinc . li . 8 . ca . 85°.*
74 James 1907, 18.

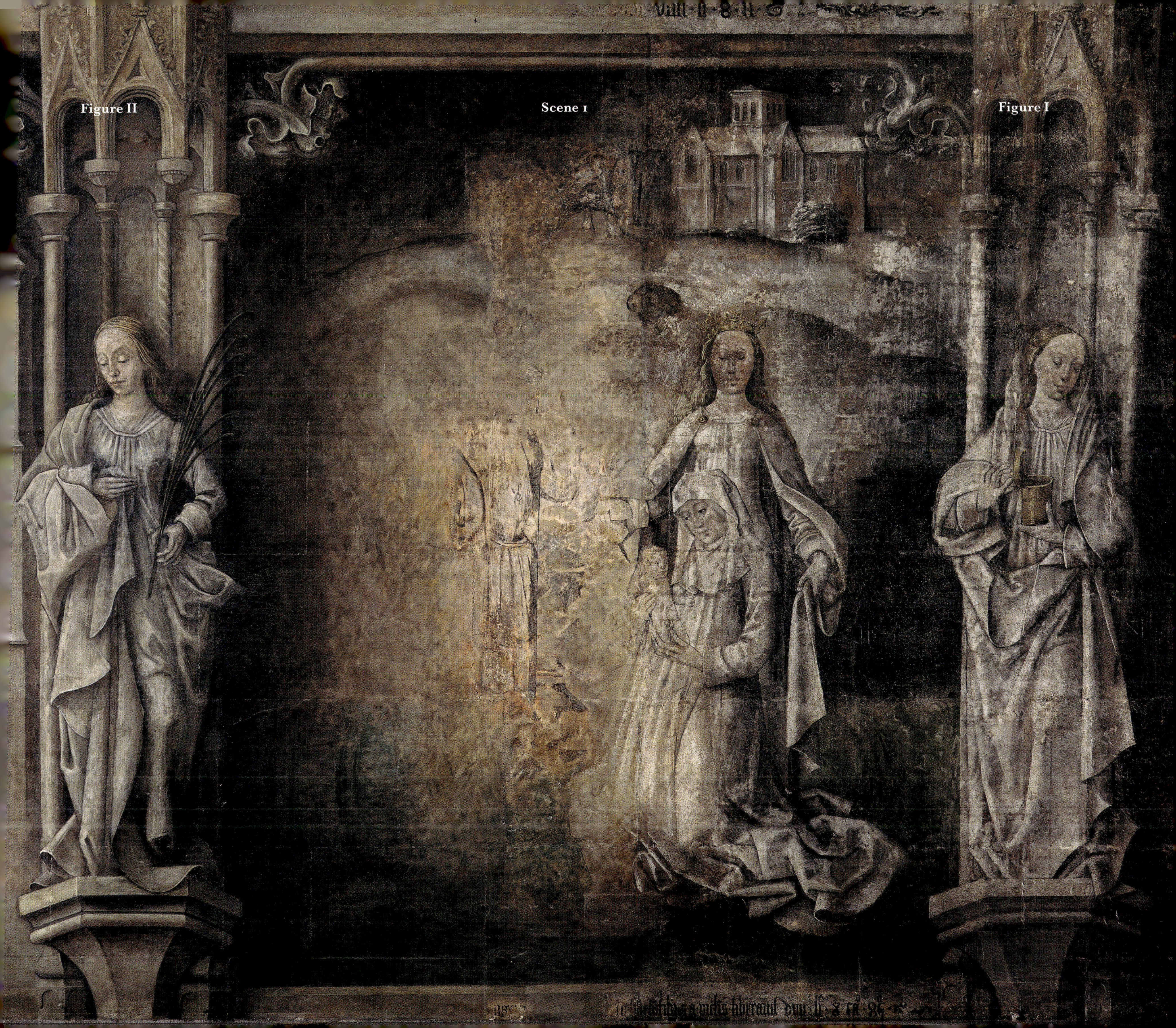
Figure II
Scene 1
Figure I

Figure II | Unidentified female saint figure (new)
The figure which originally occupied this position was completely lost during the installation of a new organ in the early seventeenth century. The current image, which was painted in the early 1970s by Pauline Plummer as part of her restoration of the wall paintings, was deliberately not identified by an attribute, lest this should imply that some traces of the original figure had been salvaged. James originally conjectured that this position was dedicated to a depiction of St Osith or St Winifred,[75] though the latter has since been identified at the west end of the south wall. A reconstruction panel, painted by Tristram in the 1920s, suggested that the missing figure might in fact have been St Agatha, but this saint has also since been identified elsewhere in the scheme (see figure V on the north wall, below) and Tristram's reconstruction has been removed.

Scene 2 | The Miracle of the wounded image
The right-hand portion of this scene was obliterated during the insertion of a new organ (see scene 1, above), but little of substance seems to have been lost. According to the legend, a soldier derided a poor woman who was praying to a statue of the Virgin and Child, and he threw a stone at the statue, hitting the Christ Child. The statue bled and the soldier dropped down dead. Here the woman, clothed in voluminous draperies and wearing a headdress, kneels in prayer before a statue of the Virgin and Child in a niche on the façade of a church (now badly effaced). To the left is the figure of a soldier, dressed in a laced doublet and hose; he is flanked on the right by an accomplice who holds a spear. In the foreground the faithless soldier lies dead.
INSCRIPTION: Qualiter. ymago. filii. beati. v[ir]g[in]is. a. p[er] fidis. percussa. [s]anguinem. dedit. *vincen[tius. libro ....] 8*[76]

Figure III | St Margaret
St Margaret of Antioch, bare-headed and holding a long crossed staff, emerges from the back of the dragon which, according to legend, swallowed her while she was in prison; the end of her robe trails from its mouth.

75 James 1907, 18.
76 James transcribes this as: *Qualiter . ymago . filii . beate . virginis . a . perfidies . percussa . sanguinem . dedit . Vince<ntius>* (probable source: *Speculum historiale*, vii, 110a; see n.8 above).

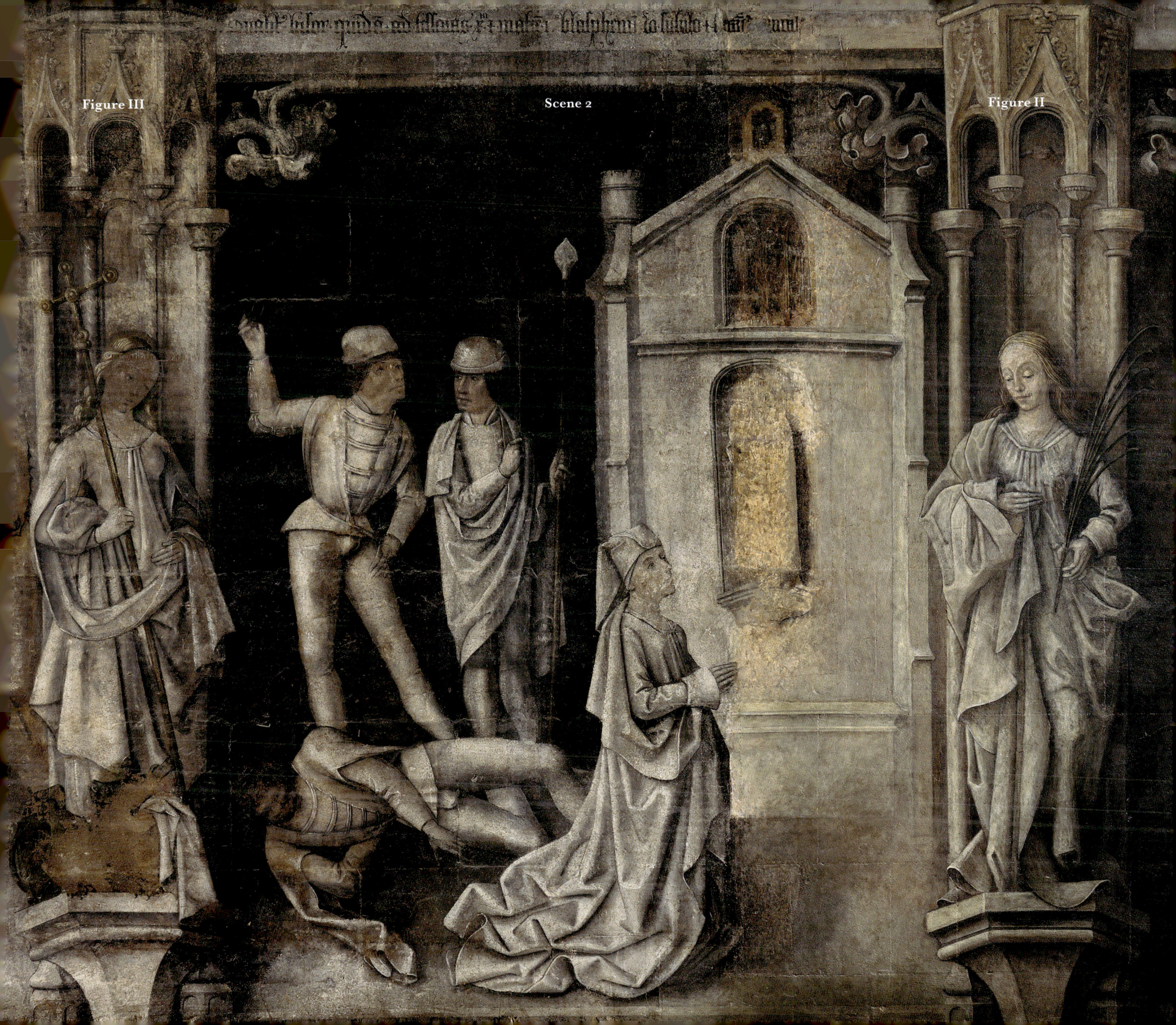
Figure III
Scene 2
Figure II

Figure III | St Margaret
St Margaret of Antioch, bareheaded and holding a long crossed staff, emerges from the back of the dragon which, according to legend, swallowed her while she was in prison; the end of her robe trails from its mouth.

Scene 3 | Amoras sells his wife to the Devil
This is the first of two consecutive scenes dedicated to this tale; the inscription reveals that the story was taken from the *Golden Legend* (119, 3). Amoras, a knight, being in dire need of money, agreed to sell his wife to the Devil. On the appointed day, the knight set off to deliver his wife. Passing a church on the way, the wife, who was devoted to the Virgin, insisted on stopping to hear Mass. While inside she fell asleep and the Virgin, assuming the guise of the wife, rejoined the knight and accompanied him to meet the Devil. The Devil was confounded and the Virgin rebuked them both, before restoring Amoras to prosperity. The left-hand section of this first scene was defaced in *c.*1700 by the insertion of a new organ screen and subsequent overpainting. On the right Amoras, dressed in a short cloak, laced doublet and cap, bargains with the Devil. On the left the knight rides out to meet the Devil, accompanied by his wife, who sports the fashionable hennin befitting her noble status.
INSCRIPTION: Qual[iter. mile] s. quida[m]. a. diabolo. deceptus. uxore[m]. eius. ad. diabolum. conducit. *legenda. sanctorum*[77]

Figure IV | St Elizabeth of Hungary
This figure was obscured until Plummer's restoration of the scheme in the 1960s and 70s; James originally ventured that the missing figure might have been either St Cecilia or St Radegund.[78] Recent scholarship suggests, however, that the figure most probably represents St Elizabeth of Hungary, patron saint to Elizabeth of York.[79] Veiled in the manner of a nun, she holds in her left hand what appear to be two crowns. While her head has been badly abraded, it is possible that she originally wore a third, the three crowns representing her status as a virgin, wife and widow. In recognition of her charity towards the poor and homeless, the saint is depicted bestowing clothes upon a small child who stands at her right knee.

77 James transcribes this as: <*Qualiter . mile*>*s . quidam . a . diabolo . deceptus . vxor(em) . eius . ad . diabolum . conducit . legenda . sanctorum .*
78 See James 1907, 18, and James & Tristram 1929, 30, respectively.
79 See Anderson 1989, 18-20 and plates 19 a & b, who draws convincing parallels with depictions of the saint in two late fourteenth- and early fifteenth-century panel paintings from the Cologne region.

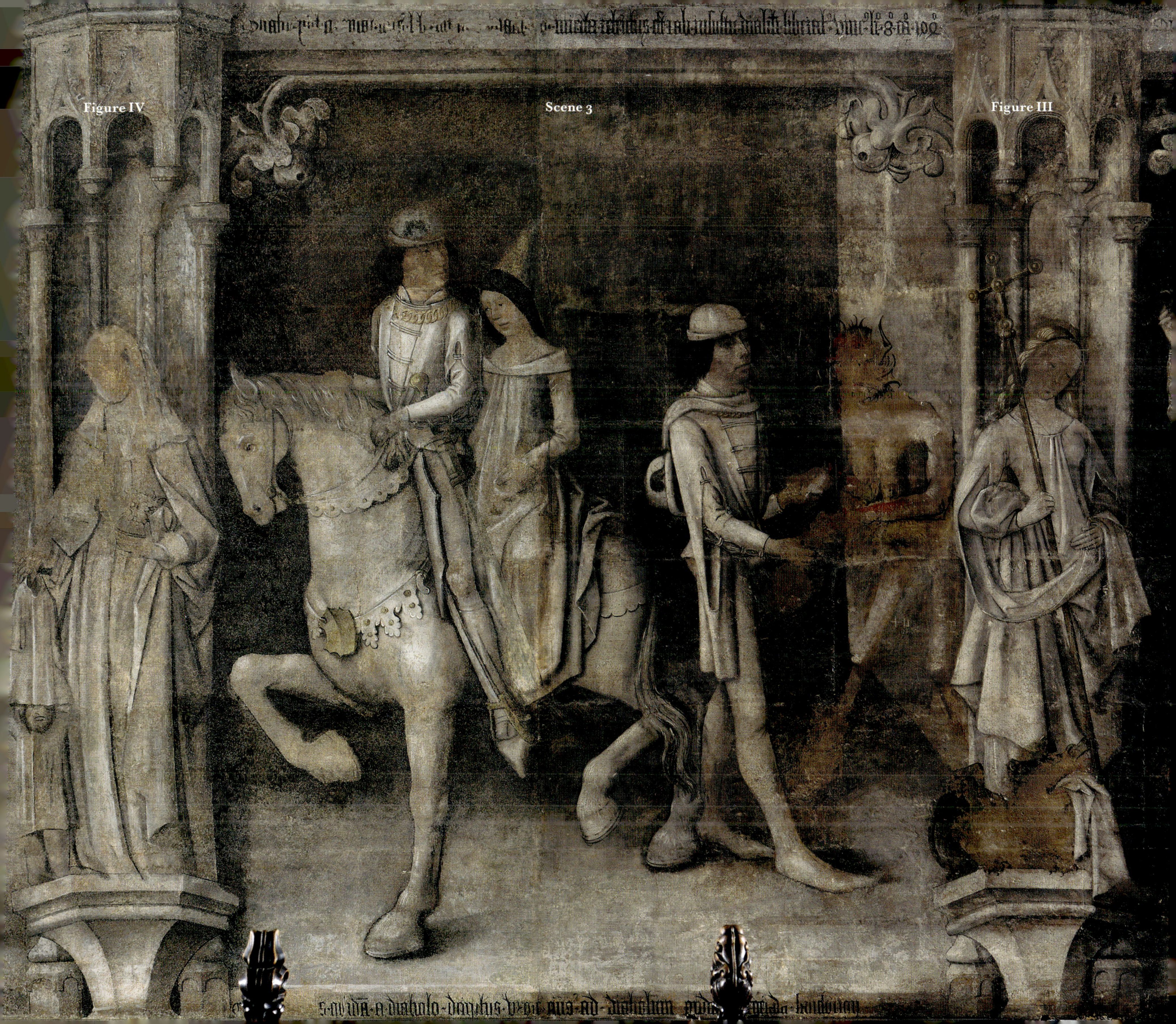
Figure IV
Scene 3
Figure III

Figure IV | St Elizabeth of Hungary
This figure was obscured until Plummer's restoration of the scheme in the 1960s and 70s; James originally ventured that the missing figure might have been either St Cecilia or St Radegund.[80] Recent scholarship suggests, however, that the figure most probably represents St Elizabeth of Hungary, patron saint to Elizabeth of York.[81] Veiled in the manner of a nun, she holds in her left hand what appear to be two crowns. While her head has been badly abraded, it is possible that she originally wore a third, the three crowns representing her status as a virgin, wife and widow. In recognition of her charity towards the poor and homeless, the saint is depicted bestowing clothes upon a small child who stands at her right knee.

Scene 4 | Amoras' wife is delivered by the Virgin
This second episode in the Amoras legend was not visible to Essex, and was only partially brought to light when James and Tristram uncovered the paintings in the mid-1920s. On the right is an archway looking through to the interior of a church. A priest, assisted by a server, celebrates Mass in front of an altar, and Amoras' wife kneels to the left. On the left of the scene, the Virgin – assuming the place of the wife – rides with Amoras to meet the Devil. Previously undetected traces of the Devil's fiery head can be made out just above the horse.[82]
INSCRIPTION: Hic. idem. miles. cu[m]. uxore. sua. [per?] beata[m]. virgine[m]. a. periculis. diaboli. liberatur. *legenda. sanctorum*[83]

Figure V | St Agatha
Only recently revealed from beneath overpainting, this figure is now thought to represent the martyr St Agatha.[84] James postulated that the figure, whose attribute seemed to have completely disappeared, might be either St Cecilia or St Mary Magdalene, both of whom have since been identified elsewhere in the scheme (figures sVII and nI respectively).[85] Post-restoration, it is clear that the saint holds the hilt of a dagger or a pair of tongs in her right hand. Her unusually low-cut and unlaced kirtle reveals a red scar which extends across the right side of her chest, a reference to the fact that, having refused to renounce Christianity and marry Quintianus, consul of Sicily, she was subjected to tortures which included the severing of her breasts.

80 See James 1907, 18, and James & Tristram 1929, 30, respectively.
81 See Anderson 1989, 18-20 and plates 19 a & b, who draws convincing parallels with depictions of the saint in two late fourteenth- and early fifteenth-century panel paintings from the Cologne region.
82 James, working from a much more obscured image than we see today, concluded that the Devil must have assumed Amoras' position on the horse.
83 This inscription was not visible to James.
84 Anderson 1989, 23-4.
85 James & Tristram 1929, 31.

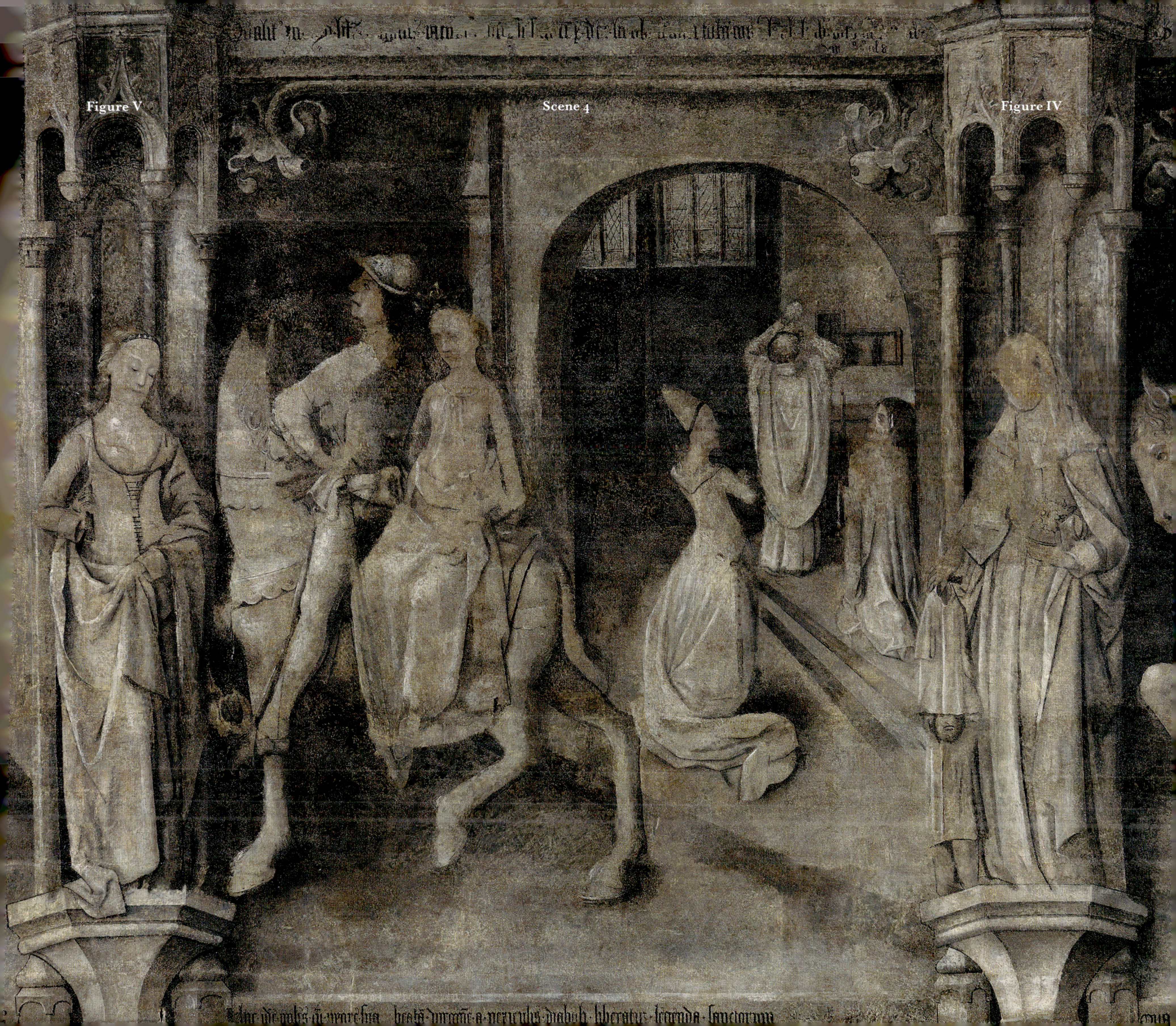
Figure V
Scene 4
Figure IV

Figure V | St Agatha
Only recently revealed from beneath overpainting, this figure is now thought to represent the martyr St Agatha.[86] James postulated that the figure, whose attribute seemed to have completely disappeared, might be either St Cecilia or St Mary Magdalene, both of whom have since been identified elsewhere in the scheme (figures sVII and nI respectively).[87] Post-restoration, it is clear that the saint holds the hilt of a dagger or a pair of tongs in her right hand. Her unusually low-cut and unlaced kirtle reveals a red scar which extends across the right side of her chest, a reference to the fact that, having refused to renounce Christianity and marry Quintianus, consul of Sicily, she was subjected to tortures which included the severing of her breasts.

Scene 5 | The Miracle of the Jewess delivered by the Virgin
The story of a Jewess endangered in childbirth; according to Vincent of Beauvais, a light appeared and a voice bade the labouring woman to call upon the Virgin, and on so doing, she was safely delivered and converted to Christianity. This scene was obscured by oil paint and not captured by Essex. Revealed following Plummer's conservation, the events can be seen to unfold within the confines of a bedchamber, with a door giving off to the right. In the centre of the room the Jewess lies in a large curtained bed; in the foreground a maid sits and puts the baby to her breast. Near her feet is a large basin on a bamboo stand; at the end of the bed stands a woman in a turban, pouring water into a basin; another maid stands in attendance behind the bed. Between these figures, hovering on a small wavy cloud, is a miniature representation of the Virgin.[88]
INSCRIPTION: Qualit[er]. beata. virgo. maria. muliere[m]. Judeam. in. partu. liberaverit. &. ad. xp[istianam … *Vincentius]. li[br]o 8°, ca[pitulo]. 100* [89]

Figure VI | St Mary of Egypt
Recent scholarship suggests that this figure, who is dressed in an exotic turban and holds three oval loaves, represents St Mary of Egypt.[90] According to the *Golden Legend*, Mary, a prostitute, was converted to a life of chastity while on pilgrimage to see the Holy Cross in Jerusalem. Retiring to the desert to live as a hermit, she is reported to have taken with her only three loaves of bread. Although James previously identified this figure as St Elizabeth, who is also sometimes depicted holding loaves of bread, it now seems more likely that she is depicted elsewhere in the scheme (figure nIV).[91]

86 Anderson 1989, 23-4.
87 James & Tristram 1929, 31.
88 The Virgin is depicted in a manner identical to that on the south wall, when she appears to the Empress in a vision (scene s5).
89 Actually cap.99; James transcribes this as: *Qualiter . beata . virgo . maria . mulierem . Judeam . in partu . liberauit . et . ad . <?christianam fidem?> . Vinc . li° . 8° . Ca° . 100°* .
90 Anderson 1989, 20; Anderson argues that her turban is an indication of the saint's Middle Eastern extraction.
91 James & Tristram 1929, 31.

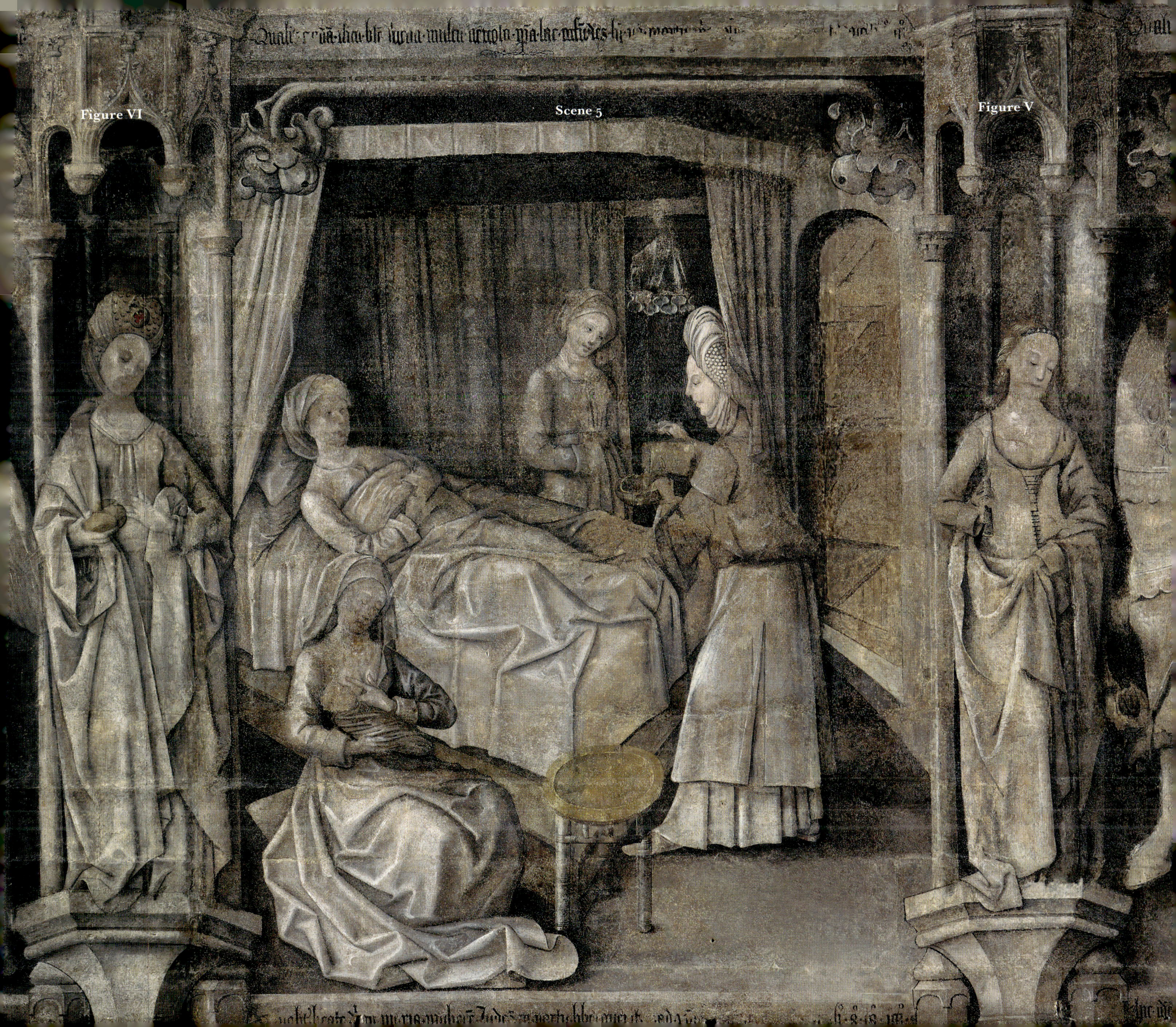
Figure VI
Scene 5
Figure V

Figure VI | St Mary of Egypt
Recent scholarship suggests that this figure, who is dressed in an exotic turban and holds three oval loaves, represents St Mary of Egypt.[92] According to the *Golden Legend*, Mary, a prostitute, was converted to a life of chastity while on pilgrimage to see the Holy Cross in Jerusalem. Retiring to the desert to live as a hermit, she is reported to have taken with her only three loaves of bread. Although James previously identified this figure as St Elizabeth, who is also sometimes depicted holding loaves of bread, it now seems more likely that she is depicted elsewhere in the scheme (figure nIV).[93]

Scene 6 | The Miracle of the candle
The story relayed in the *Golden Legend* (37, 2) is that of a devout woman who was prevented from attending the Feast of the Purification. She fell asleep at home and had a dream that she attended Mass with the Virgin and saints. In her vision, the candles used in the service were collected by an angel, but the woman refused to give hers up. In the ensuing struggle, the candle was broken and when the woman woke, she found a candle stump in her hand. In the Eton scene, the action takes place inside a church. From the left enters the crowned Virgin, who is followed in procession by four bare-headed virgins; all hold long, twisted tapers. In the foreground, on the right, the woman kneels, resting her head on her hand as if asleep. She wears a truncated hennin headdress, fashionable on the Continent at the time. She also holds a taper which an angel, to her right, attempts to seize. Behind them is an altar, in front of which two priests stand facing the procession. At the top of the scene is a two-light window filled with four figures in stained glass (from left to right): St Adrian (with an anvil and sword, and a lion at his feet); St Edmund (with a crown upon his hat and two arrows); St Paul (with a sword); and St Anthony (with crutch and a pig).
INSCRIPTION: Qualit[er]. mulier. quidam. nobilis. in. die. purificatio[n]is. be[ate. virginis… *legenda] s[anc]to[rum]*.[94]

Figure VII | St Etheldreda
St Etheldreda, seventh-century queen and abbess of Ely, wears the habit of a nun and a crown over her wimple. Facing right, she holds an ornate crozier in her right hand and clasps a book in her left.

92 Anderson 1989, 20; Anderson argues that her turban is an indication of the saint's Middle Eastern extraction.
93 James & Tristram 1929, 31.
94 James transcribes this as: *Qualiter . mulier . quedam . nobilis . in . die . purificacionis . beate . virginis . cereum . celitus . <legenda> . sanctorum.*

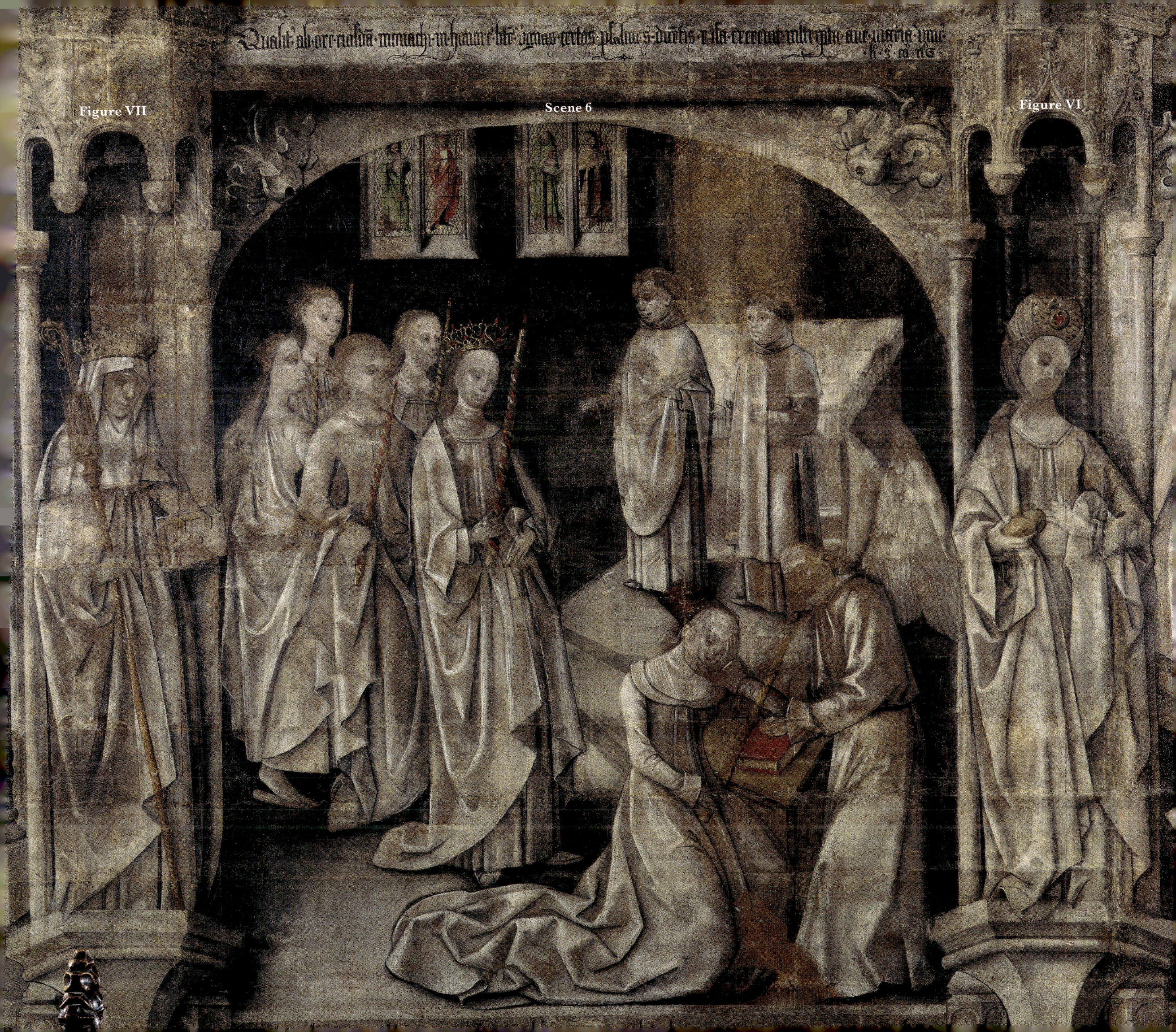
Figure VII
Scene 6
Figure VI

Figure VII | St Etheldreda
St Etheldreda, seventh-century queen and abbess of Ely, wears the habit of a nun and a crown over her wimple. Facing right, she holds an ornate crozier in her right hand and clasps a book in her left.

Scene 7 | The Miracle of the image held hostage
The source of this miracle tale is the *Golden Legend* (131, 4). When a woman's son was taken captive, she took the image of the Christ Child from the Virgin's lap as hostage, following which her own son was returned to her. On the left of the scene, the woman kneels and gazes over her right shoulder to behold her returned son; from the curved-lidded chest in front of her she takes the statue of the Christ Child. An arch on the right of the composition indicates the interior of a church. On a square pedestal sits a statue of the Virgin enthroned; the woman kneels before the Virgin, replacing the statue in its rightful place.
INSCRIPTION: Qualit[er]. mulier. queda[m]. p[er]. filiu[m]. b[ea]te. v[ir]ginis. suu[m]. filiu[m]. a. carcerib[us]. liberatu[m]. sibi. restitut[um]. meruit. *legenda. s[anc]to[rum]* [95]

Figure VIII | St Martha
St Martha holds a palm branch in her left hand and leads a dragon (the Tarasque) by her girdle with her right. According to the *Golden Legend*, Martha tamed the dragon, which had been terrorising the people of the town. It is not clear why she is depicted holding a palm, the symbol of martyrdom.

95 James transcribes this as: *Qualiter . mulier . quedam . per . filium . beate . Virginis . suum . filium . de . carceribus . liberatum . sibi . restitutum . invenit . legenda . sanctorum*

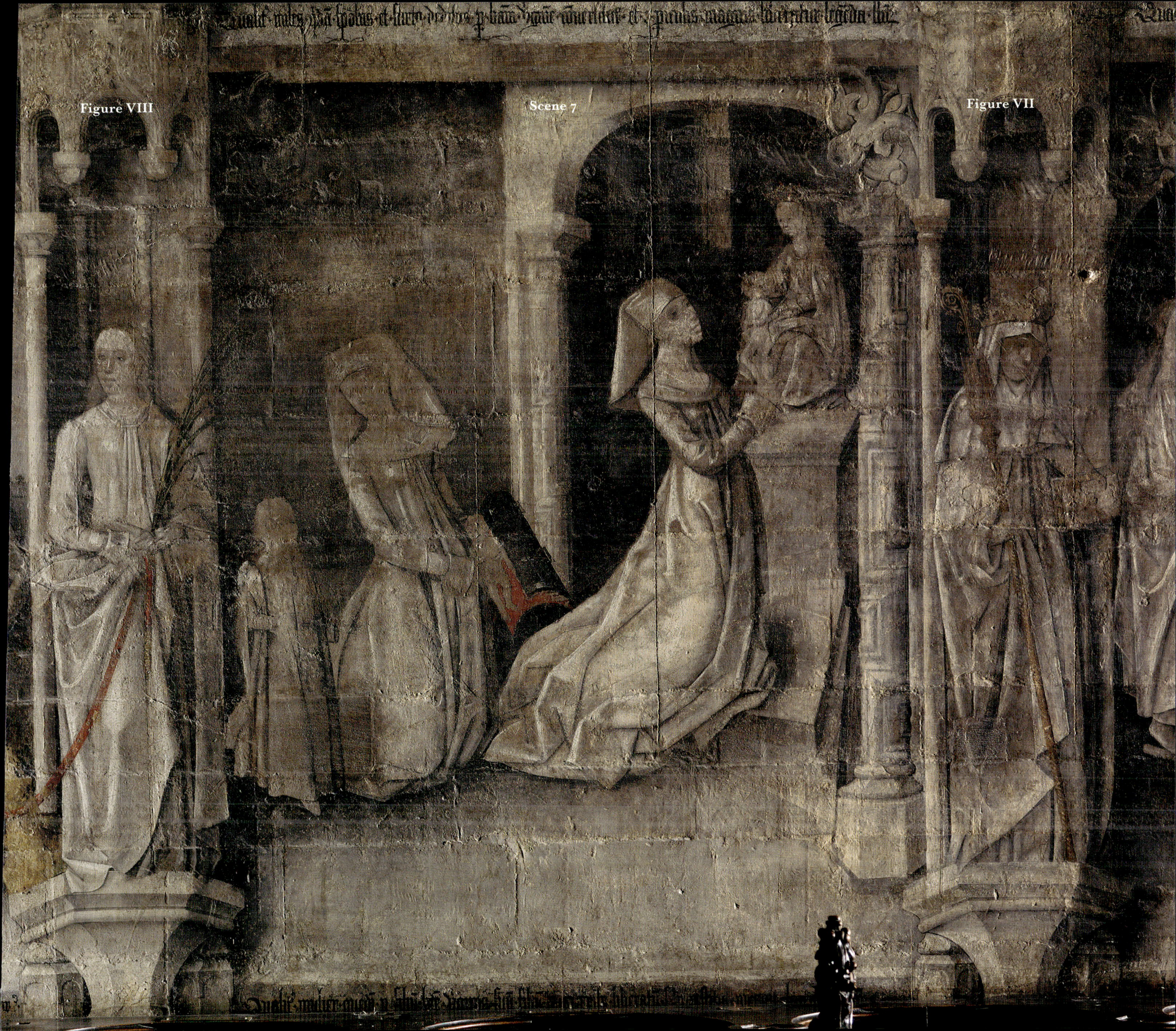
Figure VIII
Scene 7
Figure VII

Figure VIII | St Martha
St Martha holds a palm branch in her left hand and leads a dragon (the Tarasque) by her girdle with her right. According to the *Golden Legend*, Martha tamed the dragon, which had been terrorising the people of the town. It is not clear why she is depicted holding a palm, the symbol of martyrdom.

Scene 8 | The Miracle of the woman dying unconfessed
According to the legend recounted by Vincent of Beauvais, a woman dying unconfessed was revived by the intercession of the Virgin. Once she had confessed her remaining sin, she was absolved and died again. On the left kneels the Virgin, crowned and with her hands clasped in prayer, interceding for the unconfessed woman, who lies dead before her. Above them, in the centre of the scene, sits Christ in Majesty, robed in a mantle and with his feet resting on an orb. He is crowned with thorns and displays the wounds in his side, hands and feet. To the right of the scene the temporarily revived woman, still in her grave clothes, kneels with her back to the viewer, confessing her sin to a priest; he is seated in a chair, facing left.
INSCRIPTION: Qualit[er]. beata. virgo. mulier[em]. ad. morte[m]. usq[ue]. laborante[m]. de. p[e]cc[at]o. gravi. commiss[o]. non. co[n]fessa[m]. vite. restituit. &. a. p[er]ic[u]lo. da[m]pna[ti]o[n]is. liberavit. *vinc[entius]. l[ib]ro 8°. ca[pitu]lo. 117* [96]

Figure IX | St Sidwell
A youthful St Sidwell is shown bare-headed and with long hair. In her right hand she holds the haymaker's scythe which was the instrument of her martyrdom, the blade passing around the back of her neck. This figure was badly damaged by the insertion of a new organ screen at the west end of the chapel in 1881-2.[97]

96 James transcribes this as: *Qualiter . beata . virgo . mulierem . ad . mortem . usque . laorantem . de . peccato . gravi . commisso . non . confessam . vite . restituit . et . a . periculo . dampnaciois . liberauit . Vinus . li° . 8° . ca° . 117° .*
97 Anderson 1989, 22.

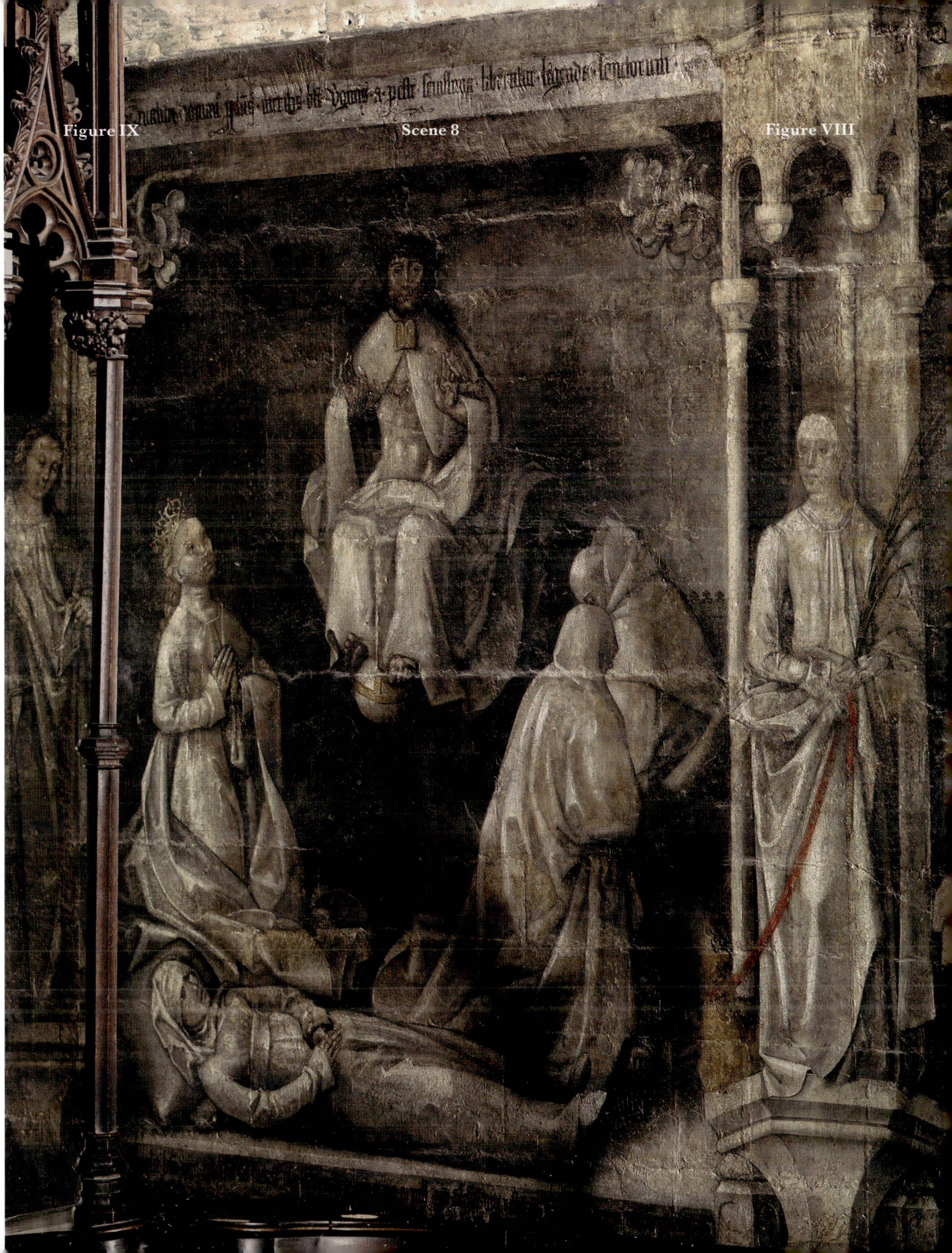
Figure IX
Scene 8
Figure VIII

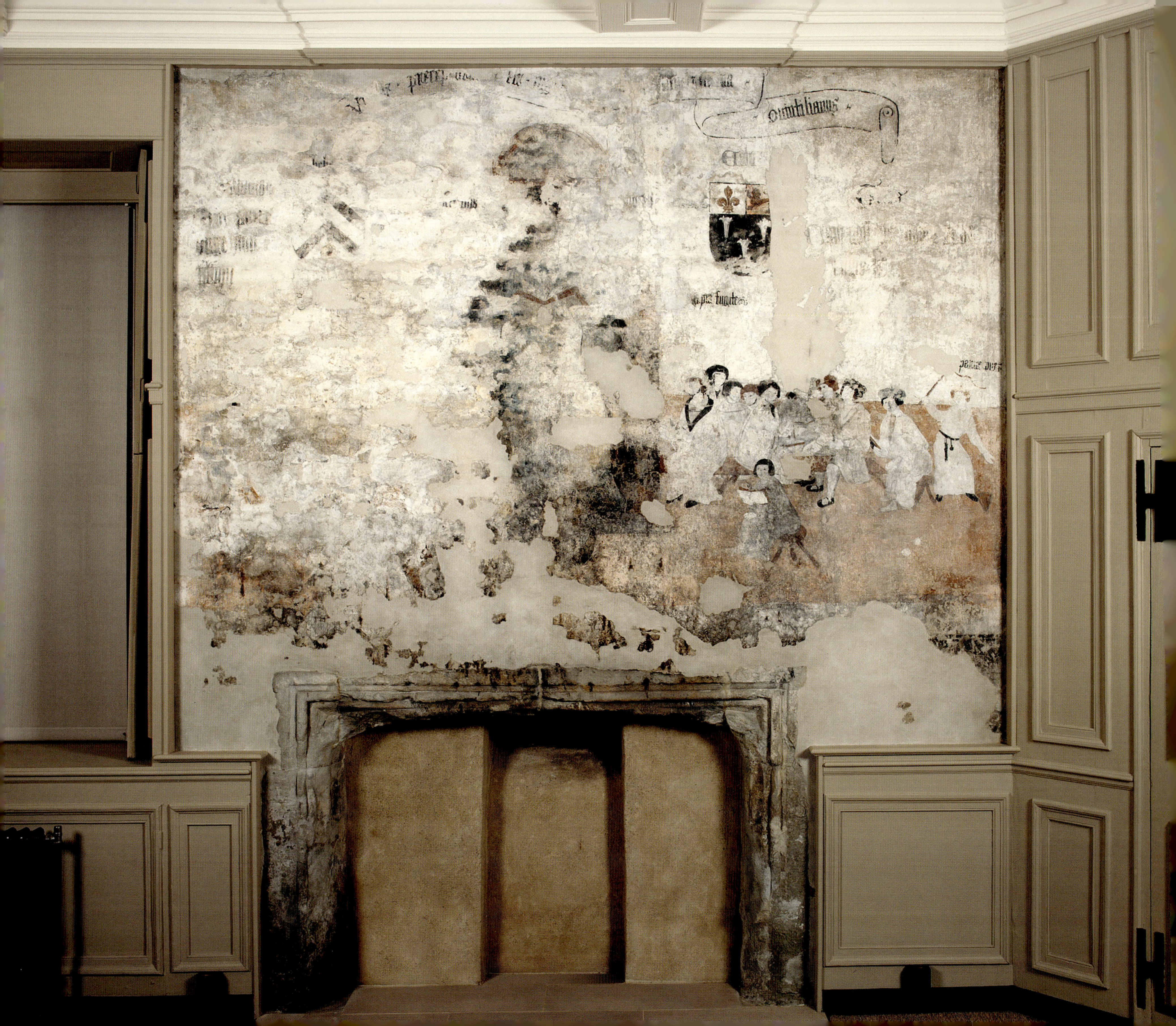

Part II: The early sixteenth-century school scene in the Head Master's Chambers

Henrietta McBurney, David Park,
Stephen Rickerby and Lisa Shekede

Fig. 1. Full view of the mural on the west wall of the Head Master's Chambers.

'Be ever occupied in redynge of good authors: and thou shalt come forwarde maruaylously'
(William Horman, *Vulgaria*, 1519)

Discovery

During renovation work in December 2005 in the room known as the Head Master's Chambers, the dismantling of eighteenth-century panelling from the west wall revealed a group of Tudor schoolboys, evidently forming part of a larger mural.[1] Subsequent removal of later limewash and plaster layers during conservation work in 2006 and 2007 brought to light many further details of this unique painting, which dates from the early sixteenth century (Figure 1).[2] The painting formed the decorative scheme of a room that had functioned, since the mid-fifteenth century, as the schoolmaster's living quarters.[3] Subsequently whitewashed out, very possibly when a successor chose a different form of wall decoration, the wall painting remained completely unknown and unrecorded until its accidental rediscovery.[4] It is without parallel in the monumental art of Renaissance Europe, and is all the more remarkable for having been discovered at Eton, already celebrated for the series of wall paintings in its chapel showing the *Miracles of the Virgin*, which constitutes the major part of the subject matter of this book.

The Head Master's Chambers forms part of the Founder's original school buildings on the north side of the quadrangle (now known as School Yard), dating from the mid-fifteenth century.[5] Located on the ground floor at the west end of the two-storey brick range, and adjacent to the original schoolroom (known as Lower School), the Head Master's Chambers is joined by a staircase to a room of the same size above, which must have functioned as the master's bedchamber.[6] This in turn has a door leading to the boys' dormitory above the schoolroom (which used to be known as Long

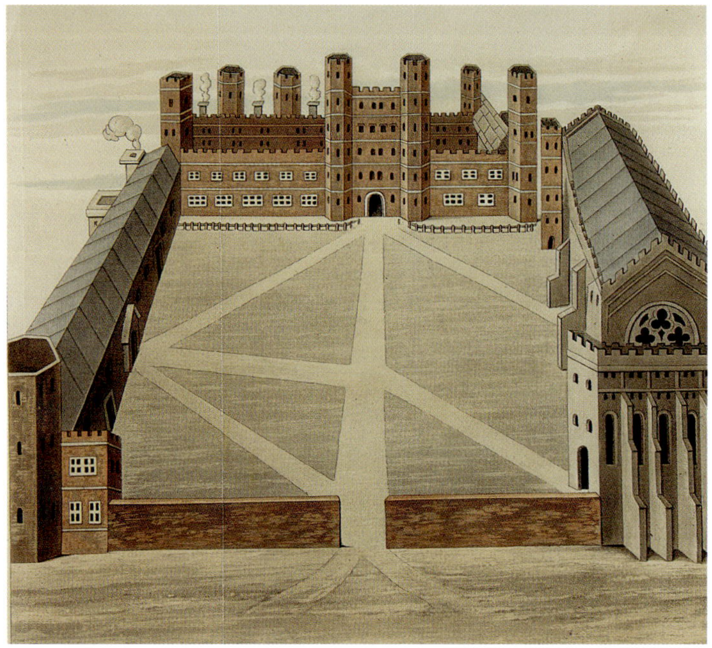

Fig. 2. View of Eton College in 1623, showing the schoolmaster's quarters in the two-storey brick building at lower left. Early nineteenth-century aquatint taken from the painted view in Sir Henry Savile's monument, Merton College, Oxford.

1 The discovery was made by Reg Harberd of the College's building department.

2 The conservation work was carried out by Stephen Rickerby and Lisa Shekede. Only bare white plaster was found on the other walls of the room (see Rickerby & Shekede 2006 and 2007). For a preliminary account of the painting, which has been left exposed following the conservation work, see McBurney 2007.

3 The term 'Head Master' was not in official use until 1791. In the sixteenth century, when there was still only one master, together with a lower master or usher, the master was usually called the 'schoolmaster' with the Latin names of 'Praeceptor', 'Informator', 'Magister', 'Moderator', etc.; the usher was given the Latin name of 'Ostiarius'.

4 There is no contemporary record of the painting in the College audit rolls. Subsequently totally concealed from view first by limewash and then, from 1702, by the panelling of the walls, it escaped the notice even of M.R. James, who, as recounted in Part I above, was notoriously thorough in his study of the College's archives and artefacts. The lack of entry in the College records would imply that the painting was a private commission, not therefore necessitating any record in the College accounts (see below p.150ff).

5 The Founder's statutes provide for a room for the master's sole use (see ECR 58/36: 'Dispositione Camerarum': 'omnes socii ejusdem et magister informator singuli in singulis cameris collocentur'; Heywood & Wright 1850, 576).

6 This upper chamber is now known as the 'Prayer Room'; no doubt it was where the master took prayers in the evening before the boys went though it to the dormitory.

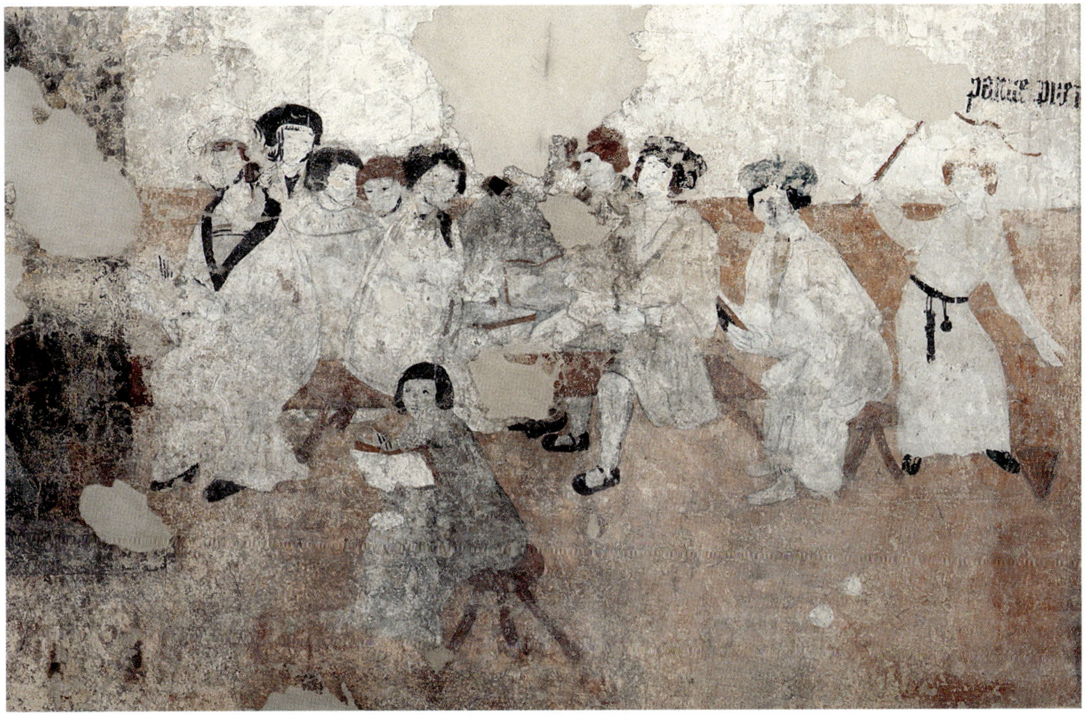

Fig. 3. Detail from the mural showing the right-hand group of boys.

Chamber), at the opposite end of which was the chamber of the usher or lower master. The master's quarters can be seen clearly in a print showing the College as it appeared in the early seventeenth century (Figure 2).[7] The Head Master's Chambers has continued to be used by the Head Master to the present day; until very recently, it was also where the Lower Master meted out punishment to boys 'in the bill'.[8]

Description

Although very fragmentary, the painting retains passages of great beauty, especially the animated group of boys at lower right (Figure 3). The surviving elements of the overall composition can be appreciated from a line drawing: a central seated figure of a schoolmaster, originally flanked by two groups of boys depicted on a much smaller scale, and accompanied by shields and inscriptions (Figure 4).[9] A watercolour reconstruction commissioned by the College from Stephen Conlin provides a good impression of how the mural might originally have appeared (Figure 5).[10]

The central figure of the schoolmaster was clearly designed to dominate the scene. Vast in scale compared to the boys, who appear diminutive grouped to his left and right, he seems even more monumental seated in his *cathedra*, the high-backed, wide, wooden chair, raised on a plinth, on which masters are typically shown in medieval and Renaissance depictions of school scenes. A particular feature of this *cathedra* is its round-headed top with an Italianate scallop-shell design. Similar examples can be seen in depictions of the enthroned Henry VIII dating from the 1520s, such as that in a 1526 patent (Figures 6 and 7).[11] This detail is the only specifically Renaissance feature in the wall painting. Although only

7 The earliest references to the fact that the master's quarters comprised both an upper and lower chamber are from the seventeenth century; see Willis & Clark 1886, 380-464 and 462, n.1. See *ibid* for a reference of 1563 indicating that the usher's quarters, by contrast, comprised only a chamber on the first floor.

8 Since the discovery and exposure of the wall painting in 2006, boys in the Lower Master's bill have been seen in Lower School; boys in the Head Master's bill are seen in the Head Master's School Room next to Upper School.

9 It should be noted that three edges of the wall on which the mural was painted are now obscured by joinery – along the top by the cornice (which covers the upper edge of the scroll bearing the Quintilian quotation), and at either side, by the window frame (to the left) and wall panelling (to the right). The limits of the original painting may have been defined by a line or border (see n.50 below) which would have given the viewer a sense of looking into the scene (rather than the present experience of its fading out at its limits).

10 Stephen Conlin's reconstruction, made in 2010, was executed in pen and watercolour, using several forms of imaging provided by S. Rickerby and L. Shekede in order to discern details and piece together fragments. The colours were established through discussion with the conservators and from the paint analyses done as part of their report.

11 Torrigiano's bust of John Colet of *c.*1520, now lost, but known from his monument in St Paul's, was contained in an Italianate niche with similar scallop-shell carving (see the engraving by Wenceslas Hollar in Dugdale's *History of St Paul's*, 1658, reproduced in Llewellyn 2000, fig.80).

a section of the master's clean-shaven chin remains of his features, he can be seen to be wearing a shaped cap, made of felted woven wool or possibly of velvet, and a long gown with a furred edge, beneath which his shirt and doublet are just visible; his black leather shoes can be seen resting on the plinth of the chair.[12] The viewer's gaze is drawn to the large open book he holds in front of him, roughly central to the whole scene and acting as its focus. His right hand is clenched, holding the other symbol of his authority, the birch rod, which, together with the book and the *cathedra*, is the usual attribute, or insignia, of the master (see Figure 5). The placing of the master on a higher level than his pupils is of course practical, so that he can see out over his class; it also, however, serves a symbolic function, together with his greatly increased scale, in denoting his elevated status and dignity.

The best preserved portion of the scene is the group of boys to the right of the master (see Figure 3). Ten are shown seated, most on or behind a long wooden form,

Left Fig. 4. Line drawing by Lisa Shekede, showing the surviving features of the mural.
Right Fig. 5. Reconstruction of the mural by Stephen Conlin, watercolour and pen and ink.

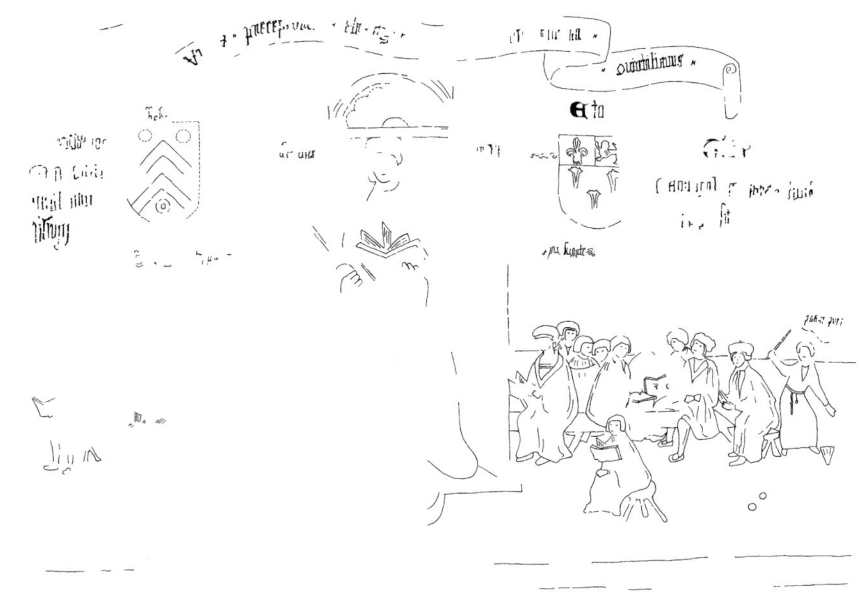

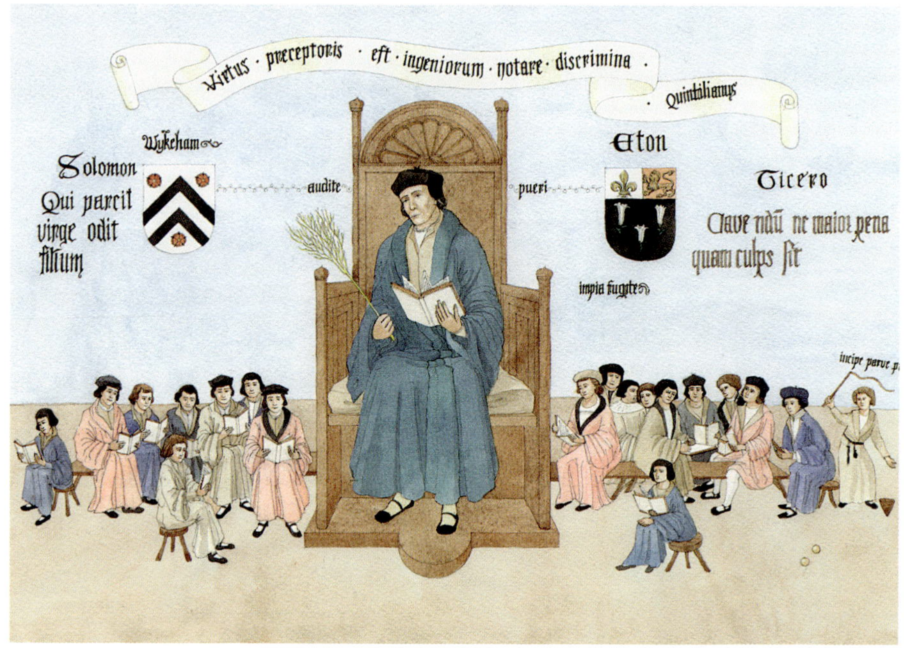

12 Susan North, Keeper of Fashion 1550–1800 in the Dept of Furniture,Textiles and Fashion, at the Victoria & Albert Museum, has kindly provided advice on the details of early sixteenth-century dress.

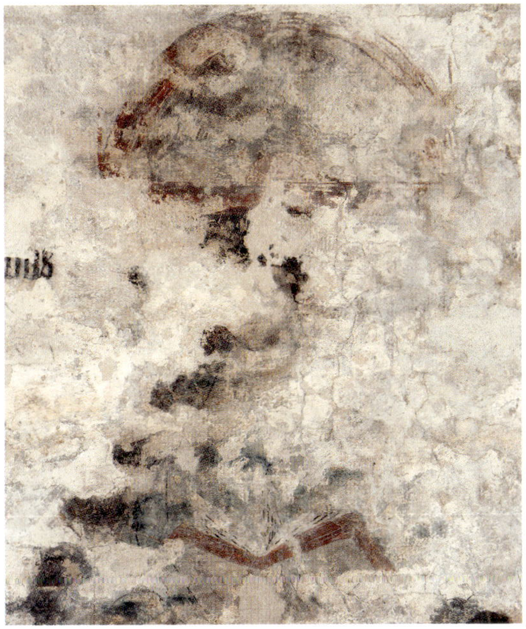

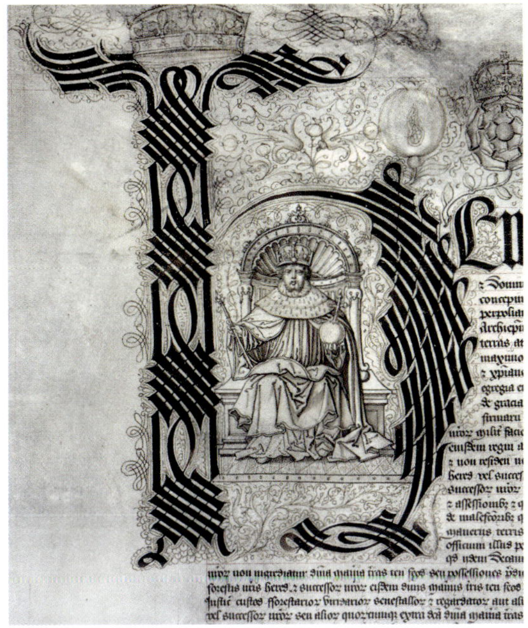

Left Fig. 6. Detail of the master seated in a chair, upper section. **Right** Fig. 7. Illuminated initial portrait of Henry VIII, from Wolsey's patent for Cardinal College, Oxford, 5 May 1526, pen and ink.

with two sitting on three-legged stools (Figure 8). Several are engaged in reading, while one, at the far end of the form, looks up at the master, and another – in the centre of the group, and facing away from the master – is shown holding a stylus and writing on a board on his lap.[13] At far right a standing boy plays with a whip and spinning top, while two balls lie on the floor in the foreground (Figure 9). Of the corresponding group of boys to the left of the master, nothing survives except traces of one or more of the books they were reading and, at far left, the fragmentary figure of a reading boy sitting on a stool and facing away from the master. While no similar master's chair or tripod stools survive at Eton, it is notable that three Tudor forms, similar to that shown in the painting although rather more elaborate, are still in use at the College; the survival *in situ* of school furniture from this date is exceedingly rare (Figure 10).[14]

The heraldry and inscriptions are dominant elements of the mural. On either side of the master, and above each group of boys, is a shield: on the right, the arms of Eton College (*Sable three lilies two and one argent a chief per pale azure and gules charged on the dexter with a fleur de lis and on the sinister a lion passant guardant or*) labelled 'Eton' (Figure 11); and on the left, the arms of Winchester College (*Argent two chevrons sable between three roses gules*) labelled 'Wykeham' (Figure 12).[15] The two schools came to have the closest connections. In 1441, the summer after he had laid the foundation stone at Eton, Henry VI paid a visit to Winchester to inspect Wykeham's buildings.[16] He then induced the schoolmaster, William Waynflete, to come to Eton with five or six scholars and perhaps a few commoners and day boys, to organise the nucleus of his new college. In 1442 a Winchester scholar, William Westbury, was brought from New College, Oxford, to be the Eton schoolmaster. And in 1443, perhaps on the advice of Waynflete, who had been made Provost in

13 Books, slates and writing boards were all used at this period: see below p.162 and n.85.

14 The forms have moulded edges to single-plank rectangular tops, and solid supports with elided ionic capitals and carved Tudor roses. Willemsen 2008, 266-7, discusses the survival of school furniture; she notes that 'benches too [like stools] have not been preserved *in situ*, but have been depicted in school scenes from Germany, England and Italy'. While these forms date from the early sixteenth century, and may indeed be a survival of the school furniture of the period, it should be noted that in 1625 Thomas Weaver, an Eton Fellow, gave a number of desks and forms for the townspeople to sit on in the chapel, and it is possible that these early forms were part of his gift (the gift is recorded on the flyleaf of a Pentateuch, Eton College Library, Dd.c.3.1; see Cust 1899, 138 for a transcription). The proposed connection between Weaver's gift and the surviving forms was made in Austen-Leigh 1988, 32. It is worth noting that the early eighteenth-century furniture in Upper School and the Head Master's School Room at Eton, as well as at Winchester College, includes masters' chairs similarly raised on plinths.

15 The arms of William of Wykeham, Bishop of Winchester (1324-1404), were adopted from the outset by Winchester College, the school he founded in 1382 (see Chitty 1923, 368-70, 378-9; 390-1; 418-19; pls.I-XIII). For a reference to Winchester College as 'Wykam colleadge' in the sixteenth century, see McGrath 1982, 240.

16 For the date of Henry's first visit to Winchester see above p.19, n.14.

1442, Henry drew up new statutes enlarging his new foundation to provide for 70 scholars (as at Winchester). The statutes, which themselves were based on those of Winchester, also brought his twin foundations of Eton and King's College, Cambridge, into the same association as Wykeham's foundations of Winchester and New College.[17] The close relationship between Eton and Winchester was exemplified above all in the person of William Waynflete, who after his promotion to the bishopric of Winchester in 1447, continued until his death in 1486 to oversee the building not only of the chapel at Eton, and the execution of its wall paintings, but also of the school.[18] He was also a prime mover in the making of the *Amicabilis concordia* between the two schools and their associate colleges.[19]

On a scroll at the top of the painting, functioning like a label to the whole scene, is an abbreviated quotation from Quintilian's *Institutio oratoria* (Book 2.8.1): 'Virtus preceptoris est ingeniorum notare discrimina' ('the excellence of a teacher is to note the difference in talents [of his pupils]') (Figure 13).[20] Enough survives of the damaged inscription to the left of the 'Wykeham' shield for it to be clear that it is labelled 'Solomon', and that it is a quotation from Proverbs 13: 24: 'Qui parcit virge odit filium' (popularly translated as 'spare the rod and spoil the child') (Figure 14); this is the only

Left Fig. 8. Detail from the mural showing a boy on a tripod stool.
Right Fig. 9. Detail of a young boy with whipping top and tennis balls.

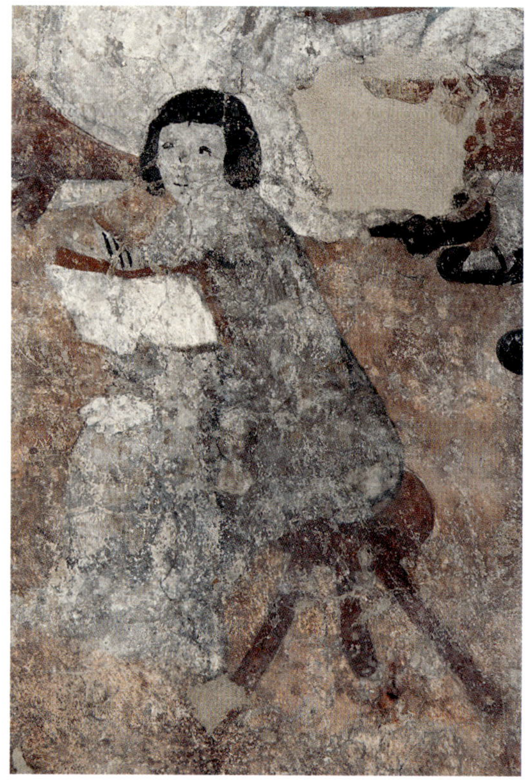

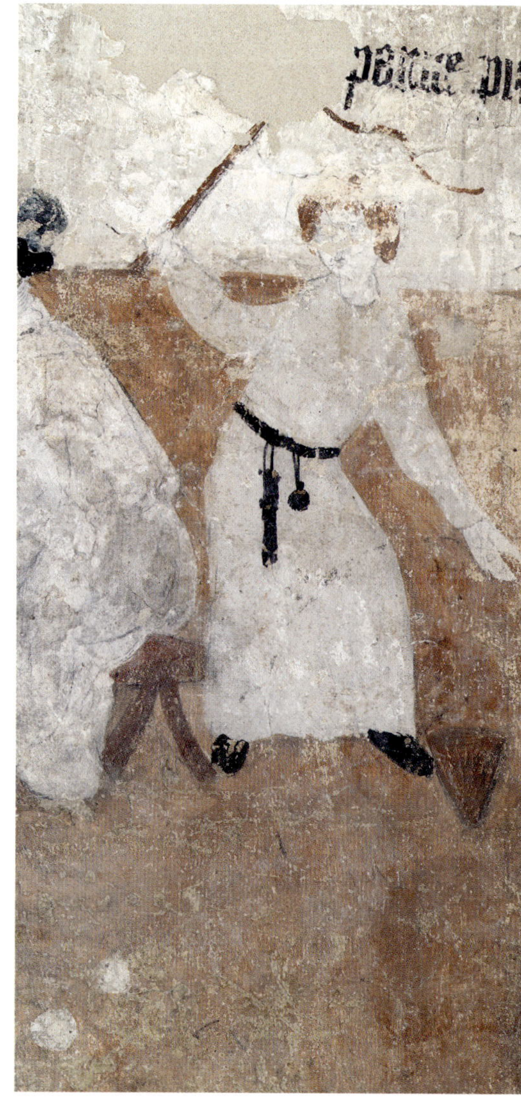

17 The Eton statutes for the most part followed the Winchester statutes literally; see Sterry 1943, xiii-xv, where he notes that Wykeham's foundation of New College, with the grammar school at Winchester to supply it with scholars, and his exclusion of regular clergy from his foundations, made it possible for 'poor scholars' and the sons of the rising commercial class to be educated. It has been noted that 'So large a part did Winchester play at Eton that the 1st 3 provosts, 12 out of the first 25 headmasters and 8 of the ushers or 2nd masters, and probably a good many more, came from Winchester' (Leach 1969, 258).

18 For the close relationship between the two foundations, see p.19 above. For Waynflete's role at Eton, see Willis & Clark 1886, ch.1-5; Davis 1993; and *ODNB*, 57, 781-5. Waynflete was an important figure in English humanist circles, his interest in education extending to his founding of Magdalen College, Oxford (in 1448), with its associated school (in or before 1479). John Anwykyll, the first master of Magdalen College School, wrote one of the most important of the early grammatical works printed at Oxford, the *Compendium totius grammaticae* (1483).

19 The *Amicabilis concordia* or 'friendly agreement', was a formal document to which the four colleges affixed their seals; by it they pledged to assist and support each other in 'actions, lawsuits and controversies' as well as in a more general way (although it did not necessarily prevent all disagreements, as for instance those between Eton and King's over Eton Fellowships). The agreement is still celebrated today, for example, in a three-yearly joint evensong by the choirs of the four colleges. See further p.19, n.18 above.

20 Quintilian's original text reads: 'Virtus praeceptoris haberi solet, nec imerio, diligenter in iis quos erudiendos susceperit notare discrimina ingeniorum', Reinhardt & Winterbottom 2006, 13.

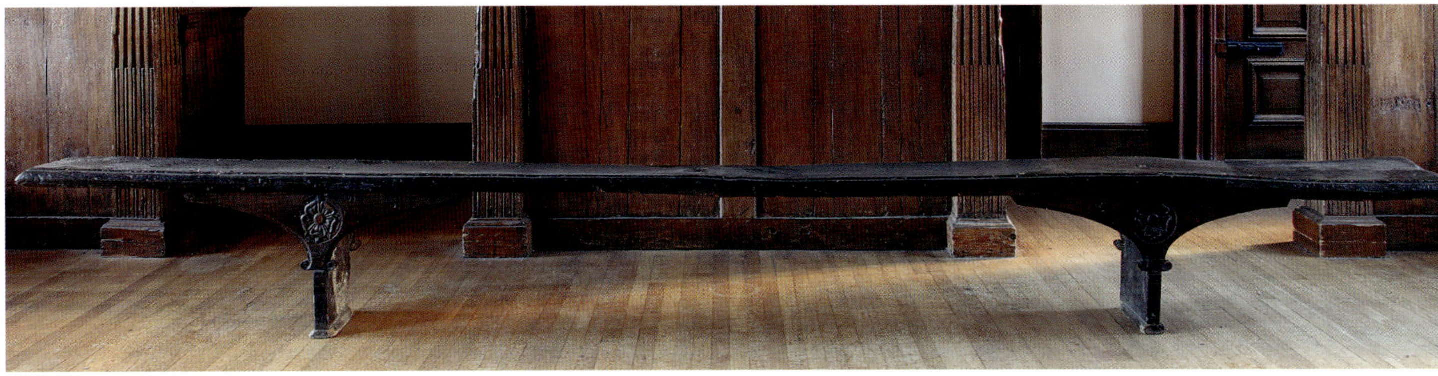

Right Fig. 10. Tudor form in Election Hall, Eton College.

biblical inscription in the painting.[21] Appropriately, the master with his birch is looking in this direction. The corresponding inscription on the right of the painting, which is somewhat deteriorated and only legible under ultraviolet illumination, softens the message. Labelled 'Cicero', and taken from his *De officiis* (Book 1.25.89), it reads: 'Cavendum ne maior poena quam culpa sit' ('Care must be taken that the punishment does not exceed the offence').[22] Of the shorter and smaller-scale inscriptions, the words flanking the master's chair are now indecipherable; a suggestion has been made in the watercolour reconstruction as to the type of phrase that might have been used (see Figure 5).[23] However, above the right-hand group of boys are the words 'impia fugite' ('flee impious thoughts') (Figure 15), and above the playing boy, 'parve puer' (small boy) (see Figure 9). Since 'parve' is in the vocative case, this latter inscription may have been a quotation from Virgil's *Eclogues* (4, line 60): 'Incipe, parve puer' ('Begin, small boy').[24]

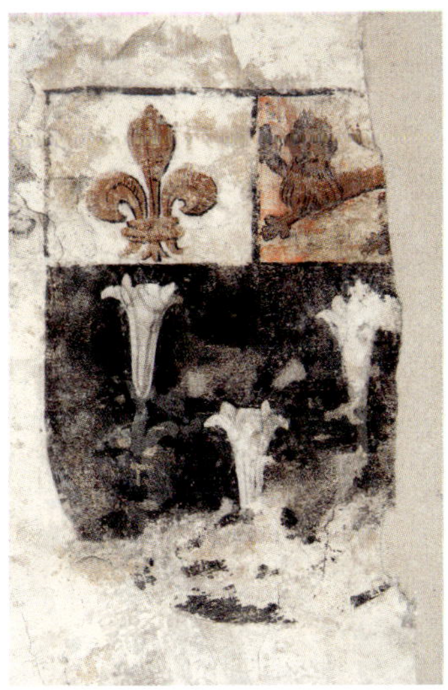

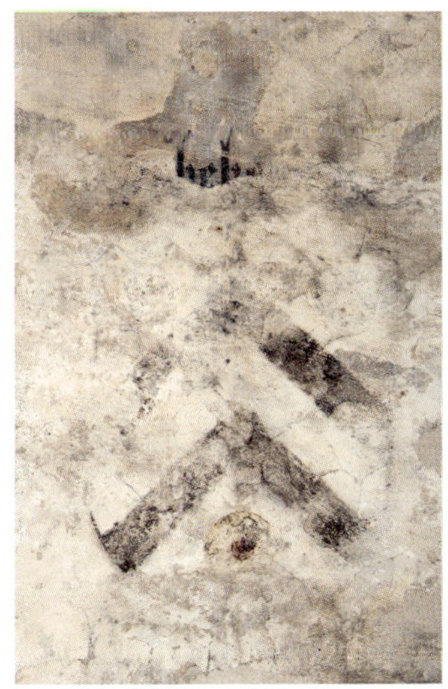

Left Fig. 11. Detail of Eton College coat of arms from the mural.
Right Fig. 12. Detail of Winchester College coat of arms.

21 The elucidation of this inscription is due to Stephen Conlin. The same verse appears on the seal of Louth grammar school in 1532, accompanying an image of a master scourging a boy; see Bagley 1993, 42.

22 This sentiment reflects the ethos expressed in the foundation statutes of Winchester and Eton, which instruct the schoolmaster to be moderate in punishment: 'But he must always be restrained by this caution, that in his chastisement he must in no wise be immoderate' (ECR 58/14, p.64).

23 The words 'audite pueri', suggested by Stephen Conlin, echo those accompanying the image of the Christ Child teaching, 'ipsum audite' (listen to me), which decorated John Colet's St Paul's School (see p.164 below). The last two letters of the first word, however, are legible as 'us'.

24 This source was kindly suggested by Andrew Maynard. In Virgil's text, the words are, however, used in a different context: 'Incipe, parve puer, risu cognoscere matrem' ('Begin, baby boy, to recognise your mother with a smile'): Rushton Fairclough & Goold 1999, 52-3.

Context, date and commissioning

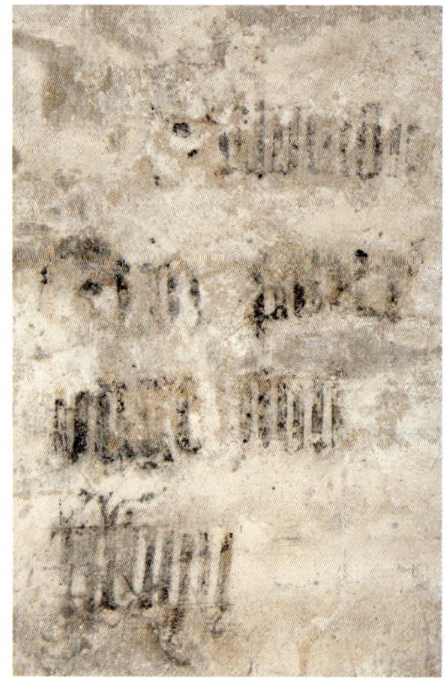

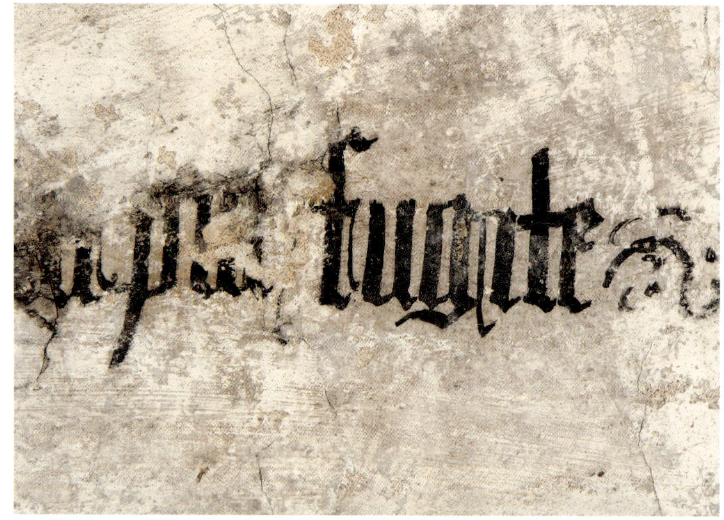

Top Fig. 13. Detail from the mural showing scroll with inscription from Quintilian. **Bottom left** Fig. 14. Detail of inscription from Proverbs. **Bottom right** Fig. 15. Detail of inscription 'impia fugite'.

The most interesting of these quotations is that from Quintilian, chosen as the 'title' to the scene, which is not in fact a direct quotation but is taken from the book of 'Vulgars', or sayings given in English and Latin, published by William Horman in 1519 as his *Vulgaria*.[25] Horman (1457-1535), at that time a Fellow of Eton, had been the schoolmaster of the College between 1486 and 1495. Originally a scholar of Winchester College, he became a scholar and Fellow of New College, Oxford, before coming to Eton as schoolmaster. In 1495 he moved to become master of Winchester, leaving in 1502 when he was elected to a Fellowship at Eton, where he remained for the rest of his life, serving various College offices, including bursar, precentor, and finally vice-provost in 1525, to which post he was continuously re-elected until his death in 1535.[26] The sayings and quotations in his book were those he had used in his teaching at Eton and no doubt at Winchester too. Among them are several direct references to the new humanist learning spreading through Europe, including the study of Greek.[27] M.R. James observes that 'for his time he was an exceedingly well and widely-read man' and 'must have read … practically the whole range of Latin literature known in his day'.[28] Horman explains that most of the phrases included in his *Vulgaria* were 'such as occurred in casual conversation and had no inner coherence. I have classified them roughly. Names of the authors are not added; usually I borrowed only a word or two from them and made a sentence of my own'.[29] The fact that he does not take his quotations verbatim from Latin authors, but rephrases them to emphasise a particular word or idi-

25 Our thanks are due to Poppy Anderson, who first recognised the connection with Horman. Vulgars or *Vulgares* were being introduced by the humanist grammarians active in Oxford in the latter part of the fifteenth century and subsequently in London from the early sixteenth century onward. They were printed textbooks of sentences, often quoting classical authors, in Latin and English, to be learned by rote as an aid to speaking Latin. A counterpart to Grammars, the use of Vulgars in schools had become standard by the 1520s. William Horman's was the most significant of these compilations, comprising 3,000 English sentences with Latin translations, arranged by subject. For the humanist grammarians and their textbooks, see Orme 2006, 118-27.

26 He served as bursar four times between 1510/11 and 1516/17; there is then a gap in the College accounts but he was bursar again in 1519/20. He then served as precentor in 1521-5, before being elected as vice-provost (ECR 62/1-62/2 *passim*). For Horman, see also *ODNB*, 28, 113.

27 For example: 'Men that be well lerned in these dayes take uppe many thynges that were of antiquyte' (p.135); 'By reading of substantial authors thou shalt bring about or attain to speak elegant and substantial Latin' (p.122); 'He applied himself with great diligence to greke' (p.137); 'Tell me in laten what he sayeth in greke'(p.145). The references to Horman's *Vulgaria* in this chapter are to M.R. James's 1926 Roxburghe Club edition (referred to as James 1926). Eton College library lacks the original 1519 edition but has a copy of the 2nd edition of 1530.

28 James 1926, xvii, further noting that Horman's *Vulgaria* 'shows [him] engaged in the real profitable work of his life, the imparting of sound learning'. He describes Horman's place in the rise of humanism as that of 'a satellite revolving around the greater figures of Colet, Erasmus, Grocyn, etc.' (James 1926, xiv).

29 Horman left a number of his own books and manuscripts to Eton. Among these is his copy of Quintilian's *Institutiones*, Venice 1494, with his neat index on the flyleaf (Eton College Library DDf.2.12).

om, helps to give the sentences their colloquial directness. The quotation from Quintilian is a good example of this, where he both contracts the original phrase as well as altering the order of the key words to give greater emphasis to the word 'discrimina', or 'differences'.[30]

Horman's *Vulgaria* was published while Robert Aldrich was the schoolmaster at Eton. Aldrich (1488/9-1556), who had been a scholar of Eton, went on to King's College, Cambridge, where he met and befriended Erasmus, remaining in contact with him after Erasmus left Cambridge. It was no doubt Erasmus who both introduced Aldrich to the new humanist learning and encouraged him in his scholarly pursuits.[31] His period as schoolmaster at Eton (1515-21) coincided with a particularly learned group of Fellows at the College, of whom Horman was one, and it is notable that it was during Aldrich's time that Greek was introduced into the curriculum. As a fellow scholar and friend of Horman, Aldrich composed a laudatory verse for his *Vulgaria*, as well as contributing a long panegyrical epistle to it; in the latter Aldrich speaks of Horman's modesty, and of the excellence of his Latin as well as his English, expressing the hope that the whole 'cohort' of his learned Eton colleagues ('omnis docta cohors Etoniensis') will encourage him to publish more. The noted grammarian William Lily, another of their circle, also contributed a laudatory verse. Lily (1468?–1522/3) had been a pupil at Magdalen College School, Oxford, under its Wykehamist master John Stanbridge, author of another *Vulgaria* (1508);[32] he later went on a pilgrimage to Jerusalem and on his return journey visited Rhodes and Rome, where he acquired an extensive knowledge of Greek and Latin. In Rome he met John Colet, friend of Erasmus and later dean of St Paul's, and other scholars later associated with humanist learning in England. In 1512 Colet appointed Lily as the first master of St Paul's School, which became one of the centres of humanist-inspired teaching in England; Lily held the position until his death in 1523.

The person responsible for commissioning the decoration of the Head Master's Chambers with a school scene that included an overt reference to Horman's *Vulgaria* and to the new humanist teaching, with which both Horman and Aldrich were connected, is very likely to have been Robert Aldrich himself.[33] The fact that the painting is not mentioned in the accounts implies that it was paid for by a private individual rather than being commissioned by the College, in the same way that Waynflete's payments for the chapel paintings are not recorded in the accounts (see Part I, chapter 1 above).

30 The whole phrase, which occurs in Horman's chapter 'De scolasticis' is translated by him as 'A principal poynt of a schole maister is to discerne the difference of wyttis in children: and to what thynge every wytte is best disposed' (James 1926, 130).

31 Bietenholz 1985, 27-8. *ODNB*, 1, 633-4, suggests incorrectly that records indicating that Aldrich retained his Fellowship at King's until 1528, '[dispute] claims that he was master of Eton for several years after 1515'. It was in fact possible for masters of Eton to retain their fellowship of King's, as happened regularly at later dates. Aldrich's name first appears in the Eton audit books in 1515 as Informator, with his leaving date as 1521 (ECR 62/1 and ECR 62/2 *passim*). Aldrich helped Erasmus collate manuscripts for his new edition of Seneca, for which he was rewarded as the dedicatee of Erasmus's Epistola 1858 (see *Collected Works of Erasmus* 1974, 11, 397 and 13, 251-73). Aldrich was Erasmus's companion and interpreter during their pilgrimage to the shrine of Our Lady at Walsingham in 1512, being commemorated in Erasmus's colloquy, *Peregrinatia religionis ergo* (1526); see Nichols 1849, 22 and 95-6.

32 Stanbridge's *Vulgaria* was used in the Eton curriculum to teach the youngest boys of the First Form; see below p.162, and Maxwell Lyte 1911, p.143.

33 Apart from Nicholas Udall, very little is known of the other schoolmasters of the period, which would suggest that none was of Aldrich's scholarly standing. The list of schoolmasters runs: Thomas Erlysman (1511-15); Robert Aldrich (1515-21); Thomas White (1521-4); John Goldwyn (1524-8); Richard Cox (1528-34); and Nicholas Udall (1534-42). Udall, who had a somewhat chequered career as master at Eton, is inherently unlikely to have commissioned the mural, with its direct quote from Horman, as his own textbook, *Floures for Latin Spekyng* (1533), superseded Horman's in its provision of conversational Latin phrases modelled on idiomatic usages by Terence. In addition, his dates would seem rather too late for the mural, both from a stylistic point of view and in terms of Lupton's architectural changes of 1517-20 (see p.153 below).

The mural's celebration of the College's close connections with Winchester can thus be read not only as an acknowledgment of the original foundation of Eton following the educational precedents set by Wykeham, but also as a personal reference by Aldrich to Horman's career; with his education as a scholar at Winchester, his posts as master at both schools, and his (then current) Fellowship at Eton, he embodied the historical and educational links between the two establishments.

Such an interpretation of the mural and its commissioning would date its creation to around 1520, a date given further credibility by the amount of significant building work and adornment to the College which was taking place precisely during this period. Roger Lupton (1456-1540), Provost of Eton from 1504 to 1535, is chiefly remembered for his '[changing] the face of Eton' and for founding a grammar school at Sedbergh, Yorkshire, the town of his birth.[34] Lupton, who had trained in canon and civil law at King's College, Cambridge, rose to a position of high standing during the reign of Henry VII and the early years of Henry VIII, being appointed chaplain to Henry VII and a canon of Windsor, and acquiring several benefices. As Christopher Hussey notes, Lupton's provostship at Eton 'witnessed the renewal of building activity which had been in abeyance since the completion of the Antechapel by Waynflete in 1482'.[35] Following the near-closure of Henry VI's foundation by Edward IV, the increase in College revenues under the Tudor monarchs made such building work possible.

Lupton was concerned not only for the visual appearance of the College, both in its overall design and decoration, but also for the educational functionality of its buildings. His works included improvements to the Founder's original school building on the north side of the quadrangle, with alterations made to the scholars' dormitory (Long Chamber), and to their schoolroom (Lower School).[36] It seems that he also undertook improving works to the schoolmaster's 'chambre' at the west end of the range at this time.[37] Although there is no reference in the accounts to significant works in the room, the style of the fireplace below the mural dates it to the early sixteenth century, and the windows in the north and west walls are of the identical square-headed type used in the major building works that Lupton was undertaking on the western range of the cloisters (see below). Such improvements to the chamber might naturally call for its enhancement by some form of decoration. If it was indeed Aldrich who commissioned the painting, both Horman and Lupton are likely to have been keen supporters of the enterprise. Horman showed a particular interest in the decoration of buildings, as

34 For Lupton see *ODNB*, 34, 784-5. He forged links between his new school at Sedbergh and Cambridge, where he founded six scholarships at St John's College.

35 Hussey 1952, 17.

36 Work is recorded in 1506-7 and 1514-15, involving either rebuilding on the original foundations or extensive repairs (Willis & Clark 1886, 430 and n.1); see also Cust 1899, 31.

37 Willis & Clark 1886, 431. The earliest specific reference to the master's chamber ('cubiculum magistri infirmatoris') is for a pair of hinges for the room, which occurs in an entry in the audit roll for 1511-12: 'Et pro pari le gemoys ad cubiculum magistri infirmatoris xiij d.' (Willis & Clark 1886, 417, n.1; Christopher Wilson kindly helped with translating this entry). The next reference to the chambers is in 1552-3 for 'Reparationes. "Item to John Kendall for workinge abowte comynge owt of the Scole Mrs Chambre in to the childers chamber… ijs. jd.; Willis & Clark 1886, 431, n.1.

demonstrated by comments in the 'De re aedificatoria' section of his *Vulgaria*, such as 'The rofe shal be celled vautwyse and with cheker work' and 'Vautynge and celynge with cunnynge caruynge and peyntynge becometh and ornatteth wonderfly lordys howsis'.[38] He was also concerned with adorning the chapel, where he was generous in his gifts of precious metalwork and textiles.[39] Lupton's building work on the western range of the cloisters between 1517 and 1521 demonstrated more dramatically than his work in the chapel his interest in adorning the new buildings as well as his encouragement of teaching and support for scholarship. His scheme involved closing in the cloisters with the creation of the gatehouse and its flanking ranges, thus bringing the design of the College into line with that of Oxford and Cambridge colleges (see Figure 2).[40] The foremost masons and craftsmen of the royal works, who had just completed the exquisite chantry Lupton had built at his own cost in the chapel, were employed to supervise the new building works: the names of William Vertue, king's master mason, Henry Redman, master mason of Westminster Abbey, and Humphrey Coke, later king's master carpenter, are all recorded in the College accounts.[41]

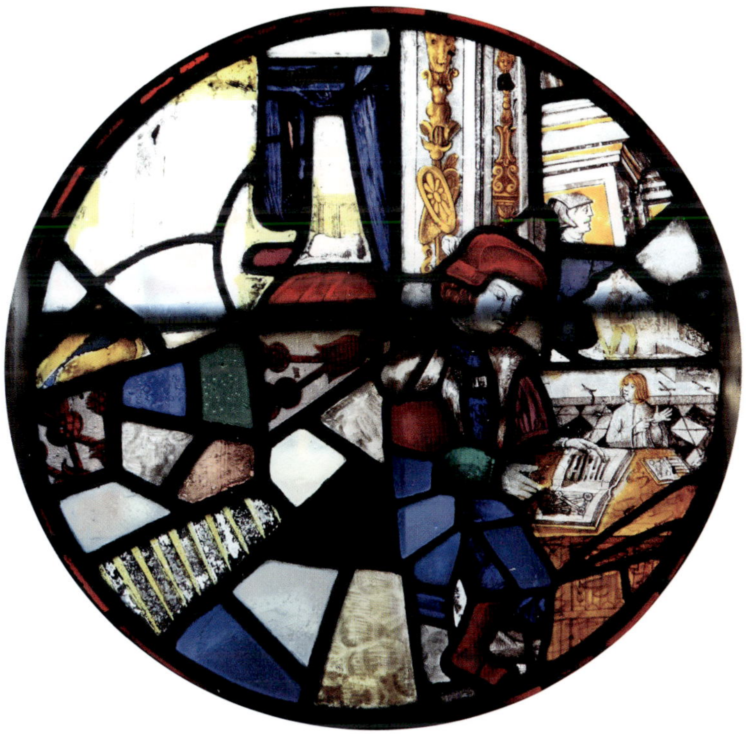

Fig. 16. Glass roundel attributed to Galyon Hone, *c.*1521, showing a master teaching mathematics, Election Hall, Eton College.

An important part of the new 'Lupton's range' was the building of the College's first library in its northern part (the room now known as Election Hall), with its typical library fenestration of pairs of windows along the two long sides of the room.[42] Horman, who shared Lupton's interests in building and adornment, may well have been useful to Lupton in advising him and helping to supervise this project.[43] He was certainly working with Lupton to increase the holdings of books and manuscripts in the Fellows' library.[44] The decoration of

38 James 1926, 349, 351.

39 His gifts included 'A ymage of the Resurrection of Christ of silver and gilt and ynamlyd' and 'A coveryng for the sepulcher of cloth of goolde with a trayll of crymsyn n velvatt' embroidered with 'scripture' (James 1926, xxviii).

40 See Goodall 2002 for the original form and design of the quadrangle to which Lupton made his additions. The College accounts record that on 2 March 1517, 'the first stone was layd yn the fundacyon of the west parte of the College, wheron ys bylded Mr. Provost's Logyn, the gate and the Lyberary'. Final payments are made to the glazier and painter in 1521 (Willis & Clark 1886, 418, n.1).

41 *Ibid*, 418, n.2. For William Vertue (d.1527), Henry Redman (1507-28) and Humphrey Coke (*fl.*1496-1531), see numerous references in Harvey 1948 and 1975.

42 Between these, bookcases would have projected from the walls on the pattern of other late medieval libraries. Unfortunately, as some of the College accounts for 1517-19 are missing, we have no records of the library furnishing. Hussey suggests the lecterns 'were probably of two storeys and longer than is usual, perhaps ten feet long, for, like Duke Humphrey's Library at Oxford, the room is exceptionally wide' (Hussey 1952, 60).

43 A suggestion made by M.R. James (James 1926, xxi). It may also be relevant that Horman held the post of College bursar during this period (see n.26 above).

44 See Hussey 1952, 60, who notes that by 1522 there were about 500 MSS and printed books in the library. For a list of those given by Horman, see James 1926, xxi-xxvii. See also Birley 1970, 9–11 for an account of Horman's significant additions to the library.

the library included the commissioning of medallions of stained glass, illustrating the various branches of learning with which the books were concerned, including the different branches of law, logic, theology, medicine, etc.[45] Unfortunately much damaged over the centuries, the medallions were reassembled at some point and inserted in the windows along the east and west walls of the room. The glass is of extremely high quality; in its sophisticated composition and use of receding perspective, it bears the hallmark of the celebrated Flemish glazier Galyon Hone, who is documented as working at Eton between 1517 and 1526.[46] Particularly interesting in relation to the mural, however, is that the subjects depicted include two fragmentary school scenes, one of them denoting the discipline of mathematics, in which a master is shown teaching a boy (Figure 16). Here the seated master, wearing a red cap and blue gown similar in style to those shown in the mural, is reading from an open book, the right-hand page of which shows a diagram, while a small boy, bare-headed and wearing a loose-sleeved tunic, sits on the other side of the table, counting on his fingers.[47] As in the mural, the boy is depicted on a diminutive scale compared to the master. The second scene is one of the more damaged fragments inserted into the windows on the west side of the room; barely legible and on a tiny scale, this shows a school scene remarkably similar to that in the mural, with a master seated in what seems to be a throne-like chair, teaching several boys who sit at his feet and hold open books (Figures 17 and 18).

Lupton's adornment of the buildings in his new range also extended to the gatehouse. A design of the 'lilie pott', the emblem of the Virgin and of Eton, was incorporated into the brickwork. A number of painted and carved sculptures were also commissioned to

Left Fig. 17. Fragment of glass *c.*1521, showing a master teaching boys, Election Hall, Eton College.
Right Fig. 18. Reconstruction of glass fragment showing a master teaching boys, line drawing by Stephen Conlin.

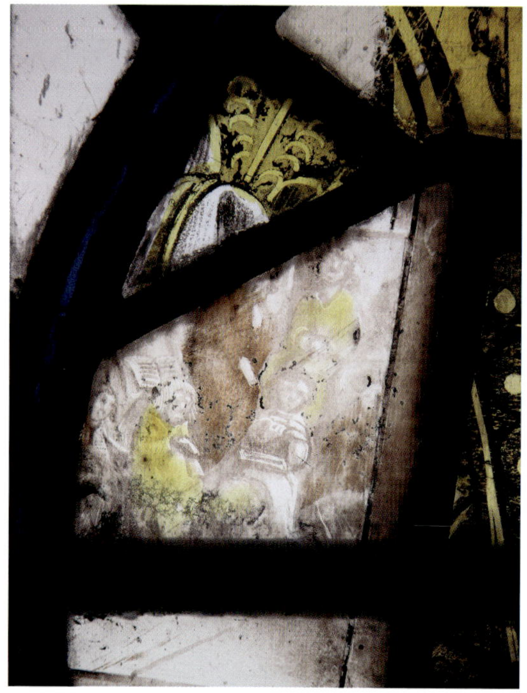

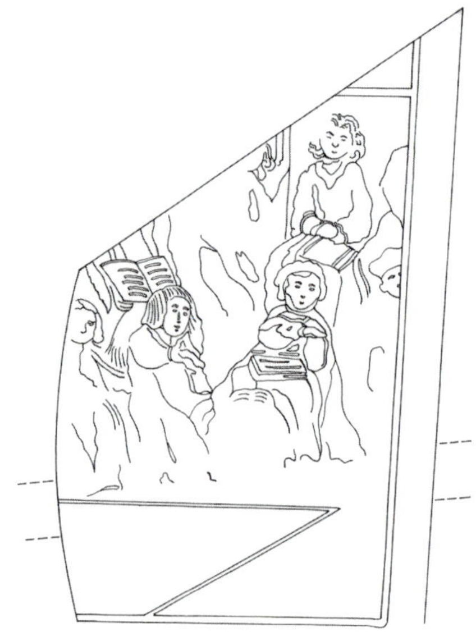

45 See James 1904. It is noteworthy that four of these roundels represent the different branches of law (one of civil law, one of canon law and two of common law), reflecting Lupton's own academic training. See also Maxwell Lyte 1911, 98.

46 Hone, who undertook royal commissions at Windsor, King's College, Cambridge, and elsewhere, is recorded as being paid £18 for completing the glass in the 'new building' in 1521, the date scratched on one of the fragments in the west windows (see ECR 62/1, 286). For Hone, see Wayment 1972, 12-13; also Marks 1993, 207, 227-8.

47 Tim Gowers has suggested (letter of 10 December 2011) that the diagram could represent an illustration of the relationship between the number of edges and the number of vertices of a tetrahedron, one of the five Platonic solids (the circles each containing three lines indicating the three edges coming out of each vertex). This would explain why one of the diagonals goes over the other (i.e. how a tetrahedron would be viewed from an appropriate angle). Interestingly, the image is the only indication of mathematics being taught in the school at this date.

embellish the great bay window over the arch: angels bearing the royal arms of the Founder; an Assumption of the Virgin; and, at the top, the royal arms of Henry VIII, surmounted by a royal crown, surrounded by the Garter, and supported by a red dragon and a white greyhound. As payments were made to the painters of these sculptures in 1520, it is not impossible that one or more of these same painters may have been employed by Aldrich for the school scene mural.[48] The shared interests of Lupton, Horman and Aldrich in the promulgation of teaching and scholarship, and their involvement in the improvements to the buildings for the use of the Fellows and the school, would make their collaboration in the design and execution of the mural a distinct possibility.

Style

In contrast to the Netherlandish style of the earlier wall paintings in the chapel, and to the exactly contemporary stained glass in Lupton's library, there is nothing in the style of the mural to suggest foreign workmanship. Apart from the detail of the round-arched top to the master's chair, it contains none of the obviously Renaissance elements, such as the sophisticated perspective or antique work ornament of Lupton's library glass, or, for example, of the contemporary wall paintings in the Oxenbridge chantry chapel of St George's Chapel (dated 1522), across the river in Windsor Castle.[49] In the Eton mural a sense of pictorial space is conveyed by the grouping and overlapping of the figures with one another and with the furnishings, and also by the plane of the floor intersecting the rear wall. The lower (foreground) edge of the floor is bordered by a light greyish band of colour; this in turn gives way to a broad black area which runs along the lower edge of the painting, which may originally have borne some sort of decorative pattern.[50] Despite the conventional medieval devices of adopting a bird's-eye view and splaying the two groups of boys to the sides, where they are out of the master's line of sight but fully visible to the viewer, each group nonetheless possesses an internal coherence and sense of solidity that reflects Renaissance spatial conventions.

The comparative lack of sophistication in the creation of spatial elements of the scene is counterbalanced by a naturalness in the depiction of the boys engaged in their various school tasks, and a lively sense of narrative. While the artist could not be described as attempting portraiture, he captures a range of expressions and achieves a real sense of characterisation among the different individuals. One boy, for example appears

48 The payment is to 'the painters of the images on the front of the new building' ('Et pictori Imaginum in Frontispicio novi edificii'): Willis & Clark 1886, 418, n.3. For a discussion of artists working on both sculptures and paintings at this period, see Auerbach 1954, 7-17. The sculptures have been subject to subsequent repainting.

49 Croft-Murray 1962, 22, pl.27. He describes these as 'the first decorative paintings probably by a native painter to show Renaissance detail'.

50 In the same way that the chapel murals are finished along their east and lower edges by decorative borders bearing a damask pattern (see p.27 above).

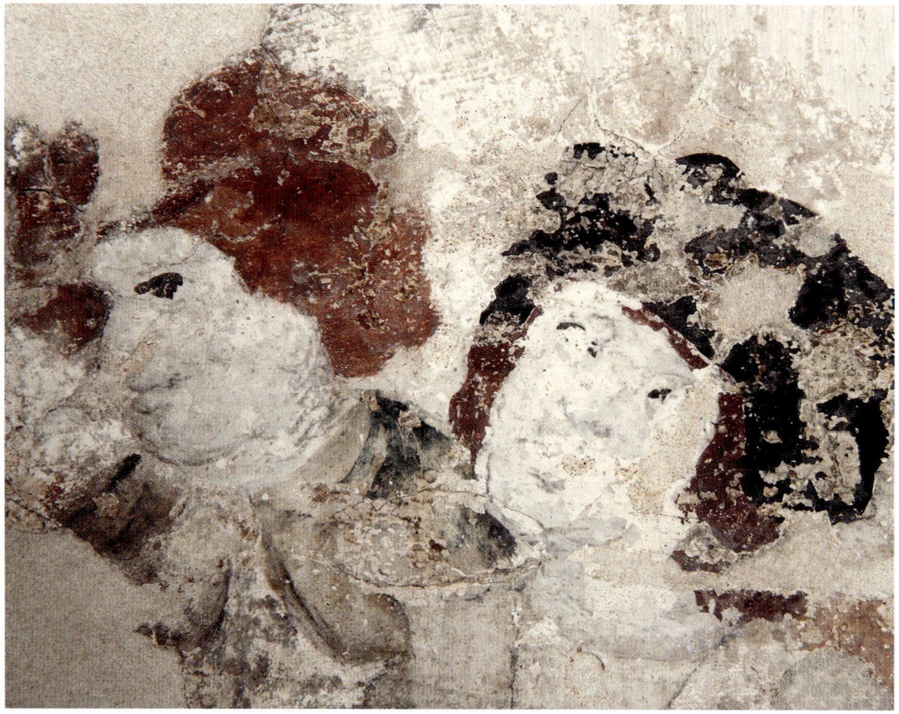

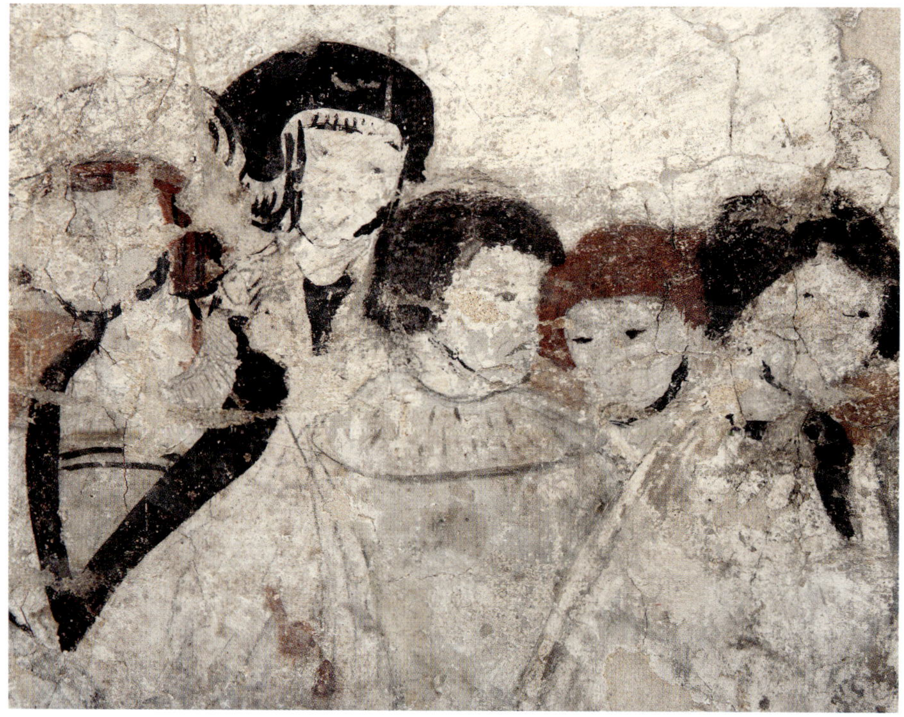

absorbed in what the master is saying (Figure 19); another, sitting alone on his stool at the far end of the bench, concentrates hard on learning from his book (see Figure 3); while yet another, sitting at the back of the class, looks distinctly cross and bored (Figure 20).

Analysis of the style and quality of the mural, must, of course, take into account the fact that we are not seeing it in its original condition. Significant damage has occurred as a result of historical events, such as the attachment of panelling in the early eighteenth century, nineteenth-century alterations to the fireplace, and 1940s bomb damage to Upper School.[51] Adverse environmental conditions in the form of salts- and moisture-related degradation of the paint layer, and photo-deterioration of organic colorants, have led to further transformations in the mural's appearance.

Left Fig. 19. Detail from the mural showing two boys, one looking intently at the master.
Right Fig. 20. Detail of a group of boys, one looking cross.

51 A bomb fell on the north end of Upper School, the part of the building abutting the Head Master's Chambers on the south side, and its effects are likely to have been a contributory factor to the greater damage sustained by the southern section of the wall painting.

Materials and technique

Since the execution of the mural was not recorded in the College accounts, we have no contemporary documentation of the materials used, as we do for the chapel wall paintings. The scientific examination carried out during the conservation of the painting in 2006-7, however, has contributed significant information about the techniques and materials employed in its creation.[52] The process included both microscopic examination of minute paint samples and multispectral imaging.[53] Most significantly, these indicate that, while the palette of the artist seems to have been intentionally restrained, it was nevertheless much richer and more varied than it now appears, on account of an extensive use of organic colorants which have now deteriorated.[54]

Overall, the examinations revealed that very different techniques were used for the mural from those employed for the chapel paintings. While the latter were executed on lead grounds over a stone support, using oil as the primary binding medium, the mural in the Head Master's Chambers was painted over two thin white ground layers of calcium carbonate applied over a lime-based plaster, which was laid over the brick support.[55] Considerable evidence of preliminary drawing in charcoal was revealed by infrared imaging.[56] Different binders were identified for different paint layers.[57] Protein (possibly indicating the use of glue) was identified as a binder both in the ground and in a paint layer containing indigo, while both oil and protein (possibly indicating the use of egg yolk) were detected in a pale pinkish-red layer.[58]

Paint application techniques were generally found to be quite simple and, by comparison with the chapel paintings, the range of mineral pigments employed was relatively limited: iron-oxide red and yellow; red lead; calcium carbonate white; and charcoal black. A significant range of organic colorants was used in addition to these, however, including indigo, madder lake and brazilwood lake, to achieve subtle translucent pinks and blues, through which the underdrawing may have been intended to remain visible.[59] Organic colorants were found mixed with inorganic pigments, as in the indigo mixed with charcoal black to suggest the folds of the boys' gowns. They were also used in combination, as with the madder lake mixed with brazilwood lake in the undergarment of the boy wearing the indigo cap. Now having a yellowish, saturated appearance, this garment would originally have been a rich pink-red. It is likely that other organic colorants were also used, mixed

52 The information included below is taken from the unpublished reports of Rickerby & Shekede 2006 and 2007; the latter report also incorporates Howe 2007.

53 For the multispectral imaging undertaken by Giovanni Verri (using UV-induced fluorescence, infrared and infrared false-colour), see Rickerby & Shekede 2007 and Verri 2007.

54 The term 'organic colorant' describes colouring matter obtained from organic dye materials, not just organic pigments. High-performance liquid chromatography (HPLC) was kindly undertaken by Jo Kirby Atkinson of the Scientific Department of the National Gallery.

55 The layer applied immediately onto the lime plaster is a slightly uneven white limewash, varying between approximately 50 and 200μm in thickness, and intended to level out the rough plaster surface. Above this is a thinner more compact white chalk-size ground up to 50μm thick, intended to provide a smooth surface for painting (see Rickerby & Shekede 2007, Technical Appendix, 3).

56 This can be seen clearly, for example, in the outlines of the legs of the boy sitting astride a form with his gown pulled up, Figure 26.

57 Identified through histochemical tests.

58 The latter was not, however, confirmed by instrumental analysis (Rickerby & Shekede 2007, Technical Appendix, 3).

59 The common use of indigo in English wall painting is discussed on p.85 above.

with organic and inorganic paint materials to produce a range of yellows, greens and purples.[60] Although the boys' faces now have a dull grey appearance, flesh tones were probably achieved with organic colorants which have also now deteriorated.

The significant colour loss in the mural means that the figures now appear somewhat flat and schematic. It is clear, however, that the handling of the brushwork and the modelling of the forms were extremely competent. Unlike the organic colorants, the brushwork in charcoal black has not faded, and shows a bold and fluid handling of paint in details such as the boys' dress, caps, and hair (Figure 21). The figures may well have been the responsibility of a different artist from the artist (or possibly several artists) employed for the lettering and heraldry.

Iconographical sources

The direct and informal style of the mural must surely have been influenced by the artist's first-hand observation of actual classes taking place in the schoolroom next door. Nonetheless, the general source of the wall painting's composition clearly lies in the many popular late medieval continental and English woodcuts showing boys being instructed by a seated master with a birch.[61] Possibly not coincidentally, two of the standard English schoolmaster woodcuts in circulation at this time were in fact used to illustrate the earliest of Horman's school textbooks, his *Introductorium lingue latine*, published in two editions in 1495 and 1499.[62] These, employed as the frontispieces of the different editions, resemble the wall painting with their centrally placed master (Figure 22 illustrates one of these). A more elaborate woodcut, used as the frontispiece of other Latin grammars, is closer to the painting in showing a larger group of boys.[63] All three are typical of schoolmaster woodcuts, however, with a simpler composition than that shown in the mural, containing fewer figures, depicting the master on the same scale as his pupils, and lacking inscriptions. A possibly unique instance of a woodcut showing two large groups of seated boys as in the Eton painting, though with the master seated to one side, is provided by a German woodcut of 1524.[64] In general, none of the woodcuts shows the characterisation of the schoolboys in the Eton mural, although such animated and individualised groups are already found in other contexts in the early sixteenth century. A carved and painted wooden group of *c.*1520 now in Paris (Figure 23) shows a startling resemblance to the Eton boys, although it has been argued convincingly that it derives from a scene

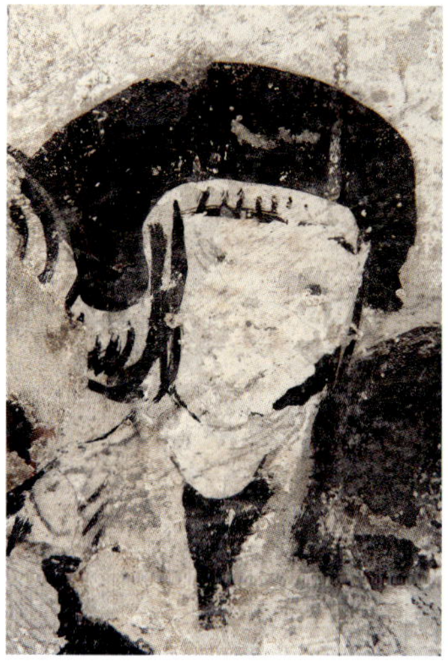

Fig. 21. Detail of a boy from the mural showing fluent painting in charcoal black.

60 It should be noted that organic colorants are notoriously difficult to identify, especially after having been exposed to light over a long period. Although hardly visible to the naked eye, false-colour infrared imaging indicates the presence of indigo (visible as bright pink) in the garments worn by the left-hand group of boys (see Howe 2007, pl.1e).

61 For German examples, see Schreiber & Heinz 1908; for English examples see Hodnett 1973, 348-9, figs 75-80.

62 See *ESTC* S112225 (1495 edition) and *ESTC* S109907 (1499 edition).

63 It was used for example as the frontispiece of John Stanbridge's *Parvulorum institutio*, 1512-13; see Hodnett 1973, fig.80.

64 Reicke 1971, Abb. 45.

from a saint's life, like the similar teaching scene from the life of St Firmin carved on the choir screen of *c.*1530 in Amiens Cathedral.[65] Both these carvings have the same charm and individualisation as the Eton painting, although they lack the classical inscriptions.

One element of the Eton painting that is derived from a different source is the young boy playing with his whip and spinning top. Such an image was a standard way of depicting childhood in medieval depictions of the *Ages of Man*, where the child was often labelled 'puer', as for example in the wall paintings of *c.*1330 in the manor house of Longthorpe Tower, near Peterborough.[66] The label, in this case 'puericia', can be seen clearly in a leaf from a mid-fourteenth-century German manuscript (Figure 24).[67] Just such a reference to a boy playing with a whip and top was used to represent childhood in the series of painted cloths for which the youthful Thomas More wrote the verses:

> I am called Chyldhood, in play is all my mynde.
> To cast a coyte, a cokstele, and a ball.
> A toppe can I set, and dryue it in his kinde.
> But would to god these hateful bookes all,
> Were in a fyre brent to pouder small.
> That myght I lede my lyfe alawayes in play:
> Which lyfe god sende me to myne endyng day.[68]

There is a similar tension between work and play in the depiction of the Eton boy who, although still engaged in the 'pursuits and trifles of boyhood',[69] has his writing accoutrements at his belt and is clearly, however reluctantly, bound for school. Just as the usual insignia of the schoolmaster are the book and birch, so the penner and inkwell – looped together and attached to the belt – are the attributes frequently used to denote the schoolboy. The artist of the mural, while using stock motifs to denote schoolboys and childhood, must have been able to observe boys at play in School Yard, just outside the room where he was painting the scene. Horman speaks of boys engaged in a number of different games, including chess, puppets, juggling, playing with

Left Fig. 22. Schoolmaster teaching three boys, woodcut used as frontispiece to William Horman, *Introductorium lingue latine*, 1495.
Right Fig. 23. Saint instructing boys, *c.*1520, carved and painted wood (Musée National du Moyen Age, Paris).

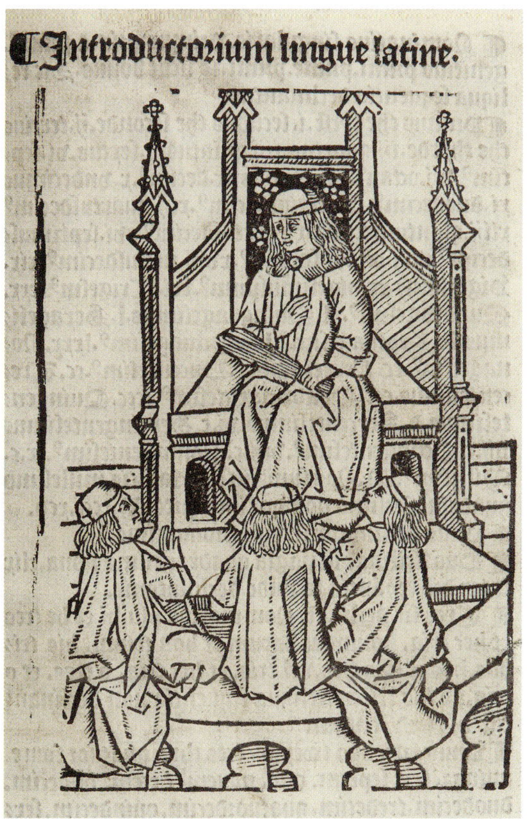

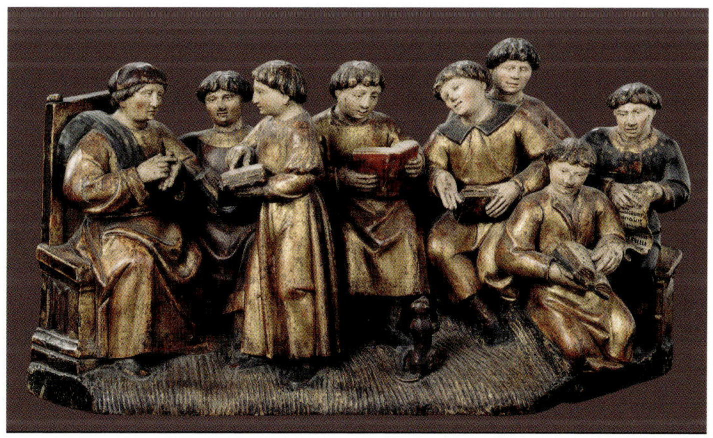

65 For both carvings, and for similar scenes from saints' lives in French stained glass of the period, see Willemsen 2008, 143, 162-5, ills.118, 140-1, 144 and cover ill. The sculpture now in Paris is reproduced in a double-page colour plate in Riché & Alexandre-Bidon 1994, 134-5.

66 Rouse & Baker 1955, 10, 33, 43, 44 n.6, pl.VII.

67 Sears 1986, 130, fig.65; see also 232 for indexed references to the terms *puer*, *pueritia* and *aetas puerilis* in descriptions and images of childhood in the Ages of Man.

68 Edwards, Gardiner Rodgers and Miller 1997, 3.

69 Malim 1560, 568.

cherrystones,[70] and several types of ball games such as playing 'with a ball full of wynde' and 'tenys'.[71] The balls shown in the mural may well be tennis balls; a tennis court is thought to have existed in the Long Walk, in front of what is now Upper School.[72] Turned wooden spinning tops and wooden balls, similar in style to those in the Eton mural, are among finds dating from the late sixteenth century excavated in 2002 at the site of a grammar school in Gorinchem in the Netherlands (Figure 25).[73]

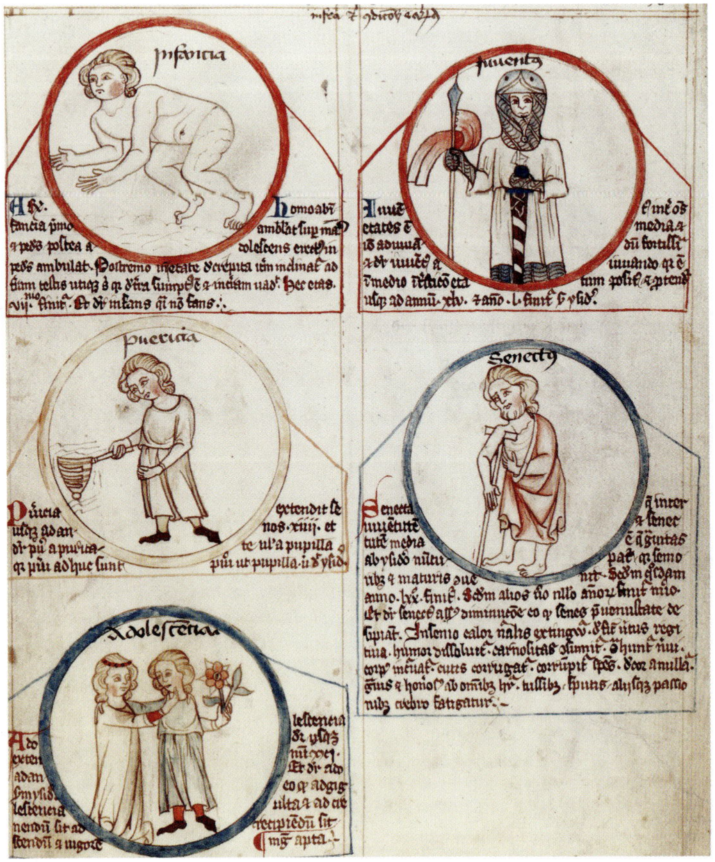

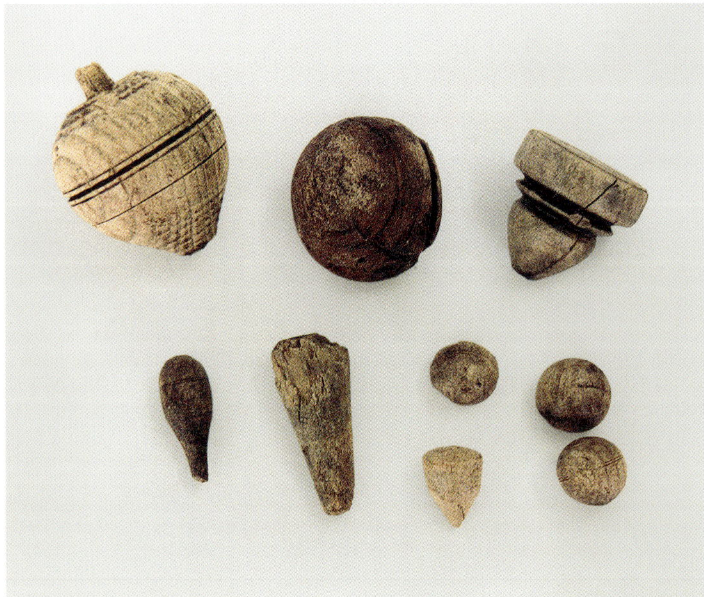

Left Fig. 24. The 'Five Ages of Man', from a mid fourteenth-century German manuscript (MS clm. 19414, f. 180*r*, Bayerische Staatsbibliothek, Munich).
Right Fig. 25. Turned wooden tops and balls dating from the late 1500s, found on the site of a grammar school at Gorinchem.

70 Orme 2001, 176-8, discusses how everyday objects such as cherrystones, cobnuts and animal bones were used by children at this period for ball games, marbles and counters.
71 'De exercitamentis et ludis': James 1926, 400-10, including a phrase with a familiar ring: 'He hyt me in the yie with a tenys balle' (409).
72 There are several references in the accounts to the repair of the tennis court. M.R. James notes that a number of what were probably tennis balls were discovered when works were being carried out to Upper School in the mid-1920s (James 1926, 454).
73 Willemsen 2008, 97-8. See *ibid*, 289, ill.255 for a very similar spinning top to that in the mural depicted in a scene of two boys playing in a Flemish MS of *c*.1500 in Munich. A moulded lead inkwell which could well date from this period has survived at Eton and can be seen among artefacts displayed in the College's museum of Eton life; we are grateful to Penny Hatfield for drawing this to our attention.

School curriculum

These human details form part of the charm of the painting, and can be set in the context of what we know of schooling at Eton and elsewhere in this period. Horman's *Vulgaria* gives us many vivid details about games and play, and also about the other activities of the pupils, their equipment and method of learning, the texts they used, and the discipline to which they were subject. From a little later we have William Malim's *Consuetudinarum vetus Scholae Etonensis* of 1560;[74] here the daily routine of school life is set out, with the teaching structure and details of the curriculum.[75] As there were no assistant masters apart from the usher responsible for the junior boys, a system of using boy-teachers, who were senior boys or prefects (known as 'praepostors'), was employed for both teaching and discipline.[76] Malim explains how:

> The boys of the Seventh Form who have been appointed by the Master to teach the other Forms begin their task and exercise those committed to their charge by explanations of their lessons and translations from English into Latin. They also read out and correct passages dictated by the Master on the same day. The Praepostors of each Form undertake this duty to enable the Schoolroom Praepostors to exercise control over all the boys as regards progress in their studies and improvement in character.[77]

He further spells out the different types of monitorial 'praepostors':

> There are appointed from among the boys: Four Praepostors of the Eton Schoolroom. One of the Hall to keep order. Two of the Church. Four of the Playing Fields. Four of the Bedchamber. Two of the Oppidans. One of the unclean and dirty boys who fail to wash their hands and faces.[78]

As the Seventh, Sixth and Fifth Forms were taught by the schoolmaster, the Fourth by both schoolmaster and usher, and the Third, Second and First by the usher,[79] it is likely that the boys represented in the mural are more senior boys from the upper forms, with perhaps the younger, bare-headed ones representing the middle year or Fourth Form. The young boy sitting out in front of the class on a tripod stool, with his book held up, could perhaps represent the 'custos', or dunce, the term applied to a boy who spoke in English during lessons, missed three words in repeating a rule in grammar, or made three mistakes in spelling. Each form had a 'custos' and he had to be the first to repeat lessons and answer questions.[80] The 'parve puer' with his writing accoutrements may also be included in the scene as a sample representative of the lower school, i.e. a boy

74 Malim 1560, 561-75.
75 Maxwell Lyte 1911, 137-58, describes the three different documents dating from the period from which we learn about the curriculum of the time. Although there are two earlier accounts than Malim's (the Cuckfield Free Grammar School account, 1528, and Eton master Richard Cox's 'Return' or guidance for Saffron Walden Grammar School, 1528-31), Maxwell Lyte notes that 'Except in the matter of certain religious observances and in the use of particular text-books, there was probably little change in the routine of the School between the years 1528 and 1560' (Maxwell Lyte 1911, 138).
76 We know from Malim, however, that some of the Fellows acted as *Magistri* (Maxwell Lyte 1911, 139). A similar system of monitorial praepostors was in use at Winchester (Cook 1917, 109-32).
77 Malim 1560, 573.
78 *Ibid*, 575.
79 See introductory text to Malim 1560, 562. A very similar form system was in operation in the smaller King's School, Canterbury (founded by Henry VIII in 1541), where the foundation statutes specify that 'there are to be five or six forms, and when boys reach the Fourth Form they are to enter the Headmaster's domain equipped with a thorough mastery of Latin, "so that no noun or verb may be found anywhere which they do not know how to inflect in every detail"' (Edwards 1957, 66).
80 Malim 1560, 575. Maxwell Lyte 1911, 139-40, notes that there was an analogy between the duty of the *custos* to begin the repetition in school, and the duties of the *custos chori* who began the singing in church.

from one of the lower forms who is still under the usher and has not yet graduated to being taught by the schoolmaster.

Writing lessons were certainly part of the curriculum for the younger boys. Malim informs us: 'Those who are not yet skilful penmen take lessons, but those who can use their hands to some purpose draw the figures of the letters of the alphabet in order, and make models for their fellows to copy'.[81] Horman includes several references to ink and inkhorns in his chapter, 'De scholasticis', including a familiar sounding, 'myn ynkehorne runneth out'; and he describes the different types of pens which might have been contained in a penner: 'poyntyllis of yron/and poyntyllis of sylver/bras boone/or stone: havynge a pynne at the ende/be putte in theyr case: and pennys of fethers and and rede in theyr case'.[82] And a vivid image of schoolboy attempts to correct writing mistakes is given in: 'I wot nat whiche is the beste of these thre: to scrape out the worde, or to streke hym through with a lyne, or to blotte hym all out'.[83] The boy sitting centrally on the form, who is shown writing, perhaps personifies the pupil identified as 'He that writteth upon his knee hath more labour than he that writteth upon a writtynge bourde'.[84] Although the paint losses make it difficult to be sure, it would appear that he is writing on a wax-coated wood tablet with a stylus or writing peg in his right hand.[85] Horman gives us a description of such tablets: 'tables be made of leves of yvery/boxe/cypress and other stouffe daubed with waxe to wrytte on'.[86] He also speaks of both paper and parchment (vellum), and the need for ruled lines and a margin to help pupils to write neatly.[87]

Not every boy was equipped with printed school books. Much teaching was done by dictation, either by the master or usher or by the *praepostors*, with the boys writing out rules and sentences and learning them by heart. Different authors and works were studied in different forms, as well as different grammars and 'vulgars'.[88] Thus in the First Form, John Stanbridge's grammar books were used, including his *Vocabula* and *Parvulorum institutio*,[89] and the boys also did small and easy 'Latins' 'such as the children may understand and have a delight in'.[90] The Second Form also composed 'Latins', and they learned grammar out of Robert Whittington's treatises *De nominum generibus* and *De heteroclites nominibus* and *Cato*.[91] The Third Form studied Whittington's grammar books, and construed from Terence or from Erasmus's *Similitudines* and *Colloquia*; the Fourth Form continued with grammar from one of Whittington's treatises and read Martial and Catullus, and for versification studied the epigrams of Sir Thomas More.[92] The Fifth Form advanced to the composition of Latin

81 Malim 1560, 564.
82 James 1926, 124; Willemsen 2008, 274-5, contains useful information about pen cases and inkwells excavated from grammar schools of this period in the Netherlands.
83 James 1926, 126.
84 Horman, in James 1926, 124.
85 Willemsen observes (pers. comm.) that the fact that the board is flat and that the stylus is curved and appears to be painted brown (styluses were made of copper alloy at this time) would seem to point to this conclusion. For a general discussion of writing materials, see Willemsen 2008, 274-5.
86 James 1926, 124.
87 *Ibid*, 'Parchement leves be wonte to be ruled: that ther may be a comly margent: also streyte lynes of equal distance be drawe withyn: that the writtyng may shewe feyre'.
88 Malim gives us an account of which texts were studied by each form; Malim 1560, 571-4.
89 Maxwell Lyte 1911, 143, notes that 'By 1528, the time-honoured Grammar of Donatus, mentioned in the statutes of Henry the Sixth, had been entirely superseded at Eton. The "babies" in the First Form were at that date [the date of the Cuckfield Free Grammar School document] taught out of books by the Wykehamist, John Stanbridge…'.
90 Maxwell Lyte 1911, 143.
91 The grammarian Robert Whittington (*c*.1480-1553?), a pupil of John Stanbridge, was famous in his day as the author of elementary Latin school books. He had a high opinion of himself, and his abilities as a poet and grammarian were mocked by Horman and Lily in their *Antibossicon* (1528) (see *ODNB*, 58, 773-4).
92 Texts from Martial, Catullus and Thomas More are recorded as part of their curriculum by the time of Malim (see Malim 1560, 574).

verses, and construed Virgil, Sallust, Horace and Ovid; and the Sixth and Seventh Forms read Virgil, Lucan and Cicero's *De officiis*, the text from which one of the inscriptions in the painting is taken.[93]

School dress

The mural depicts the master, and all the boys apart from one, wearing similar long gowns with fur-edged, wide neck openings.[94] These were uniformly worn by boys and men in an academic context, with tunic and hose beneath, and linen shirts as the undergarment; in the painting, shirts can be seen on most of the boys.[95] The boy third from the left behind the form (see Figure 20) appears to be wearing a tunic with a separate ermine collar.[96] One boy sitting astride the form has his gown pulled up over his knees, showing his white stockings or nether hose, and wears black, flat, open leather shoes with square toes (Figure 26). The boys' hair is uniformly bobbed, with seven out of the eleven wearing berets;[97] the four bare-headed boys, including the young boy at play, would seem to be junior to the others.[98]

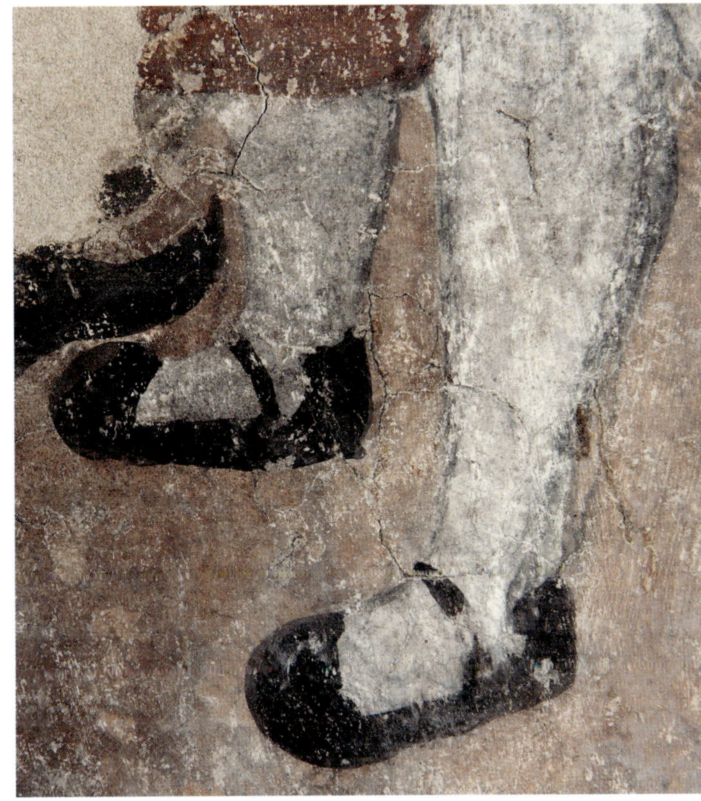

Fig. 26. Detail of boy's legs showing his open leather shoes and white nether hose.

The three colours of gown apparently shown – blue, pinkish-red and a tawny colour – appear uncharacteristically pale for this period, when deep, rich, and sometimes bright, colours were more usually worn.[99] This discrepancy is partly due to fading of the once strong and vibrant effects achieved by the use of organic colorants. Although the different coloured gowns may have had a particular significance – for example in differentiating whether a boy was a scholar, a commensal

93 Malim mentions Cicero's *De officiis*; see Malim 1560, 571. By 1528, the date of the Cuckfield document, the boys were also studying Erasmus's '*De copia verborum*', a new edition of which 'freshly revised and enlarged by the author' had been published in 1526 (Maxwell Lyte 1911, 144).

94 In the sixteenth century, gowns were almost always either lined completely or edged with fur, hare or lambskin being worn by poorer people, and marten by the aristocracy.

95 Gowns could be taken off on occasion, for instance for sport, as recounted in Horman's phrase, 'He caste awey his gowne lest it shulde lette hym of his rennynge' ('De exercitamentis et ludis': James 1926, 402).

96 The tunic, known by the Latin *tunica* in the sixteenth century, was a standard piece of clothing for young children in the later Middle Ages, while the ermine collar was a typical attribute of a wealthy scholar; it is frequently shown in manuscripts of the period (see, for example, Willemsen 2008, ill.105). We are grateful to Annamarieke Willemsen for her observations about the school clothing shown in the mural.

97 These berets, typical attributes of scholars, would have been made of woven or knitted wool. Similar headgear is worn by a number of Holbein's sitters, including Erasmus and Thomas More.

98 Clearly by this period the requirement of the statutes that the boys should be tonsured ('we … will that all and singular scholars and choristers of our said Royal College having the first tonsure shall receive a becoming tonsure [ECR 58/2,4]) was no longer observed.

99 Dark colours were favoured partly for the practical reason that none of the garments apart from the linen shirt was easily washable.

(commoner), or chorister, or in signifying a position of authority such as the *praepostors*[100] – artists at this period tended to employ more varied colours than might actually have been worn.[101] The Founder's statutes required that 'the school master of the scholars in grammar, the clerks, scholars and choristers... are to have... a livery, or becoming clothes, of cloth of similar or nearly similar colour, though of unequal quality according to the inequality of status', it being stipulated further that 'there shall however not be any such cloth of white or black russet or grayish or red colour, and so much of such cloth is to be given to each of them as will be able to make becomingly one long gown with a hood...'.[102] The master and boy in the contemporary glass roundel in Election Hall can be seen to be wearing very similar garments; while the boy is shown wearing a tunic of a pale tawny colour, much deeper colours are used for the master's robes (see Figure 16).

Comparable depictions of school scenes

Similar wall paintings may once have existed in other schools, but no comparable examples survive in England or elsewhere in Europe. A mid-sixteenth-century painted ceiling was discovered in the original Warden's lodgings at Winchester College,[103] but this is a more common type of decorative scheme comprising antique work and classicising and contemporary busts in roundels.[104] We know from woodcuts and contemporary descriptions that the walls of schoolrooms were sometimes hung with boards or rolls covered with texts, inscriptions, or music; such teaching aids are shown in a German woodcut of 1592 (Figure 27). Remarkably, a late fifteenth-century wall painting of musical notation survives in a room once used by the choristers of St George's Chapel, Windsor Castle.[105] At Colet's school, St Paul's, Erasmus himself was involved in the decoration of the schoolroom with a biblical scene; in a letter of 1521, he describes how:

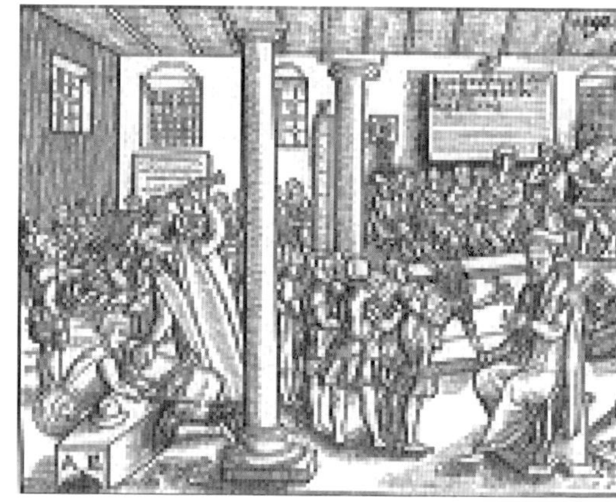

Fig. 27. Schoolroom interior with wall charts, German woodcut, 1592 (reproduced from Reicke 1971).

> Above the high master's desk sits a remarkable representation of the boy Jesus in the attitude of a teacher, which is greeted by the whole body with a hymn when they enter or leave the school. Above is the Father's face, saying 'Hear ye Him': for he added these words at my suggestion.[106]

Other verses may well have been attached to the walls.[107] Extensive use of inscriptions on walls, recalling those in the Eton mural, was also made by the social elite, whose children were educated at home rather than at

100 The term 'commensal' derived from the Founder's statutes, where the phrase 'generosorum filii pueri commensales' occurs, explained further in the provision for 'the reception, teaching, and boarding of sons of noble persons, friends of the College, up to twenty in number' (see James 1926, 609-14). There was also a lower level of commensal, the number of whom was not restricted; the two types ate at different tables in College Hall (see Card 2001, 13). Oppidans were boys who boarded in town and paid their school fees. The Winchester statutes allowed for ten 'commoners' or 'oppidans' to live in College.

101 This observation was made by Willemsen.

102 ECR 58/29, 100-02. 'Russet' in this context denotes a coarse, homespun, woollen cloth (rather than the reddish-brown colour). Just as the fashion in hair style had changed since the 1440s, so the style of gown had evolved over 60 years, from more monastic gowns with hoods to the gowns we see here. The gown would have served the double function of distinguishing boys who were being educated at the school, and as a necessary way of keeping warm.

103 The dismantled ceiling was discovered in 1885, during the removal of a partition wall in the original Warden's lodgings; it is now in the Westgate Museum in Winchester.

104 It also bears inscriptions perhaps referring to the marriage of Philip of Spain and Mary Tudor at Winchester in 1554 (Lewis 1996).

105 Bowers 2001, 203-5, St George's Chapel choristers sometimes went on to attend Eton; *ibid*, 207-8.

106 Correspondence of Erasmus 1988, 236, no.1211.

107 Rieger 1962, 187.

schools; an example is the remarkable series of moralising verses painted in various rooms of the great Percy houses of Leconfield and Wressle in Yorkshire.[108] In a similar vein, the stuccowork of the inner court of Nonsuch Palace, apparently intended for the edification of the future Edward VI, included mottoes in gilded lead derived from grammatical textbooks by Erasmus, such as his *Dicta septem sapientum*.[109] The one biblical and several classical texts included in the Eton mural reflect this same tradition of teaching by wall texts; indeed the quantity of texts employed may suggest that, while the mural functioned primarily as a room decoration with a portrait of school life as its chosen subject, in its proximity to the actual schoolroom it might also itself have been used for teaching.[110]

Fig 28. Schoolmaster's signboard, 1516, attributed to Ambrosius Holbein and Hans Holbein the Younger, oil on board (Inv. no. 311, Kuntsmuseum, Basel).

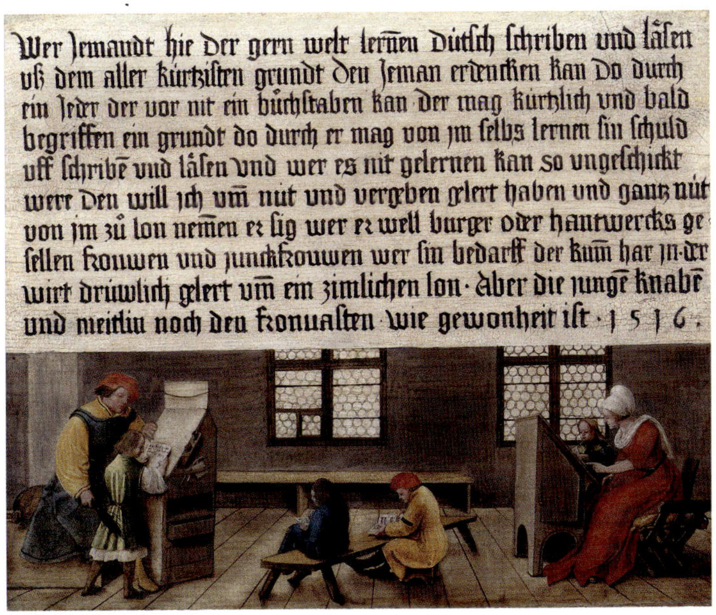

A remarkable description from 1523 of a schoolroom at Zwickau, in Germany, demonstrates the type of visual didactic scheme that once existed on the Continent, recalling library schemes such as that in the Lupton's library glazing; the description reads that the schoolroom was 'well decorated to support teaching...with a wheel of fortune...histories, verses, Proverbs, and the four disciplines Music, Geometry, Arithmetic, and Astronomy, together the whole of the universe'.[111] But the only surviving continental wall painting that is in any way comparable to that at Eton is the early fifteenth-century painting on the façade of the former grammar school at Memmingen in southern Germany.[112] This shows a personification of Grammar, holding a birch and originally teaching at least three pupils from a book, and is the type of image from which the schoolmaster woodcuts were ultimately derived. Much closer in spirit to the Eton painting, however, is a schoolmaster's signboard now in the Kunstmuseum at Basel, dated 1516 and attributed to Ambrosius Holbein and Hans Holbein the Younger (Figure 28).[113] Here two pupils concentrating on their book are seated on or beside a wooden form, in a similar manner to the boys in the Eton mural, while another boy reads to the master, who is ready with his birch, and a female instructress helps the smallest child at the back of the class.[114] Such signboards may also have existed in England, but they were by their nature ephemeral and, like the majority of wall paintings from this period, have not survived.[115]

108 Flügel 1892, 471-97; Lancashire 1980, 28-9.
109 Colvin 1982, 199-201; Turquet 1983; Biddle 1984, 411-17.
110 Fleming 2001, 44, discusses the place of writing on walls, or graffiti, in Elizabethan decorative schemes as 'that which frames truth to catch the eye or memory'. Izaak Walton's description of Sir Henry Wotton's colonnade in Lower School, as hung with 'choicely drawn pictures ... of divers of the most famous Greek and Latin poets, historians and orators [in order to persuade boys] not to neglect rhetorick' may hark back to this very tradition (Walton 1651, 51).
111 The quote from the 1523 *Schulordnung* of Zwickau is cited in Willemsen 2008, 266-8.
112 Wirth 1983, 256-8, ills.Ia and b. Willemsen 2008, 265, ill.238 shows the somewhat deteriorated painting in its present condition.
113 The use of signboards by schoolmasters to advertise their premises and vaunt their qualifications is described in Alexandre-Bidon & Lett 1999, 126-8.
114 Müller & Kemperdick 2006, 158-60, no.22. This signboard may have been made for the famous humanist scholar 'Myconius', for whom both Holbeins illustrated a copy of Erasmus's *In Praise of Folly*; however this is undocumented.
115 A large board hung above the panelling in the school at Winchester reads 'Aut disce aut discede. Manet sors tertia, caedi' ('Either learn or get out; there remains a third option, to be beaten'), with the appropriate images: a bishop's crozier and mitre as the reward of learning, a sword and penner with inkhorn as the emblems for departure, and a 'bibling rod' (birch) as the third option. The board derives from a sixteenth-century original which hung in the Old Schoolroom, where it was probably installed by Christopher Johnson, headmaster 1561-71. This information was kindly supplied by John Falconer, Suzanne Foster and Christopher Rowell.

Conclusion

The importance of the Eton mural lies partly in its rare survival as an example of a very fragile form of domestic room decoration. It is even more remarkable, however, as a portrait of school life, the incidental detail and activity of which, while doubtless familiar to the artist from late fifteenth- and early sixteenth-century illustrations, he could also have observed taking place in the adjacent schoolroom and yard. This was how school life actually was at Eton, and indeed to a certain extent still is, in that the room has continued from that time to the present to be used by the Head Master, as well as until very recently functioning as one of the places where punishment was meted out to boys. Most probably commissioned by Robert Aldrich and his associates, the painting both commemorates Eton's historical alliance with Winchester and at the same time makes an overt statement – or indeed a celebration – of the new humanist learning of which Aldrich, his colleagues and the school were a part. Just as, through William Horman's *Vulgaria*, 'we live again in the very human atmosphere of early Tudor times',[116] so also in the mural, functioning as the visual counterpart of Horman's book, we are given a direct and human glimpse into the style of education, thought and manners of the school in about 1520. The master in the painting holds his book out in front of him (Figure 29) so that his pupils, and indeed the viewers of the scene, may be encouraged in the 'redynge of good authors', a gesture as persuasive now as it was then.

Fig. 29. Detail from mural showing book held by master.

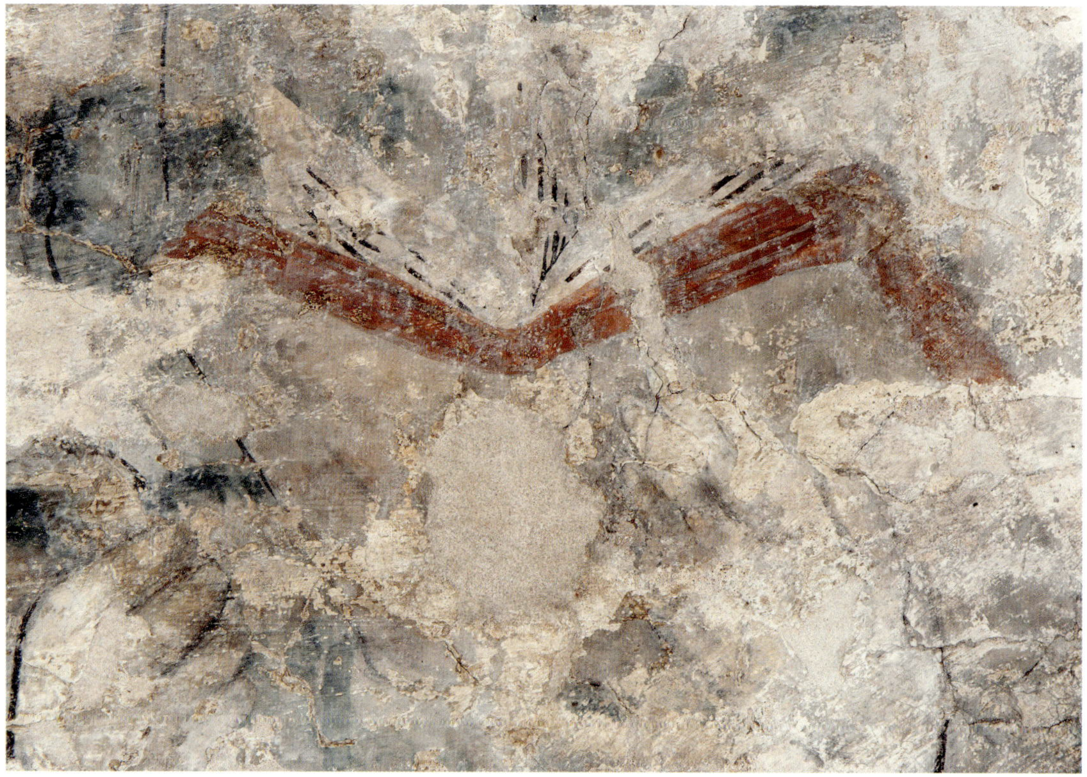

116 James 1926, ix.

Appendix: Technical summary of the chapel programme paint analysis

Minute paint samples were taken following a systematic strategy, to characterise the range of painting materials used and the ways in which they had been employed.

All samples were examined under a binocular microscope (10x to 45x magnification) and their stratigraphy documented. A portion of each was then mounted as a cross-section in clear polyester embedding resin (Tiranti clear casting resin) and examined with a Leica DMRX optical microscope at 100x to 500x. The microscope was equipped with Leica 10x and 20 PL Fluotar™ objectives and a 50x PL Apo™ objective. For UV examination, excitation filter BP 340-380nm, dichroic mirror (RKP 400nm) and suppression filter LP 425nm were used. Photomicrographs were taken with a Nikon Coolpix™ 4500 camera at 100x to 500x. Many of the paint layers were also examined in dispersion in Meltmount™ (n=1.662), and their behaviour in incident, transmitted and ultraviolet light, and under crossed polars, recorded. Where further analysis proved necessary, microchemical tests were undertaken to identify characteristic metal ions and functional groups (see Plesters 1956). Where confirmation of inorganic components proved necessary, elemental analysis using scanning electron microscopy coupled with energy-disruptive x-ray (SEM-EDX) analysis was undertaken using a Jeol JSM-6480LV high-performance, variable pressure analytical scanning electron microscope with a high resolution of 3.0nm, along with EDS (energy-dispersive system) and EBSD (electron backscatter diffraction) using the Oxford Link system. High-performance liquid chromatography (HPLC) analysis of organic colorants was generously undertaken by Jo Kirby and Dr David Peggie at the National Gallery, London. The presence of organic binding media was assessed using histochemical tests capable of detecting oil- and protein-based media (Sudan Black B and acid fuchsin), and confirmation of these findings sought through Fourier transform infrared spectroscopy (FTIR) and gas chromatography coupled with mass spectrometry (GC-MS), analyses kindly undertaken by Dr Brian Singer at the University of Northumbria.

Sample ECC01
South wall, fictive textile

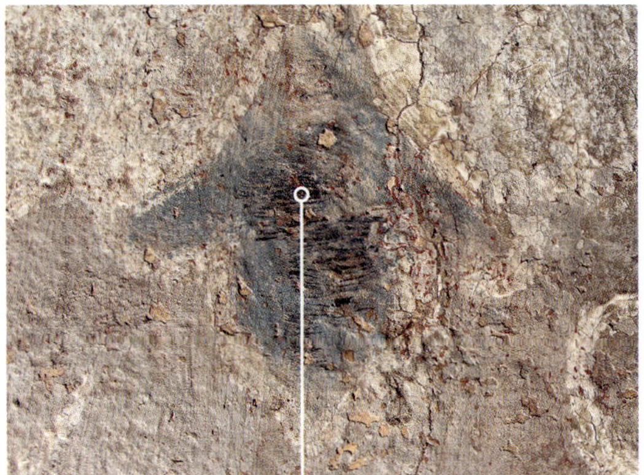

Sample location

Blue floral bud

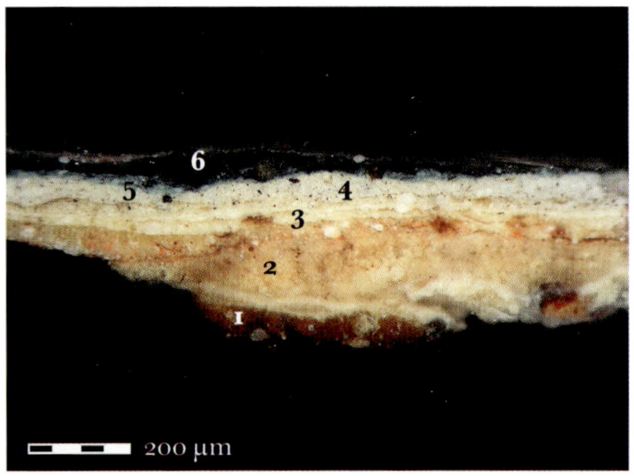

Stratigraphy

6 Indigo blue glaze
5 Pale blue layer (lead white + indigo)
4 Grey (lead white + carbon black with small amounts of red lake and indigo)
3 Lead white ground (with a little calcium carbonate) applied in 2 layers
2 Medium-rich sealant with red and white lead (+ a little calcium carbonate white)
1 Fragments of limestone support?

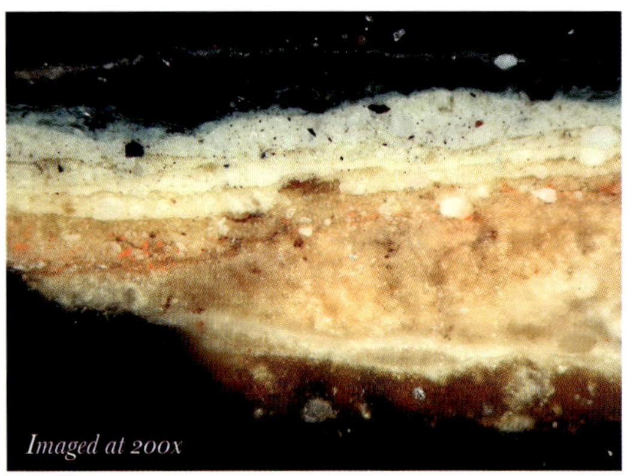

Imaged at 200x

Notes

The blue was identified as indigo using FTIR and HPLC analysis. It is not, however, possible to determine whether the original source of the dyestuff was the plant native to India (*Indigofera tinctoria* L.) or the European plant woad (*Isatis tinctoria* L.)

Sample ECC02
South wall, fictive textile

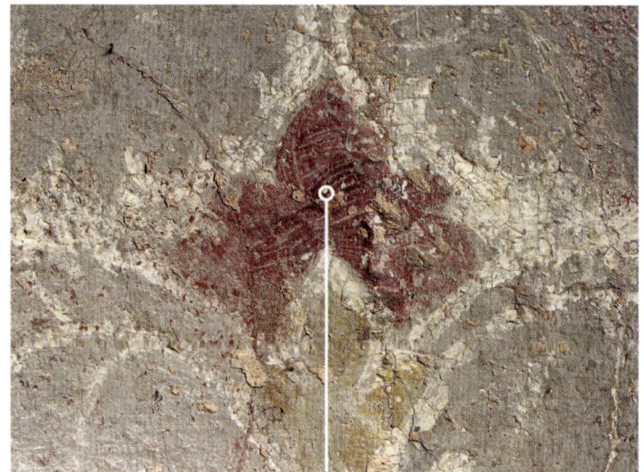

Sample location

Red floral bud

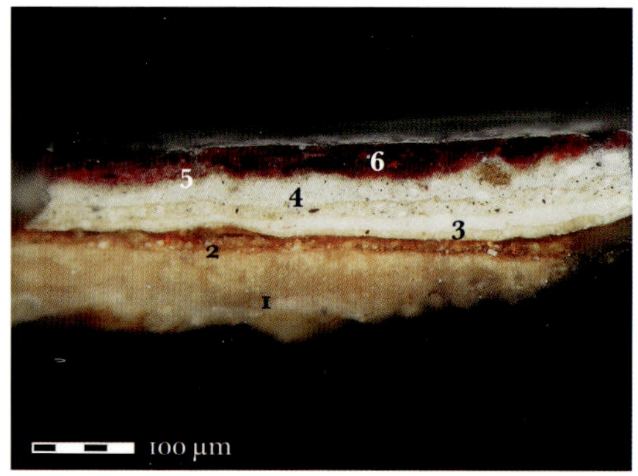

Stratigraphy

6 Madder lake glaze (extended with calcium carbonate white)
5 Pale pink layer (lake with lead white and a little calcium carbonate white)
4 Grey layer (lead white + carbon black, with a little calcium carbonate) – 2 layers
3 Lead white ground (with a little calcium carbonate) – 2 layers
2 Medium-rich sealant with red lead and lead white inclusions (plus a little calcium carbonate)
1 Limestone support

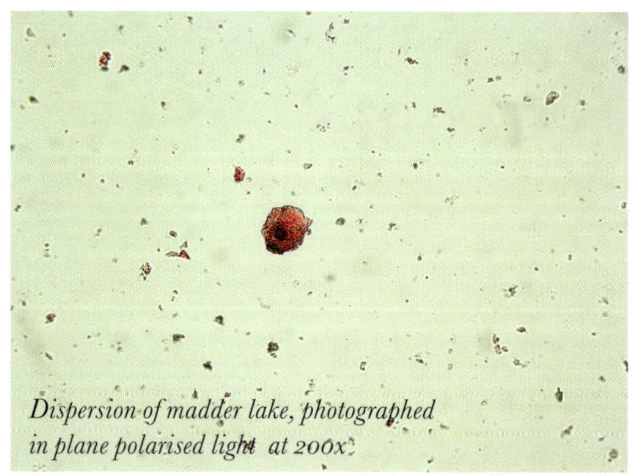

Dispersion of madder lake, photographed in plane polarised light at 200x

Notes

HPLC analysis has identified the red lake as madder; SEM-EDX analysis of the substrate indicates that the dyestuff was precipitated onto a substrate of hydrated alumina; the high levels of sulphur present suggests that the dyestuff may have been extracted from dyed wool clippings (see also sample 9).

Sample ECC03
South wall, fictive textile

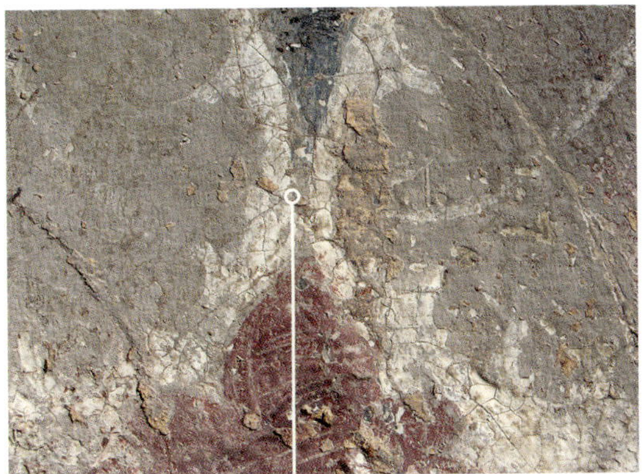

Sample location

White damask pattern over grey

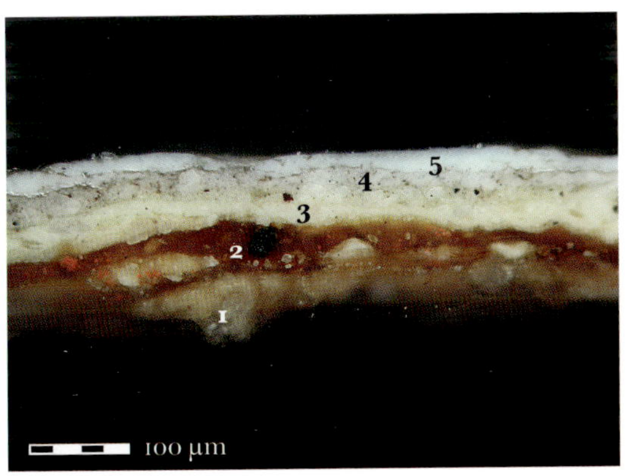

Stratigraphy

5 Impasto lead white
4 Pale grey (lead white + carbon black)
3 Lead white ground (with a little calcium carbonate)
2 Medium-rich sealant with red lead and lead + calcium carbonate white inclusions
1 Fragments of limestone support

Sample ECC04
South wall, fictive textile

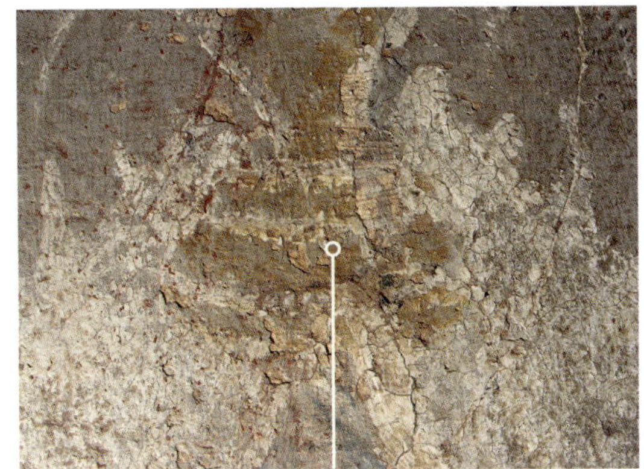

Sample location

Yellow over grey

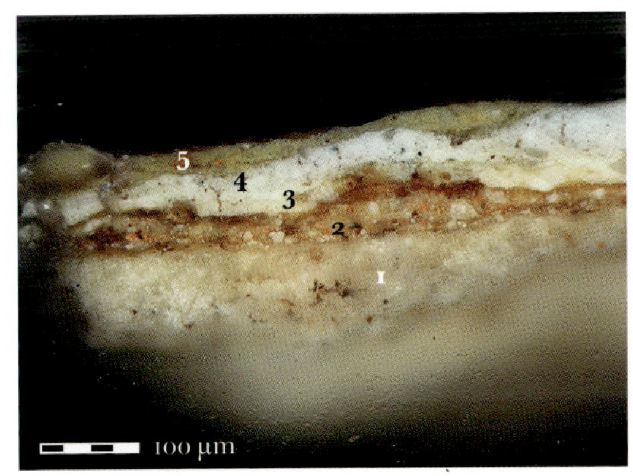

Stratigraphy

5 Yellow iron oxide layer
4 Grey layer (lead white + carbon black, with a little calcium carbonate)
3 Lead white ground (with a little calcium carbonate)
2 Medium-rich sealant with red lead and lead white inclusions (plus a little calcium carbonate)
1 Limestone support

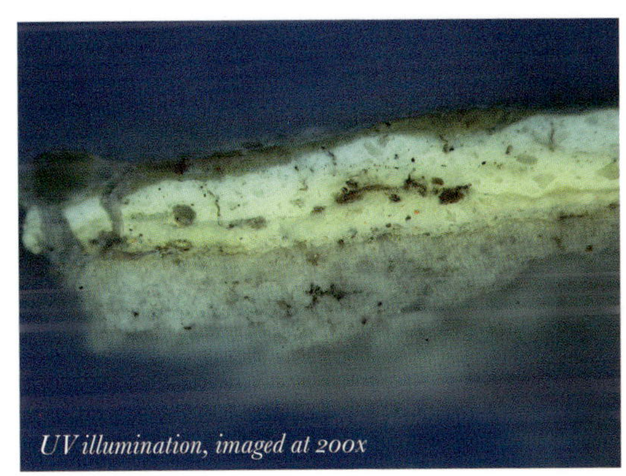

UV illumination, imaged at 200x

Notes

The medium-rich (oil-based?) sealant layer fluoresces yellow under UV illumination.

Sample ECC05

South wall, Scene 2

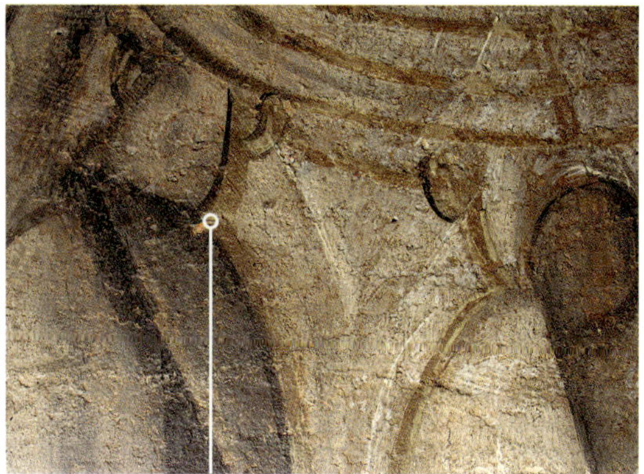

Sample location

Emperor's right hip with red ground

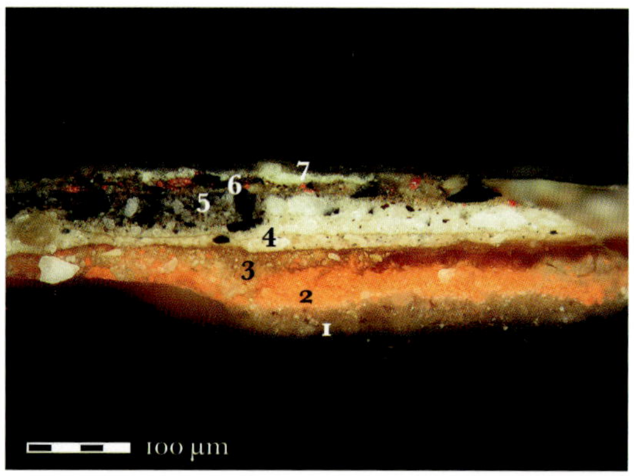

Stratigraphy

7 Lead-tin yellow highlight
6 Black-brown layer (carbon black + vermilion)
5 Dark grey (lead and/or calcium carbonate white + carbon black)
4 Pale grey (lead white + carbon black)
3 Medium-rich sealant with red and white lead + calcium carbonate inclusions
2 Red lead ground
1 Fragments of limestone support

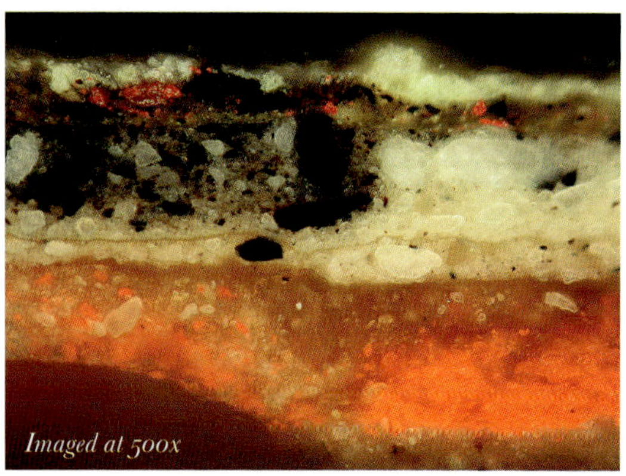

Imaged at 500x

Notes

The sealant layer fluoresces brightly under UV illumination, and is probably oil-based.

Sample ECC06

South wall, Scene 2

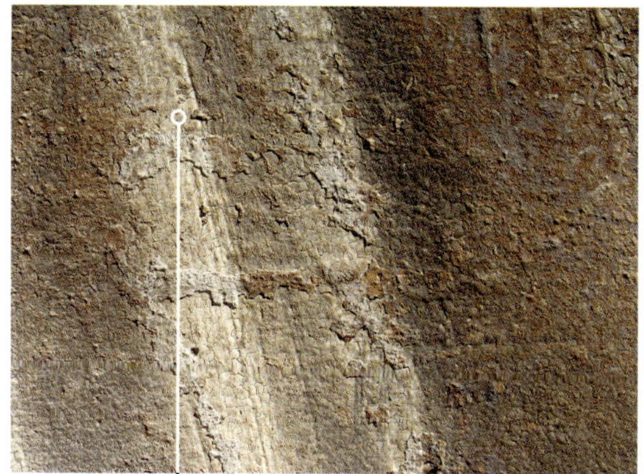

Sample location

Empress figure, draperies with impasto white highlight

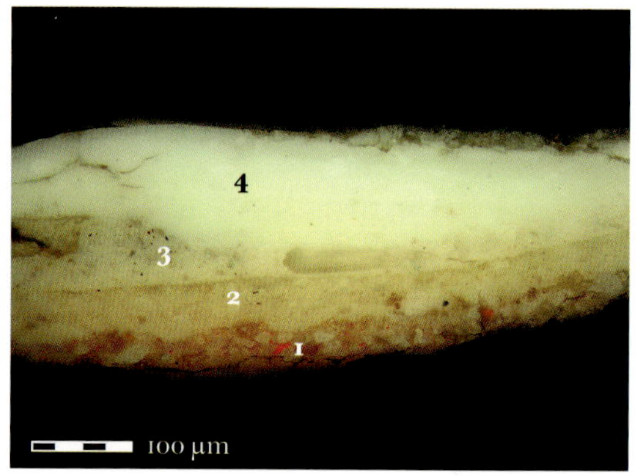

Stratigraphy

4 Lead white
3 Pale grey layer (lead white and a little carbon black)
2 Lead white ground + a little calcium carbonate
1 Medium-rich sealant with red lead and lead white inclusions (+ a little calcium carbonate)

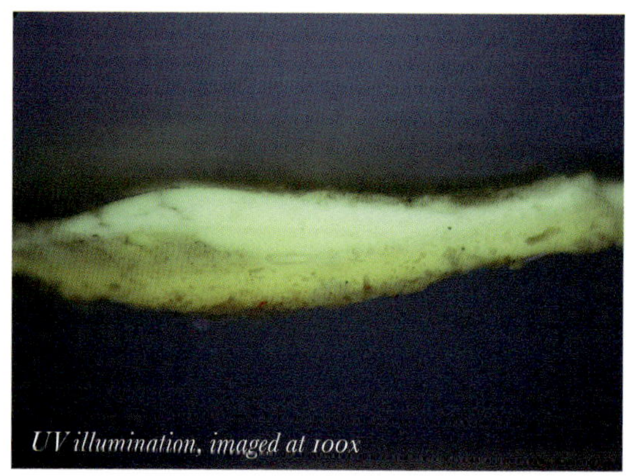

UV illumination, imaged at 100x

Notes

The medium-rich (oil-based?) sealant and ground layers fluoresce yellow under UV illumination

Sample ECC07
South wall, Figure V

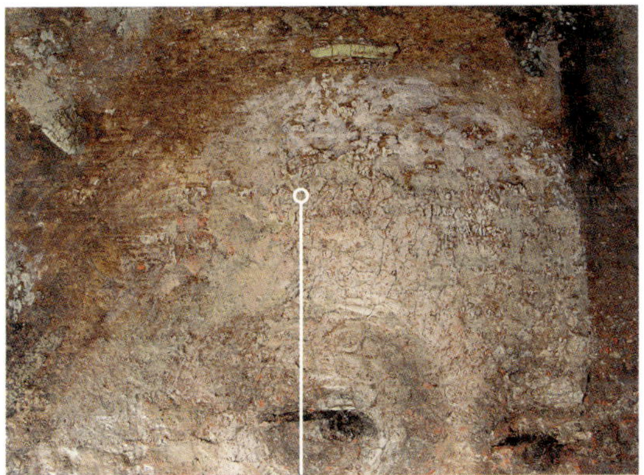

St Ursula, flesh modelling on face

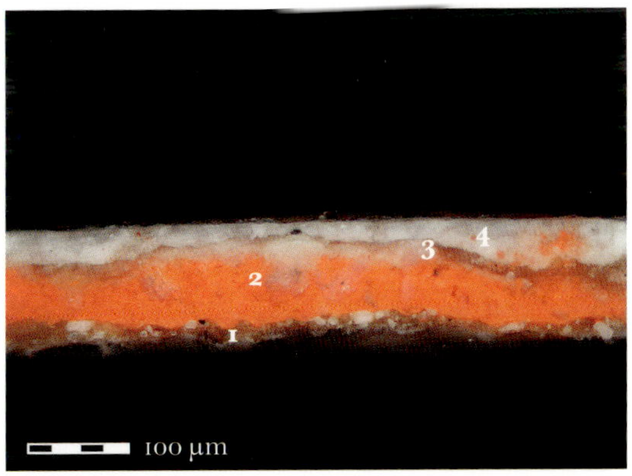

Stratigraphy

4 Pale pink (lead white matrix with red lead and tiny lake inclusions)
3 Possible further sealant layer?
2 Thick red lead ground with lead white inclusions
1 Fragments of medium-rich sealant layer

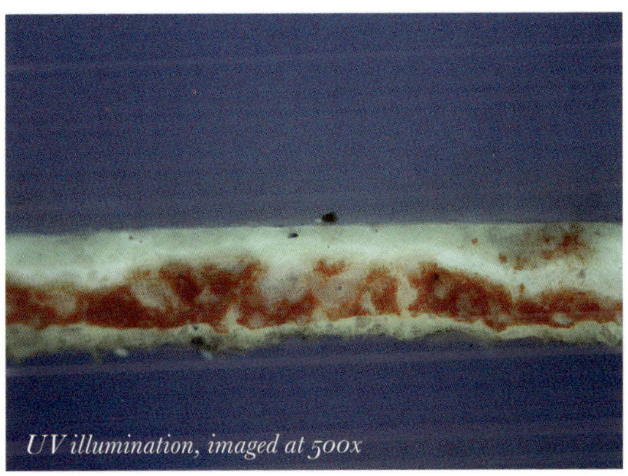

UV illumination, imaged at 500x

Notes

The oil-based sealant layer fluoresces brightly under UV illumination.

Sample ECC08
South wall, Scene 5

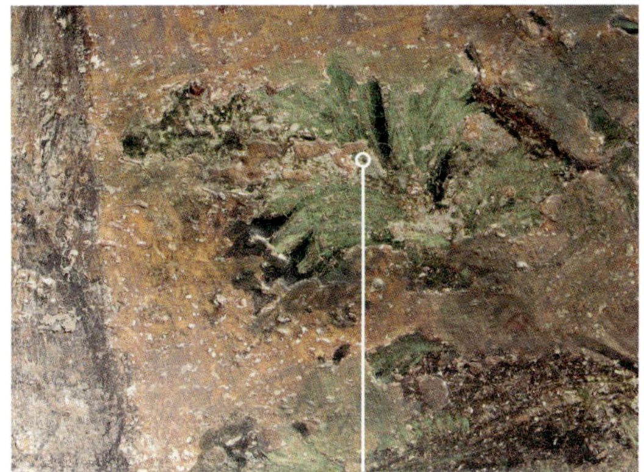

Miraculous green plant with pale green highlights

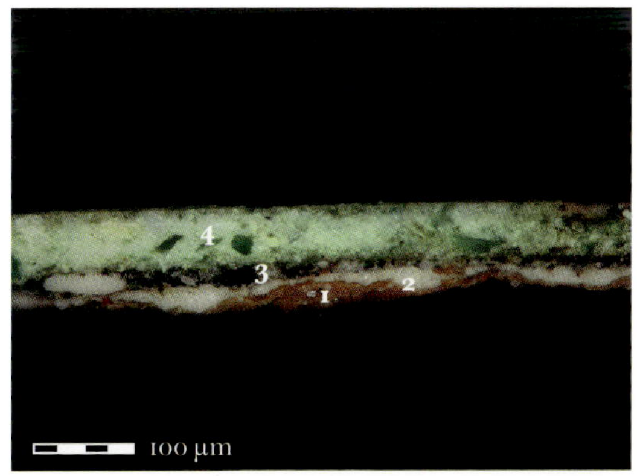

Stratigraphy

4 Pale green layer (unidentified copper green in a matrix of lead white and lead-tin yellow)
3 Grey layer (lead white and coarsely ground carbon black)
2 Lead white ground
1 Medium-rich sealant with red lead and lead white inclusions (+ a little calcium carbonate)

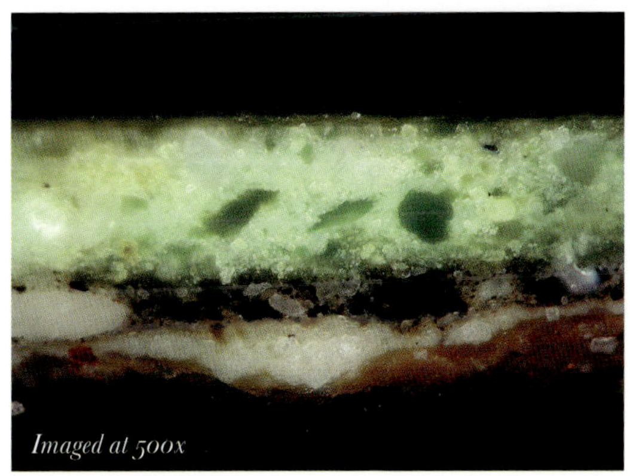

Imaged at 500x

Notes

Lead-tin yellow confirmed by SEM-EDX analysis; analysis of material from this area using GC-MS and FTIR analysis confirmed the presence of a linseed oil binding medium.

Sample ECC09

South wall, Figure VI

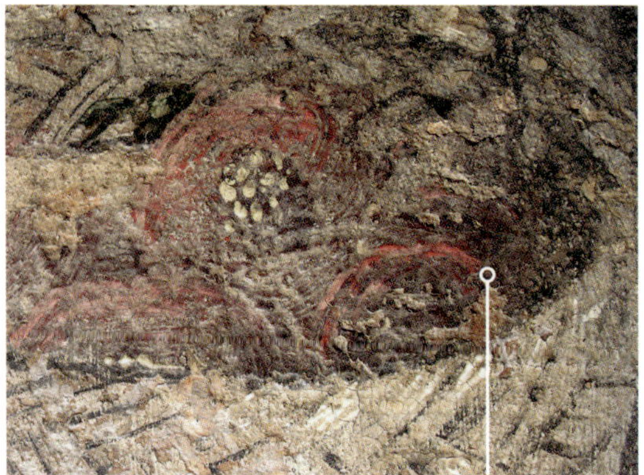

Sample location

St Dorothy, red flower from basket

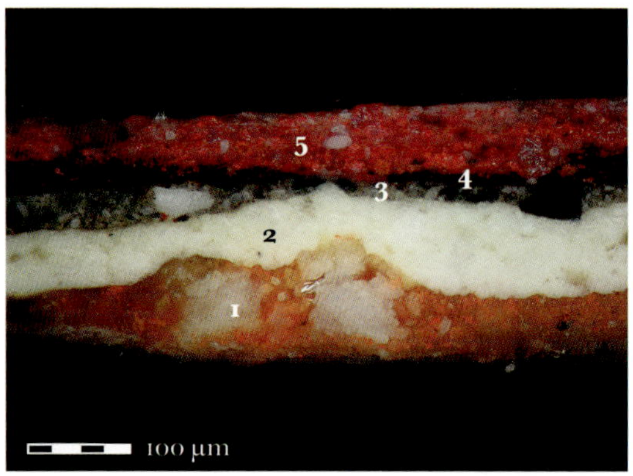

Stratigraphy

5 Pink layer (madder + vermilion in a lead white matrix)

4 Fine madder lake glaze (with a little lead and calcium carbonate white)

3 Grey layer (lead white + carbon black)

2 Lead white ground

1 Medium-rich sealant with red lead and lead white inclusions (plus a little calcium carbonate)

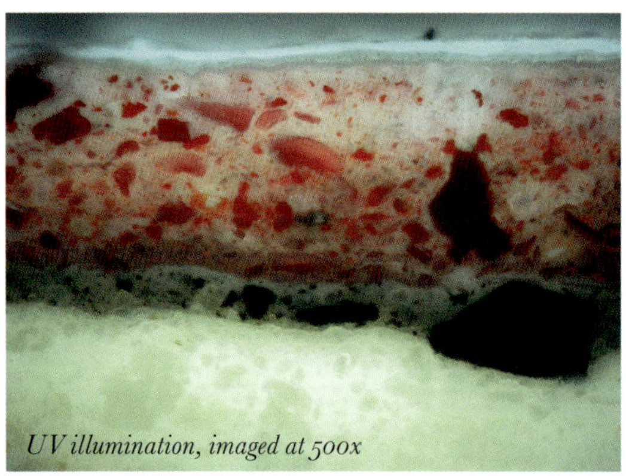

UV illumination, imaged at 500x

Notes

HPLC analysis has identified the red lake dyestuff as madder. SEM-EDX analysis of the lake substrate suggests that the colorant was precipitated onto a ground of hydrated alumina; the high levels of sulphur present suggest that the dyestuff may have been derived from dyed wool clippings.

Sample ECC10

South wall, Scene 6

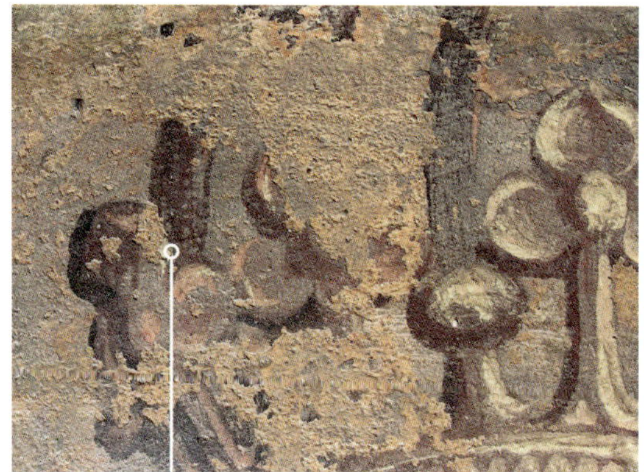

Sample location

Impasto decoration on Empress's crown

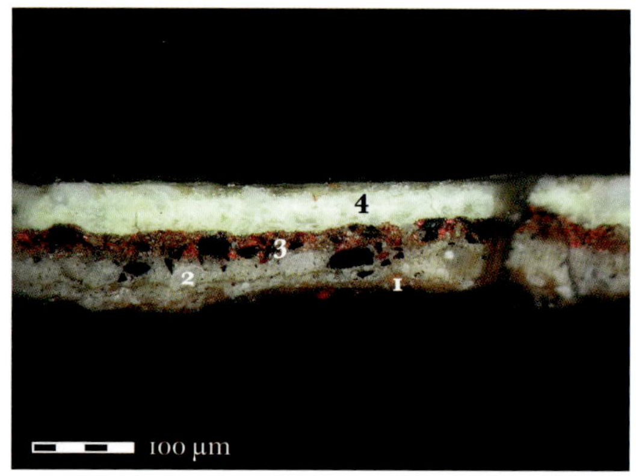

Stratigraphy

4 Lead-tin yellow highlight

3 Brown (admixture comprising carbon black, vermilion, madder, yellow iron oxide + lead white)

2 Background grey (lead white + carbon black)

1 Medium-rich sealant with red and white lead + calcium carbonate inclusions (fragmentary)

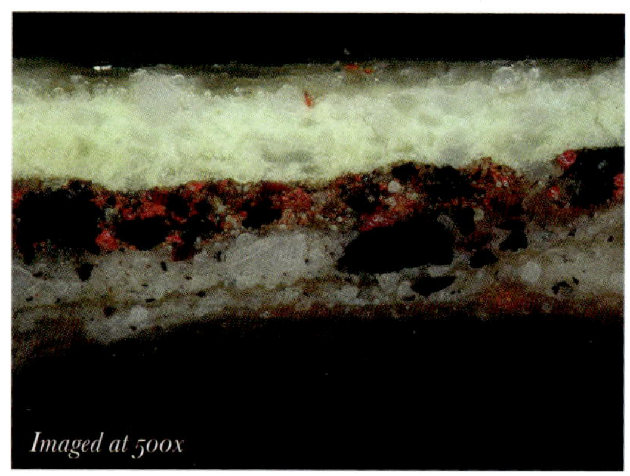

Imaged at 500x

Notes

The lead-tin yellow layer contains lead soaps which are characteristic of a lead-based pigment interacting with an oil-based medium (see also sample 20).

Sample ECC11

South wall, Scene 6

Empress's hair

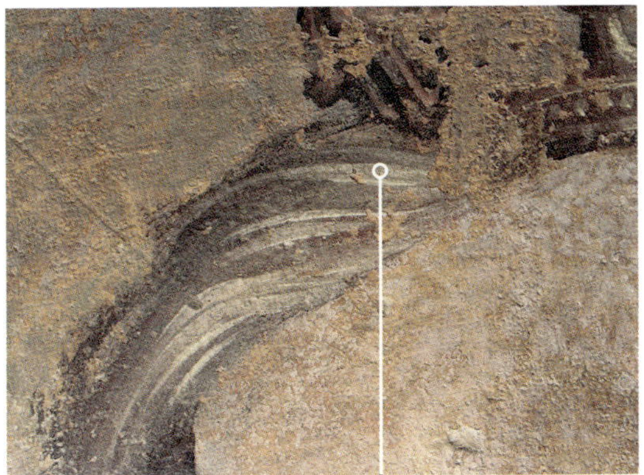

Sample location

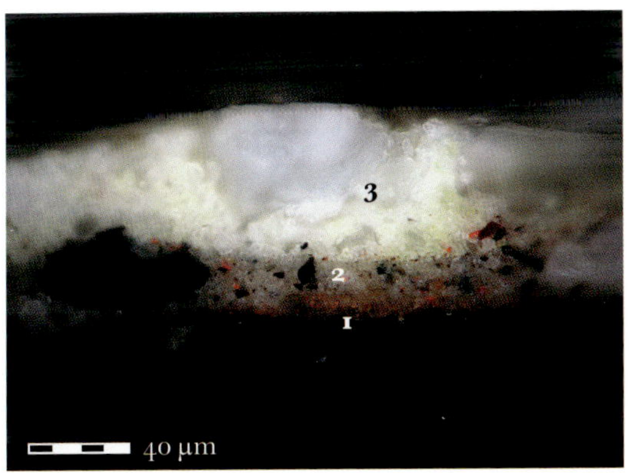

Stratigraphy

3 Lead-tin yellow highlight
2 Light brown hair (lead white matrix with carbon black, vermilion and madder inclusions)
1 Medium-rich sealant with red lead and lead white inclusions (plus a little calcium carbonate)

Sample ECC12

South wall, Scene 7

Emperor's black hair

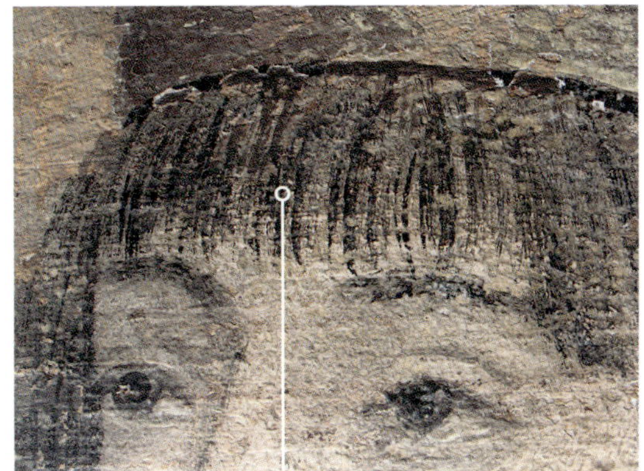

Sample location

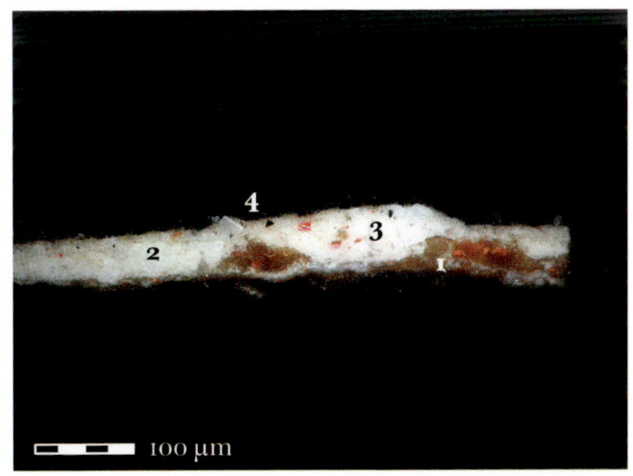

Stratigraphy

4 Carbon black layer
3 Pink flesh layer (lead white matrix, possibly with some calcium carbonate white, with vermilion + red lead inclusions)
2 Partial lead white ground?
1 Medium-rich sealant with red lead inclusions

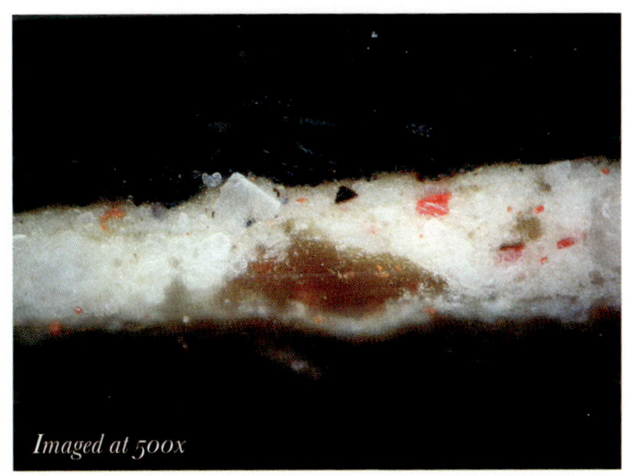

Sample ECC13
South wall, Scene 7

Brother-in-law's pink belt

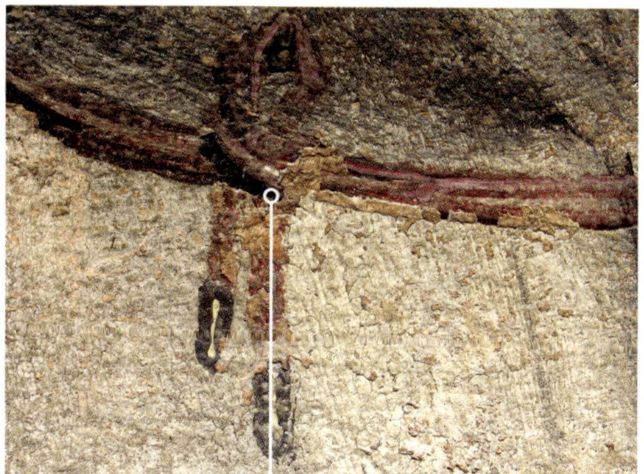

Sample location

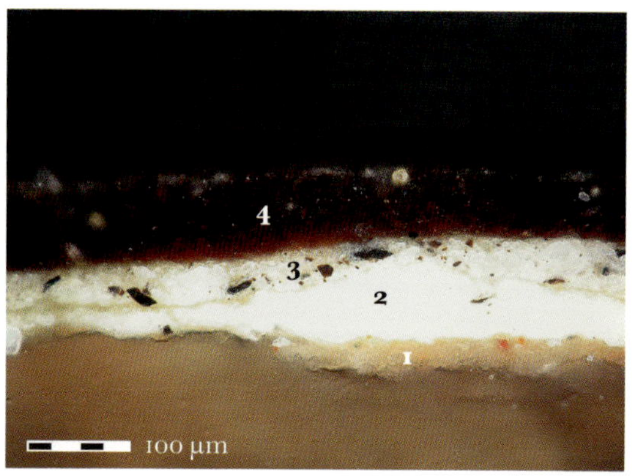

Stratigraphy

4 Dark madder lake glaze
3 Grey draperies (lead white + carbon black)
2 Lead white ground
1 Medium-rich sealant with red lead and lead white inclusions (fragmentary)

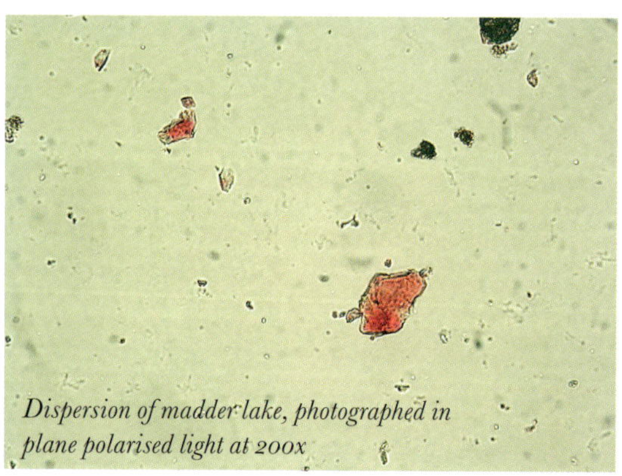

Dispersion of madder lake, photographed in plane polarised light at 200x

Notes

HPLC analysis has identified the red lake dyestuff as madder. SEM-EDX analysis of the lake substrate suggests that the colorant was precipitated onto a ground of hydrated alumina; the high levels of sulphur present suggest that the dyestuff may have been derived from dyed wool clippings.

Sample ECC14
South wall, Scene 8

Attendant's red and yellow hat

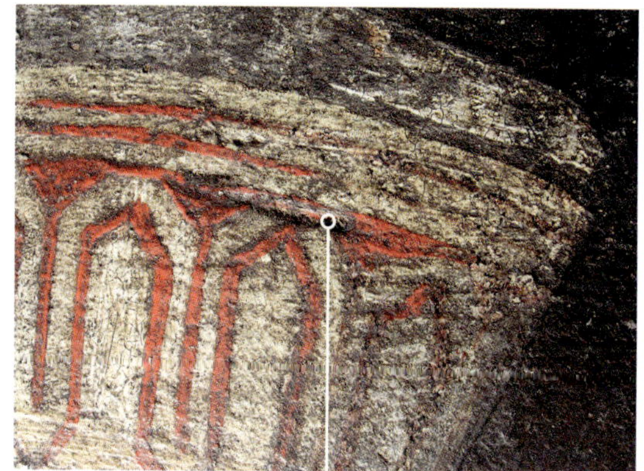

Sample location

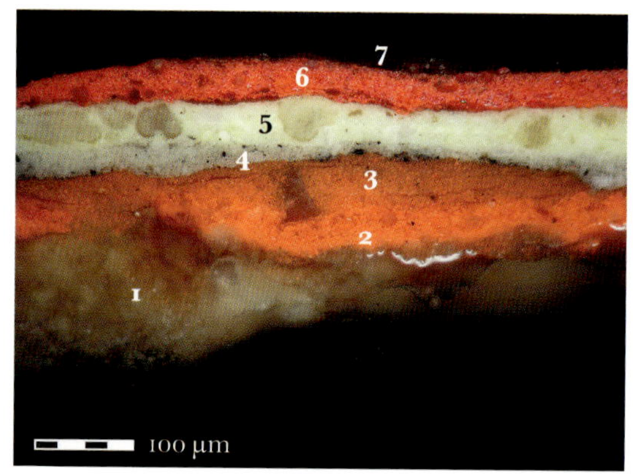

Stratigraphy

7 Varnish residue?
6 Red (vermilion + lake + lead white)
5 Lead-tin yellow
4 Grey (lead white + finely ground carbon black, with a little calcium carbonate)
3 Red lead ground (mixed with calcium carbonate extender)
2 Red lead ground (with lower proportion of calcium carbonate)
1 Limestone support

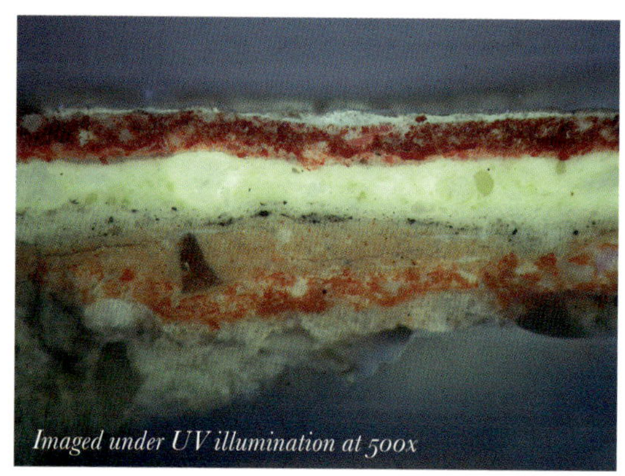

Imaged under UV illumination at 500x

Notes

The difference between the two red lead ground layers – which comprise varying proportions of red lead and calcium carbonate white – is more evident when viewed under UV illumination.

Sample ECC15
South wall, Scene 8

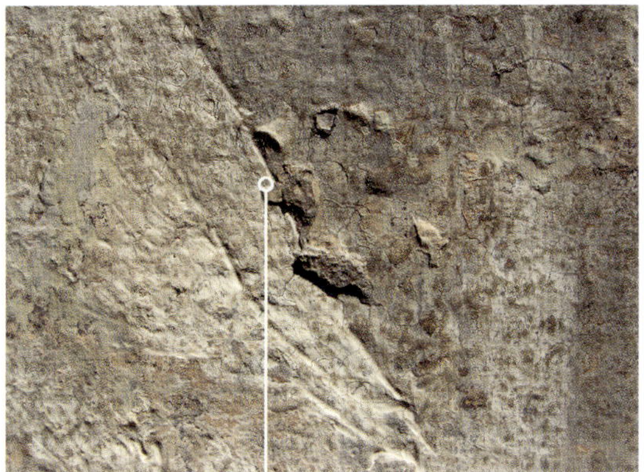

Sample location

Empress's draperies with white impasto highlight

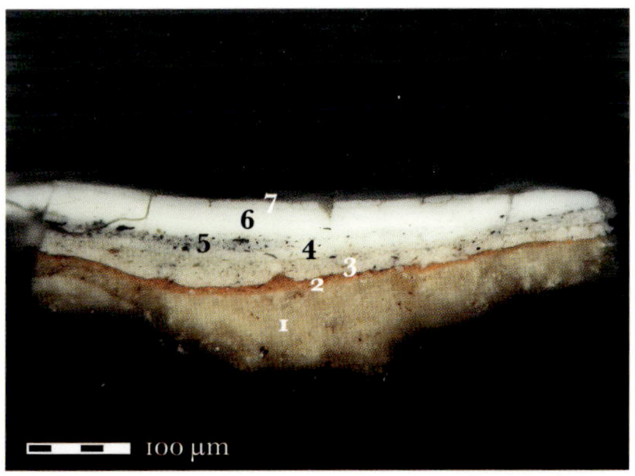

Stratigraphy

7 Fine lead white layer
6 Impasto lead white layer
5 Grey draperies (lead white and carbon black)
4 Lead white layer
3 Pale grey (carbon black, lead white and a little calcium carbonate)
2 Red lead underdrawing (with calcium carbonate and red earth inclusions?)
1 Limestone support

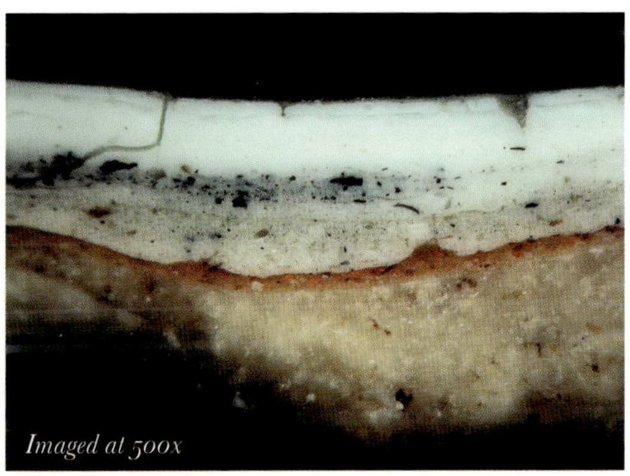

Imaged at 500x

Notes
FTIR and GC-MS analysis of the painting medium in this scene detected raw linseed oil.

Sample ECC16
South wall, Scene 8

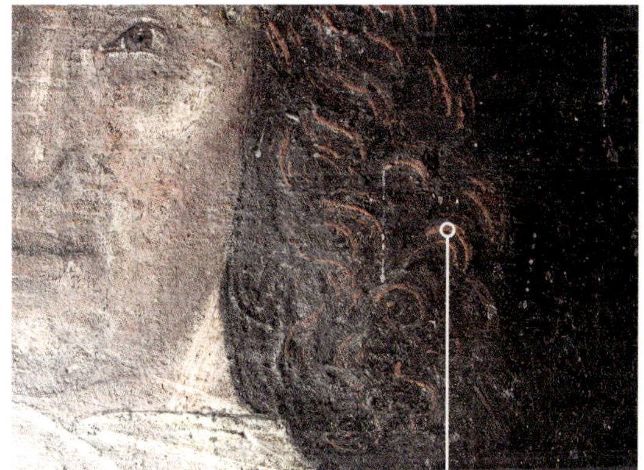

Sample location

Attendant's brown hair

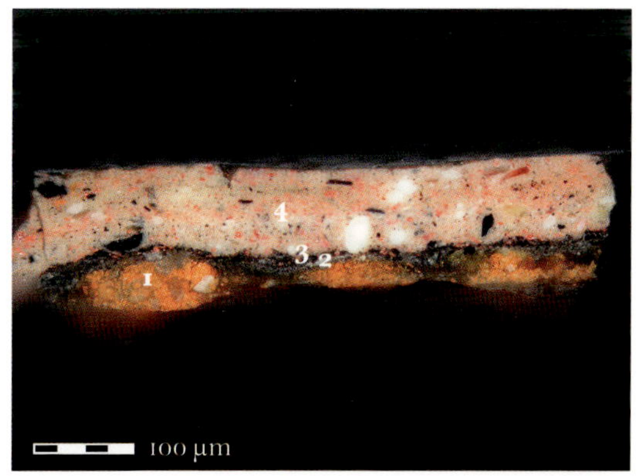

Stratigraphy

4 Orangey-red highlight (white matrix with madder, vermilion, red lead and carbon black inclusions)
3 Black/brown hair (carbon black + vermilion)
2 Very fine grey layer (carbon black + lead white?)
1 Medium-rich red lead ground (with some calcium carbonate white?)

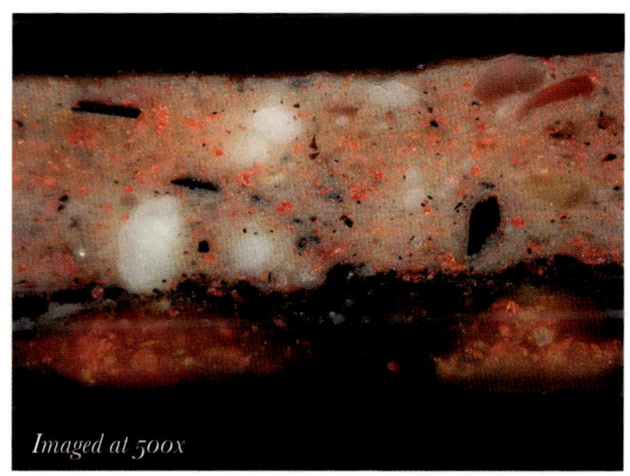

Imaged at 500x

Notes
FTIR and GC-MS analysis of the painting medium in this scene detected raw linseed oil.

Sample ECC17
South wall, Scene 8

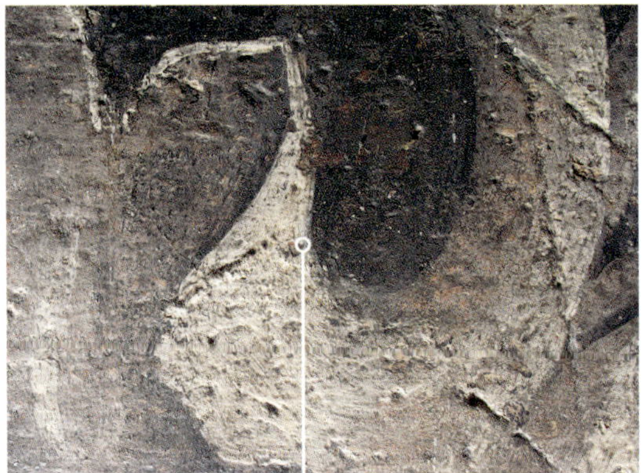

Sample location

Micro-architectural leaf, top right

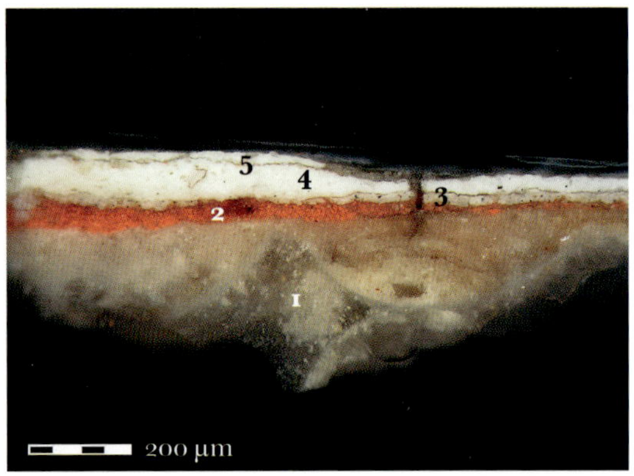

Stratigraphy

5 Fine lead white layer (delaminated from lower layer?)
4 Thick white layer (lead white with calcium carbonate inclusions?)
3 Fine grey layer (carbon black + calcium carbonate/ lead white?)
2 Red lead ground or underdrawing?
1 Limestone support

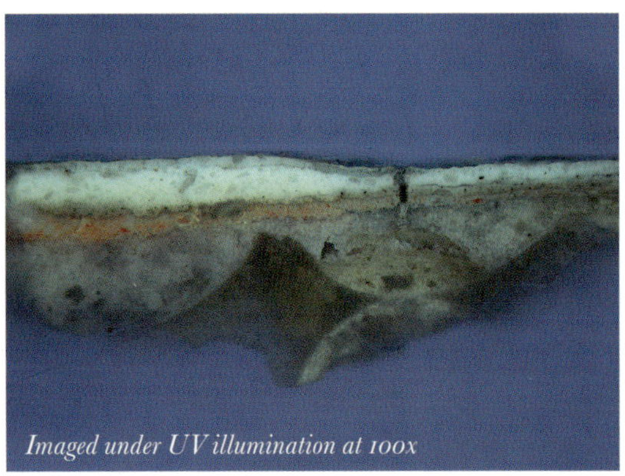

Imaged under UV illumination at 100x

Notes
Examination of the impasto white paint layer under UV illumination suggests that lead white was bulked out and extended using calcium carbonate – this would need to be verified using SEM-EDX analysis.

Sample ECC18
South wall, Scene 8

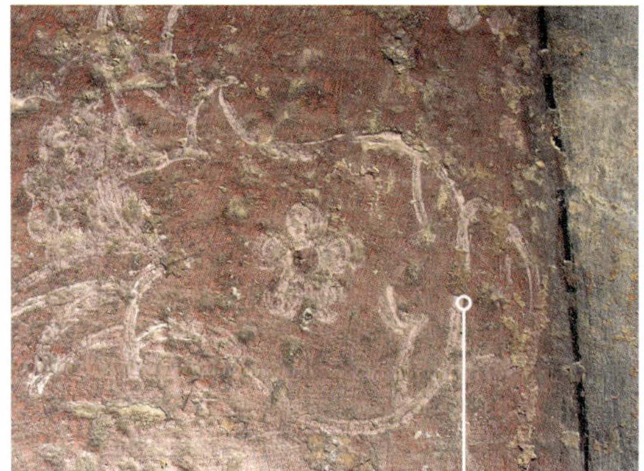

Sample location

Damask cushion holding Empress's crown

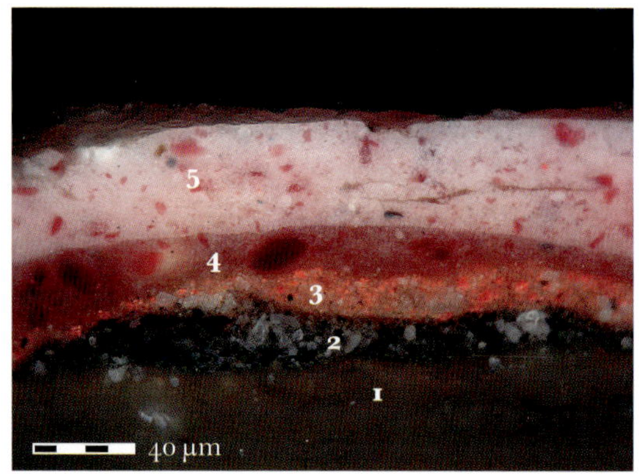

Stratigraphy

5 Pale pink (madder lake in a lead white matrix + a little calcium carbonate)
4 Dark pink (madder lake mixed with lead white and calcium carbonate)
3 Medium-rich red layer (comprising vermilion, calcium carbonate + lead white)
2 Grey background (carbon black + lead white, with some calcium carbonate)
1 Traces of limestone and sealant layer

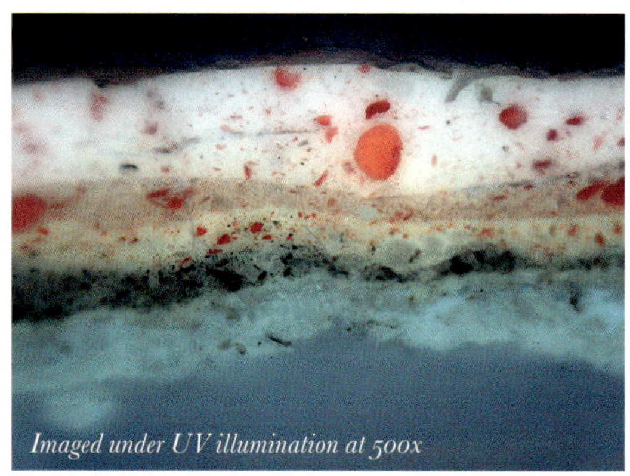

Imaged under UV illumination at 500x

Notes
Under UV illumination, the large lake particles fluoresce salmon pink. HPLC and SEM-EDX analysis of these particles reveal the lake to comprise madder dye precipitated onto a substrate of hydrated alumina. FTIR and GC-MS analysis suggests that the binding medium is raw linseed oil.

Sample ECC19

South wall, Scene 8

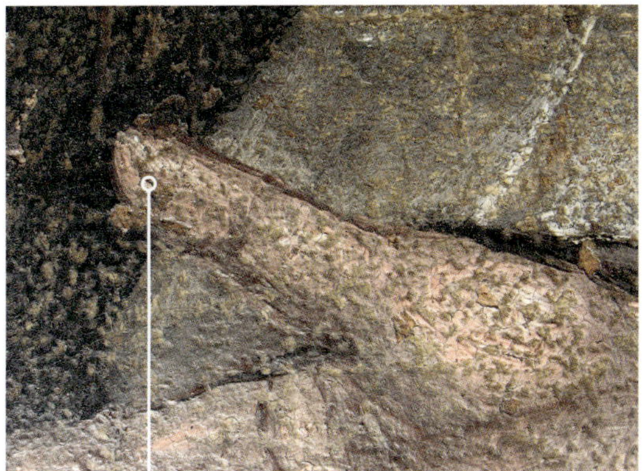

Sample location

Emperor's hand, flesh modelling

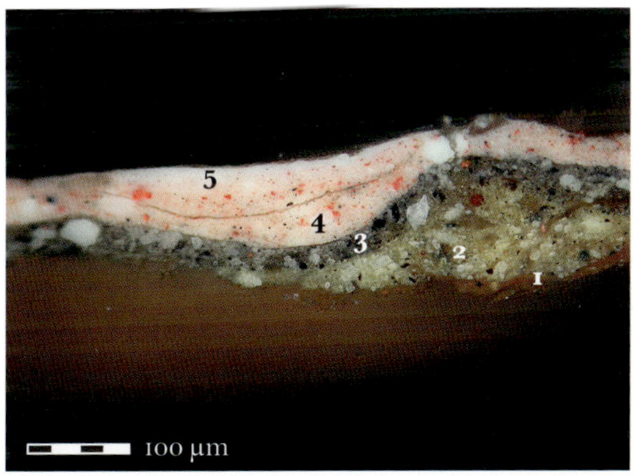

Stratigraphy

5 Fine lead white highlight
4 Pink flesh layer (lead white matrix + vermilion + red lead?), delaminated
3 Grey draperies (lead white? + carbon black)
2 Brownish-grey ground (carbon black + lead/calcium carbonate white)
1 Fragmentary red ground

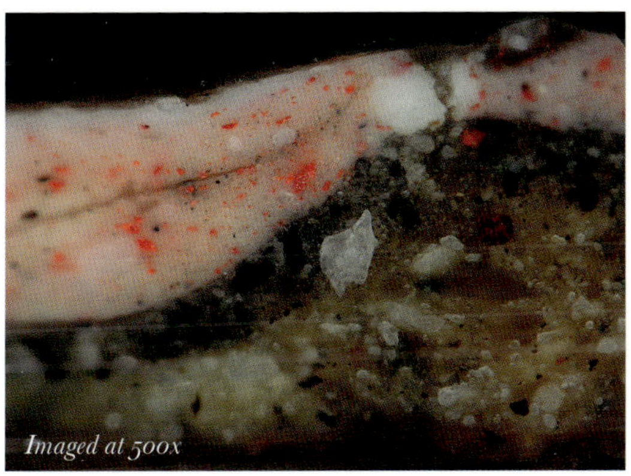

Sample ECC20

North wall, Scene 8

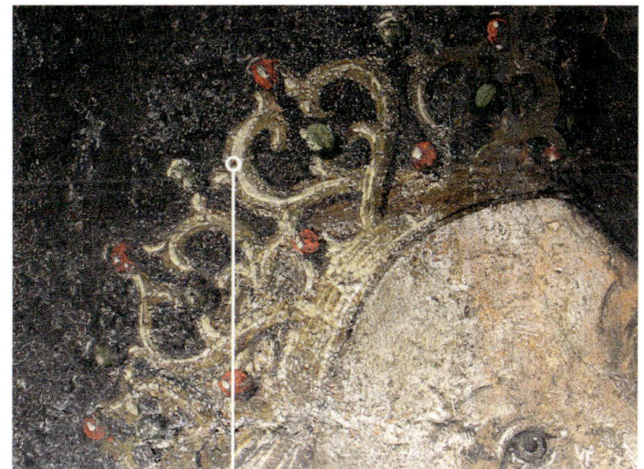

Sample location

Virgin's crown

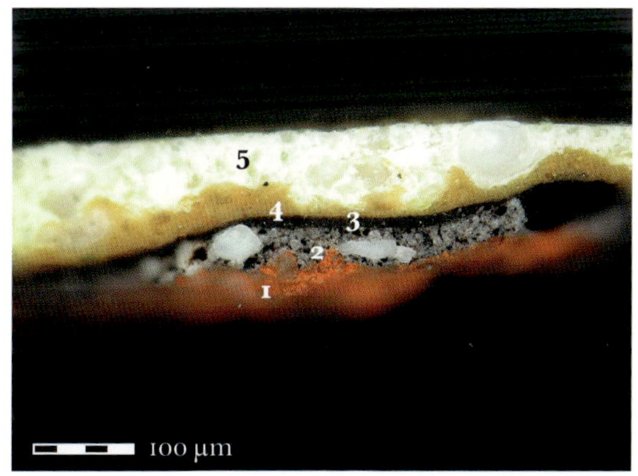

Stratigraphy

5 Lead-tin yellow
4 Iron oxide yellow
3 Carbon black with a little lead white + calcium carbonate white
2 Grey background (lead white + carbon black + a little calcium carbonate white)
1 Fragmentary red lead ground

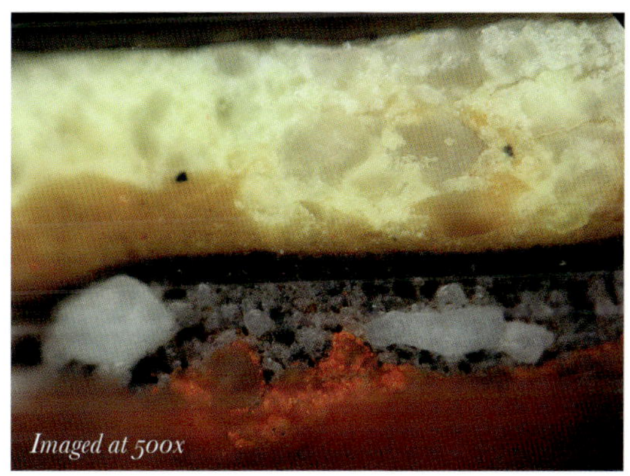

Notes

Examination of the cross-section at high magnification reveals that the lead-tin highlights were painted in while the yellow iron oxide layer was still wet. Note also the characteristic lead soaps in the lead-tin layer, which are the product of interaction between the pigment and an oil-based medium.

Sample ECC21

North wall, Scene 8

Micro-architectural leaf, top left corner

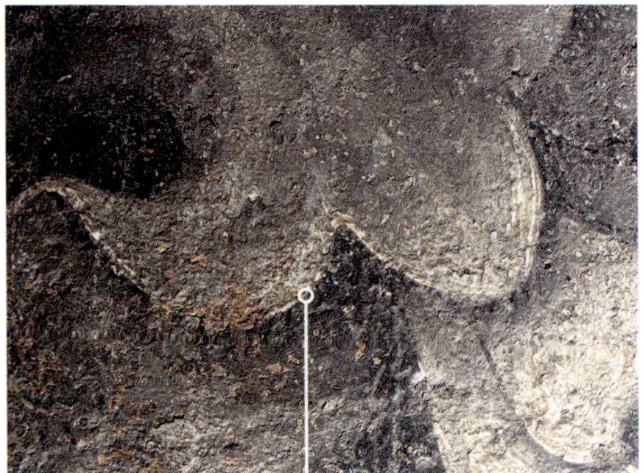

Sample location

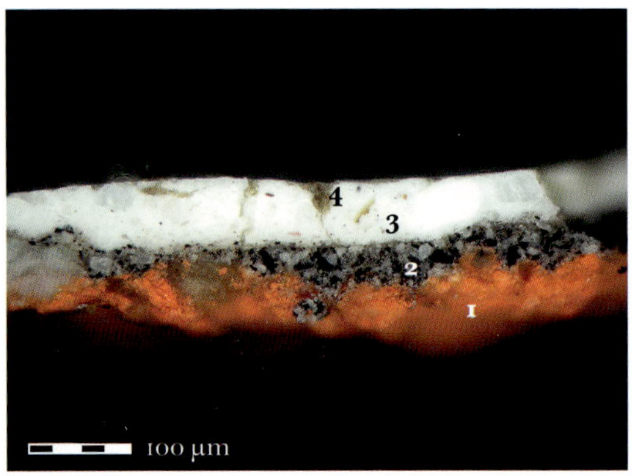

Stratigraphy

4 Varnish residue
3 Impasto lead white – possibly bulked out with calcium carbonate white
2 Grey background (comprising lead white + carbon black + a little calcium carbonate white)
1 Red lead ground

Sample ECC22

North wall, Figure VIII

St Martha, palm leaf

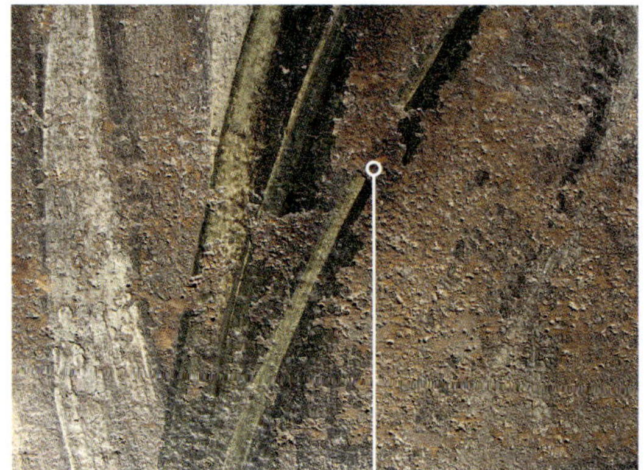

Sample location

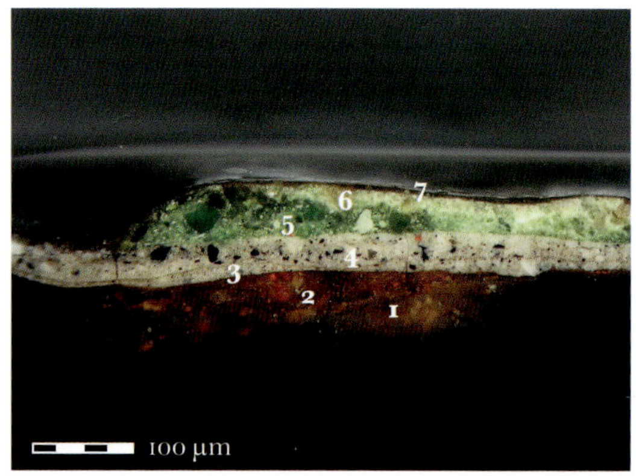

Stratigraphy

7 Varnish residue
6 Pale green highlight (copper green mixed with lead-tin yellow)
5 Dark green layer (copper green mixed with lead white and/or lead-tin yellow)
4 Thick grey layer (coarsely ground carbon black particles in a lead white matrix)
3 Fine grey layer (lead white matrix + finely ground carbon black)
2 Medium-rich sealant layer, with lead inclusions + some calcium carbonate
1 Limestone support

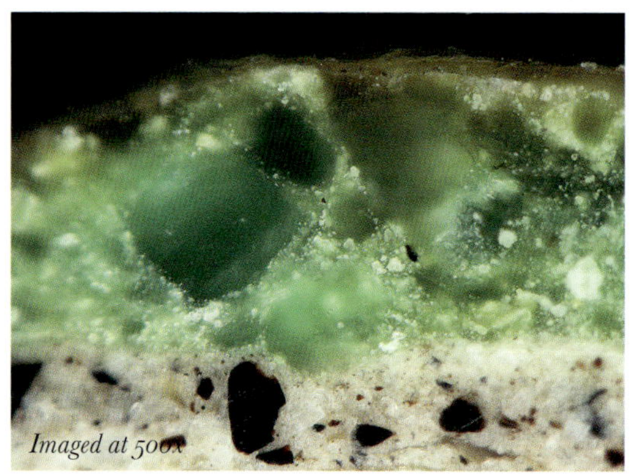

Notes

FTIR and GC-MS analysis of the binding medium of this sample suggests that elements of the painting were undertaken in walnut oil. Traces of a proteinaceous medium such as egg were also discovered in one of the lower paint layers.

Sample ECC23

North wall, Figure VIII

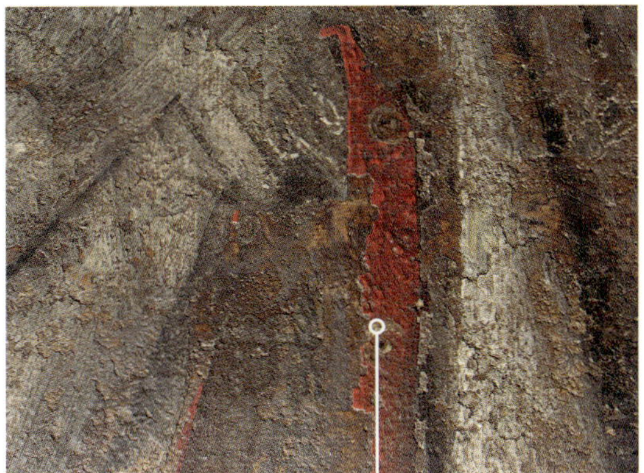

Sample location

St Martha, red lead with yellow rivets

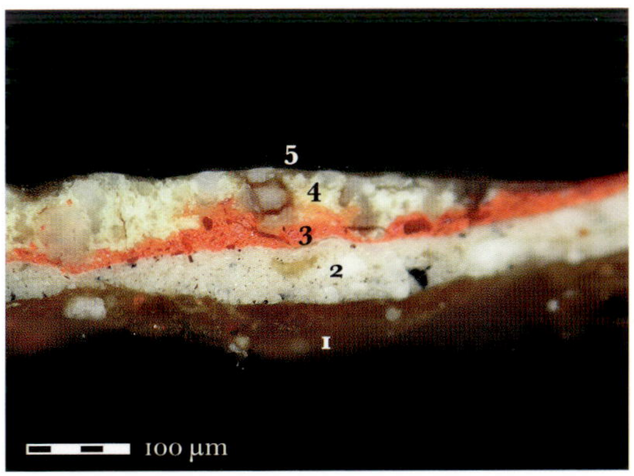

Stratigraphy

5 Varnish residue
4 Lead-tin yellow
3 Coarsely ground vermilion particles and some madder particles in a matrix of red lead
2 Grey draperies (lead white matrix with some calcium carbonate + finely ground carbon black)
1 Medium-rich sealant layer, with calcium carbonate + white and red lead inclusions

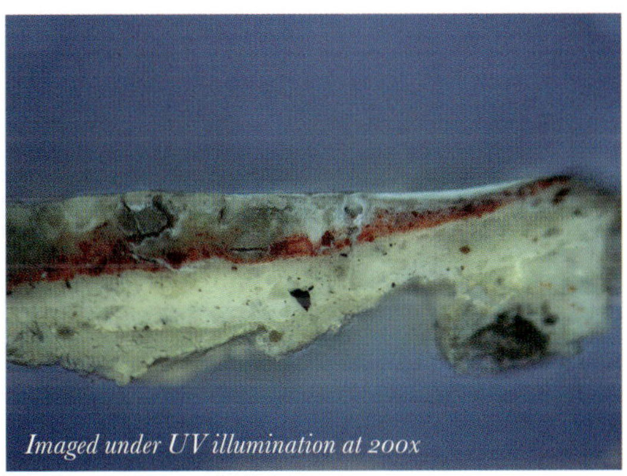

Imaged under UV illumination at 200x

Notes

The lead-tin layer contains a large proportion of lead soaps, which are characteristic of the interaction of lead-based pigments with an oil-based binding medium. Note also how the sealant layer fluoresces under UV illumination.

Sample ECC24

North wall, Scene 6

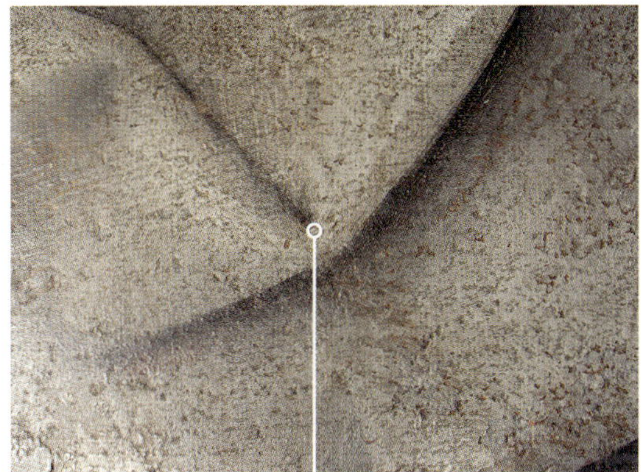

Sample location

Kneeling woman, draperies with grey outline

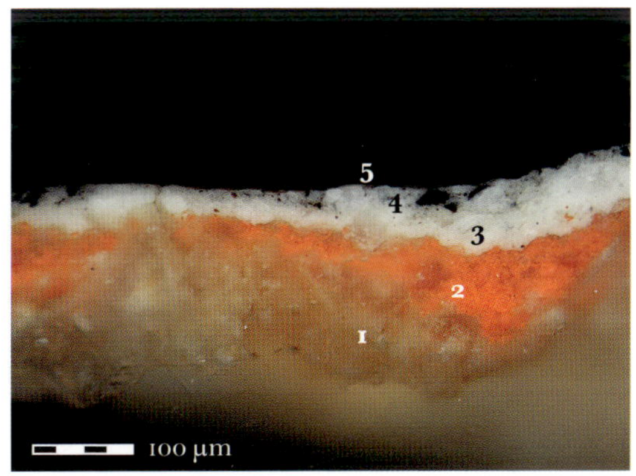

Stratigraphy

5 Wax and varnish residues
4 Grey of draperies (carbon black in a lead white matrix)
3 Lead white
2 Red lead underdrawing
1 Limestone saturated with sealant?

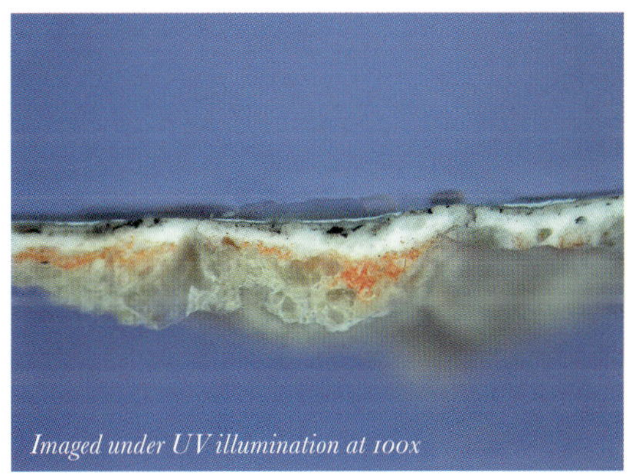

Imaged under UV illumination at 100x

Notes

Note how the sealant layer fluoresces under UV illumination.

Sample ECC25
North wall, Scene 6

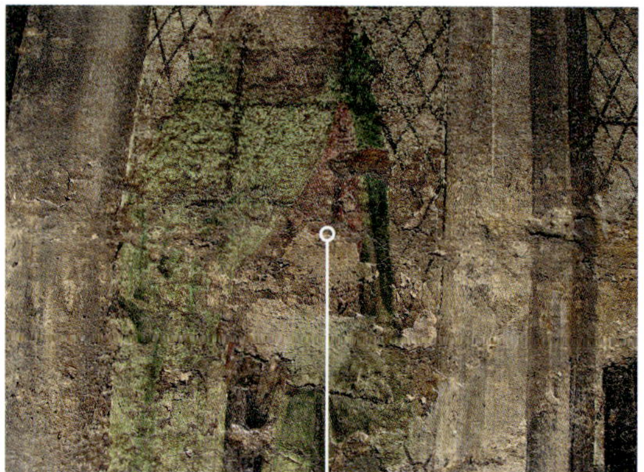

Sample location

Stained glass window, second figure from right, lake robe

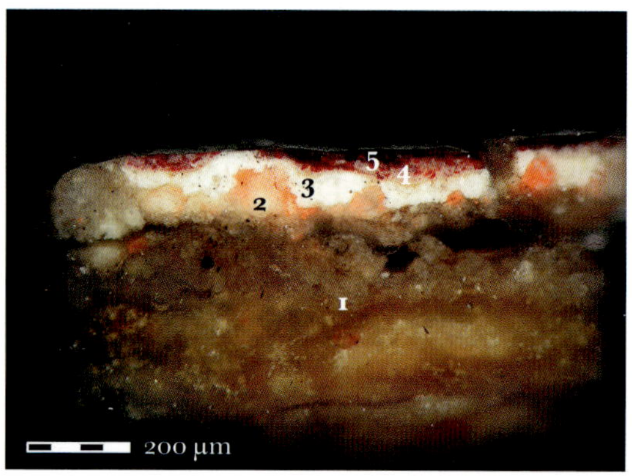

Stratigraphy

5 Madder lake glaze
4 Pink (lead white matrix with madder inclusions)
3 Lead white ground
2 Red lead underdrawing or ground (mixed with lead white?)
1 Limestone support (decohesive at interface with paint layer)

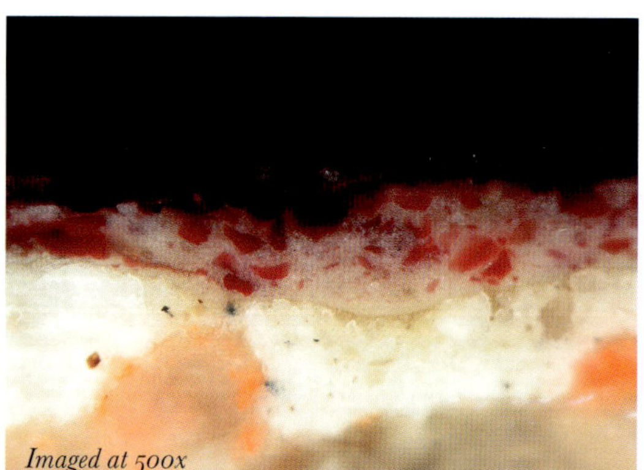

Imaged at 500x

Notes

Viewed at high magnification, it is possible to discern the madder glaze applied over a reflective opaque underlayer of the same lake combined with lead white. The lake dyestuff was identified as madder by HPLC analysis. The high levels of sulphur detected in SEM-EDX analysis of the lake substrate suggests that the dyestuff may have been extracted from dyed wool clippings.

Sample ECC26
North wall, Figure V

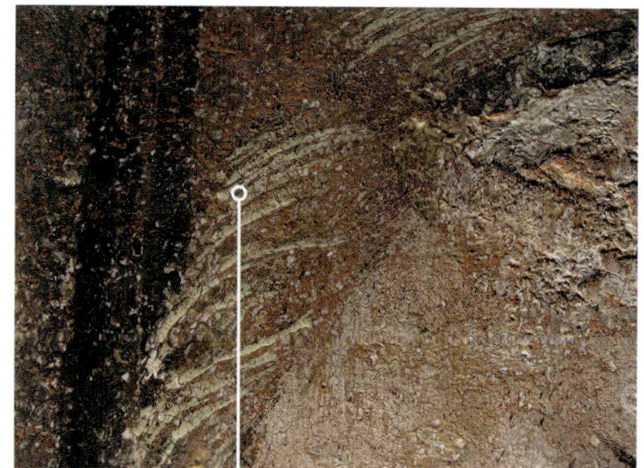

Sample location

St Agatha, blonde hair

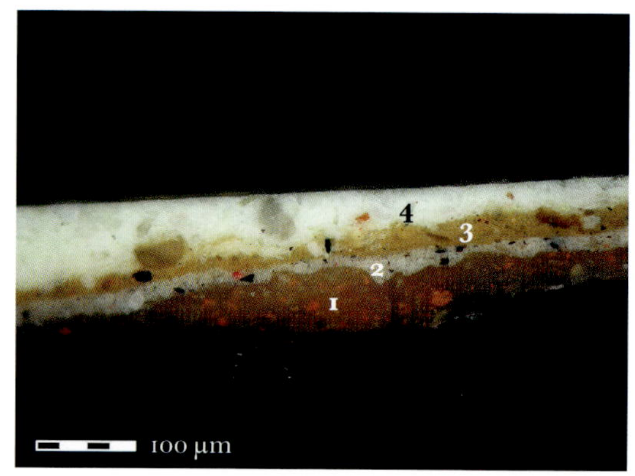

Stratigraphy

4 Lead-tin yellow highlight (almost white)
3 Iron oxide yellow
2 Grey background (lead white (+ calcium carbonate?) with carbon black and a few vermilion inclusions)
1 Medium-rich sealant layer with red lead inclusions

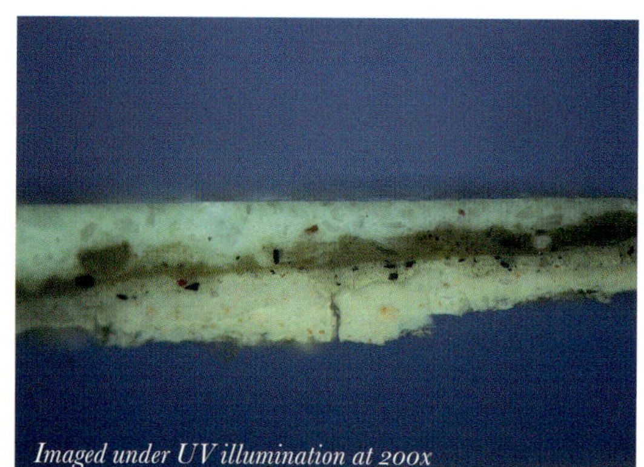

Imaged under UV illumination at 200x

Notes

Note how the medium-rich sealant layer fluoresces under UV illumination.

Sample ECC27

North wall, Scene 2

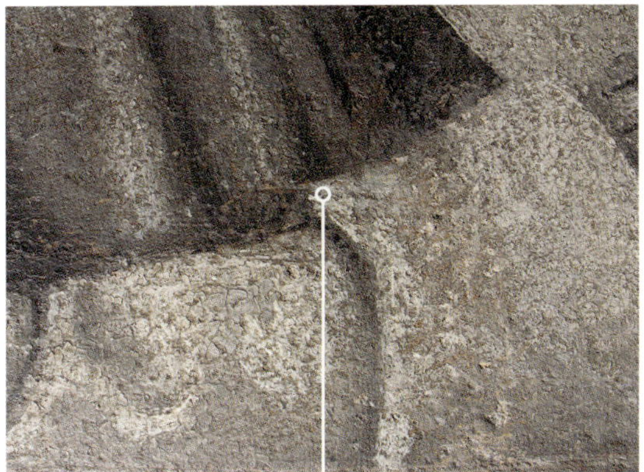

Sample location

Kneeling woman, cuff of robe with white highlight

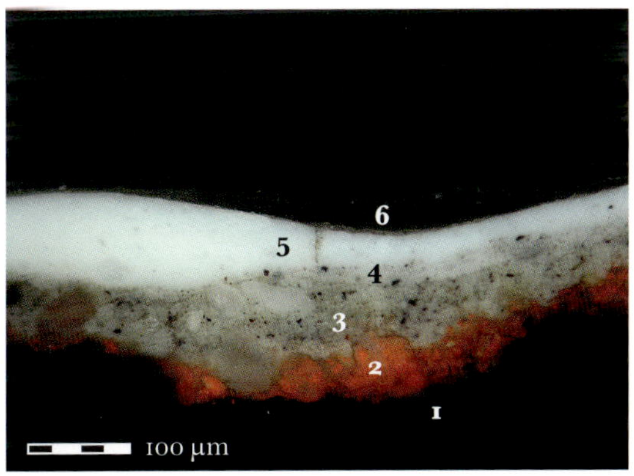

Stratigraphy

6 Wax
5 Lead white highlight
4 Grey draperies (carbon black in a lead white matrix + a little calcium carbonate)
3 Grey draperies (greater proportion of carbon black in a lead white matrix + a little calcium carbonate)
2 Red lead mixed with lead white (underdrawing?)
1 Traces of a sealant layer?

Sample ECC28

North wall, Scene 2

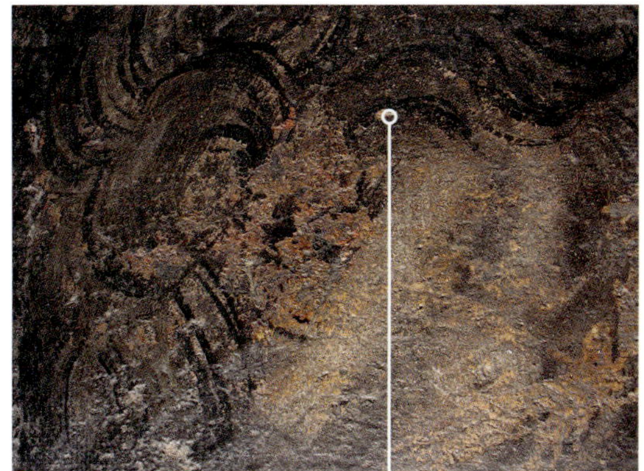

Sample location

Dead man, brown hair

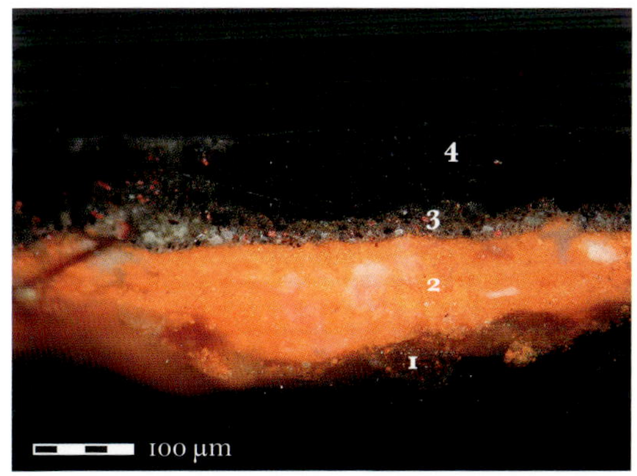

Stratigraphy

4 Thick charcoal black layer
3 Fine brown layer (carbon black, vermilion, iron oxides/clay minerals, calcium carbonate + lead pigments)
2 Red lead mixed with white lead + a little calcium carbonate white
1 Traces of sealant layer with lead and calcium carbonate inclusions

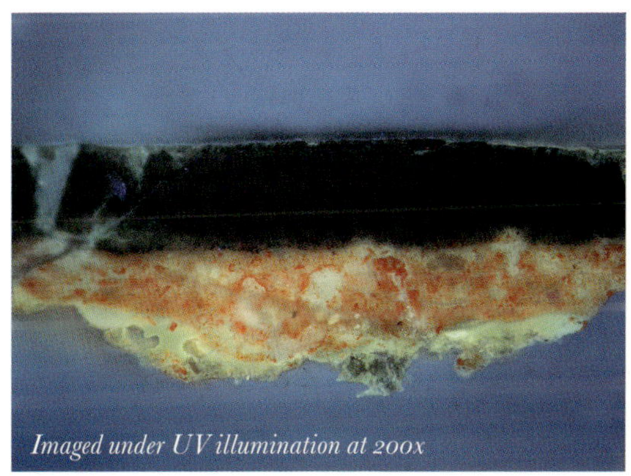

Imaged under UV illumination at 200x

Notes

SEM-EDX analysis of the black layer detected unusually high levels of copper, which may have been added as a siccative to expedite the drying of this layer (see also sample 31). Note also how the sealant layer fluoresces under UV illumination.

Sample ECC29
North wall, Scene 2

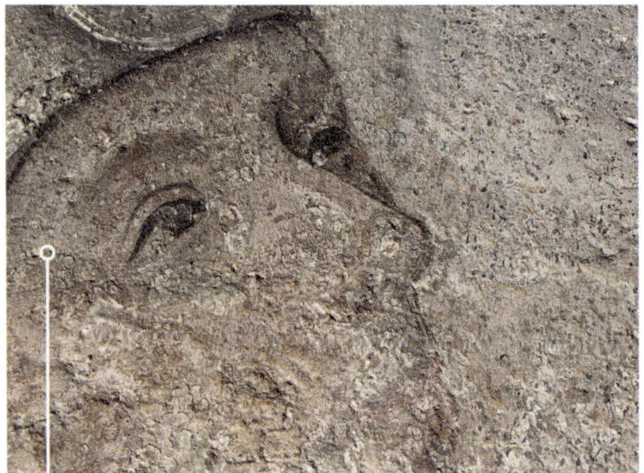

Sample location

Kneeling woman, flesh modelling on face

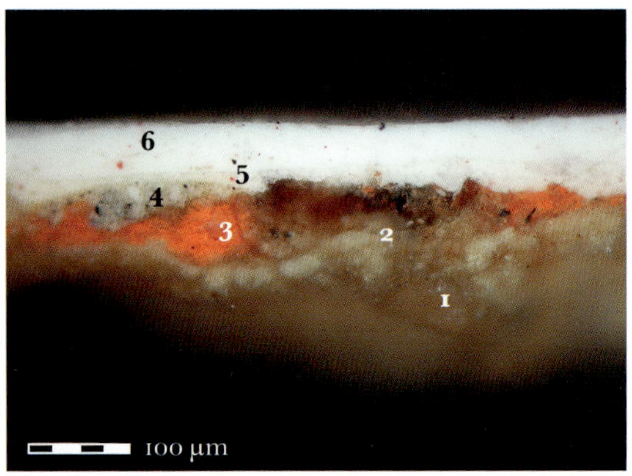

Stratigraphy

6 Pale pink layer (lead white + vermilion)
5 Lead white + few red particles
4 Fragmentary grey layer (lead and/or calcium carbonate white + carbon black)
3 Patchy layer of red lead underdrawing?
2 Patchy area of sealant
1 Traces of limestone

Sample ECC30
North wall, fictive textile

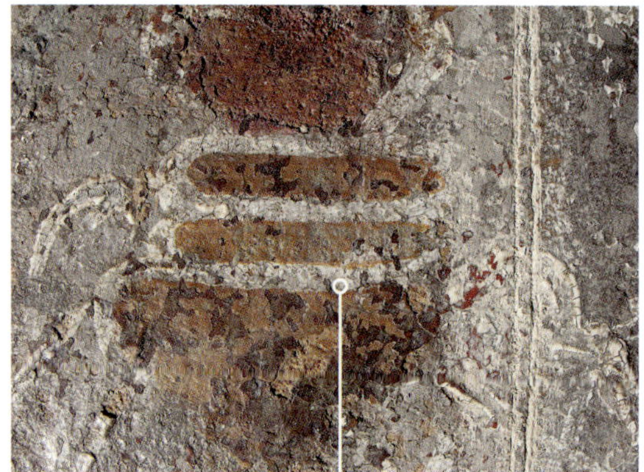

Sample location

Yellow over grey

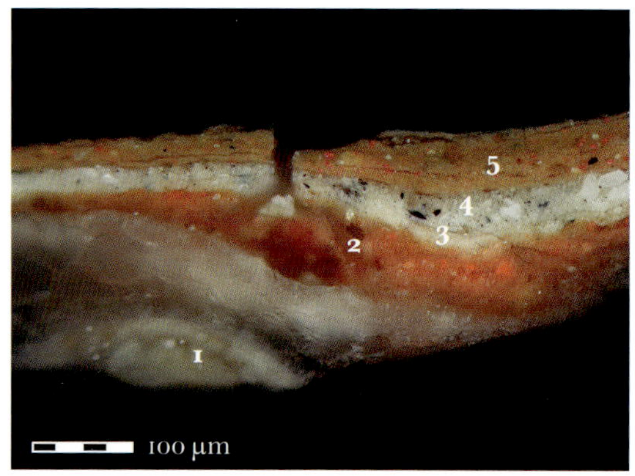

Stratigraphy

5 Thick iron oxide yellow layer with vermilion, lead white, lead-tin yellow and carbon black inclusions
4 Grey background layer (lead white matrix with carbon black inclusions)
3 Fine lead white layer
2 Medium-rich sealant layer, with lead, calcium carbonate + clay inclusions
1 Limestone support

Sample ECC31
North wall, Scene 3

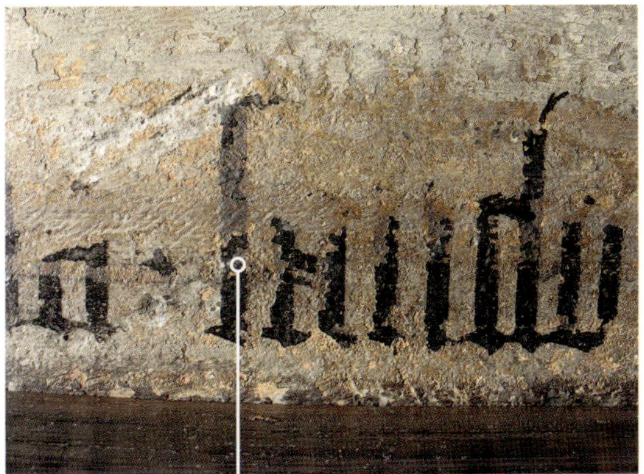

Sample location

Inscription, black text

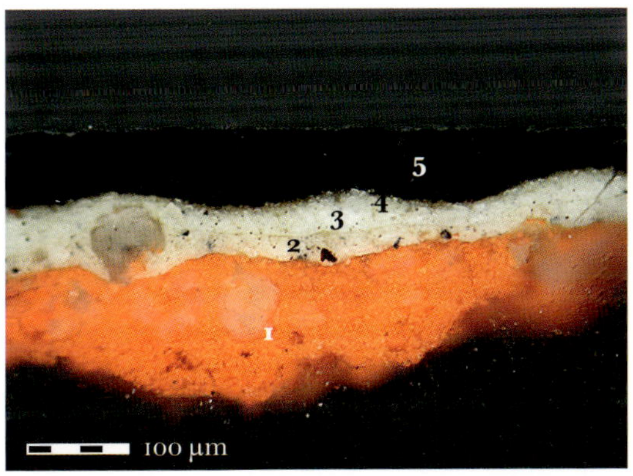

Stratigraphy

5 Thick carbon black layer (script)
4 Fine (original?) varnish layer?
3 Lead white (of scroll) with calcium carbonate inclusions
2 Grey background layer (lead white matrix with carbon black inclusions)
1 Red lead ground (with lead white inclusions)

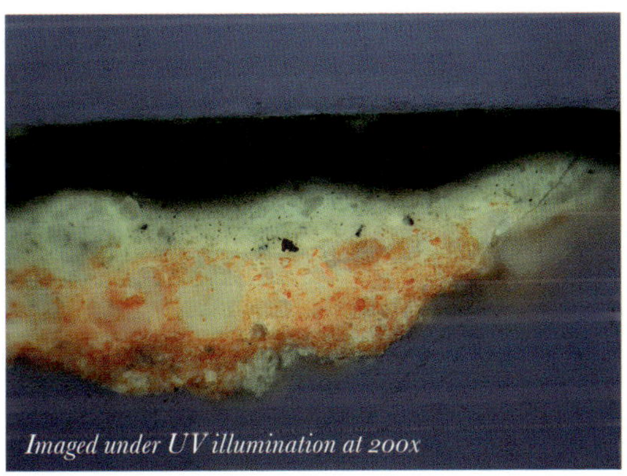

Imaged under UV illumination at 200x

Notes
SEM-EDX analysis of the black layer detected unusually high levels of copper, which may have been added as a siccative to expedite the drying of this layer (see also sample 28).

Sample ECC32
South wall, Scene 1

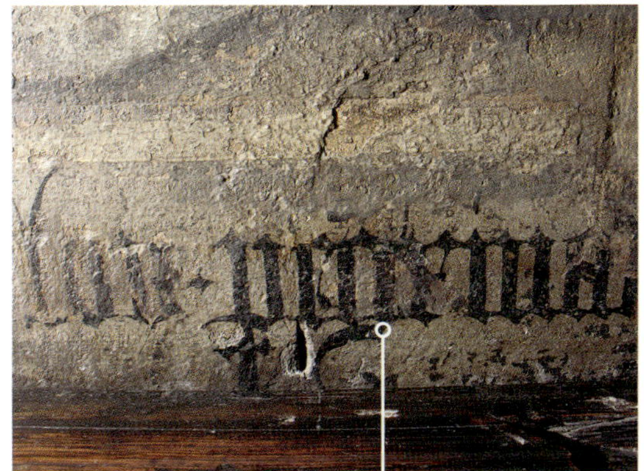

Sample location

Inscription, black text

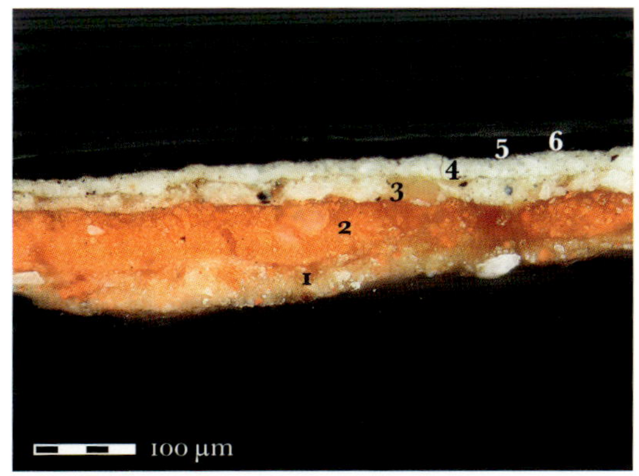

Stratigraphy

6 Wax residues?
5 Black layer (script)
4 Lead white (of scroll)
3 Grey background layer (lead white matrix with carbon black inclusions)
2 Red lead ground (with lead white inclusions)
1 Medium-rich sealant layer with red and white lead inclusions

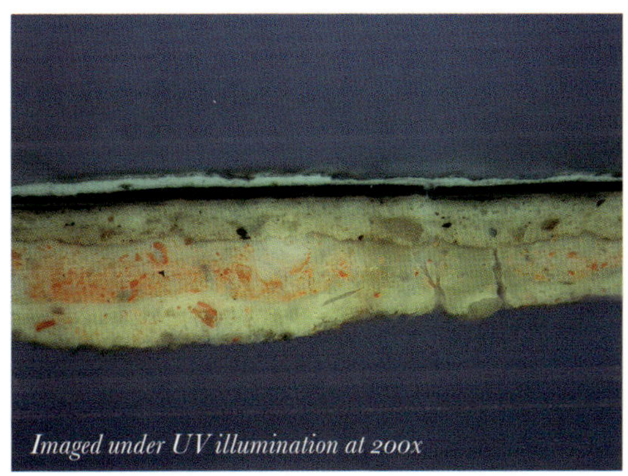

Imaged under UV illumination at 200x

Notes
Fluorescence under UV illumination suggests that an oil-based medium was used throughout; the bright uppermost layer would appear to be a non-original wax coating.

Bibliography

Archival Sources

ECR: Eton College Records

ECR 39/30
Eton College, contract of alliance between Eton and Saint Mary and St Nicholas' College (later King's College), Cambridge, 15 September 1443

ECR 39/57
Eton College, Consolidation Charter, 5 March 1446

ECR 58
Typescript translation by N. Blakiston, 1973, held in the College library, of ECR 60/1/1, Eton College Founder's Statutes, *Liber originalis*, 1452-3

ECR 61/AR/C/6
Eton College, audit roll, 1479-80

ECR 61/AR/D/1
Eton College, audit roll, 1482-3

ECR 61/AR/D/2
Eton College, audit roll, 1484-5

ECR 61/AR/F/2
Eton College, audit roll, 1486-7

ECR 61/BR/K/6
Eton College, bursar's roll, dating from the reign of Elizabeth I (of which the wrapper is a fragment of the lost audit roll for 1477)

ECR 61/NR/2
Eton College, nominal roll, 1485-6

ECR 62/3
Eton College, audit book, 1551-62

ECR 62/38
Eton College, bursar's book, 1544-53

COLL/HB1
Eton College, household accounts of Provost Bost, 1477-1504

Printed Primary Sources

Cal. Pat. Rolls 1436-41
H.C. Maxwell Lyte (ed.), *Calendar of the Patent Rolls*, 1436-41, HMSO, London (1907).

Cennini 1960
Cennino Cennini, *Il Libro dell'Arte, the Craftsman's Handbook of Cennino d'Andrea Cennini*, trans. D.V. Thompson, New Haven (1933), repr. Dover Publications, New York (1960).

Cennini 1982
Cennino Cennini, *Il Libro dell'Arte*, ed. F. Brunello, Vicenza (1982).

Collected works of Erasmus 1974
Collected Works of Erasmus, 42 vols, Toronto (1974-).

Correspondence of Erasmus 1988
The Correspondence of Erasmus, 8, Letters 1122 to 1251, 1520 to 1521, trans. R.A.B. Mynors, annotated P.G. Bietenholtz, Toronto, Buffalo and London (1988).

Golden Legend
The Golden Legend of Jacobus de Voragine, trans. G. Ryan and H. Ripperger, London/New York/Toronto (1941).

Malim 1560
W. Malim, *Consuetudinarium Vetus Scholae Etonensis*, trans. H. Perry, *Etoniana*, 36, 6 December 1923, 561-75.

Nicolas 1830
N. Nicolas, *Privy purse expenses of Elizabeth of York and wardrobe accounts of Edward the Fourth: with a memoir of Elizabeth of York and notes*, London (1972, reprint of 1830 edition).

Speculum historiale
V. Bellovacensis, *Speculum Quadruplex sive Speculum Maius. Speculum Historiale*, Douai (1624).

Sterry 1943
W. Sterry, *The Eton College Register, 1441-1698*, Eton (1943).

Strasbourg MS 1966
V. and R. Borradaile (eds), *The Strasbourg Manuscript: A Medieval Painter's Handbook*, London (1966).

Walton 1651
I. Walton, *The Life of Sir Henry Wotton*, London (1651).

Weatherly 1936
E.H. Weatherly (ed.), *Speculum sacerdotale, edited from British Museum MS Additional 36791*, London (1936).

William of Malmesbury
William of Malmesbury, Gesta regum Anglorum (Deeds of the English Kings), vol.1, ed. and trans. R.A.B. Mynors, R.M. Thomson and M. Winterbottom, Oxford (1998); vol.2, general introduction and commentary, M. Winterbottom and R.M. Thomson, Oxford (2002).

Williams 1872
G. Williams (ed.), *Correspondence of Thomas Bekynton Secretary to Henry VI and Bishop of Bath and Wells*, 2 vols, Rolls Series (1872).

Secondary Literature

Alexander 1975
J. Alexander, 'The Middle Ages', in D. Piper (ed.), *The Genius of British Painting*, London (1975), 13-61.

Alexander 1994
J. Alexander, 'The pulpit with the Four Doctors at St James's, Castle Acre, Norfolk', in N. Rogers (ed.), *England in the Fifteenth Century. Proceedings of the 1992 Harlaxton Symposium*, Stamford (1994), 198-206.

Alexandre Bidon & Lett 1999
D. Alexandre-Bidon and D. Lett, *Children in the Middle Ages, Fifth–Fifteenth Centuries*, Notre Dame (1999).

Allardyce 1984
F.M. Allardyce, 'The painting of the legend of St Eustace in Canterbury', *Archaeologia Cantiana*, 101 (1984), 115-30.

Allardyce *et al.* 1983
F. Allardyce, L. Medhurst and T. Organ, 'The Deanery wall painting, Durham', unpublished report, 1983.

Anderson 1989
D. J. Anderson, 'The Eton College Chapel wall paintings', unpublished MA dissertation, Courtauld Institute of Art, London, 1989.

Aston 1984
M. Aston, *Lollards and Reformers: Images and Literacy in Late Medieval Religion*, London (1984).

Aston 1993
M. Aston, *Faith and Fire: Popular and Unpopular Religion 1350-1600*, London and Rio Grande (1993).

Auerbach 1954
E. Auerbach, *Tudor Artists: A Study of Painters in the Royal Service and of Portraiture on Illuminated Documents from the Accession of Henry VIII to the Death of Elizabeth I*, London (1954).

Austen-Leigh 1988
R.A. Austen-Leigh, rev. R.C. Martineau and T.P. Connor, *An Illustrated Guide to Eton College*, Eton (1988).

Backhouse 1987
J. Backhouse, 'Founders of the royal library: Edward IV and Henry VII as collectors of illuminated manuscripts', in D. Williams (ed.), *England in the Fifteenth Century. Proceedings of the 1986 Harlaxton Symposium*, Woodbridge (1987), 23-42.

Backhouse 2005
J. Backhouse, 'The Psalter of Henry VI (London, BL, MS Cotton Dom. A. XVII)', in F. Buttner (ed.), *The Illuminated Psalter: Studies in the Content, Purpose and Placement of its Images*, Turnhout (2005), 329-36.

Bagley 1993
A. Bagley, 'Some pedagogical uses of the emblem in sixteenth- and seventeenth-century England', *Emblematica*, 7 (1993), 39-60.

Barron 1995
C. Barron, 'England and the Low Countries, 1327-1477', in C. Barron and N. Saul (eds), *England and the Low Countries in the Late Middle Ages*, Stroud (1995), 1-28.

Behrens 1982
G.H. Behrens, 'Conservation work on the Cartmel Fell figure of Christ', *Transactions of the Cumberland and Westmorland Antiquarian and Archaeological Society*, 82 (1982), 125-34.

Biddle 1984
M. Biddle, 'The stuccoes of Nonsuch', *Burlington Magazine*, 126 (1984), 411-17.

Bietenholz 1985
P.G. Bietenholz, *Contemporaries of Erasmus: A Biographical Register of the Renaissance and Reformation*, 1, Toronto (1985).

Billinge *et al.* 1997
R. Billinge, L. Campbell, J. Dunkerton, S. Foister, J. Kirby, J. Pilc, A. Roy, M. Spring and R. White, 'Methods and materials of Northern European painting in the National Gallery, 1400-1550', *National Gallery Technical Bulletin*, 18 (1997), 6-55.

Binski & Panayotova 2005
P. Binski and S. Panayotova (eds), *The Cambridge Illuminations: Ten Centuries of Book Production in the Medieval West*, exhib. cat., London and Turnhout (2005).

Binski & Park 1986
P. Binski and D. Park, 'A Ducciesque episode at Ely: the mural decorations of Prior Crauden's chapel', in W.M. Ormrod (ed.), *England in the Fourteenth Century. Proceedings of the 1985 Harlaxton Symposium*, Woodbridge (1986), 28-41.

Birch 1887-1900
W. de G. Birch, *Catalogue of Seals in the Department of Manuscripts in the British Museum*, 6 vols, London (1887-1900).

Birley 1970
R. Birley, *The History of Eton College Library*, Eton (1970).

Blair & Ramsay 1991
J. Blair and N. Ramsay (eds), *English Medieval Industries: Craftsmen, Techniques, Products*, London (1991).

Bomford *et al.* 1990
D. Bomford, J. Dunkerton, D. Gordon and A. Roy, *Art in the Making: Italian Painting before 1400*, National Gallery, London (1990).

Bornstein 1983
D. Bornstein, *The Lady in the Tower: Medieval Courtesy Literature for Women*, Hamden, Conn. (1983).

Bowers 2001
R. Bowers, 'The music and musical establishment of St George's Chapel in the 15th century', in C. Richmond and E. Scharff (eds), *St George's Chapel, Windsor, in the Late Middle Ages*, Windsor (2001), 171-214.

Brodrick & Darrah 1986
A. Brodrick and J. Darrah, 'The fifteenth-century polychromed limestone effigies of William Fitzalan, 9th Earl of Arundel, and his wife, Joan Nevill, in the Fitzalan Chapel, Arundel', *Church Monuments*, 1 (1986), 65-94.

Brodrick & Darrah 1989
A. Brodrick and J. Darrah, 'A description of the polychromy on the fragments of limestone figure-sculpture from the Great Screen at Winchester Cathedral', *Burlington Magazine*, 131 (1989), 615-17.

Brown & MacDonald 1997
S. Brown and L. MacDonald (eds), *Life, Death and Art: The Medieval Stained Glass of Fairford Parish Church*, Stroud (1997).

Burmester & Krekel 1998
A. Burmester and C. Krekel, 'The relationship between Albrecht Dürer's palette and fifteenth/sixteenth-century pharmacy price lists: the use of azurite and ultramarine', in A. Roy and P. Smith (eds), *Painting Techniques: History, Materials and Studio Practice* (Preprints of the IIC 17th International Congress, Dublin, 1998), London (1998), 101-5.

Burns 2011
T. Burns, 'Cennino Cennini's Il Libro dell'Arte: a historiographical review', *Studies in Conservation*, 56 (2011), 1-13.

Camille 1998
M. Camille, *Mirror in Parchment: The Luttrell Psalter and the Making of Medieval England*, London (1998).

Card 2001
T. Card, *Eton Established*, London (2001).

Cather & Howard 1994
S. Cather and H. Howard, 'St Gabriel's Chapel, Canterbury Cathedral: its technique, condition and environment reassessed', in *Forschungsprojekt Wandmalerei-Schäden, Arbeitshefte zur Denkmalpflege in Niedersachsen*, 11, Hanover (1994), 141-56.

Cather *et al.* 2000
S. Cather, D. Park and R. Pender, 'Henry III's wall paintings at Chester Castle', in A. Thacker (ed.), *Medieval Archaeology, Art and Architecture at Chester* (British Archaeological Association Conference Transactions, 22), London (2000), 170-89.

Childs 2010
W. Childs, 'Painters' materials and the northern international trade routes of late medieval Europe', in J. Kirby, S. Nash and J. Cannon (eds), *Trade in Artists' Materials: Markets and Commerce in Europe to 1700*, London (2010), 29-41.

Chitty 1923
H. Chitty, 'The College arms', *The Wykehamist*, nos 636-40 (24 July-23 November 1923), 368-70, 378-79, 390-91, 418-19.

Chrisman 1995
K. Chrisman, 'Dress in fifteenth-century English wall paintings', unpublished paper presented at the Courtauld Institute of Art, London, 29 November 1995.

Clarke 2001
M. Clarke, *The Art of All Colours: Medieval Recipe Books for Painters and Illuminators*, London (2001).

Clayton 1990
M. Clayton, *The Cult of the Virgin in Anglo-Saxon England* (Cambridge Studies in Anglo-Saxon England, 2), Cambridge (1990).

Colvin 1963
H.M. Colvin (ed.), *The History of the King's Works: The Middle Ages*, 2 vols, London (1963), vol. I.

Colvin 1982
H.M. Colvin (ed.), *The History of the King's Works: 1485-1660*, 2 vols, London (1982), vol. 2.

Cook 1917
A.K. Cook, *About Winchester College*, London (1917).

Cox 1916
J.C. Cox, *Bench-Ends in English Churches*, London/New York (1916).

Cox 1923
J.C. Cox, *English Church Fittings, Furniture and Accessories*, London (1923).

Cragoe 2010
C.D. Cragoe, 'The custom of the English Church: parish church maintenance in England before 1300', *Journal of Medieval History*, 30 (2010), 1-19.

Croft-Murray 1962
E. Croft-Murray, *Decorative Painting in England 1537-1837, I, Early Tudor to Sir James Thornhill*, London (1962).

Cunnington & Cunnington 1969
C.W. Cunnington and P. Cunnington, *Handbook of English Mediaeval Costume*, 2nd ed., London (1969).

Cust 1899
L. Cust, *A History of Eton College*, London (1899).

Davidson 1988
C. Davidson, *The Guild Chapel Wall-Paintings at Stratford-upon-Avon*, New York (1988).

Davis 1993
V. Davis, *William Waynflete: Bishop and Educationalist*, Woodbridge (1993).

Demailly *et al.* 2001
S. Demailly, W. Nowik and J.D. Mertz, 'Étude stratigraphique et analyses physico-chimiques', rapport no. 835B:28/09/2001, Dijon, ancienne Chartreuse de Champmol – Puits de Moïse – sculptures polychromes, unpublished report, 2001.

Dhanens 1998
E. Dhanens, *Hugo van der Goes*, Anvers (1998).

Duffy 1990
E. Duffy, 'Holy Maydens, Holy Wyfes: the cult of women saints in fifteenth- and sixteenth-century England', in W.J. Sheils and D. Wood (eds), *Women in the Church* (Studies in Church History, 27), Oxford (1990), 175-96.

Duffy 1992
E. Duffy, *The Stripping of the Altars; Traditional Religion in England, c.1400-c.1580*, New Haven and London (1992).

Edgren 1993
H. Edgren, *Mercy and Justice: Miracles of the Virgin Mary in Finnish Medieval Wall Paintings*, Helsinki (1993).

Edwards 1957
D.L. Edwards, *A History of the King's School, Canterbury*, London (1957).

Edwards, Gardiner Rodgers & Miller 1997
A.S.G. Edwards, K. Gardiner Rodgers and C.H. Miller (eds), *The Complete Works of St Thomas More*, New Haven and London (1997).

van Eikema Hommes 2001
M. van Eikema Hommes, 'Verdigris glazes in historical oil paintings: recipes and techniques', *Zeitschrift für Kunsttechnologie und Konservierung*, 15 (2001), 163-95.

ESTC
English Short Title Catalogue (electronic resource including the two print Short Title Catalogues), London (1992-).

Feller & Curran 1975
R.L. Feller and M. Curran, 'Changes in solubility and removability of varnish resins with age', *Bulletin of the American Institute for Conservation of Historic and Artistic Works*, 15 (1975), 17-26.

Fleming 2001
J. Fleming, *Graffiti and the Writing Arts of Early Modern England*, London (2001).

Flügel 1892
E. Flügel, 'Kleinere Mitteilungen aus Handschriften', *Anglia*, 14 (1892), 471-97.

French 1998
K. French, '"I Leave My Best Gown as a Vestment": women's spiritual interests in the late medieval English parish', *Magistra: A Journal of Womens' Spirituality in History*, 4 (1998), 57-77.

Fryer 1935
A. Fryer, 'Theophilus, the Penitent, as represented in art', *Archaeological Journal*, 92 (1935), 287-333.

Furlan *et al.* 1981
V. Furlan, R. Pancella and T. Hermanès, 'Portail peint de la Cathédrale de Lausanne: analyses pour une restauration', *Chantier*, 12 (1981), 13-20.

Gee 1984
E. Gee, *Glossary of Building Terms used in England from the Conquest to c.1550*, Frome (1984).

Geijer 1979
A. Geijer, *A History of Textile Art*, London (1979).

Gilderdale Scott 2005
H. Gilderdale Scott, '"this little Westminster": the chantry-chapel of Sir Henry Vernon at Tong, Shropshire', *Journal of the British Archaeological Association*, 158 (2005), 46-81.

Gill 2002
M. Gill, 'Late medieval wall painting in England: content and context, c.1300-c.1530', unpublished PhD thesis, Courtauld Institute of Art, London, 2002.

Gill 2003
M. Gill, 'The wall paintings in Eton College Chapel: the making of a late medieval Marian cycle', in P. Lindley (ed.), *Making Medieval Art*, Donington (2003), 173-201.

Gill & Howard 1997
M. Gill and H. Howard, 'Glimpses of Glory: paintings from St Mark's Hospital, Bristol', in L. Keen (ed.), *'Almost the Richest City': Bristol in the Middle Ages* (British Archaeological Association Conference Transactions, 19), London (1997), 97-106.

Glasscoe 1987
M. Glasscoe, 'Late medieval paintings in Ashton church, Devon', *Journal of the British Archaeological Association*, 140 (1987), 182-90.

Glover 2007
S. Glover, 'The Marian miracle cycle in the chapel of Eton College: text and context', in L.U. Alfonso and V. Serrão (eds), *Out of Stream: Studies in Medieval and Renaissance Mural Painting*, Newcastle (2007), 335-59.

Goodall 2002
J.A.A. Goodall, 'Henry VI's court and the construction of Eton College', in L. Keen and E. Scarff (eds), *Windsor. Medieval Archaeology, Art and Architecture of the Thames Valley* (British Archaeological Association Conference Transactions, 25), Leeds (2002), 247-63.

Gostling 1825
W. Gostling, *A Walk in and about the City of Canterbury, with many observations not to be found in any description hitherto published*, Canterbury (1825).

Graves & Rollason 2010
P. Graves and L. Rollason, 'The medieval prior's chapel at Durham: its development and its use', *Monastic Research Bulletin*, 16 (2010), 25-43.

Green 1992
G. Green, *British Regional Geology: Bristol and Gloucestershire Region*, British Archaeological Survey, 1992.

Griffiths 2004
R.A. Griffiths, *The Reign of King Henry VI*, Stroud (2004).

Harvey 1948
J. Harvey, *Gothic England: A Survey of National Culture, 1300-1550*, London (1948).

Harvey 1975
J. Harvey, *Mediaeval Craftsmen*, London (1975).

Harvey 1984
J. Harvey, *English Mediaeval Architects: a biographical dictionary down to 1550 including master masons, carpenters, carvers, building contractors and others responsible for design*, 2nd ed., Gloucester (1984).

Heck 2003
C. Heck (ed.), *L'art flamand et hollandais: le siècle des primitives, 1380-1520*, Paris (2003).

Helbig 1968
J. Helbig, *Les vitraux de la première moitié du XVIe siècle conservés en Belgique. Province d'Anvers et Flandres* (Corpus Vitrearum Medii Aevi, Belgique, II), Brussels (1968).

Heywood & Wright 1850
J. Heywood and T. Wright, *The Ancient Laws of the Fifteenth Century for King's College, Cambridge, and for the Public School of Eton College*, London (1850).

Higgitt *et al.* 2005
C. Higgitt, M. Spring and D. Saunders, 'Pigment-medium interactions in oil paint films containing lead-based pigments', *WAAC Newsletter*, 27:2 (2005), 12-16.

Hind 1935
A. Hind, *An Introduction to a History of Woodcut, with a detailed survey of work done in the fifteenth century*, 2 vols, London (1935).

Hluvko 1991
S. Hluvko, 'Red pigments in English medieval wall painting', unpublished dissertation, Conservation of Wall Painting Department, Courtauld Institute of Art, London, 1991.

Hodnett 1973
E. Hodnett, *English Woodcuts 1480-1535*, 2nd ed., Oxford (1973).

Holmes 1923
C. Holmes, 'The wall paintings in Eton College Chapel', *Burlington Magazine*, 43 (1923), 229-36.

Horie 1987
C.V. Horie, *Materials for Conservation: Organic Consolidants, Adhesives and Coatings*, Oxford (1987).

Howard 1988
H. Howard, 'Blue pigments in English medieval wall painting', unpublished dissertation, Conservation of Wall Painting Department, Courtauld Institute of Art, London, 1988.

Howard 1996
H. Howard, 'Scientific examination of the "Doom" wall painting in Holy Trinity Church, Coventry', unpublished report, Conservation of Wall Painting Department, Courtauld Institute of Art, London, 1996.

Howard 2003
H. Howard, *Pigments of English Medieval Wall Painting*, London (2003).

Howard *et al.* 1998
H. Howard, T. Manning and S. Stewart, 'Late medieval wall painting techniques at Farleigh Hungerford Castle and their context', in A. Roy and P. Smith (eds), *Painting Techniques: History, Materials and Studio Practice* (Preprints of the IIC 17th International Congress, Dublin, 1998), London (1998), 59-64.

Howe 2005
E. Howe, 'A report on the wall paintings in St Peter's Church, Raunds, Northamptonshire', unpublished report for the PCC of St Peter's Church, Raunds, 2005.

Howe 2006
E. Howe, 'Wall painting technology at Westminster Abbey c.1260–1300: A comparative study of the murals in the south transept and the Chapel of St Faith', in J. Nadolny with K. Kollandsrud, M.-L. Sauerberg and T. Froysaker (eds), *Medieval Painting in Northern Europe: Techniques, Analysis, Art History. Studies in Commemoration of the 70th Birthday of Unn Plahter*, London (2006), 91-113.

Howe 2007
E. Howe, 'A technical study of samples from the wall paintings in the Head Master's Chambers, Eton College, Berks', unpublished report in Rickerby and Shekede, 2007.

Hussey 1923
C. Hussey, 'Old wall paintings in Eton College Chapel', *Country Life*, 54 (1923), 303-5.

Hussey 1952
C. Hussey, *Eton College*, London (1952).

Hutchinson 1949
F. Hutchinson, *Medieval Glass at All Souls College: A History and Description, based upon the notes of the late G. McN. Rushforth*, London (1949).

James 1895a
M.R. James, *The Sculptures in the Lady Chapel at Ely*, London (1895).
James 1895b
M.R. James, 'On the frescoes in Eton College Chapel', *Proceedings of the Cambridge Antiquarian Society*, 8 (1895), 92-106.
James 1895c
M.R. James, *On the Abbey of S. Edmund at Bury. I. The Library. II. The Church* (Cambridge Antiquarian Society, octavo series VIII), Cambridge (1895).
James 1904
M.R. James, 'Description of the stained glass in the windows of Election Hall', *Etoniana*, 3 (November 1904), 38-9.
James 1907
M.R. James, *The Frescoes in the Chapel at Eton College. Facsimiles of the drawings by R.H. Essex with explanatory notes*, Eton (1907).
James 1915
M.R. James, 'Castrianus: an address of the Eton Commensals of the fifteenth century', *Etoniana*, 39 (1915), 609-14.
James 1920
M.R. James, 'Chapel inventories', *Etoniana*, 26 (1920), 401-8.
James 1926
M.R. James, *Vulgaria, by William Horman*, Oxford (Roxburghe Club) (1926).
James 1930
M.R. James, 'The carved bosses in the cathedral church and cloisters', in D.H.S. Cranage (ed.), *Thirteen-Hundredth Anniversary of the Diocese of East Anglia Official Handbook*, Norwich (1930), 55-63.
James 1933
M.R. James, *St George's Chapel Windsor. The Woodwork of the Choir*, Windsor (1933).
James & Tristram 1929
M.R. James and E.W. Tristram, 'The wall paintings in Eton College Chapel and in the Lady Chapel of Winchester Cathedral', *Walpole Society*, 17 (1928-9), 1-43.
Jones 1995
R. Jones, 'The methods and materials of three Tudor artists: Bettes, Hilliard and Ketel', in K. Hearn (ed.), *Dynasties: Painting in Tudor and Jacobean England, 1530-1630*, exhib. cat., Tate Gallery, London (1995), 231-40.
Kahsnitz 2006
R. Kahsnitz, *Carved Altarpieces: Masterpieces of the Late Gothic*, London (2006).
Kamerick 2002
K. Kamerick, *Popular Piety and Art in the Late Middle Ages: Image Worship and Idolatry in England 1350-1500*, New York and Basingstoke (2002).
Karras 1988
R. Karras, 'The Virgin and the Pregnant Abbess: miracles and gender in the Middle Ages', *Medieval Perspectives*, 3 (1988), 112-32.
Kidd 1987
P. Kidd, 'The Miracles of the Virgin series of wall-paintings in Eton College Chapel and related works', unpublished BA dissertation, University of East Anglia, 1987.
Kirby 2010
J. Kirby, 'Trade in painters' materials in sixteenth-century London', in J. Kirby, S. Nash and J. Cannon (eds), *Trade in Artists' Materials: Markets and Commerce in Europe to 1700*, London (2010), 339-55.
Kirby & White 1996
J. Kirby and R. White, 'The identification of red lake pigment dyestuffs and a discussion of their use', *National Gallery Technical Bulletin*, 17 (1996), 56-80.
Kirby *et al.* 2005
J. Kirby, M. Spring and C. Higgitt, 'The technology of red lake pigment manufacture: study of the dyestuff substrate', *National Gallery Technical Bulletin*, 26 (2005), 71-87.
Kirby *et al.* 2006
J. Kirby, D. Saunders and M. Spring, 'Proscribed pigments in Northern European Renaissance paintings and the case of Paris red', in D. Saunders, J.H. Townsend and S. Woodcock (eds), *The Object in Context: Crossing Conservation Boundaries* (Preprints of the IIC 21st International Congress, Munich 2006), London (2006), 235-43.
Kirby *et al.* 2010
J. Kirby, S. Nash and J. Cannon (eds), *Trade in Artists' Materials: Markets and Commerce in Europe to 1700*, London (2010).
Knoop & Jones 1933
D. Knoop and G. Jones, 'The building of Eton College 1442-1460: a study in the history of operative masonry', *Transactions of the Quatuor Coronati Lodge*, 46 (1933), 70-114.
Knoop & Jones 1938
D. Knoop and G. Jones, 'The English medieval quarry', *Economic History Review*, a9 (November 1938), 17-37.
Knowles 2002
R. Knowles, 'Medieval livery collars', web article for the Richard III Foundation (http://www.richardiii.com/medieval_livery_collars.htm accessed 11/04/2012).
Kühn 1993
H. Kühn, 'Lead-tin yellow', in A. Roy (ed.), *Artists' Pigments: A Handbook of their History and Characteristics*, II, New York and Oxford (1993), 83-112.
Laborde 1929
A. de Laborde (ed.), *Les miracles de Nostre-Dame compilés par Jehan Miélot*, Paris (1929).
Lancashire 1980
I. Lancashire (ed.), *Two Tudor Interludes: The Interlude of Youth; Hick Scorner*, Manchester (1980).
Leach 1903
A.F. Leach, *Early Yorkshire Schools*, II (Yorkshire Archaeological Society Record Series, 33), Leeds (1903).
Leach 1969
A.F. Leach, *The Schools of Medieval England*, reprinted London (1969).
Lees-Milne 1915
J. Lees-Milne, *Tudor Renaissance*, London (1915).
Lewis 1996
E. Lewis, 'A sixteenth-century painted ceiling from Winchester College', *Proceedings of the Hampshire Field Club and Archaeological Society*, 51 (1996), 137-65.
Lindley 1988
P. Lindley, 'Two late-medieval statues at Eton College', *Journal of the British Archaeological Association*, 141 (1988), 169-78.
Lindley 1989
P. Lindley, 'The Great Screen of Winchester Cathedral. Part I', *Burlington Magazine*, 131 (1989), 604-15.
Lindley 1993
P. Lindley, 'The Great Screen of Winchester Cathedral. Part II: style and date', *Burlington Magazine*, 135 (1993), 796-807.
Llewellyn 2000
N. Llewellyn, *Funeral Monuments in Post-Reformation England*, Cambridge (2000).
Long 1972
E.T. Long, 'Mediaeval wall paintings in Oxfordshire churches', *Oxoniensia*, 37 (1972), 86-108.
Mairinger & Schreiner 1986
F. Mairinger and M. Schreiner, 'Deterioration and preservation of Carolingian and medieval mural paintings in the Müstair Convent, Switzerland. Part II: Materials and rendering of the Carolingian wall paintings', in N. Brommelle and P. Smith (eds), *Case Studies in the Conservation of Stone and Wall Paintings* (Preprints of the IIC 11th International congress, Bologna, 1986), London (1986), 195-6.
Marks 1979
R. Marks, 'The glazing of the collegiate church of the Holy Trinity, Tattershall (Lincs.): a study of late fifteenth-century glass-painting workshops', *Archaeologia*, 106 (1979), 133-56.
Marks 1987
R. Marks, 'Stained Glass, 1200-1400', in J. Alexander and P. Binski (eds), *Age of Chivalry: Art in Plantagenet England 1200-1400*, exhib. cat., Royal Academy of Arts, London (1987), 137-47.
Marks 1993
R. Marks, *Stained Glass in England during the Middle Ages*, London (1993).
Marks & Williamson 2003
R. Marks and P. Williamson (eds), *Gothic: Art for England 1400-1547*, exhib. cat., Victoria & Albert Museum, London (2003).
Martens 1992
M. Martens, *Lodewijk van Gruuthus. Mecenas en Europees Diplomaat ca.1427-92*, Bruges (1992).
Martindale 1971
A. Martindale, 'The early history of the choir of Eton College Chapel', *Archaeologia*, 103 (1971), 179-98.
Martindale 1995
A. Martindale, 'The wall-paintings in the chapel of Eton College', in C. Barron and N. Saul (eds), *England and the Low Countries in the Late Middle Ages*, Stroud (1995), 133-52.
Maxwell Lyte 1899
H.C. Maxwell Lyte, *A History of Eton College (1440-1898)*, 3rd ed., London (1899).
Maxwell Lyte 1911
H.C. Maxwell Lyte, *A History of Eton College (1440-1910)*, 4th ed., London (1911).
McBurney 2007
H. Ryan (McBurney), 'A portrait of school life in the early 16th century: a wall painting uncovered in the Head Master's Chambers', *Eton Collections Review* (Journal of the Friends of the Eton College Collections), 1 (April 2007), 9-16.
McConnell 1970
J. McConnell, *Eton Repointed: the new structures of an ancient foundation*, London (1970).
McConnell 1976
J. McConnell (ed.), *Treasures of Eton*, London (1976).
McGrath 1982
P. McGrath, 'Winchester College and the old religion', in R. Custance (ed.), *Winchester Cathedral: Sixth-centenary Essays*, Oxford (1982) 240.
Monnas 1998
L. Monnas, '"Tissues" in England during the fifteenth and sixteenth centuries', *Bulletin du CIETA*, 75 (1998), 62-80.
Monnas 2008
L. Monnas, *Merchants, Princes and Painters. Silk Fabrics in Italian and Northern Paintings 1300-1500*, New Haven and London (2008)
Morgan 1991
N. Morgan, 'Texts and images of Marian devotion in thirteenth-century England', in W.M. Ormrod (ed.), *England in the Thirteenth Century. Proceedings of the 1989 Harlaxton Symposium*, Stamford (1991), 69-103.
Morgan 1993
N. Morgan, 'Texts and images of Marian devotion in fourteenth-century England', in N. Rogers (ed.), *England in the Fourteenth Century. Proceedings of the 1991 Harlaxton Symposium*, Stamford (1993), 34-57.
Müller & Kemperdick 2006
C. Müller and S. Kemperdick *et al.*, *Hans Holbein the Younger: the Basle Years 1515-1532*, exhib. cat., Basle (2006).
Nash 2000
S. Nash, 'The Parement de Narbonne: context and technique', in C. Villiers (ed.), *The Fabric of Images: European Paintings on Textile Supports in the Fourteenth and Fifteenth Centuries*, London (2000), 77-87.
Nash 2008
S. Nash, *Northern Renaissance Art*, Oxford (2008).
Nash 2010
S. Nash, '"Pour couleurs et autres chose prise de lui…": The supply, acquisition, cost and employment of painters' materials at the Burgundian Court, c.1375-1419', in J. Kirby, S. Nash and J. Cannon (eds), *Trade in Artists' Materials: Markets and Commerce in Europe to 1700*, London (2010), 97-182.
Nicholls 1985
J. Nicholls, *The Matter of Courtesy: Medieval Courtesy Books and the Gawain-poet*, Woodbridge (1985).
Nichols 1849
J.G. Nichols, ed., *Pilgrimages to Saint Mary of Walsingham and Saint Thomas of Canterbury by Desiderius Erasmus*, Westminster (1849).
Nichols 2002
A. Nichols, *The Early Art of Norfolk: a subject list of extant and lost art including items relevant to early drama* (Early Drama, Art and Music Reference Series, 7), Kalamazoo (2002).
Noad 1997
T. Noad, '"The imagery worke upon the walles": aspects of Early Netherlandish influence on the wallpaintings of Eton College', unpublished BA dissertation, Birkbeck College, University of London, 1997.
Nord & Tronner 2000
A.G. Nord and K. Tronner, 'Chemical analysis of medieval mural paintings in Sweden', in J. Goupy and J.P. Mohen (eds), *Art et chimie, la couleur* (Actes du Congrès, Paris, 16-18 septembre 1998, CNRS), Paris (2000), 97-101.
Norris 1999
H. Norris, *Medieval Costume and Fashion*, New York (1999).
ODNB
Oxford Dictionary of National Biography, Oxford (2004).
Orme 2000
N. Orme, *The Saints of Cornwall*, Oxford (2000).
Orme 2001
N. Orme, *Medieval Children*, New Haven and London (2001).
Orme 2006
N. Orme, *Medieval Schools: From Roman Britain to Renaissance England*, New Haven and London (2006).
Owst 1961
G. Owst, *Literature and Pulpit in Medieval England: A Neglected Chapter in the History of English Letters and of the English People*, 2nd ed., Oxford (1961).

Park 1993
D. Park, 'The interior decoration of the cathedral', in D. Pocock (ed.), *Durham Cathedral. A Celebration*, Durham (1993), 57-67.

Park & Welford 1993
D. Park and P. Welford, 'The medieval polychromy of Winchester Cathedral', in J. Crook (ed.), *Winchester Cathedral: Nine Hundred Years 1093-1993*, Chichester and Winchester (1993), 123-38.

Parker 1873
W. Parker, *The History of Long Melford*, London (1873).

Parshall 2009
P. Parshall, *The Woodcut in Fifteenth-Century Europe*, New Haven and London (2009).

Perry 1998
M. Perry, 'St Alban's Cathedral. The upper west wall of the presbytery', unpublished report, Perry Lithgow Partnership (1998).

Pfaff 1980
R.W. Pfaff, *Montague Rhodes James*, London (1980).

Plesters 1956
J. Plesters, 'Cross-sections and chemical analysis of paint samples', *Studies in Conservation*, 2 (1956), 110-55

Plummer 1976
P. Plummer, 'The wall paintings in Eton College Chapel', unpublished paper, March 1976.

Plummer 1986
P. Plummer, 'The wallpaintings in Eton College Chapel', in P. Burman (ed.), *Conservation of Wall Paintings: the international scene: a collection of papers given at the International symposium on the Conservation of Wallpaintings organised jointly by the Council for the Care of Churches and the Cathedrals Advisory Commission for England, with the support of the International Centre for the Study of the Preservation and the Restoration of Cultural Property (ICCROM) in 1979*, London (1986), 36-40.

Randall 1980
G. Randall, *Church Furnishing and Decoration in England and Wales*, London (1980).

Reader 1936
F.W. Reader, 'Tudor domestic wall-paintings, Part II', *Archaeological Journal*, 93, London (1936), 220-62.

Reicke 1901
E. Reicke, *Magister und Scholaren: Illustrierte Geschichte des Unterrichtswesens*, Leipzig (1901), (reprinted Düsseldorf and Cologne (1971).

Reinhardt & Winterbottom 2006
T. Reinhardt and M. Winterbottom (eds), *Quintilian: Istitutio Oratoria. Book 2*, Oxford (2006).

Riché & Alexandre-Bidon 1994
P. Riché and D. Alexandre-Bidon, *L'Enfance au Moyen Age*, Paris (1994).

Rickerby 1988
S. Rickerby, 'Conservation of medieval wall paintings in Rochester Cathedral', *Friends of Rochester Cathedral, Report for 1988*, Rochester (1988), 9-12.

Rickerby & Shekede 2006
S. Rickerby and L. Shekede, 'Eton College, Head Master's Chambers: Wall Painting Investigation', unpublished report, 2006.

Rickerby & Shekede 2007
S. Rickerby and L. Shekede, 'Eton College, Head Master's Chambers: Wall Painting Conservation Programme', unpublished report, 2007.

Rickert 1965
M. Rickert, *Painting in Britain: The Middle Ages*, 2nd ed., Harmondsworth (1965).

de la Rie & Shedrinsky 1989
E.R. de la Rie and A.M. Shedrinsky, 'The chemistry of ketone resins and the synthesis of a derivative with increased stability and flexibility', *Studies in Conservation*, 34 (1989), 9-19.

Rieger 1962
H. Rieger, 'Erasmus, Colet and the schoolboy Jesus', *Studies in the Renaissance*, 9 (1962), 187-94.

Rose 1996
M. Rose, 'The vault bosses', in I. Atherton, E. Fernie, C. Harper-Bill and H. Smith (eds), *Norwich Cathedral: Church, City and Diocese, 1096-1996*, London and Rio Grande (1996), 363-78.

Rose-Troup 1933
F. Rose-Troup, 'St Sidwell and Henry VI', *Devon and Cornwall Notes and Queries*, XVII (1933), 291-5.

Rossi-Manaresi 2002
R. Rossi-Manaresi, 'Observations à propos de la polychromie de la sculpture monumentale romaine et gothique', in D. Verret and V. Steyaert (eds), *La couleur et la pierre: polychromie des portails gothiques. actes du colloque, Amiens 12-14 octobre 2000*, Paris (2002), 57-64.

Rouse & Baker 1955
E.C. Rouse and A. Baker, 'The wall-paintings at Longthorpe Tower near Peterborough, Northants', *Archaeologia*, 96 (1955), 1-57.

Rubin 2009
M. Rubin, *Mother of God: A History of the Virgin Mary*, London (2009).

Rushton Fairclough & Goold 1999
H. Rushton Fairclough (ed. and trans.), G. P. Goold (rev.), *Virgil: Eclogues. Georgics. Aeneid I-VI*, Cambridge (Mass) and London (1999).

Salzman 1952
L. Salzman, *Building in England down to 1540*, Oxford (1952).

Schreiber & Heinz 1908
W.L. Schreiber and P. Heinz, *Die Deutschen 'Accipies' und Magister cum Discipulis: Holznitte als Hilfsmittel zur Inkunabel-Bestimmung* (Studien zur Deutschen Kunstgeshichte, 100), Strasbourg (1908).

Scott 1996
K.L. Scott, *Later Gothic Manuscripts, 1390-1490* (A Survey of Manuscripts Illuminated in the British Isles, 6), 2 vols, London (1996).

Sears 1986
E. Sears, *The Ages of Man: Medieval Interpretations of the Life Cycle*, Princeton (1986).

Shekede 1997
L. Shekede, 'English domestic wall paintings on earthen supports: materials and deterioration', unpublished MA dissertation, Courtauld Institute of Art, London, 1997.

Simon 1967
J. Simon, *Education and Society in Tudor England*, Cambridge (1967).

Sinclair 1991
E. Sinclair, 'The west front: II. The west front polychromy', in F. Kelly (ed.), *Medieval Art and Architecture at Exeter Cathedral* (British Archaeological Association Conference Transactions, 11), Leeds (1991), 116-33.

Sinclair 1992
E. Sinclair, 'Exeter Cathedral: exterior polychromy', in *The Conservator as Art Historian* (Proceedings of the UKIC Wall Paintings Section Conference, June 1992), London (1992), 7-14.

Singer 2011
B. Singer, 'Investigation of paint samples from Eton College Chapel', unpublished report, University of Northumbria, 2011.

Skinner 2004
D. Skinner, 'The Marian anthem in late medieval England', in R. Swanson (ed.), *The Church and Mary* (Studies in Church History, 39), Woodbridge (2004), 168-80.

Smith 2005
K. Allen Smith, 'Mary or Michael? Saint-switching, gender, and sanctity in a medieval miracle of childbirth', *Church History*, 74 (2005), 758-83.

Southern 1958
R.W. Southern, 'The English Origins of the Miracles of the Virgin', *Medieval and Renaissance Studies*, 4 (1958), 176-216.

Spencer 1990
B. Spencer, *Pilgrim Souvenirs and Secular Badges* (Salisbury Museum Medieval Catalogue, Part 2), Salisbury (1990).

Spencer 1998
B. Spencer, *Pilgrim Souvenirs and Secular Badges* (Medieval Finds from Excavations in London, 7), London (1998).

Stone 1972
L. Stone, *Sculpture in Britain: the Middle Ages*, 2nd ed., Harmondsworth (1972).

Stratford 1994
J. Stratford, 'The royal library in England before the reign of Edward IV', in N. Rogers (ed.), *England in the Fifteenth Century. Proceedings of the 1992 Harlaxton Symposium*, Stamford (1994), 187-97.

Swanson 1995
R.N. Swanson, *Religion and Devotion in Europe, c.1215 c.1515*, Cambridge (1995).

Swanton 1986
M. Swanton, *St Sidwell: An Exeter Legend*, Exeter (1986).

Tatton-Brown 1989
T. Tatton-Brown, *Great Cathedrals of Britain*, London (1989).

Tatton-Brown 2001
T. Tatton-Brown, 'The quarrying and distribution of Reigate stone in the Middle Ages', *Medieval Archaeology*, 45 (2001), 189-201.

Teasdale Smith 1959
M. Teasdale Smith, 'The use of grisaille as a Lenten observance', *Marsyas. Studies in the History of Art*, 8 (1957-9), 43-54.

Thomson 1965
J. Thomson, *The Later Lollards 1414-1520*, London (1965).

Tristram 1950
E.W. Tristram, *English Medieval Wall Painting: The Thirteenth Century*, 2 vols, London (1950).

Tristram 1955
E.W. Tristram, *English Wall Painting of the Fourteenth Century*, London (1955).

Tudor-Craig 1973
P. Tudor-Craig, *Richard III*, exhib. cat., National Portrait Gallery, London (1973).

Tudor-Craig 1992
P. Tudor-Craig, 'Painting in medieval England: the wall to wall message', in N. Saul (ed.), *Age of Chivalry: Art and Society in late Medieval England*, London/New York/Sydney/Toronto (1992), 106-119.

Turquet 1983
J.C. Turquet, 'The inner court of Nonsuch Palace', unpublished PhD thesis, Courtauld Institute of Art, London, 1983.

VCH Cambridgeshire III
Victoria History of the Counties of England: A History of the County of Cambridge and the Isle of Ely, vol. III, The City and University of Cambridge, ed. J.P.C. Roach, London (1959).

Verri 2007
G. Verri, 'An investigation of corrected UV-induced fluorescence for the examination of polychromy', unpublished MA dissertation, Courtauld Institute of Art, London, 2007.

Wayment 1972
H. Wayment, *The Windows of King's College Chapel, Cambridge* (Corpus Vitrearum Medii Aevi, Great Britain, Supplementary Vol. I), London (1972).

Wayment 1984
H. Wayment, *The Stained Glass of the Church of St Mary, Fairford, Gloucestershire*, Occasional Paper (New Series) V, Society of Antiquaries of London, London (1984).

Weed 2002
S. Weed, 'The *Virgo inter virgines*: art and the devotion to virgin saints in the Low Countries and Germany, 1400-1530', unpublished PhD thesis, University of Pennsylvania, 2002.

Whittingham 1981
A.B. Whittingham, *Norwich Cathedral, Bosses and Misericords*, Norwich (1981).

Willemsen 2008
A. Willemsen, *Back to the Schoolyard: the Daily Practice of Medieval and Renaissance Education*, Tournhout (2008).

Williams Boyarin 2010
A. Williams Boyarin, *Miracles of the Virgin in Medieval England: Law and Jewishness in Marian Legends*, Cambridge (2010).

Williamson 2000
M. Williamson, 'Pictura et scriptura: the Eton Choirbook in its iconographical context', *Early Music*, 28 (2000), 359-80.

Williamson 2002
P. Williamson, *Netherlandish Sculpture 1450-1550*, Victoria & Albert Museum, London (2002).

Willis & Clark 1886
R. Willis and J. Willis Clark, *The Architectural History of the University of Cambridge and of the Colleges of Cambridge and Eton*, Cambridge (1886, reprinted 2009).

Wilson 2003
C. Wilson, 'The arts of the great church', in R. Marks and P. Williamson (eds), *Gothic: Art for England 1400-1547*, exhib. cat., Victoria & Albert Museum, London (2003), 348-74.

Winter 1983
J. Winter, 'The characterisation of pigments based on carbon', *Studies in Conservation*, 28 (1983), 49-66.

Wirth 1983
K-A. Wirth, 'Von Mittelalterlichen Bildern und Lehrfiguren im Dienste der Schule und des Unterrichts' in B. Moeller, H. Patze and K. Stackmann (eds), *Studien zum Städtischen Bildungswesen des Späten Mittelalters und der Frühen Neuzeit* (Bericht über Kolloquien der Kommission zur Erfoschung der Kultur des Spätmittelalters, 1978 bis 1981), Göttingen (1983), 256-370.

Wolffe 2001
B. Wolffe, *Henry VI*, New Haven and London (2001).

Woodforde 1950
C. Woodforde, *The Norwich School of Glass Painting in the Fifteenth Century*, London (1950).

Woods 2007
K. Woods, *Imported Images: Netherlandish Late Gothic Sculpture in England, c.1400-c.1550*, Donington (2007).

Index

Figures in italics indicate illustrations.

Credits

First published in 2012 by
Scala Publishers Ltd
Northburgh House
10 Northburgh Street
London EC1V 0AT
www.scalapublishers.com

In association with Eton College
Windsor SL4 6DW
www.etoncollege.com

ISBN 978-1-85759-787-5
rin e Singapore

Project editor Jessica Hodge
Proofreader Julie Pickard
Designer James Alexander/Jade Design
Printed in Singapore

10 9 8 7 6 5 4 3 2 1

Every effort has been made to acknowledge correct copyright of images where applicable. Any errors or omissions are unintentional and should be notified to the Publisher, who will arrange for corrections to appear in any reprints.

Frontispiece: St Catherine, patron saint of Henry VI, Eton's founder, as depicted on the south wall of the chapel.

All images © Eton College and reproduced by the permission of the Provost and Fellows of Eton College unless stated otherwise.

Front and back cover: Photographs by James Davies

Introduction and Part I
Frontispiece, Figs 1, 7, 9, 11, 12, 13, 14, 15, 16, 17, 18, 20, 21, 22, 23, 24, 29, 40, 51, 52, 53, 54: Photograph by James Davies
Ground plan, p.4, courtesy of Yale University Press
Fig. 3: © The British Library Board
Fig. 6: Reproduced from A. Martindale, 'The early history of the choir of Eton College Chapel', *Archaeologia*, CIII (1971), 179-98, fig.2, by kind permission of the Society of Antiquaries of London, © reserved
Fig. 8: Photograph by Dennis Wallis
Figs 10, 19, 55, 56, 57, 58, 59, 60, 61, 62, 63, 64, 65, 66, 67, 68, 69, 70, 71, 72, 73, 74, 75, 76, 77, 78, 79: © Emily Howe and Eton College
Fig. 25: © Bibliothèque nationale, France
Fig. 26, 41, 44: © Crown copyright, NMR
Fig. 27: © Edelmann – Städel Museum/ ARTOTHEK
Fig. 28: © Soprintendenza Speziale per il Polo Museale Fiorentino, Gabinetto Fotografico
Fig. 30: © Dr John Crook
Figs 31, 80: © Conservation of Wall Painting Department, Courtauld Institute of Art
Figs 33, 34: Photograph by Emily Howe, reproduced with the kind permission of The Dean and Chapter of Winchester Cathedral
Fig. 35: Photograph by Emily Howe
Fig. 36: © Glasgow City Council (Museums)
Fig. 37: © KIK-IRPA, Brussels
Fig. 38: © 2011 Bayerische Staatsbibliothek
Fig. 42: © V&A Images, all rights reserved
Figs 43, 82, 83: Photograph © National Gallery, London
Figs 45, 48, 49, 50: Photograph © Pauline Plummer, image by courtesy of the Conway Library, Courtauld Institute of Art, London
Fig. 46: Image by courtesy of the Conway Library, Courtauld Institute of Art, London
Fig. 81: Photograph © Alan Wright, image by courtesy of Granville & Burbidge

Catalogue
All images © Eton College; photographs of paintings by James Davies, photographs of drawings by Dennis Wallis

Part II
Figs 1, 3, 6, 8, 9, 11, 12, 13, 14, 15, 19, 20, 21, 26, 29: Photograph by James Davies
Figs 2, 10, 16, 17: Photograph by Dennis Wallis
Fig. 7: The National Archives, ref. E24/6/1
Fig. 22: © The Pepys Library, Magdalene College, Cambridge
Fig. 23: © RMN / Jean-Gilles Berizzi
Fig. 24: © 2011 Bayerische Staatsbibliothek
Fig. 25: Photograph by Annamarieke Willemsen
Fig. 28: © Kunstmuseum Basel, Martin P. Bühler

Appendix
All images © Emily Howe & Eton College

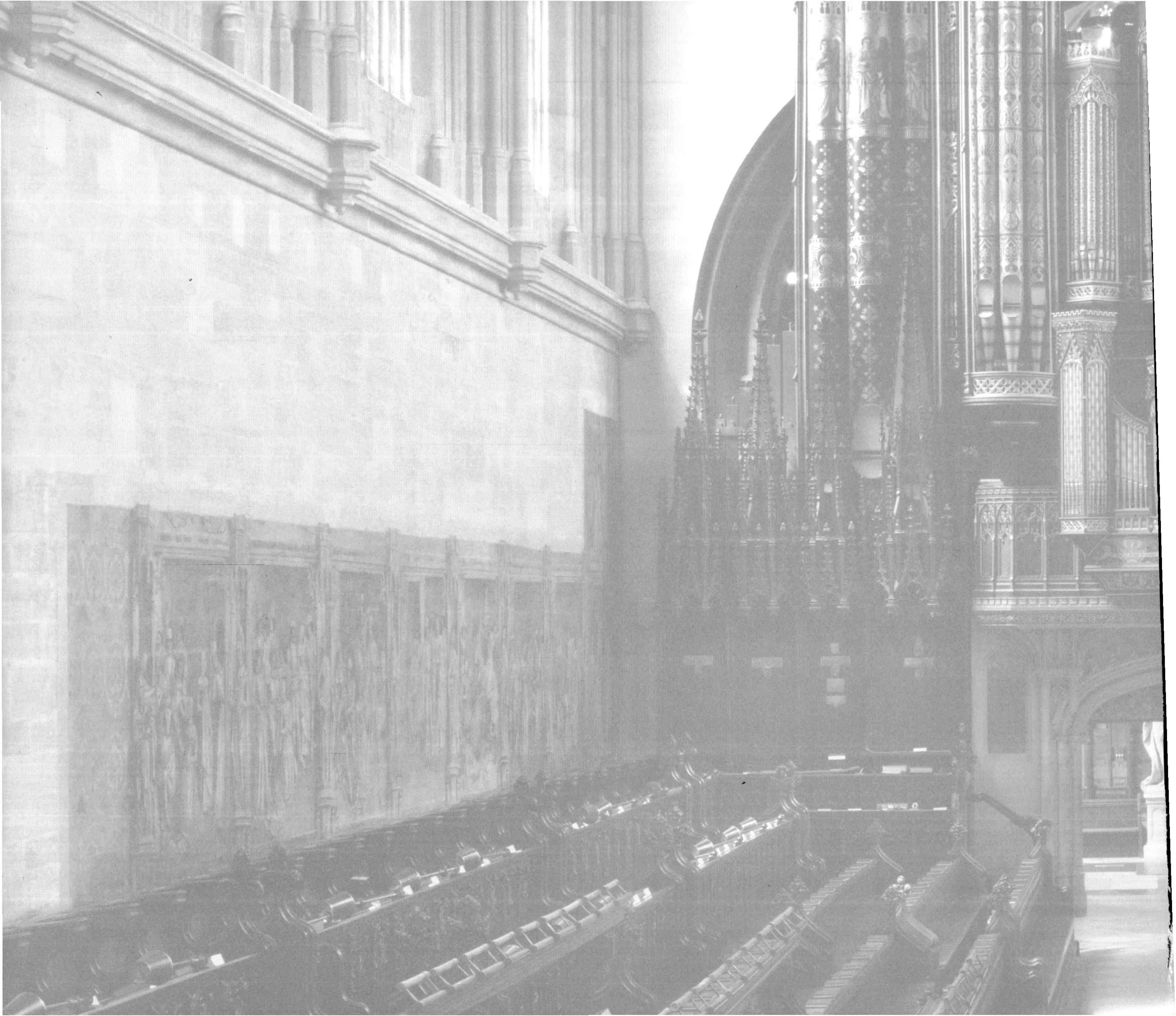